THE
SAMSON
OPTION

THE SAMSON OPTION

Israel's Nuclear Arsenal
and American Foreign Policy

Seymour M. Hersh

Random House New York

Library of Congress Card Catalogue Number: 91-52678
ISBN 0-394-57006-5

Manufactured in the United States of America

9 8 7 6 5 4 3 2

First Edition

For Elizabeth, Matthew, Melissa, and Joshua

Author's Note

This is a book about how Israel became a nuclear power in secret. It also tells how that secret was shared, sanctioned, and, at times, willfully ignored by the top political and military officials of the United States since the Eisenhower years.

In it, you will find many senior American officials being quoted—most of them for the first time—about what they knew and when they knew it. These officials spoke to me not because of animosity toward the Israeli government, but because they realized the hypocrisy of the American policy of publicly pretending that Israel's nuclear arsenal does not exist. That policy remains in effect as this is written.

I chose not to go to Israel while doing research for this book. For one thing, those Israelis who were willing to talk to me were far more accessible and open when interviewed in Washington, New York, or, in some cases, Europe. Furthermore, Israel subjects all journalists, domestic and foreign, to censorship. Under Israeli rules, all material produced by journalists in Israel must be submitted to military censors, who have the right to make changes and deletions if they perceive a threat to Israeli national security. I could not, for obvious reasons, submit to Israeli censorship. Those in the past who have broken the rules have been refused reentry to Israel.

Those Israelis who talked were not critics of Israel's nuclear capability, nor would they feel secure without the bomb. They spoke because they believe that a full and open discussion of the Israeli nuclear arsenal—and of the consequences of its deployment—is essential in a democratic society.

SEYMOUR M. HERSH
August 1991
Washington, D.C.

Contents

17. Nuclear Blackmail   225

18. Injustice   241

19. The Carter Malaise   259

20. An Israeli Test   271

21. Israel's Nuclear Spy   285

22. An Israeli Asset   307

     Epilogue   317

     Acknowledgments   321

     Notes   323

     Index   335

THE
SAMSON
OPTION

1

A Secret Agreement

America's most important military secret in 1979 was in orbit, whirling effortlessly around the world every ninety-six minutes, taking uncanny and invaluable reconnaissance photographs of all that lay hundreds of miles below. The satellite, known as KH-11, was an astonishing leap in technology: its images were capable of being digitally relayed to ground stations where they were picked up—in "real time"—for instant analysis by the intelligence community. There would be no more Pearl Harbors.

The first KH-11 had been launched on December 19, 1976, after Jimmy Carter's defeat of President Gerald R. Ford in the November elections. The Carter administration followed Ford's precedent by tightly restricting access to the high-quality imagery: even Great Britain, America's closest ally in the intelligence world, was limited to seeing photographs on a case-by-case basis.

The intensive security system was given a jolt in March 1979, when President Carter decided to provide Israel with KH-11 photographs. The agreement gave Israel access to any satellite intelligence dealing with troop movements or other potentially threatening activities as deep as one hundred miles inside the borders of neighboring Lebanon, Syria, Egypt, and Jordan. The Israelis were to get the real thing: the raw and spectacular first-generation imagery as captured by the KH-11, some of it three-dimensional—and not the deliberately fuzzed and dulled photographs that were invariably distributed by the American intelligence community to the bureaucracy and to overseas allies in an effort to shield the superb resolution of the KH-11's optics.*

It was a significant triumph for the Israeli government, which had been seeking access to the KH-11 since the moment of launch three years before. Jimmy Carter's decision to provide that high-tech imagery was suspected by some American intelligence officials as being a reward for Prime Minister Menachem Begin's successful Camp David summit with Egyptian President Anwar Sadat the year before. These officials understood what many in the White House did not: adding an Israeli dimension to the system was a major commitment—and one that would interfere with the KH-11's ability to collect the intelligence its managers wanted. The KH-11 was the most important advance of its time, explained a former official of the National Security Agency (NSA), the unit responsible for all communications intelligence, and every military and civilian intelligence agency in the government seemed to have an urgent requirement for it. The goal of the KH-11's managers was to carefully plan and "prioritize" the satellite's schedule to get it to the right place at the right time, while avoiding any abrupt shifts in its flight path or any sudden maneuver that would burn excess fuel. With good management, the multimillion-dollar satellite, with its limited fuel supply, would be able to stay longer in orbit, provide more intelligence, and be more cost-efficient. Carter's decision to give Israel direct access to the KH-11 completely disrupted the careful scheduling for the satellite's future use; it also meant that some American intelligence agencies were going to have less access to the satellite. "It was an unpopular decision in many, many ways," said the former NSA official.

There were no official protests inside the administration, however: those few who were distressed by the KH-11 agreement understood that any disquiet, or even second-guessing,

---

* The KH-11 was at the time known to be the most significant advance in outer-space reconnaissance. The key element of the sixty-four-foot-long satellite was a downward-looking mirror in front of the camera that rotated from side to side, like a periscope, enabling the satellite to track a single location as it moved across the atmosphere. The result was a stereoscopic image of unusually high quality that could be even further enhanced by computer.

could jeopardize their own access to such information and thus reduce their status as insiders.

The Israelis, not surprisingly, viewed the KH-11 agreement as a reaffirmation of respect and support from the Carter administration, whose director of central intelligence, retired Admiral Stansfield Turner, had abruptly cut back intelligence liaison with Israel and other friendly nations as part of a restructuring of the Central Intelligence Agency. The Israelis, accustomed to far warmer treatment by Presidents Richard M. Nixon and Gerald R. Ford, saw the men running the Carter administration as naïve and anti-Semitic; as men who perhaps did not fully understand how entwined Israel's primary foreign intelligence service, Mossad, had become with the CIA during the Cold War. The 1979 agreement on the KH-11 was no less than the twenty-eighth in a series of formal Israeli-American cooperative ventures in strategic intelligence since the 1950s.

Nothing has ever been officially disclosed about these arrangements, many of which were financed off-the-books—that is, from a special contingency fund personally maintained by the director of central intelligence. Through the 1960s, for example, one of the most sensitive operations in the Agency was code-named KK MOUNTAIN (KK being the CIA's internal digraph, or designation, for messages and documents dealing with Israel) and provided for untold millions in annual cash payments to Mossad. In return, Mossad authorized its agents to act, in essence, as American surrogates throughout North Africa and in such countries as Kenya, Tanzania, and the Congo. Other intelligence agreements with Mossad revolved around the most sensitive of Israeli activities in the Middle East, where American dollars were being used to finance operations in Syria, and inside the Soviet Union, where the CIA's men and women found it difficult to spy. Some of the Soviet activities apparently were financed by regular Agency disbursements— and thus cleared through the appropriate CIA congressional oversight committees—but the complex amalgamation of American financing and Israeli operations remains one of the great secrets of the Cold War.

The Israelis had responded to Admiral Turner's 1977 cutback

in liaison—in essence, his refusal to pay for the continuing operations in Africa and elsewhere—by sharply reducing their flow of intelligence back to Washington. In the Israeli view, the KH-11 agreement in March 1979 was made inevitable not by the success of Camp David but by the CIA's failure to anticipate the steadily increasing Soviet pressure on Afghanistan in 1978 and the continuing upheavals in Iran. There were large Jewish communities in both nations—many shopkeepers in Kabul, Afghanistan's capital, were Jewish—and Mossad's information was far superior to the CIA's. Most galling to the President and his top aides was the CIA's embarrassingly inept reporting on Iran, where Shah Mohammed Reza Pahlavi, a U.S. ally of long standing, had been overthrown in February 1979 in a popular uprising—despite a year-long series of upbeat CIA predictions that he would manage to cling to power.* The CIA had rejected the Israeli view, provided in a trenchant analysis in 1978 by Uri Lubrani, a former Israeli ambassador to Iran, that the shah would not survive. The CIA had failed the President and forced the American leadership to turn once again to Israeli help in trying to anticipate world events. It was no accident that Lubrani was attached to the Israeli delegation that negotiated the March 1979 KH-11 agreement in Washington.

The KH-11 imagery provided Israel—depicting any military activity inside the border of Israel's four neighbors—is known as I&W, for intelligence and warning, and carries the highest classification marking in the American intelligence community. The photographs, once processed, were to be picked up by Israeli military attachés at a special Pentagon office controlled by the Defense Intelligence Agency (DIA), the military's joint intelligence service. There was one significant caveat in all this: Israelis were not to be given any intelligence that could help them plan preemptive strikes on their neighbors.

"I set up the rules," one senior American intelligence official

---

* In August 1977, for example, the CIA produced a sixty-page study for the President, entitled "Iran in the 1980s," that was predicated on the assumption that the shah would "be an active participant in Iranian life well into the 1980s." Five months later, Carter, to his everlasting embarrassment, publicly toasted Iran at a 1977 New Year's Eve state dinner in Tehran as "an island of stability in a turbulent corner of the world."

recalled. "The system was designed to provide [the Israelis] with everything they could possibly use within [the one-hundred-mile] striking distance. If it was inside Syria or Egypt, they got it all. If it was Iraq, Pakistan, or Libya, they didn't."

The official added, however, that he and his colleagues anticipated from the outset that the Israelis would do everything possible to get around the restrictions of the agreement. One of the immediate Israeli arguments was that the limitations should not apply to the joint enemy of the United States and Israel—the Soviet Union. In the months ahead, there would be constant Israeli pressure for access to satellite intelligence on the Soviet supply lines to Syria and the Soviet involvement in the training of Iraqi combat divisions in western Iraq. Those requests were flatly turned down by the Carter administration.

Nonetheless, Israel was once again an essential ally, and even if it could not get unfettered access to KH-11 imagery, the 1979 agreement did include language permitting Israel to make specific requests for satellite intelligence. Each request would be handled on a case-by-case basis.

The package was too much for British intelligence officials, involved Americans recalled, who were described as "mad as hell" about Israel's being provided with the chance to obtain intelligence that they—World War II allies and fellow members of NATO—could not get.*

* The British were denied full access, American officials explained, in part because of concern about what turned out to be a major leak inside the British communications intelligence establishment, known as GCHQ (for Government Communications Headquarters). American intelligence officials had learned by the end of the Carter administration that the existence and capability of the KH-11 system were known to the Soviets, and there were suspicions that someone in a senior position in British intelligence was funneling vast amounts of technical information to Moscow. In the fall of 1982, a former high-level GCHQ employee named Geoffrey A. Prime, of Cheltenham, was arrested on sex charges, and he subsequently confessed to spying for the Soviets. Prime, who was sentenced to a thirty-five-year jail term, was said by British authorities to have had access to "matters of the utmost secrecy." There were British newspaper reports that senior British officials had known of Prime's betrayal for two years before the arrest but had not told their American counterparts. The incident led to inevitable tension between the intelligence services of the two allies. "We were holding back the Brits for a definite reason," one American said. "We knew they had a real problem there and we were very, very sensitive about what we gave them." The stern American position was more than a little offset by the fact that a junior CIA clerk named William T. Kampiles had been sentenced to forty years in jail in 1978 after his conviction for the sale of a top-secret KH-11 technical manual to the Soviets. Kampiles received $3,000 for the manual, which included no KH-11 photographs—and thus presumably did not reveal just how good the satellite's optics could be. The trial of Kampiles raised a

Israel, as the British may have suspected, did have a secret agenda in its constant maneuvering for KH-11 access, but that agenda only became clear to a few top Reagan administration policymakers in the fall of 1981. The unraveling began with a bombing raid in Iraq.

It was a Sunday afternoon in early June 1981, and Richard V. Allen, President Ronald Reagan's national security adviser, was taking it easy, sipping iced tea on the sundeck of his suburban Virginia home and shuffling through a week's worth of unread cables, many of them highly classified.

An aide in the White House situation room, which is staffed around the clock, telephoned to report that the Israelis had informed Washington that they had successfully bombed the Iraqi nuclear reactor at Osirak, twelve miles southeast of Baghdad. Allen immediately telephoned Reagan, who was spending the weekend at the presidential retreat at Camp David, in the nearby Catoctin Mountains of Maryland.

The President, he was told, had just boarded his helicopter for the trip back to the White House. "Get him off," Allen ordered. It was, after all, the new administration's first Middle East crisis. The President took the telephone call amid the background thumping of the helicopter blades.

"Mr. President, the Israelis just took out a nuclear reactor in Iraq with F-16s." Israel, aided by long-term, low-interest American credits, had been authorized in 1975 to begin the purchase of seventy-five F-16s "for defensive purposes only."

"What do you know about it?"

"Nothing, sir. I'm waiting for a report."

"Why do you suppose they did it?"

The President let his rhetorical question hang for a moment, Allen recalled, and then added:

"Well. Boys will be boys."*

---

number of embarrassing questions about security at CIA headquarters, where Kampiles worked; at least sixteen other KH-11 technical manuals were missing, and there was testimony to the effect that Kampiles—and others, if they wished—were able to leave the premises without any security check.

* Moments later, Allen added, Secretary of State Alexander M. Haig, Jr., who had competed from inauguration day with all senior officials for influence in the administration, telephoned and excitedly demanded to know where the then-airborne Presi-

The next morning, according to Allen, there was a meeting of Reagan's high command at which Secretary of Defense Caspar Weinberger proposed canceling the F-16 aircraft sale. Others at the meeting, including Vice President George Bush and Chief of Staff James A. Baker III, agreed that some sanctions against Israel were essential. Reagan glanced at Allen at one point and with a gesture made it clear he had no intention of taking any such step: "He rolled his eyes at me," Allen said.

The President's private acceptance of the raid was not reflected in the administration's public actions. That afternoon the State Department issued a statement, said to have been cleared by the President and Secretary of State Alexander M. Haig, Jr., formally condemning the bombing, "which cannot but seriously add to the already tense situation in the area." Nonetheless, recalled Allen, "Reagan was delighted . . . very satisfied" by the attack on the reactor at Osirak. "It showed that the Israelis had claws, a sense of strategy, and were able to take care of problems before they developed. Anyway, what did Israel hurt?" Haig similarly was forbearing in private.

The Israeli bombing triggered worldwide protest, and a few days later the White House announced the suspension of a scheduled delivery of four more F-16s, a continuation of the 1975 sale. Two months later, with little fanfare, the administration's real policy emerged: the suspension was lifted and the aircraft were delivered without incident.

There was controversy inside Israel, too, over the bombing, which had been debated at the highest levels of the Israeli government since late 1979. Yitzhak Hofi, the director of Mossad, and Major General Yehoshua Saguy, chief of military intelligence, both opposed the attack, primarily because there was no evidence that Iraq was as yet capable of building a bomb.* They

---

dent was: "Dick, I've got to talk to him right away." Allen asked why. "I've just got to talk to him." "Is it about the reactor?" Haig said yes. Allen said he was too late: he had just briefed Reagan. "What?" exclaimed Haig. "How did you find out?" Allen laughed at the recollection and added that Haig wouldn't know it, but he had wasted his time in rushing to tell Reagan: "The fact is you couldn't score brownie points that way. Ronald Reagan never remembered who told him first."

* That issue also was hotly debated inside the American intelligence community, whose experts on nonproliferation did not have "complete information"—as one involved official put it—about Iraq's capabilities. After the Israeli strike, the American

were joined in futile dissent by Yigael Yadin, the deputy prime minister. At a late-1980 planning session, Saguy continued to inveigh against the mission, arguing that the adverse reaction in Washington would be a more serious national security threat to Israel than was the Iraqi reactor.* He took exception to the view that any Israeli military steps to avoid a "second Holocaust" were permissible. Saguy suffered for his dissent; the chief of military intelligence was not told of the mission until June 4, three days before it was scheduled to take place. Saguy responded by renouncing any responsibility for the raid and threatening—briefly—to withhold intelligence.

The mission planners, anxious to avoid international protest, had gone to extremes to mask the operation: it was hoped that Iraq and the rest of the world would be unable to fix blame for the bombing on the unmarked Israeli Air Force planes. The attack had been carried out, as planned, in two minutes, and the likelihood of any detection was slight. But Menachem Begin, buoyed by the success, stunned his colleagues on June 8 by unilaterally announcing the Israeli coup. On the next day, as Israel was besieged with protests, the prime minister defended the operation and vowed that Israel was ready to strike again, if necessary, to prevent an enemy from developing the atomic bomb. "If the nuclear reactor had not been destroyed," Begin said, "another Holocaust would have happened in the history of the Jewish people. There will never be another Holocaust. . . . Never again! Never again!"

Two days later, at a British diplomatic reception, Begin again shocked the senior officials of his government, as well as the intelligence community, by bragging that the Israeli planes also had destroyed a secret facility buried forty meters—130 feet—below the reactor at Osirak that was to serve as the assembly point for the manufacture of Iraqi nuclear bombs. The appalled Israeli officials knew that Begin's remarks were descrip-

---

experts concluded that Israel had bombed only one of two major targets at the site; it had destroyed the reactor as planned but left the nearby reprocessing plant untouched. It was in the reprocessing facility that plutonium could be chemically recovered from spent reactor fuel rods.

* Many in the Israeli military also were glad to see Iraq sink hundreds of millions of dollars into the reactor rather than purchasing more tanks, planes, and other conventional arms.

tive not of the nonexistent underground weapons facility at Osirak, but of one that did exist in Israel. Begin also told newsmen at the reception that the Iraqi government had hidden the facility from the International Atomic Energy Agency (IAEA), which had inspected the reactor at Osirak in January 1981, under provisions of the 1968 Nuclear Nonproliferation Treaty, to which Iraq was a party.

Israeli government spokesmen attempted to recoup the next day by telling newsmen that Begin had misspoken; the underground facility was only four meters, not forty, below the surface. The government's worst fears, however, were not publicly realized in the subsequent days and weeks: Israel's biggest secret remained a secret.[*]

By 1981, Israeli scientists and engineers had been manufacturing nuclear bombs for thirteen years at a remote site known as Dimona, located in the barren Negev region south of Jerusalem. Aided by the French, Israel had constructed a nuclear reactor as well as a separate facility—hidden underground—for the complex process of chemically separating the reactor's most important by-product: weapons-grade plutonium. Begin had visited the underground facility at Dimona at least once since becoming prime minister in 1977 and, Israeli officials told me, had been provided in the days before the raid at Osirak with a detailed memorandum about it. The officials suggested that Begin, in his public remarks, had simply transferred what he had seen and read about Dimona to Osirak. "He confused one with the other," said one Israeli, acknowledging that his interpretation was a charitable one.

Yitzhak Hofi, the Mossad chief, was not as charitable. Two weeks after the Osirak bombing, he gave an unprecedented newspaper interview—Hofi was cited only by title in the article, under the rules of Israeli censorship—to complain about politicians who were compromising secret intelligence. There was no doubt in the Israeli intelligence community about which politician Hofi was criticizing.

. . .

---

[*] Some American intelligence analysts instantly understood that Begin had made a mistake, but their reports were highly classified and never reached the public.

The secrets of Dimona may have been safe from the Western press, but Dimona itself was facing a much more immediate threat. Israeli officials acknowledged that their intelligence services saw evidence in the days after the June 7 raid that Iraq, obviously seeking revenge, had begun moving some of its Soviet-supplied Scud missiles closer to the Iraq-Jordan border. If the Scuds were to be moved farther west into Jordan, Dimona would be in range of a retaliatory strike by the Iraqis. Unlike the reactor at Osirak, which had not yet begun full-scale operation, Dimona had operated around the clock for eight months a year to produce and reprocess weapons-grade plutonium for nuclear weapons. An Iraqi strike could scatter deadly radioactive contamination for dozens of miles.

Well before the bombing at Osirak, however, Israeli officials had ordered the dome-shaped reactor and underground reprocessing plant at Dimona to cease all operations; both were kept out of service through the end of the year. The Israeli Air Force was also instructed to keep intelligence aircraft in the sky on a twenty-four-hour alert. There is no evidence that Washington saw or understood any of the Israeli defensive actions.

A few British intelligence officials immediately suspected that Israel had used the high-resolution KH-11 photography to target Osirak, and they complained to their American counterparts about it. In essence, one involved American recalled, they were saying, "We told you so." The brilliant reputation of the KH-11 system was reinforced, ironically, by Israel's successful raid: high-resolution satellite photographs of the destroyed research reactor were on the desks of Washington decision-makers within a few hours of the mission.

The British were right, as a subsequent highly secret investigation showed: Israel had gotten much valuable intelligence from the KH-11. There was evidence that William J. Casey, Ronald Reagan's director of central intelligence, had inadvertently played a key role.

Casey was an enthusiastic supporter of the imagery-sharing program from the moment he took office, and early in his tenure he ordered that the Israeli liaison officers be provided with a private office near CIA headquarters. The goal, apparently, was to give the Israelis direct access to the American intelligence officers who processed the KH-11 imagery to make sure that all essential intelligence was turned over. Only Israelis, so the reasoning went, would know what was important to Israel. "Casey was prepared to show them a little thigh," one high-ranking American official explained. "But he didn't roll over and play dead for the Israelis."

The CIA director, suddenly confronted after Osirak with serious questions about Israel's abuse of the KH-11 intelligence-sharing agreement, authorized a small, ad hoc committee of experts to review the matter.* The group was ordered to operate with the heightened security that always surrounded Israeli intelligence issues.

What the review group found was stunning.

In little more than two years, the Israelis had expanded what had been a limited agreement to the point where they were able to extract virtually any photograph they wished from the system. Most surprisingly, the Israelis had requested and received extensive KH-11 coverage of western Russia, including Moscow. "The Israelis did everything except task [target] the bird," one disturbed military man acknowledges. There was anger at the senior officials of the Central Intelligence Agency and Defense Intelligence Agency for what some officials considered their "very lax" management of the liaison agreement: "We set up the system and we didn't bother to monitor what they [the Israelis] were doing," the military man said.** William B. Bader, who was serving in 1979 as assistant deputy un-

---

* Casey had made his first secret trip to Israel as CIA director a few months earlier and, according to Israelis, put in motion an ambitious list of joint intelligence operations aimed at rolling back Communism—actions, Casey believed, that had all but ceased during the Carter years. These included renewed espionage activities inside the Soviet Union, aid for the anti-Communist Solidarity movement in Poland, and economic and military support—in violation of a congressional ban—for Jonas Savimbi's UNITA resistance movement in Angola. Casey also insisted upon and apparently received Israeli promises of support for what emerged in the early 1980s as one of his near-obsessions—covert aid to the anti-Communist Renamo insurgency in Mozambique. (A 1988 State Department study placed the number of civilians murdered by Renamo at more than 100,000, with an estimated one million Mozambicans forced into refugee status.) Despite the successful visit, Casey was embarrassed and rankled by the fact that his newfound colleagues in Israel had not seen fit to inform him in advance of the planned attack on Osirak. His CIA thus had failed to anticipate the first serious foreign policy crisis in the Reagan administration.

** Adding to the dismay, surely, was the fact that President Carter, as a security measure, had, shortly after taking office, ordered a freeze on the number of codework clearances in the government. The freeze led to enormous complications throughout

der secretary of defense for policy, recalled his frustration at knowing that the Israelis were "edging deeper into the overhead" and not knowing how to stop it. "You didn't know where to complain," Bader said. "We knew that these guys [the Israelis] had access that went around the colonels and the deputy assistant secretaries." If a complaint got to the wrong office, he explained, "you might get your head handed back to you."

A former high-ranking NSA official recalled his anger upon subsequently learning early in the Reagan administration that Israeli military officers were permitted to attend Pentagon meetings at which future missions and orbital flight paths for the KH-11 were discussed. "People who knew about it wanted to puke," the former official said. "With the care this [the KH-11] got everywhere else, this blew our minds." However, another senior American intelligence officer, agreeing that "a lot of guys were shocked and dismayed," explained that he was less troubled by the Israeli encroachment: "It was in our national interest to make sure in 1981 that the Israelis were going to survive." This officer depicted the direct access provided to Israel as "a compromise. Israel wanted to make sure that nothing important was passed by. It needed to make sure it got all it needed." The Israeli officer assigned to the Pentagon, the intelligence officer said, was only relaying Israel's intelligence needs to the men in charge of the KH-11 program. The Israeli, in return, was allowed to "stand by" as the KH-11 funneled its real-time imagery back to Washington.

A State Department official who was involved said he and Secretary Haig viewed the arguments about Israeli access as "an intelligence community theological debate. Why have a fight? Give them the pictures. It's a confidence builder." It was a zero-sum issue for the Israelis, this official added: if the Reagan administration refused them access to the KH-11, they would turn to Congress "and get the money [inserted into the foreign aid budget] for a satellite, launching pad, and downlink."

To Richard Allen as well, Israel's manipulation of the KH-11 agreement was no big deal: "I figured they had friends"

---

the intelligence world, because many analysts were not permitted access to the information—such as that collected by the KH-11—they needed to do their job.

in the Pentagon who informally had provided the expanded access.

It was finally agreed in the White House after the ad hoc review that the photographs could continue to flow to Israel, but with the initial 1979 restrictions emphatically back in force. "We were going to narrow the aperture," Allen said; Israel would no longer be permitted to get KH-11 imagery of the Soviet Union or any other country outside the hundred-mile limit. Allen personally relayed that message in the fall of 1981 to Ariel Sharon, the controversial and hard-line Israeli general and war hero who had been named defense minister in August by the newly reelected Begin government.

Begin and Sharon were in Washington in September to lobby the White House in support of a far-reaching Israeli plan for a U.S.–Israeli strategic cooperation against a shared enemy: the Soviet Union. An Israeli memorandum for Washington argued that the two nations needed to cooperate "against the threat to peace and security of the region caused by the Soviet Union or Soviet-controlled forces from outside the region introduced into the region." To meet that need, the Israelis sought Reagan's approval for the pre-positioning of American military forces, joint use of airfields, joint planning for military and political contingencies in the Middle East and Persian Gulf, and the U.S. financing of a receiving station, or downlink, for the KH-11 satellite imagery, to be located in Tel Aviv.

The Israeli proposals were understandably viewed as excessive and were much watered down during negotiations over the next few months, to Sharon's dismay. Sharon pushed especially hard on the downlink issue, also insisting that the receiving station be "dedicated"—meaning that the encoded signals to and from the satellite to the downlink could be read only by Israel. The United States thus would be in the untenable position of not being able to know what intelligence the Israelis were obtaining from its own satellite system.

It was a preposterous suggestion, and Allen privately told Sharon so. "It was rough," Allen recalled. "He started bitching about American aid being Band-Aids and mustard plaster. He kept on saying, 'You want to give us Band-Aids. If that's what you mean by strategic alliance, we're not interested.' " Allen, a strong supporter of Israel, said he wasn't intimidated: "I saw Sharon as a big tough swashbuckler who did a lot of bellowing."

The bombing at Osirak led to no significant changes in the U.S.–Israeli relationship, nor were any serious questions raised about Israel's need for so many KH-11 photographs from so many places—a need that risked a breach in Israel's relations with the United States. Despite the brief flap over Israeli access, there were no lessons learned and KH-11 photographs continued to flow to Israel. Some far-reaching changes were triggered, however, for Israel.

The French, who had also been the chief suppliers of nuclear materials and expertise to Iraq in return for oil, were embarrassed as well as outraged by the Israeli attack. There were a few officials in Paris who sought revenge by breaking long-held vows of silence, and they began to tell about an earlier French nuclear relationship in the Middle East: as secret partners in the making of the Israeli bomb.

Ariel Sharon concluded after the cabinet room meeting that the United States was not a reliable strategic ally. He turned to a clandestine Israeli intelligence agency controlled by his defense ministry, whose operations at the time were not fully understood by Washington, and stood by as it intercepted intelligence on the Middle East and Soviet Union from the most sensitive agencies in America—the kind of intelligence that Israel had been told it would no longer be able to get. An American Jew working in the U.S. intelligence community had volunteered his services to the agency several years earlier; he would soon be put to work spying on his country for Israel.

It's almost certain that no one in Ronald Reagan's White House considered Sharon's request for a KH-11 downlink in Tel Aviv in terms of Israel's nuclear ambitions. Similarly, the ad hoc review group that William Casey had set up after Osirak to monitor compliance with the 1979 intelligence-sharing agreement blithely accepted Israel's explanation for its violation of the rules: it had obtained the off-limits KH-11 imagery of the Soviet Union solely to monitor the ongoing supply links between Russia and its allies in Syria and Iraq.

Indeed, there were not many, even in the American intelligence community, who understood in 1981 why Israel had collected satellite imagery of the Soviet Union and why Sharon was so insistent on continued access to that intelligence: Israel was itself a nuclear power that was targeting the Soviet Union with its warheads and missiles.

2

The Scientist

The scientific father of the Israeli bomb, its J. Robert Oppenheimer, was a slight, pale, chain-smoking scientist named Ernst David Bergmann, a rabbi's son who was a refugee from Nazi Germany.

The international scientific community came to know Bergmann after Israel's successful War of Independence in 1948—the first Arab-Israeli War—as a brilliant organic chemist and director of the chemistry division at the Weizmann Institute of Science, Israel's preeminent research facility. He was chairman of Israel's Atomic Energy Commission, set up in 1952, and, on those few occasions when he appeared in public, an outspoken advocate of nuclear research for peaceful purposes. Cigarette constantly in hand, Bergmann was a picture of charm and wit at international conferences on nuclear science. His high intelligence seemed obvious. So did Israel's need for nuclear power: there would be no oil available for purchase from Arab neighbors.

By 1947, Bergmann was telling friends that the large phosphate fields in the Negev desert contained meager, but recoverable, traces of natural uranium. Within two years, a department of isotope research was established at the Weizmann Institute and young Israeli scientists were being sent abroad to study the new fields of nuclear energy and nuclear chemistry. A joint research program also was begun with the nascent French Atomic Energy Commission. By 1953, Israeli researchers at Weizmann had pioneered a new process for creating heavy water, needed to modulate a nuclear chain reaction, as well as devising a more efficient means of extracting uranium from phosphate fields.

In November 1954, Bergmann introduced himself to the Israeli citizenry in a radio address and reported on Israel's progress in peaceful nuclear research. He announced—two years
after the fact—that an Israeli Atomic Energy Commission had
been established. The next year Israel signed an agreement
with the United States, under the Eisenhower administration's
Atoms for Peace program, for cooperation in the civilian uses
of atomic energy. Washington helped finance and fuel a small
nuclear reactor for research, located at Nahal Soreq, south of
Tel Aviv. The agreement called for the United States to have
inspection rights to the small reactor under the Atomic Energy
Act of 1954, which provided for an Israeli guarantee, to be verified by inspections, that the nuclear materials would not be
diverted to weapons research.

These were years in which David Ben-Gurion—Israel's
white-maned "Old Man," who served, with one brief interlude,
as prime minister and defense minister from 1948 to 1963—repeatedly bragged to visitors that Israel would build its own
atomic reactor, utilizing its own natural uranium and locally
manufactured heavy water. Nuclear energy, Ben-Gurion
promised, would soon be producing the electricity and creating
the desalinated water needed to make the Negev desert bloom.

Bergmann's dream of nuclear power plants was sincere, but
it also amounted to a totally effective cover for his drive to
develop the bomb. Ben-Gurion was the man in charge of all of
this, with the aid of his brilliant young protégé Shimon Peres,
who was thirty years old when Ben-Gurion appointed him director general of the ministry of defense in late 1953.
Bergmann's Israeli Atomic Energy Commission, as the public
was not told in the radio address, was under the direct jurisdic-
tion of Peres and the defense ministry. Nuclear power was not
Ben-Gurion's first priority; the desert would glow before it
bloomed.

These three men would find an international ally to help
create the bomb and, equally important, would accept from the
beginning that the bomb would have to be privately financed
by wealthy American and European Jews who shared their
dream of an ultimate deterrent for Israel. Any other approach
would make the bomb impossible to keep secret.

. . .

Israel's nuclear bomb ambitions in the early 1950s were not foreseen in Cold War Washington. The United States was preoccupied with the Korean War, economic and social conditions in Europe, the strength of the Communist Party in France and Italy, fears of internal Communist subversion, and the continuing political battle with the Soviet Union.

There were crises in the Middle East, too. Egypt's corrupt King Farouk was overthrown in a coup in 1952, and a radical new leader, Gamal Abdel Nasser, emerged in 1954 as premier. British troops, after a stay of more than seventy years in Egypt, were on their way out of North Africa. So were the French. By 1955 the French government was facing insurrection from three former colonies, Morocco, Tunisia, and Algeria. Morocco and Tunisia would gain their independence by 1956, but Algeria, whose opposition National Liberation Front (FLN) was strongly supported by Nasser, became the main event. The bloody war, with its 250,000 dead, came close to destroying France over the next five years and provided inspiration to Arab revolutionaries throughout the Middle East.

Nasser, with his talk of Pan-Arabism, also rattled the Israelis, who instinctively turned to the United States. American Jews were Israel's lifeline: hundreds of millions of American dollars were pouring in every year. Ben-Gurion had tried for years to join in a regional security pact with Washington—to somehow be included under the American nuclear umbrella—with no success. Israel had publicly supported the American position in the Korean War and secretly went a step further: Ben-Gurion offered to send Israeli troops to fight alongside the United Nations' forces in South Korea.* President Harry S. Truman said no, apparently in fear of backing into a security arrangement with Israel. The United States, England, and France had agreed in their 1950 Tripartite Agreement that all three nations would maintain the status quo in the Middle East by not providing any significant quantity of military equipment to Arabs

---

* Israel's position on the Korean War enraged Moscow and led to a rupture in diplomatic relations. The Soviet Union, which had been the first nation to recognize the State of Israel in 1948, would for the next thirty years castigate Israel for its "racist and discriminatory" treatment of Palestinians and ties to American "imperialism."

or Israelis. The Eisenhower administration came into office in
1953 with no intention of changing the policy.

Israel tried, nonetheless, to establish some kind of a special
relationship with President Eisenhower, with no luck. In the
mid-1950s, a year-long series of renewed talks on a mutual security treaty with Washington went nowhere. At one point, as
Ben-Gurion told his biographer, Michael Bar-Zohar, he considered offering Eisenhower American bases in Israel in return
for a security commitment. That idea was dropped when the
talks faltered. There were equally unsuccessful strategems to
purchase fighter planes and other weapons, but Eisenhower
essentially maintained the 1950 embargo on arms sales to Israel
throughout the eight years of his presidency. The effect was to
limit America's influence in the Middle East and deny Washington a chance to have an impact on Israeli foreign policy.
The policy suited the men around Eisenhower, many of them
Wall Street lawyers who thought that America's oil supply
would be jeopardized by arms trafficking with Israel.

Ben-Gurion's private nightmare in these years—as his close
aides knew—was of a second Holocaust, this time at the hands
of the Arabs. Israel's only security, Ben-Gurion repeatedly
warned, would come through self-defense and self-reliance.
"What is Israel?" he was quoted by an aide as asking.
". . . Only a small spot. One dot! How can it survive in this
Arab world?" Ben-Gurion believed that he understood Arab
character and was persuaded that as long as Arabs thought they
could destroy the Jewish state, there would be no peace and no
recognition of Israel. Many Israelis, survivors of the Holocaust,
came to believe in *ein brera,* or "no alternative," the doctrine
that Israel was surrounded by implacable enemies and therefore had no choice but to strike out. In their view, Hitler and
Nasser were interchangeable.

For these Israelis, a nuclear arsenal was essential to the survival of the state. In public speeches throughout the 1950s, Ben-
Gurion repeatedly linked Israel's security to its progress in science. "Our security and independence require that more young
people devote themselves to science and research, atomic and
electronic research, research of solar energy . . . and the like,"
he told the Israeli parliament, the Knesset, in November 1955.

Ernst Bergmann explicitly articulated the *ein brera* fears in a letter two years later: "I am convinced . . . that the State of Israel needs a defense research program of its own, so that we shall never again be as lambs led to the slaughter."

Ben-Gurion, Shimon Peres, and Ernst Bergmann believed that Israel's independent arsenal finally could provide what President Eisenhower would not—the nuclear umbrella.

No outsider—not the international scientific community, the Israeli public, nor American intelligence—could understand the significance of Bergmann's two other government portfolios in the early 1950s: as scientific adviser to the minister of defense and as director of research and planning for the defense ministry. The Israelis in charge of those posts knew Bergmann to be the most uncompromising and effective advocate for nuclear weapons, the man most directly responsible—along with the French—for Israel's status by the end of the 1960s as a nuclear-weapons state. Bergmann and the French not only got it done in the Negev desert, but they kept it secret, just as J. Robert Oppenheimer and his colleagues had kept the Manhattan Project undiscovered in the desert at Los Alamos.

The young Bergmann had been introduced in the early 1920s to the world of the atom as a student of organic chemistry at the Emil Fischer Institute of the University of Berlin. He was on the fringe of a circle of eminent scientists, including Ernest Rutherford in England and Marie Curie of France, who were the cutting edge of what would become an international race in the prewar years to unravel the mystery of nuclear fission. Bergmann's colleagues in Berlin included Herman F. Mark, an Austrian who later became an eminent chemist and dean of the Brooklyn Polytechnic Institute (and whose son, Hans M., served as secretary of the Air Force in the Carter administration).* "We were not theoreticians," recalled Mark, who during

* Herman Mark was ninety-five years old when interviewed in 1990 at his son's home in Austin, Texas. Hans Mark, then chancellor of the University of Texas, was himself no stranger to the world of intelligence and nuclear weapons. As Air Force secretary, he also wore what is known in the government as the "black hat": he was head of the executive committee, or Ex-Com, of the National Reconnaissance Office (NRO), a most-secret unit that is responsible for the development, procurement, and targeting of America's intelligence satellites. As a nuclear physicist, Hans Mark had

his career published twenty books and more than five hundred papers on polymer science. "We were interested in making things. The important thing for us was synthetics. First you have to make something nobody else has—and then you can use it." While in Berlin, Bergmann and Mark worked together and published joint papers on the chemical structure of rubber, paint, and adhesives.

Bergmann's father was one of the most eminent rabbis in Berlin and a close friend of Chaim Weizmann, the Russian-Jewish biochemist and Zionist then living in England. In 1933, when a series of sweeping Nazi decrees made it impossible for Bergmann or any other Jew to continue in an academic job in Germany, Weizmann arranged for young Bergmann to join him on the faculty at Manchester University in England, where he continued his research on synthetics and his close association with those scientists racing to split the atom. Like Weizmann, Bergmann came to the attention of Frederick A. Lindemann, later Lord Cherwell, a German-born Oxford scientist who became Winston Churchill's chief science adviser in the years before World War II.

Little is known of Bergmann's defense work for the British before the war; it is in those years that he first became involved with the defense of Palestine. One of the Weizmann biographies reports that the Hagannah, the military arm of the Zionist movement in Palestine, asked Weizmann in 1936 for a chemist to help produce an effective high explosive for use in the underground war against the Arabs and the British. Dynamite was far too dangerous to handle in the climate of the Middle East. Weizmann assigned the mission to Bergmann, who got it done and then signed on as a member of the Hagannah's technical committee. In 1939, the biography adds, Bergmann traveled to Paris on behalf of the Hagannah and shared his findings with the French, whose army was then operating in North Africa.

Bergmann left England shortly after Germany invaded Poland in the fall of 1939. Weizmann had intervened once again and found him a job with old friends who owned a chemistry

---

worked for twelve years beginning in 1955 for the Lawrence Livermore Laboratory in California, one of America's main nuclear weapons facilities. For four of those years he served as a division leader in experimental physics.

laboratory in Philadelphia. It didn't work out, and another old friend from Germany, Herman Mark, came to his rescue: "He had no space. So we invited him to come to Brooklyn." Mark had been driven out of Europe in 1938 and ended up doing research for a Canadian paper company in Ontario. By 1940 he was running a laboratory at the Polytechnic Institute of Brooklyn; two years later he became dean of faculty and turned the institute into a haven for Jewish refugees, including Chaim Weizmann. "The whole gang came to America," said Mark, who, when interviewed for this book, was the sole known survivor of that period.

With the defeat of Hitler, there was one final migration for Bergmann: to Palestine to help establish what would become the Weizmann Institute of Science at Rehovot, south of Tel Aviv. Israeli ambitions seemed unlimited. Oppenheimer and his colleagues in the Manhattan Project, including John von Neumann, the mathematician and early computer theoretician, were being wooed—unsuccessfully—by Weizmann as early as 1947, and were repeatedly asked to spend time doing research in Israel.*

Bergmann was Weizmann's first choice to become director of the institute, but Weizmann's wife, Vera, successfully objected on the oldest of grounds: she was offended at Bergmann's long-standing affair with Hani, her husband's private secretary (whom Bergmann eventually married).** Bergmann instead was named head of the organic chemistry division. He could take solace, if needed, at the eminence of his colleagues. Amos Deshalit, who headed the physics division, subsequently was considered a quantum researcher in a class with Oppenheimer

---

* Oppenheimer's personal papers, on file at the Library of Congress, show that he went to Israel in May 1958 to participate in ceremonies marking the opening of the Institute of Nuclear Science in Rehovot. He also took a military flight with Bergmann and Shimon Peres to visit the port city of Elat at the southern reach of the Negev, according to newspaper reports at the time. Israeli officials who worked in 1958 at Dimona, then in the early stages of construction, recall no visit then or in later years by Oppenheimer.
** It was Bergmann's second missed opportunity to direct a Weizmann research institute. Weizmann had been instrumental in the 1930s in setting up Palestine's first research facility, the Daniel Sieff Institute. According to Shimon Peres, Weizmann approached Albert Einstein, then teaching at Princeton, and asked him to recommend one of his students to run the institute. Einstein instead suggested Bergmann, who didn't get the job for reasons not known.

and Niels Bohr, the Danish Nobel Prize winner. Inorganic chemistry was directed by Aharon Katchalsky, later Katzir, who was a specialist in the electrolytic properties of chain molecules and a pioneer researcher in the related field of muscle-powered robotics. (Like Bergmann, Katzir had a secret life: at his death in 1972, he was one of the driving forces in the then flourishing Israeli nuclear weapons program.) There was one final move for Bergmann, at Ben-Gurion's request, after Israel's Independence in 1948—to the ministry of defense, where, under Shimon Peres, Bergmann established the nation's first institute for defense research. More than forty years later, Peres would tell an Israeli newspaper reporter that Bergmann, even in 1948, was constantly speaking about a missile capability for Israel. "I might be ready to tell the full truth about him in one hundred years, maybe," Peres added. "We worked thirteen years together, perhaps the best years of my life."

Without Bergmann, insisted Herman Mark, there would have been no Israeli bomb: "He was in charge of every kind of nuclear activity in Israel. He was the man who completely understood it [nuclear fission], and then he explained it to other people." Mark became a constant commuter between Brooklyn and Israel after World War II, serving on planning boards and as a scientific adviser to the fledgling Weizmann Institute. He remained close to Bergmann and shared his view of the inevitability of Israeli nuclear weapons research: "We were both of the same opinion—that eventually Israel has to be in full cognizance and knowledge of what happens in nuclear physics. Look, a new type of chemical reaction was discovered at Los Alamos. Whether it's desalination, a power plant, or a bomb makes no difference—it's still fission."

Bergmann had made the same point in a 1966 interview—after he was forced out of government service—with an Israeli newspaper: "It's very important to understand that by developing atomic energy for peaceful uses, you reach the nuclear option. There are no two atomic energies." That interview, nine years before his death, was as close as Bergmann ever came to publicly discussing the bomb. "Bergmann was anxious, rightly so," said Mark, "that there shouldn't be too much talk. It was super-secret—just like the Manhattan Project."

There was at least one early occasion, however, when Bergmann couldn't resist sharing what he knew. Abraham Feinberg, a wealthy New York businessman and ardent advocate of statehood for Israel, was one of Ben-Gurion's most important and trusted allies in the United States. By 1947, Feinberg was playing a major—and highly discreet—role in fund-raising and White House lobbying for Israel as well as for the Democratic Party. He would operate at the highest levels between Washington and Jerusalem for the next two decades. Bergmann was in New York that fall and, as usual, joined Abe Feinberg and his family at Friday-night synagogue services; the group would later return to Feinberg's apartment. "Bergmann was always hungry," recalled Feinberg. "He loved my wife's scrambled eggs." One night over dinner, added Feinberg, "Bergmann's eyes lit up and he said, 'There's uranium in the desert.' " There was no question about the message—that a path was now cleared for Israel to develop the atomic bomb. Feinberg was astonished at such indiscreet talk: "I shushed him up."

Israel's needs in the late 1940s and early 1950s coincided perfectly with France's. Both nations were far from having any technical capacity to build a bomb, nor was there any internal consensus that a bomb was desirable.

Ben-Gurion, Peres, and Bergmann would spend much of their careers engaged in a bitter fight inside the Israeli government over their dreams of a nuclear weapons program. Most senior members of the ruling Mapai (Israel Workers') Party viewed an Israeli bomb as suicidal, too expensive, and too reminiscent of the horrors that had been inflicted on the Jews in World War II.

The French debate revolved around the Cold War. France's high commissioner for nuclear matters, Frédéric Joliot-Curie, a Nobel laureate who had done important research in nuclear physics before the war, was a member of the Communist Party who was opposed to a French role in NATO and any French link to nuclear weapons. In 1950, he was the first to sign the Stockholm Appeal, a Soviet-backed petition calling for a ban on all nuclear weapons. French scientists, despite extensive involvement in prewar nuclear fission research, had been excluded from a major role in the American and British bomb programs of World War II, and Joliot-Curie's politics kept France isolated. Joliot-Curie was dismissed after signing the Stockholm Appeal, and he was eventually replaced by Pierre Guillaumat, who had served during the war with the French secret intelligence service, and Francis Perrin, a Joliot associate who in 1939 had been the first to publish a formula for calculating the critical mass of uranium—the amount needed to sustain a chain reaction. The French plowed ahead with no help from the United States, which viewed France's Atomic Energy Commission as being riddled with Soviet agents.

Perrin also was important to the Israeli connection. A socialist who fled to England in 1940 at the fall of France, he became friendly with Bergmann—how the two met is not known—and traveled to Tel Aviv in 1949. It was after that visit that some Israeli scientists were permitted to attend Saclay, the newly set up French national atomic research center near Versailles, and participate in the construction of Saclay's small experimental reactor. It was a learning experience for the nuclear scientists of both countries.

In an unpublished interview with an American graduate student in 1969, Bergmann spoke elliptically of the ambitions he shared with Ben-Gurion and Peres for the French-Israeli connection: "We felt that Israel . . . needed to collaborate with a country close to its own technical level. First it was important to train Israeli experts. Then we would decide exactly what sort of collaboration to seek and what kind of contribution could be made in a joint endeavor, considering Israel's capacities and resources. Every effort was to be made to keep cooperation from being entirely one-directional."

A critical decision for France, and thus Israel, came in 1951 when, over the objections of Perrin, Guillaumat authorized the construction of a natural uranium–fueled reactor capable of producing, after chemical reprocessing, about twenty-two pounds of weapons-grade plutonium a year. The chain reaction would be moderated by graphite, a technique used by the United States and the Soviet Union in their huge plutonium-

producing reactors. Surveyors had found large deposits of natural uranium a few years earlier near Limoges, in central
France, and that discovery made it easy for Guillaumat and
Perrin to discard an alternative method for powering the reactor—using uranium that had been artificially enriched. Enriched fuel, if available at all, would have to be imported, since
French technicians did not yet know how to enrich natural
uranium. But relying on foreign suppliers—and inevitable international controls—would rob France of any chance to
achieve its basic goal of atomic independence. "France,"
Charles de Gaulle wrote in his World War II memoirs, "cannot
be France without greatness." The decision to produce weapons-grade plutonium would irrevocably propel France down
the road to a nuclear bomb, as Guillaumat, Perrin, and the
Israelis had to know—but the French public and its military
leaders did not.

Construction began the next year at Marcoule, in the southern Rhône Valley. Saint-Gobain Techniques Nouvelles (SGN),
a large chemical company, subsequently was granted a contract
to build a chemical reprocessing plant on the grounds at
Marcoule. Such plants are the critical element in the making of
a bomb. The natural uranium, once burned, or irradiated, in
the reactor, breaks down into uranium, plutonium, and highly
toxic wastes. The irradiated fuel needs to be transported,
cooled, and then treated before the plutonium can be separated
and purified. These steps can be accomplished only by remote
control and in a specially built separate facility—the reprocessing plant—containing elaborate and very expensive physical
protection for the work force.

Bergmann's men were able to contribute to all of this. There
was renewed controversy inside Israel over the constantly expanding Israeli presence in France, but Ben-Gurion held firm.
"In 1952," Shimon Peres told an Israeli interviewer, "I was
alone as favoring the building of an Israeli nuclear option. I
. . . felt terrible. Everyone was opposed—only Ben-Gurion
said, 'You'll see, it will be okay.' There were people who went
to Ben-Gurion and told him, 'Don't listen to Shimon; he and
Bergmann are spinning tales. Israel won't be able to launch a
project like this.' They said, 'Buy from the Canadians, from the

Americans.' But I wanted the French, because Bergmann was well known among the community of French atomic scientists."

French officials reciprocated the Israeli trust: Israeli scientists were the only foreigners allowed access throughout the secret French nuclear complex at Marcoule. Israelis were said to be able to roam "at will." One obvious reason for the carte blanche was the sheer brilliance of the Israeli scientists and their expertise, even then, in computer technology. The French would remain dependent for the next decade—the first French nuclear test took place in 1960—on Israeli computer skills. A second reason for the Israeli presence at Marcoule was emotional: many French officials and scientists had served in the resistance and maintained intense feelings about the Holocaust. And many of France's leading nuclear scientists were Jewish and strong supporters of the new Jewish state, which was emerging—to the delight of these men—as France's closest ally in the Middle East.

No Frenchman had stronger emotional ties to Israel than Bertrand Goldschmidt, a nuclear chemist who had served during World War II with the handful of French scientists who were permitted—despite being foreigners—to work directly with the Americans doing nuclear research. He had become an expert in the chemistry of plutonium and plutonium extraction. He also had helped build an experimental reactor fueled with natural uranium and moderated by heavy water. As a first-rate chemist, he had been offered a chance to stay in the American bomb program after the war, but instead chose to return to France and join its Atomic Energy Commission. After intense negotiations, American security officials permitted him to do so, but refused to release him from his wartime pledge of secrecy. "It was tacitly understood," Goldschmidt subsequently wrote, "that we could use our knowledge to benefit France by giving information to our research teams, but without publishing and only to the extent necessary for the progress of our work. That was a reasonable compromise"— and one that was quickly disregarded.

Goldschmidt was a Jew whose family had suffered, as had most Jewish families in Europe, during the war. His ties to

Israel were heightened by marriage; his wife was a member of
the eminent Rothschild banking family, whose contributions to
Israel and Jewish causes were measured in the tens of millions
of dollars. Goldschmidt and his wife had made the pilgrimage
to Israel in the early 1950s and been taken by Ernst Bergmann
for a memorable meeting with Ben-Gurion at his frame home
in the Negev.* By then, Goldschmidt was serving as director of
chemistry for France's Atomic Energy Commission; in the
1970s he would become a widely respected French spokesman
on nonproliferation and other international atomic energy issues. He also was among the few outsiders permitted to visit
the completed reactor at Dimona in the 1960s—then a classic
example of illicit proliferation.

"We weren't really helping them [the Israelis]," Goldschmidt
explained years later. "We were just letting them know what
we knew—without knowing where it would lead. We didn't
know ourselves how difficult it would be." The important fact
to understand, he added, with some discomfort, is that "in the
fifties and sixties having a nuclear weapon was considered a
good thing—something to be congratulated for. Not like the
stigma it is now."

By 1953, the scientific team at the Weizmann Institute had developed the improved ion exchange mechanism for producing
heavy water and a more efficient method for mining uranium.**
Both concepts were sold to the French; the sales led to a formal
agreement for cooperation in nuclear research that was signed
by the two nations. Goldschmidt recalled that Bergmann himself came to France to negotiate the mining sale with Pierre
Guillaumat. He demanded 100 million francs for the new process, but refused to describe it fully in advance, claiming that if

---

* "We had a long discussion about atomic energy," Goldschmidt recalls. "Ben-Gurion asked me how long would it take [for nuclear desalinization] to make the Negev
desert bloom?"—a favorite Ben-Gurion question. "I said fifteen years. He started scold-
ing me and said if we brought in all the Jewish scientists we could do it much faster."

** Israel's much-ballyhooed breakthrough in heavy-water production, which involved distillation rather than the previously used electrolysis method, was a disappointment, however. The procedure did produce heavy water far more easily and
much more cheaply than other methods, as advertised, but also much more slowly.

he did so it would lose half its value. There was an impasse. Finally, said Goldschmidt, "Guillaumat told me, 'I have the greatest respect for those people,' and we bargained." Bergmann settled for sixty million francs. Israel would remain on a cash-and-carry basis with the French in its nuclear dealings.

The French Connection

  In late 1953, a disillusioned Ben-Gurion, convinced that Israeli society was losing its pioneering, volunteerist spirit, retired to his desert kibbutz at Sdeh Boker, in the Negev, near the future site of Dimona. He believed he could revive that spirit and set an example by resettling in the desert with his wife. His political control over the Mapai Party remained total, however—like that of a Mafia don—and the government that was left behind was one of his creation. Ben-Gurion would be replaced by not one but two people, for he decreed that his jointly held positions of prime minister and defense minister be separated. Ben-Gurion then appointed Moshe Sharett as the new prime minister. No two men could have differed more in their approach to the Arab question. Sharett, who had lived in an Arab village as a child and who, unlike Ben-Gurion, spoke Arabic, believed that peace with the Arab world was possible, but only through military restraint and with the possible intervention of the United Nations. As prime minister, he would begin secret peace negotiations with Nasser.

  Before leaving office, Ben-Gurion also designated Pinhas Lavon, more hard-line than Sharett on the Arab question, as the new defense minister. His goal, obviously, was to ensure that Sharett's views would not go unchallenged. Ben-Gurion also arranged for another hard-liner, Moshe Dayan, to become the new army chief of staff. Shimon Peres would stay on the job as director general of the defense ministry: he was a known Ben-Gurion favorite.

  Ben-Gurion's concerns about Sharett did not extend to the nuclear question. Sharett, as his voluminous personal diaries—as yet unpublished in full in English—make clear, shared the

Old Man's ambition for the "Enterprise," without sharing Ben-
Gurion's confidence in Bergmann. In one typical entry,
Sharett wrote off Bergmann "as a chemist sunk in research and
teaching with no ability to oversee the 'problem' "—one of
many synonyms for the bomb. Bergmann's lack of administrative skills, added Sharett, would "limit and disrupt the hori-
zons of the 'Enterprise' and sabotage its development."

How to handle the Arab question was the dominant issue,
however, and over the next year there was inevitable tension as
Dayan and Peres, in almost constant contact with Ben-Gurion
at his kibbutz, sought to stifle Sharett's dovish policies and his
secret talks with the Egyptians. Scandal broke in mid-1954
when Egyptian authorities announced the arrest of an Israeli
spy ring that had bombed and sabotaged American, British,
and Egyptian targets earlier in the year in what became known
as the Lavon Affair. The goal of the bombings had been to
derail pending British and American negotiations—and possible rapprochement—with the Nasser government; Egypt was
to remain isolated from the Western powers. An internal Israeli
investigation was unable to determine who had given the order
for the sabotage activities, and Sharett, who had not known of
the operation, accepted Lavon's resignation in January 1955.
Ben-Gurion was recalled a few days later from retirement to
replace Lavon as defense minister.* Sharett remained as prime
minister, although there was little doubt about who would be
running the government.

The Old Man's immediate public mission was to restore the
army's morale and the citizens' confidence in the government.
He entered office, however, more convinced than ever that a
policy of military reprisal was essential; any interference with
defense planning, he warned Sharett in writing, would force
him once again to resign and call for new elections. Six days

* Lavon, one of the intellectual leaders of the Mapai Party, maintained that Dayan
and other witnesses against him in the various internal Israeli inquiries had perjured
themselves in an effort to shift the blame to him alone. He was exonerated by a cabinet
committee inquiry seven years later. Sharett, in his diaries, made it clear that he was
convinced that Dayan was involved in both the original unauthorized operations inside
Egypt and the subsequent attempt to shift the blame to Lavon. Any involvement of
Dayan, of course, inevitably raises the possibility that Ben-Gurion had personal knowledge of the operation and, in fact, had approved it.

after taking office, on February 28, 1955, Ben-Gurion responded
to a cross-border attack by Palestinian guerrillas, or *fedayeen*, by
authorizing a large-scale retaliation against an Egyptian military camp at Gaza. The Israeli attack, which killed thirty-six
Egyptians and Palestinians, was led by Lieutenant Colonel
Ariel Sharon, whose reputation for skill and brutality already
was well established. The Gaza attack escalated what had been
a series of skirmishes into something close to guerrilla war;
Arab casualties were four times greater than Sharett had been
told to expect. The raid ended the secret contacts between
Sharett and Nasser and resulted in an Egyptian decision to step
up its *fedayeen* attacks from Gaza. The Israeli historian Avi
Shlaim has written that Sharett viewed the subsequent increases in Gaza Strip border clashes as the "inevitable consequence" of the February 28 raid, while Ben-Gurion saw them
"as a sign of growing Egyptian bellicosity which, if allowed to
go unchallenged, would pose a threat to Israel's basic security."

Nasser responded to the increased tension by turning to the
Communist world for military aid. He traveled in April 1955 to
the Bandung Conference of African and Asian nations and received a promise from Chou En-lai, the Chinese premier, for as
many arms as Egypt could afford. In July, Soviet delegations
arrived in Cairo to offer military aid. In September, Nasser
announced that Egypt would receive the staggering total of 200
modern Soviet bombers, 230 tanks, 200 troop carriers, and more
than 500 artillery pieces. Soviet advisers also were promised.

In Tel Aviv, there was dismay. Israel's third temple was in
danger.* Ben-Gurion, still denied American support, turned
anew to the French. The Israelis wanted more than guns. The
French had their needs, too.

In late 1954, the coalition government led by Pierre Mendès-
France, one of fourteen coalitions that held office during the
chaotic Fourth Republic, had granted authority for a nuclear

---

* The first temple and Jewish state, as every Israeli schoolchild knows, was destroyed in 537 B.C. by the Babylonians. The second temple was destroyed by the Romans in A.D. 70, although Jews continued to live in the area through the centuries.
Modern Zionist resettlement of Palestine began in the 1880s, and Jews had become a
political force in Palestine by 1917, when Britain, in the Balfour Declaration, pledged to
establish in Palestine "a national home for the Jewish people," with safeguards for the
other, i.e., Arab, inhabitants.

weapons planning group to be formed inside the French Atomic Energy Commission. Senior officials of the ministry of defense thus were brought into nuclear planning for the first time. Many French military men had been skeptical of an independent nuclear deterrent, but that attitude was changed by France's disastrous defeat at the hands of Ho Chi Minh at Dienbienphu, North Vietnam, in 1954, and the subsequent collapse of French colonialism in the wars of liberation in North Africa. It was clear to many Frenchmen that France could not depend on its NATO allies to protect purely French interests. This was especially true in Algeria, where the bloody revolution and French repression were turning the casbahs and deserts into a killing field.

In January 1955, the French government fell again and a new socialist government headed by Guy Mollet assumed power. Mollet took a much harder line on the war in Algeria and those Arab leaders, such as Nasser, who supported the revolutionaries. Israel, which had been intensively waging guerrilla war against Egypt, was now widely seen as one of France's most dependable allies. Mollet agreed later in the year to begin secretly selling high-performance French bombers to Israel; the sales, arranged by Shimon Peres, were from one defense ministry to another, with no diplomatic niceties and no involvement of the French or Israeli foreign ministries. Arms continued to flow from France to Israel for the next twelve years.

In return, Israel agreed to begin sharing intelligence on the Middle East, the United States, and Europe with the French. The Israeli intelligence networks in North Africa were particularly good, former Israeli officials recalled, because the Jews there tended to live and work as merchants and businessmen in the Arab quarters. Of special significance were the more than 100,000 Jews in Algeria, many of them trapped by the violence and irrationality of both sides. Those Jews were encouraged by the Israeli government to provide intelligence on the leadership of the National Liberation Front and in other ways to cooperate with the French.

It was inevitable that Bergmann and Peres would conclude that Israel now had enough leverage to seek French help for the Israeli bomb: would the Mollet government match the extraordinary Israeli support in Algeria and elsewhere by agreeing to construct a large reactor—and a chemical reprocessing plant— in Israel? The Israelis understood that no plutonium weapon could be made without a reprocessing plant, and they also understood that the construction of the plant would be impossible without a French commitment. The French Atomic Energy Commission was scheduled to begin construction in mid-1955 on its own chemical reprocessing plant at Marcoule, and Israeli scientists had been involved at every step along the way.

Having the French say yes could, ironically, trigger a crisis inside the top ranks of the Israeli government. A French commitment would force Peres and Bergmann to inform the cabinet that Israel was going to build a secret nuclear complex. There already were plenty of objections from those few who knew. Levi Eshkol, the finance minister, shared Ben-Gurion's belief in *ein brera*, but also was convinced that a nuclear-armed Israel would be financial madness. Eshkol would hold on to that view after becoming prime minister in 1963. There were concerns other than financial among the Israeli leadership. How could Israel keep the reactor secret? Was it moral for Israel, whose citizens had suffered so much from indiscriminate slaughter, to have a weapon of mass destruction? What would the American government say? Would America continue to be the land of deep pockets?

The nuclear advocates got a huge break in September 1955. The Canadian government announced that it had agreed to build a heavy-water research reactor for the Indian government. The Canadian offer included no provision for international inspections, since no international agreement on nuclear safeguards had yet been promulgated. India promised to utilize the reactor only for "peaceful purposes." There was now international precedent for an Israeli reactor.

In late 1955, a new Israeli government was formed with Ben-Gurion once again serving as both defense minister and prime minister. Moshe Sharett, despite misgivings, stayed on as foreign minister. National elections that summer had eroded the Mapai plurality in the Knesset and provided more evidence that the Israeli public was dissatisfied with the dovish policies

of Moshe Sharett.* An American attempt, authorized by Eisenhower, to mediate a settlement between Nasser and Ben-Gurion failed early in 1956 when the Egyptian president refused to
negotiate directly with Jerusalem and presented demands, as
many Israelis thought, that he knew to be unacceptable. A few
months later, the long-standing direct talks between Jerusalem
and Washington also collapsed; there would be no American
security agreement with Israel. On June 10, Ben-Gurion authorized General Moshe Dayan to open secret negotiations with
Paris on a joint war against Egypt. In July, Nasser, as expected,
nationalized the Suez Canal, bringing the outraged British government into the secret planning for war. Shimon Peres was
now shuttling between Paris and Tel Aviv on behalf of Ben-
Gurion; the line between public policy and personal diplomacy
was eroding daily, to the muffled protests of many inside each
government.

* Pocketbook politics played a significant role in these politically complicated years,
along with the always important Arab question. Within the labor movement there
were three main parties, the dominant one Mapai, the most centrist and pragmatic
faction of Israel's socialist-Zionist movement. Achdut Avodah, the Unity of Labor, was
domestically more socialistic than Mapai, and more hawkish and nationalistic in foreign policy. Mapam, the United Workers' Party, was far more dovish in foreign policy,
and even opposed the creation of Israel in 1948 as an exclusively Jewish state; it urged,
instead, a secular bi-national Jewish and Palestinian state. (The three main elements of
the labor movement joined forces in the late 1960s to create the Labor Party.) Ben-
Gurion's Mapai Party had lost seats in the 1955 election to the right-wing Herut Party
in what amounted to a voter backlash by new immigrants, resentful of their treatment
by the Mapai leadership. The General Zionists, conservative on economic matters and
moderate on defense and military issues, lost seats. (The free-market General Zionists
would merge in 1966 with the Herut Party, Menachem Begin's populist-conservative
party, to form the Gahal Party. Gahal, in turn, merged in 1973—after relentless pressure from newly retired General Ariel Sharon—with three right-wing factions to create the Likud Party, which took office in 1977—ending twenty-nine years of Labor
control of the government.) The most hawkish political factions in the mid-1950s, in
terms of military policy toward the Arabs, were the group led by Moshe Dayan and
Shimon Peres, Mapai; Achdut Avodah, led by Yisrael Galili and former 1948 War of
Independence hero Yigal Allon; and Herut. Both groups were opposed by moderate
members of the Mapai Party such as Moshe Sharett, Levi Eshkol, Abba Eban, and
Pinhas Sapir. Even among the hawks there were divisions, with Begin and his Herut
Party followers believing the primary task of Israel to be the redemption of biblical
lands in order to reestablish Greater, or Eretz, Israel. Ben-Gurion, Dayan, Peres, and
Galili (who played a major and secret role in future governments) were hawks of
Realpolitik considerations—a belief in force as a necessary ingredient of international
relations. They were thus adamantly opposed to the fundamentalist views of Begin and
his Herut Party. In essence, the Mapai Party's loss of seats in the 1955 elections reflected
economic worries as well as a move within the Labor faction away from the dovish
policies of Sharett and toward the more hawkish views of Ben-Gurion, Dayan, Peres,
and Allon.

That summer Moshe Sharett quietly resigned as foreign minister. He had sought an open debate on Israel's foreign policy in front of Mapai Party members, but Ben-Gurion fought it off by threatening to resign. The Israeli public would not learn of the deep divisions at the top of its government until the publication of Sharett's personal diaries in 1980. Sharett's replacement was Golda Meir, the minister of labor, whose main qualification, Ben-Gurion would later acknowledge, was her ignorance of international affairs. Meir endorsed Ben-Gurion's argument for preventive war; nonetheless, her ministry would be repeatedly bypassed by Ben-Gurion, Peres, Dayan, and Ernst David Bergmann as Israel broadened its involvement with France.

In mid-September, with the Suez War against Egypt six weeks away and with no international protest over the Canadian reactor sale, Ben-Gurion decided it was time to formally seek French help for the Israeli bomb. Israeli nuclear scientists working at Saclay had been involved since 1949 in planning and constructing the French experimental reactor, known as EL 2, which was powered by natural uranium and moderated by heavy water. Building a similar reactor in Israel was eminently feasible. Uranium was indigenous to Israel, and there was some heavy water available locally in Israel; more heavy water, if needed, as seemed likely, could be supplied by the French or illicitly purchased from Norway or the United States, then the world's largest producers. Ben-Gurion already had picked out a location for the Israeli reactor—in the basement of an old deserted winery at Rishon LeZion, a few miles from the Weizmann Institute.

It was decided to send Shimon Peres with Ernst Bergmann to Paris. Bertrand Goldschmidt vividly recalled a subsequent meeting of the French Atomic Energy Commission: "They came to me and said they'd like to buy a heavy-water research reactor similar to the one the Canadians were building in India. They said that when the Americans will realize we have a nuclear capacity, they will give us the guarantee of survival. All of this was decided before the Suez affair."

Four days later, on September 17, Bergmann and Peres had dinner with Francis Perrin and Pierre Guillaumat at the home of Jacob Tzur, the Israeli ambassador to France. Once again France was asked to provide a reactor. "We thought the Israeli bomb was aimed against the Americans," Perrin later explained. "Not to launch it against America but to say, 'If you don't want to help us in a critical situation we will require you to help us. Otherwise we will use our nuclear bombs.' "

Goldschmidt remained convinced years later that the basic decision to help Israel get the bomb was made during those two meetings in mid-September. There is no written record of the meetings, and it is impossible to determine what happened when. What is clear, nonetheless, is that Israel sought French help for the bomb—and got it—at least six weeks before the shooting started in the Suez War.

Many Israelis viewed the conduct of their partners in the Suez War as a betrayal. Israel's immediate tactical goal in the war was to destroy the Egyptian Army and its ability to support and train the growing Palestinian *fedayeen* movement. The strategic goal was far more ambitious: to destroy Nasser's ability to achieve Arab unity. Keeping the Arab world in disarray has always been a focal point of Israeli strategy, and Nasser, with his calls for Pan-Arabism—Egyptian hegemony, in Israeli eyes —was a serious national security threat. The Israelis further believed that a humiliating Egyptian defeat in the Suez War inevitably would lead to Nasser's overthrow.

The battle plan called for Israel to initiate the attack on October 29, sending paratroopers into the Sinai and destroying the ability of Egypt to operate from Gaza. France and Britain would then demand that both sides halt hostilities and withdraw ten miles from the Suez Canal, creating a buffer zone. When the Egyptians, who owned the canal, refused to do so—a refusal that was inevitable—France and England would launch bombing and airborne assaults on November 6 to neutralize and occupy the canal.

The battle plan went much better than scheduled. Israel stormed through the Egyptian Army and had captured all of the Sinai by November 4. There was nothing, other than a United Nations call for a cease-fire, to stop the Israeli Army from crossing the Suez and taking Cairo. Guy Mollet began urging Anthony Eden, Britain's prime minister, to move up the date of their combined assault, but Eden, made anxious by the fast pace of the Israeli Army and the United Nations cease-fire call, refused. The British and French finally landed, as pre-arranged, on the morning of November 6 at Port Said, only to stop again when the Soviet Union, then involved in the bloody suppression of the Hungarian revolution, issued what was perceived in Israel to be a nuclear ultimatum in separate notes to Ben-Gurion, Mollet, and Eden.

The Soviet telegram to Ben-Gurion accused Israel of "criminally and irresponsibly playing with the fate of peace, with the fate of its own people. It is sowing a hatred for the state of Israel among the people of the east such as cannot but make itself felt with regard to the future of Israel and which puts in jeopardy the very existence of Israel as a State." A separate note signed by Prime Minister Nikolai Bulganin explicitly warned Ben-Gurion that the Soviet Union was capable of attacking with "remote-controlled vehicles." There also was a threat to send troops as "volunteers" into the Middle East.

Anthony Eden, already under extreme pressure to pull out of the war from the Eisenhower administration as well as from the opposition Labor Party at home, was the first to break ranks, informing Paris that he had ordered his troops to cease firing. The French followed. Israel, deserted by its two allies, was forced a few days later to agree to a cease-fire and the eventual deployment of the United Nations' peacekeeping force in the Sinai.

The Israelis were disappointed by the French and enraged by Eisenhower, who, so Ben-Gurion had believed, would never turn away from supporting Israel in the weeks before the presidential elections. There was a widespread belief in Israel and in France that the United States, considered to be Israel's superpower friend, had backed down in the face of the Soviet nuclear threat.* For Ben-Gurion, the lesson was clear: the Jewish community in America was unable to save Israel.

---

* Eisenhower's refusal to back the attack on Egypt had nothing to do with the Bulganin threat, which was analyzed at an all-night meeting at CIA headquarters and subsequently discounted as a bluff. The Suez War was viewed by Washington not as an anti-Soviet or anti-Communist move, but as a last-ditch attempt by two powers—

"You Americans screwed us," one former Israeli government official said, recalling his feelings at the time. "If you hadn't intervened, Nasser would have been toppled and the arms race in the Middle East would have been delayed. Israel would have kept its military and technological edge. Instead, here comes the golf player Ike, dumb as can be, saying in the name of humanity and evenhandedness that 'we won't allow colonial powers to play their role.' He doesn't realize that Nasser's reinforced and Israel's credibility is being set back."

The Israeli, who has firsthand knowledge of his government's nuclear weapons program, added bitterly: "We got the message. We can still remember the smell of Auschwitz and Treblinka. Next time we'll take all of you with us."

On November 6, after learning of the French and British cease-fire, Ben-Gurion sent Peres, accompanied by Golda Meir, to Paris. Mollet had fought against the cease-fire but, when faced with Britain's insistence on withdrawal, felt he had no choice but to go along. Even worse, Mollet was now going to have to persuade Ben-Gurion to accept a United Nations peacekeeping role in the Sinai. Israel would have to withdraw from the land for which its paratroopers had fought and died.

Peres later told a biographer of his feelings toward Eisenhower at the time: ". . . [A] man with healthy teeth, beautiful eyes and a warm smile who hadn't the vaguest notion what he was talking about. And what he did know, he couldn't express properly. There was no connection between one sentence and

---

England and France—to stanch their continuing international decline. Eisenhower and his senior aides believed that Nasser and other Third World leaders much preferred alliances with the United States rather than with the Soviets, and thus were more likely to become pro-American if the administration disassociated itself from the Middle East colonialism of England and France. The President was distressed at the two American allies for continuing to practice what he viewed as their colonialistic policies; he also resented the obvious Israeli belief that he would pander to the American Jewish vote by endorsing the Suez War. (Eisenhower, as the French and British knew only too well, was perfectly prepared to act as a colonialist himself—as he did in ordering the CIA to help overthrow governments in Iran in 1953 and Guatemala in 1954 —to protect what he believed to be vital American interests.) CIA officials recalled another point of White House concern in 1956: Eisenhower's realization from the secret U-2 overflights—the first U-2 spy mission had taken place a few months earlier—that Israel had purchased sixty Mystère attack aircraft from the French, and not the twenty-four they had publicly announced. No public mention was made of the larger-than-reported Israeli purchase—the new aircraft were seen on runways—since the existence of U-2 overflights was then the government's biggest national security secret.

the next. The only question he could answer well was 'How are you?' "

One American defense analyst, in a conversation many years later about Israel's drive for the nuclear option after Suez, posed this rhetorical query and answer: "What is the lesson the United States draws from the Suez Crisis?

"It is terribly dangerous to stop Israel from doing what it thinks is essential to its national security."

Israel's unhappiness with Eisenhower was matched by Guy Mollet's sense of guilt and shame at France's failure to carry out commitments made to his fellow socialists in Israel. There was an obvious trade-off: Ben-Gurion agreed to withdraw his troops from the Sinai and accept a United Nations peacekeeping role in return for France's help in building a nuclear reactor and chemical reprocessing plant. Israel was no longer interested in an experimental reactor, such as at Saclay, but in the real thing—a reactor patterned after Marcoule. Mollet, obsessed with the consequences of France's failure, was quoted as telling an aide at the time of meetings with Peres and Meir: "I owe the bomb to them. I owe the bomb to them." The deal was struck, although it would be nearly a year before Peres would conclude the final negotiations.* The formal agreement between France and Israel has never been made public.

Mollet also formally cleared the way later in 1956 for the French nuclear weapons program by establishing a committee on the military use of atomic energy, to be led by the army chief of staff. Israeli scientists were on hand as observers when the first French nuclear test took place in 1960.

Over the next few years, as weapons-grade plutonium began rolling out of Marcoule, the French strategic goal would incor-

* A major complication for Peres in working out the official government-to-government agreement was the continuing collapse of the French governments. Guy Mollet's government fell in mid-1957 and was replaced by one led by Maurice Bourges-Maunoury. There were last-minute qualms about the Israeli reactor expressed by Christian Pineau, the new foreign minister. Peres would later tell a biographer that he had overcome Pineau's doubts by insisting that the reactor—already understood by engineers and officials throughout the French nuclear bureaucracy to be for a bomb— would be utilized only for "research and development." Pineau's meeting with Peres and his signed authorization for the reactor came in late September 1957, precisely at the time that the Bourges-Maunoury administration—that is, Pineau's government— was being voted out of office by the French National Assembly. In essence, the formal authorization for Dimona was signed by an official who was already out of office.

porate the lesson learned in Suez: avoid reliance on the United States—and the NATO allies. The nuclear tests in the South Pacific, although marred by misfires, enabled France to develop its nuclear deterrent, the *force de frappe*, by the mid-1960s, with ambitions—not reached until the 1980s—of independently targeting the Soviet Union with intercontinental missiles. Charles de Gaulle would stun Washington and its allies by pulling France out of NATO in 1966. The intellectual spokesman for the French nuclear program was a retired general named Pierre Gallois, whose argument, as eventually published, came down to this: "When two nations are armed with nuclear weapons, even if they are unequally armed, the status quo is unavoidable." The Soviets would conclude, so Gallois's reasoning went, that there was no military target in Paris or anywhere in France that was worth the risk of having one nuclear bomb falling on Moscow. A nuclear-armed France would no longer need to wonder, as did all of Europe, whether the United States would come to its defense—and risk a Soviet retaliation—in a nuclear crisis.

Gallois was taken very seriously by the Israelis, and France's *force de frappe* became the role model for Israel's strategic planning—and its ultimate decision not to count on the American nuclear umbrella. Israel would complement its new reactor with a major research effort to design and manufacture long-range missiles capable of targeting the Middle East and, eventually, the Soviet Union. The reactor at Dimona was just the beginning for Ernst Bergmann; he would now have to begin putting together a nuclear arsenal.

Herman Mark explained years later why Ben-Gurion had picked the right man: "Bergmann was one of the few scientists who saw the lamp and knew how to make a light bulb. He understood that different types of activity would be necessary. The first part is to prepare new and unknown materials. Then you make them in ample quantities and store them. Finally there's delivery—how to put it somewhere."

Bergmann's role in developing Israel's nuclear arsenal remains a state secret today. In the years after his death, as the Israeli nuclear arsenal became fixed, he became a virtual nonperson, a victim of stringent Israeli security and the self-censorship that such security involves. For example, in a book he wrote that was published in the United States in 1979, Shimon Peres eulogized Bergmann, with whom he worked closely for thirteen years, as one of the seven founders of the State of Israel. Peres, of course, did not mention nuclear weapons, but he did report that Chaim Weizmann considered Bergmann to be "a future candidate for the presidency" of Israel. And yet Bergmann is not even cited once in a biography of Peres published in 1982 and written by Matti Golan, a former government official who had access to Peres's papers; nor is he mentioned in the English edition of Michael Bar-Zohar's definitive biography of Ben-Gurion.

By the spring of 1957 it was clear that the old winery at Richon-el-Zion wouldn't do and a new site was needed for the larger reactor, known then only as EL 102. It wasn't difficult for Peres to convince Ben-Gurion to locate it at Dimona, near the ancient city of Beersheba in his beloved Negev. Money was transferred directly to Paris from the prime minister's account and Saint-Gobain, the French chemical firm, then two years away from completing the reprocessing plant at Marcoule, was selected to build the Israeli reprocessing facility—underground. As they began work, Saint-Gobain's engineers were given access to the initial construction plans for the reactor, and were stunned by what they learned. The French-Israeli agreement called for the plant to be capable at its peak of producing 24 million watts (twenty-four megawatts) of thermal power, but its cooling ducts, waste facilities, and other specifications suggested that the plant would operate at two to three times that capacity.* If so, it could produce more plutonium than the re-

* The reactor at Dimona did not produce any electrical power; its output is measured therefore in terms of thermal power. It takes three megawatts of thermal power to produce one megawatt of electrical power; Dimona's electrical power output thus would be eight megawatts. The average electricity-producing nuclear power station operates at one thousand megawatts of electrical power (or three thousand megawatts of thermal power). The first U.S. weapons-grade plutonium plants, built during and after World War II, operated at about 250 megawatts. Nuclear scientists have determined that one megawatt-day of production (that is, energy output) will produce one gram of plutonium. Dimona's reported output of twenty-four megawatts would produce, if the reactor were operating 80 percent of the time, about seven kilograms of enriched plutonium per year, enough for two low-yield weapons.

actor at Marcoule—more than twenty-two kilograms a year, enough for four nuclear bombs with the explosive force of those dropped at Hiroshima and Nagasaki.

Ground-breaking for the EL 102 reactor took place in early 1958. Over the next few years, thousands of tons of imported machinery and hundreds of imported technicians, engineers, wives, children, mistresses, and cars turned a quiet corner of the Negev desert into a French boom town. Nothing comparable—or as secret—had been created since Los Alamos.

4

First Knowledge

General Dwight D. Eisenhower's reliance on aerial photography as Allied Commander in Chief in World War II was reaffirmed by the exhaustive postwar bombing surveys of Germany and Japan, which concluded that as much as 80 percent of the most useful intelligence had come from overhead reconnaissance. Eisenhower came into the presidency in 1953 concerned about the lack of aerial intelligence on the Soviet Union and ordered the CIA to do something about it. A Photographic Intelligence Division was promptly set up, and CIA officials selected a University of Chicago graduate named Arthur C. Lundahl to direct it. Lundahl had analyzed reconnaissance photos for the Navy during the war and stayed in the business afterward. One of his first moves was to entice Dino A. Brugioni, then compiling dossiers on Soviet industry for the CIA, to join his staff. Brugioni was another World War II veteran who had served as an aerial photographer and radio and radar specialist in lead bombers with the Twelfth Air Force in Italy. He had been recruited by the CIA in 1948, the year after it was established; like Lundahl, Brugioni was very good at what he was doing. The two men would remain colleagues and close friends for the next forty years.

Eisenhower's next major step was to authorize a daring reconnaissance program—primarily targeted at the Soviet Union—and assign the development of the revolutionary airplane that would make it work jointly to the CIA and the Air Force. The aircraft, built under cover by the Lockheed Aircraft Company in Burbank, California, and known as the U-2, would be able to fly and glide for almost eleven hours—covering more than five thousand miles—at heights greater than 65,000 feet,

while utilizing only one thousand gallons of fuel. Special
lenses, cameras, and thin film were developed, enabling the spy
plane to photograph a path from Moscow to Tashkent, southeast of the Ural Sea, in one take. The U-2 went operational
from a secret base in West Germany on July 4, 1956. Its initial
targets: Soviet long-range bomber bases and Leningrad. Moscow was overflown on the next day, and dramatic photographs
—code-named CHESS—of the Kremlin and the Winter Garden
were later shown to the President and his advisers. A second
U-2 base was authorized in Turkey; later there would be more
bases in Pakistan and Norway.

It was a spectacular asset: Soviet sites were photographed,
mapped, and targeted, all within a few days, by American missiles and bombers from the Strategic Air Command. There
was, however, an equally essential mission in those first years:
to locate and photograph the industrial elements of the Soviet
nuclear program. Where were the reactors, the heavy-water-
production facilities, and the uranium- and plutonium-process-
ing plants? Where were the Soviets machine-tooling the
nuclear warheads and assembling the actual weapons?*

By the mid-1950s, it was clear that Soviet technology, to
American dismay, had done a brilliant job of catching up in the
nuclear arms race. By August 1949, four years after Hiroshima
and Nagasaki, the Soviets had managed to explode their first
atomic bomb, using plutonium. That first bomb, like its American predecessor, was the most basic in the atomic arsenal—a
fission weapon. Such weapons consist of a small core of fissile
material surrounded by high explosives. The explosives are
triggered inward in a precise sequence (measured in nanosec-
onds), suddenly and intensely compressing, or imploding, the
core. The fissile material goes "supercritical" and begins discharging neutrons at a much faster rate than they can escape

---

* American intelligence had been unable to locate all the Soviet nuclear facilities in
the early 1950s, before the U-2 went operational, and the Pentagon's nuclear war planners had to emphasize Soviet airbases and missile fields in their primary targeting. The
1954 war plan of the Strategic Air Command (SAC), for example, called for as many as
735 bombers to hit the Soviets in a single massive nuclear blow. Despite the tonnage,
SAC could not guarantee that the Soviets' nuclear retaliatory capacity would be destroyed, leaving American cities open to retaliation.

from the core. The sudden release of energy produces the violent explosion.

Well before the end of the war, Edward Teller and other American nuclear weapons designers understood that a far more powerful nuclear device, with fission as merely a first step, was theoretically possible. The new weapon, developed under the code name of "Super," was the hydrogen bomb, known to today's physicists as a fusion device. There were two central problems in the development of a high-yield hydrogen bomb: how to ignite the fusion material and how to make it burn efficiently. After much trial and error, scientists at Los Alamos developed a two-stage device, with two separate components inside a single warhead case. A fission bomb would be triggered (the first stage) inside the warhead. Much of the radiation from the fission device would be contained in the warhead case and compress and ignite a special thermonuclear fuel in the separate compartment (the second step). Deuterium, a hydrogen isotope twice the weight of hydrogen, or lithium deuteride could be used as the thermonuclear fuel. Deuterium is the main fuel of the sun, and is burned there at temperatures of 18 to 36 million degrees Fahrenheit. American physicists conducted experiments and came to understand, with appropriate awe, that a thermonuclear fuel, once ignited by fission inside a hydrogen bomb, would burn at a speed, temperature, and pressure greater than it burned at in the center of the sun. A key to the hydrogen bomb was the initial triggering of a fission device, for only fission was capable of generating the heat and, as the scientists later came to understand, the radiation needed to burn the thermonuclear fuel. The thermonuclear device, when successfully tested in 1952 at Eniwetok, an atoll in the western Pacific, produced a crater 6,240 feet in diameter—more than a mile—and 164 feet deep. It was 650 times as powerful as the primitive device dropped at Hiroshima. The Los Alamos team later determined that the fusion of deuterium and tritium, another heavy hydrogen isotope that is a by-product of lithium, could produce a thermonuclear explosion of fifteen megatons— that is, one thousand times greater than the Hiroshima bomb.

The Soviets, at one point known to be at least three years behind the American thermonuclear bomb program, moved ahead rapidly in the science of making doomsday weapons. The first Soviet two-stage hydrogen bomb was successfully tested in 1955, and six years later Soviet scientists detonated the largest known hydrogen bomb, with an explosive force of fifty-eight megatons. At its height in 1988, the Soviet nuclear stockpile totaled an estimated 33,000 warheads, slightly more than the United States maintained in 1967, its peak year.

In the beginning, everything was secret—even the existence of the CIA as well as its Photographic Intelligence Division.

The first U-2 flights over the Soviet Union had provided dramatic evidence that the Soviets were not nearly as advanced in conventional arms as the Pentagon had assumed. There was no "bomber gap" or "missile gap." These revelations were of the utmost importance and were immediately presented to President Eisenhower himself, as well as to other top officials. Lundahl, as head of the U-2 intelligence unit, soon found himself becoming the American government's most listened-to briefing officer. "I was a courier on horseback," he recalled. "I'd spend my nights soaking up the lore and then gallop around Washington in the morning."* The man in charge of providing him with information gained from the U-2 flights was Brugioni.

The United States also was keeping its eyes on the Israeli desert. Eisenhower and the men around him, including John Foster Dulles, the secretary of state, and his brother Allen, the CIA director, had been infuriated by Israel's attempt to mask the extent of its military buildup prior to the 1956 Suez invasion. The administration's truth-teller continued to be the U-2, whose pilots, including Gary Francis Powers, later to be shot down, were usually assigned to overfly the Soviet Union. But there were other standing U-2 targets in sensitive areas and

---

* Lundahl briefed President John F. Kennedy in the Oval Office in October 1962, after a U-2 overflight produced evidence of Soviet missiles in Cuba. He recalled standing behind the President, who was studying the enlarged photos—which are essentially meaningless to a layperson—with a magnifying glass: "I showed him the various pieces of equipment that supported the medium-range missiles, about ten items in all. He listened to all that and was obviously unsure. He looked up from the U-2 photos, turned in his chair and looked me straight in the eye, and said, 'Are you sure of all this?' I replied, 'Mr. President, I am as sure of this as a photo interpreter can be sure of anything and I think you might agree that we have not misled you on the many other subjects we have reported to you.'" The Cuban missile crisis had begun.

especially in moments of crisis—and that description fit the Middle East in 1958. Egypt and Syria had merged early in the year to form the United Arab Republic, and the Arab world was immediately thrown into political turmoil. Muslim opposition, sparked by Egypt and Syria, led to violence in pro-Western Lebanon, where American marines waded ashore in July to protect the regime of President Camille Chamoun. The Iraqi monarchy, also pro-Western, was overthrown in a bloody coup d'état and replaced by a military dictator, Abdel Karim Qassem.

Gary Powers and his colleagues, who had continued intermittently to overfly the Middle East, were now steadily back at work in the area. The CIA's photo interpreters were suddenly seeing a lot of activity at an Israeli Air Force practice bombing range south of Beersheba, an old Bedouin camel-trading center.

Photo interpretation was still a fledgling science in 1958, a hands-on business. The developed film from the U-2 missions was rushed to the CIA's Photographic Intelligence Division, printed, analyzed, mounted on boards if necessary, cleared with Allen Dulles, and then immediately taken to the White House. Eisenhower remained an avid consumer until the last days of his presidency, and access to the photographs and briefings often was limited to the President and his immediate aides. Secrecy was paramount, although the Soviet Union eventually learned of the U-2 operations and began to complain bitterly, in private, about the American violations of its airspace.*

---

* It was widely known that the Soviets were able to track a U-2 flight by radar once it passed over a border point. Much more disturbing to Washington was evidence that the Soviets were aware in advance of the take-off time for each mission. The National Security Agency, responsible for monitoring Soviet signals intelligence, reported— precisely when could not be learned—that the Soviet military and civilian aviation authorities had established a pattern of abruptly grounding all air traffic before a U-2 flight was scheduled to depart. The elimination of all airplane traffic, of course, made it much easier for the Soviet radar system to plot the U-2 flight paths, and thus provided more time for the intended targets of the U-2 cameras to take countermeasures. How did the Soviets know the approximate schedule of U-2 activity? The mystery was solved early in the U-2 program by a group of Air Force communications technicians at Kelly Field in Texas—none of whom had any knowledge of the U-2 operation or any clearance for such knowledge. The Air Force analysts were able to deduce that a special intelligence operation was in existence as well as predict each flight simply by monitoring the extensive and poorly masked preflight communications between Washington and the U-2 airfields. The U-2 communications system did not change, and, one of the never-ending ironies of the intelligence world, the high-level American intelligence officer who brought the evidence of Soviet awareness to the attention of the U-2 plan-

There also was a continuing and essential need for close co-
ordination between exotic groups such as America's nuclear
planners and the men authorizing U-2 operations. Plutonium
and tritium, for example, occur in nature only in minute
amounts and thus must be manufactured by irradiating lithium
in a nuclear reactor. Among the inevitable by-products of the
manufacturing process are radioactive gases, which are vented
into the atmosphere. The analysts of the early U-2 photography
learned to look for huge or distinctive chimneys, or "smoke-
stacks," as the photo interpreters called them, all of which were
studied intently to see if they were linked to a nuclear weapons
facility.

It was Brugioni who recalled seeing the first signs of what
would become the Israeli nuclear reactor. "Israel had a bombing range in the Negev, and we'd watch it," Brugioni said. "It
was a military training spot—where they'd stage exercises."
One clue, not immediately understood, was the fencing off of a
large, barren area a dozen or so miles outside the small desert
town of Dimona. Brugioni and the photo interpreters assumed
that the Israelis were setting up an ammunition-testing site. A
new road from Beersheba, twenty-five miles to the north, was
observed, leading directly to the fenced area. Construction
workers and heavy machinery suddenly showed up. The site
was no longer just another point of reference amid the thousands of feet of U-2 negatives flowing into CIA headquarters.
The subterranean digging began in early 1958; soon afterward,
cement began to pour into heavy foundations. Brugioni and his
colleagues had studied and visited nuclear weapons reactors in
the United States and knew something unusual was going on:
"We spotted it right away. What the hell was that big of a plant,
with reinforced concrete, doing there in the middle of the desert?"
The deep digging was another major clue. "After the '56
war," Brugioni explained, "it was all sub rosa in Israel. But
man builds by patterns. For example, you can draw a circle

---

ners was accused of a security violation. The incident reinforces a basic rule of the
intelligence community: never bring information that is not wanted—such as word of
an Israeli bomb—to the attention of higher-ups.

twenty-five miles in diameter in most areas of the world and understand how man spends his life by studying that circle. You see cattle grazing, hog and poultry pens, and conclude that people eat meat. You can also spot industries, schools, churches, homes, etc., by what we call their 'signatures.' The military are even more patterned. Whenever you build something nuclear you build it thick and deep. They were pouring a hell of a lot of concrete. We knew they were going deep."

The Eisenhower administration was sympathetic to Israel's precarious international position in 1958, Brugioni recalled: "The United Arab Republic was seen as a great threat. There was a fear that Nasser would get together [with the Arab world] and they'd take Israel. It'd have been a real coup if Nasser had taken Lebanon in '58." Eisenhower secretly authorized the U.S. Air Force to provide fighter pilot training and courses in aerial reconnaissance and photo interpretation to the Israelis. Some of the Americans operated under cover: "The attitude was help them [Israel] out—wink, but don't get caught."

There was no way that Lundahl and Brugioni could wink at the imminent construction of a secret nuclear reactor. They and their colleagues in the U-2 shop believed strongly in Israel's right to exist, but were equally convinced that an Israeli bomb would destabilize the Middle East. They also knew that they were dealing with political dynamite, and chose to wait; speculation would be deadly. "Whenever you get something on the Israelis and you move it along," said Brugioni, "you'd better be careful. Especially if you've got a career."

The pouring of concrete footings for the reactor's circular dome was all the evidence Lundahl needed. Lundahl rushed the early raw photographs to the White House; it was late 1958 or early 1959.* Lundahl understood the rules: he carried no written report—paper was never to be generated in the U-2 briefings. "Ike didn't want any notes—period," recalled Lundahl. The special secrecy of the U-2 was heightened by the fact

---

* The lack of any written notes or documents inevitably made it difficult for Brugioni and Lundahl to recall the dates of specific events, such as the date of Lundahl's briefing on Dimona to President Eisenhower. No declassified documents about such briefings are available to the public in the Eisenhower Library in Abilene, Kansas. The dates cited herein are reasonable approximations, based on all the available data.

that Lundahl's unit had been given unusually broad access to all of America's secrets, including reports from defectors and covert agents in the Soviet Union and elsewhere. The photo interpreters also were provided with communications intercepts and reports of Soviet and Eastern European refugee interrogations, as compiled by special American and Israeli intelligence teams. The assumption was that since most of the nuclear weapons installations behind the Iron Curtain were carefully camouflaged, the photo interpreters needed all the help possible. A refugee's random comment about a secret factory somewhere in the Soviet Union often triggered a major discovery.

The White House briefings on important issues followed a set pattern, Lundahl recalled: he would tell the President, usually accompanied by Allen Dulles, the CIA director, and John Foster Dulles, the secretary of state, what he knew and then get a presidential request for further intelligence. The CIA's Photographic Intelligence Division offered three categories of follow-up. Phase One was the immediate report—presented as soon as possible, as were the early photos of the Israeli reactor. A Phase Two report, to be presented overnight, would require Lundahl's shop to enlarge the intelligence photos and mount them for display. There would be annotation and perhaps some text. A Phase Three report called for extensive analysis based on many more overflights over many weeks. There would be special assignments for the U-2s, and an extensive series of photographs.

Lundahl anticipated a Phase Two or Three request on the Israeli intelligence. Instead, he recalled—still amazed, more than thirty years later—there was "no additional requirement. No request for details." In fact, added Lundahl, over the next years, "nobody came back to me, *ever*, on Israel. I was never asked to do a follow-up on any of the Israeli briefings."

But no one told him not to do so, and so the U-2 continued to overfly the Negev. Lundahl also relayed the findings on Dimona to Lewis L. Strauss, chairman of the Atomic Energy Commission, and a few AEC aides who were among the handful of officials in the Eisenhower administration cleared for U-2 intelligence. Lundahl's standing orders called for him to pro-

vide all nuclear intelligence to the White House and then, unless directed otherwise, to the AEC commissioner. Something
as important as Dimona was rushed over, Lundahl recalled.

"The way I look at it," Lundahl said, "I reported all that I
knew to my masters. They sit at a higher place on the mountain."

None of the communications between Eisenhower and Ben-
Gurion about the ominous construction in the Negev has been
made public, but such letters are known to have been written.
In July 1958, at the Israeli height of concern over Nasser's Pan-
Arabism, Ben-Gurion privately requested American "political,
financial, and moral" assistance as Israel was standing up to
Nasser and "Soviet expansion." Eisenhower responded, according to Ben-Gurion's authorized biographer, Michael Bar-
Zohar, with a lukewarm note telling Ben-Gurion that "you can
be confident of the United States' interest in the integrity and
independence of Israel." Ben-Gurion had hoped to be invited
to visit Washington for direct talks with the President. A former Israeli government official interviewed for this book revealed that Eisenhower privately raised the issue of Dimona at
least once in this period, prompting Ben-Gurion to request that
the United States "extend its nuclear umbrella to Israel."
There was no subsequent reply from Eisenhower, the former
official said.*

Brugioni remained fascinated by the Israeli construction at
Dimona: "We kept on watching it. We saw it going up. The
White House," he confirmed, also mystified, "never encour-
aged us to do further briefings. It was always 'Thank you,' and
'This isn't going to be disseminated, is it?' It was that attitude."

Brugioni prepared the presidential briefing materials for
Lundahl and knew that the intelligence on Israel was getting to

---

* Few of the private messages between Eisenhower and Ben-Gurion on any subject
have been made public by the Eisenhower Library. Retired Army General Andrew J.
Goodpaster, Eisenhower's military aide in the White House, explained that the diplomatic exchanges between the two were "very closely held" and not available at the
time to even close subordinates. Goodpaster, who also served as military aide to President Nixon, added that while there was presidential concern about "what they were
doing at Dimona," he could remember no "specific exchange about a nuclear umbrella."

the top. "The thing is," Brugioni said, "I never did figure out whether the White House wanted Israel to have the bomb or not."

Lundahl's interpreters had watched, via the steady stream of U-2 imagery, as the construction teams (the Americans did not immediately know, of course, that they were French-led) dug two separate sites in the desert. There was an early attempt to estimate how large the sites were going to be by measuring the "spoil"—the amount of cubic feet of dirt unearthed each day. It was old hat for the American photo interpreters, who had watched in World War II as the Germans moved their industrial plants and factories underground in futile attempts to avoid the heavy Allied bombing. One clue that remained consistent was freshly unearthed dirt: it was always a dead giveaway of an underground operation. The CIA profited from the World War II experience: its team in charge of the 1956 Berlin tunnel that was dug from West to East Germany successfully masked its extensive digging by trucking away the dirt in military C-ration boxes.*

One fact became clear over the next few years: Israel knew about the U-2 overflights and didn't like them. At some point after 1958, the Israelis, using covered trucks, could be seen hauling away the dirt and debris from each day's digging. There was very strong circumstantial evidence by then that the second underground site at Dimona was being readied for the chemical reprocessing plant that was essential in order to make weapons-grade plutonium—and the bomb. The best evidence of Israel's intent came from an analysis of the striking similarities in layout, as seen from aerial photography, between Dimona and the French nuclear facility at Marcoule. The French facility was being constantly overflown in the late 1950s by civilian transport planes—equipped with hidden cameras—that belonged to American diplomats and military officers assigned to the American embassy in Paris. By 1959, the reactor and the chemical reprocessing plant at Marcoule were known to be in full operation. "It was obvious that the Israelis were

---

* The Berlin operation was compromised from within, however, by British intelligence officer and Soviet spy George Blake.

following the French pattern," Brugioni recalled. "We saw enough to know that it [the second site at Dimona] was going to be a chemical reprocessing plant," just as the reprocessing plant at Marcoule was separate.

As the Dimona reactor was completed, there was less to be learned from the U-2 overflights. The U-2 imagery could only depict what was on the surface, and the intelligence community would spend years trying to find out for certain whether Israel had taken the next step—construction of a chemical reprocessing plant. American military attachés were assigned to find a reason to travel to the desert—the CIA station even offered to buy the wine for any seemingly casual group that wanted to picnic—and take photographs. Special automatic cameras with preset lens settings were developed by the CIA for the attachés. "All they had to do was push the trigger," recalled Lundahl. In the early years, he added, a few of the attachés "snuck in and got some good shots." Later, in an attempt to determine whether the chemical reprocessing plant was in operation, the CIA began urging attachés to pick up grass and shrubs for later analysis. The theory was that traces of plutonium and other fission products, if being produced, would be in the environment. "A guy would go where there were clumps of grass and pretend to take a crap," recalled Brugioni with a laugh. "While pretending to wipe his butt he'd grab some grass and stick it in his shorts."

The Israelis responded by planting large trees to block the line of vision of any would-be candid photographers and increasing their perimeter patrols around Dimona. One American military attaché was nearly shot by Israeli guards after overstepping the ground rules that had been set up by the American embassy in Tel Aviv.

The cat-and-mouse game would continue for the next ten years, with the Israelis shielding the expanding construction at Dimona while the United States remained unable to learn categorically whether the Israelis were operating a chemical reprocessing plant. "We knew they were trying to fool us," said Brugioni, "and they knew it. The Israelis understood [aerial] reconnaissance. Hell, most of them were trained by the U.S. Air Force. It was an Alphonse and Gaston act."

There was much more intelligence, Brugioni believed, that did not filter down to the interpreters: "Allen Dulles would occasionally ask me if I'd seen 'the Jewish information' "—referring to CIA agent reports dealing with the Israeli bomb. "I'd say no," Brugioni added, "and his office would call later and tell me to forget it." One of the most complicated issues involved the question of American Jews who were also intensely committed—as many were—to the security of Israel. A few American nuclear physicists were known to have emigrated to Israel after World War II; one was a veteran of the Manhattan Project who had worked until 1956 in the most sensitive areas of nuclear reactor design. "We knew there were Jews going to Israel who were telling them how to do it," said Brugioni. On the other hand, he said, "We were getting information from Jews who went to Israel and never told the Israelis they talked to us." Jewish physicists and scientists began returning from visits to Israel by the late 1950s with increasingly specific information about Israeli interest in nuclear weapons. The CIA had even been tipped off about the fact that Israel was raising large sums of money for Dimona from the American Jewish community.

By the end of 1959, Lundahl and Brugioni had no doubt that Israel was going for the bomb. There also was no doubt that President Eisenhower and his advisers were determined to look the other way.

Brugioni said he and the others also chose in the end not to raise any questions about Dimona: "There was a lot of policy that we didn't know about—and we didn't care to know. We weren't stupid; we could put two and two together. But the hierarchy decided to play it cool—and that's the way it was. If you're a senior officer, you learn to read the tea leaves quickly —and keep your mouth shut. Period."

5

Internal Wars

Israel's nuclear bomb project was besieged with enemies—from within and without—in its early history. The vast majority of those senior officials who knew what was going on at Dimona thought it folly to waste such prodigious amounts of money on a doomsday weapon that might or might not work when conventional weapons such as tanks, guns, and aircraft were desperately needed. The concept of underdeveloped and underfinanced Israel as a superpower seemed ludicrous. By the early 1960s, Dimona, with its huge manpower needs, had hired many of the most skilled Israeli scientists and technicians away from local research and manufacturing companies, resulting in a much-criticized slowdown in the growth of the nation's industrial base. There also were moral objections from a few members of the scientific and academic community, including two of the original members of the Israeli Atomic Energy Commission. By 1957, as construction began on the reactor, four more members of the commission had resigned, essentially because they had nothing to do. The only commission member still on the job was its chairman, Ernst David Bergmann.

Bergmann, David Ben-Gurion, and Shimon Peres were waging what amounted to constant war—all in secret—to keep the Israeli bomb project alive. The most threatening problem came from Israel's partner in secrecy—the French. General Charles de Gaulle had won a seven-year term as president of France's newly constituted Fifth Republic in December 1958 by promising to find an acceptable compromise for ending the war in Algeria. The war, which de Gaulle continued to prosecute, had sharply divided the nation, as the Vietnam War would later divide the United States; all other issues, such as the question

of continued support for Israel, seemed secondary. De Gaulle
was known to be emphatically in favor of an independent nuclear deterrent for France, but it was not known how he might
react to the profound French commitment to Dimona. It was a
worrisome matter for those members of the French Atomic
Energy Commission who supported the Israeli bomb, and they
handled the issue in the time-honored way of the bureaucracy:
they did not tell de Gaulle what was going on. Contracts had
been signed and money paid, and the work was proceeding at
Dimona.

The French on the job at Dimona were also a source of turmoil.
Hundreds of French engineers and technicians had begun
pouring into the Negev in 1957, and Beersheba bustled with
construction as new apartment complexes and residential units
were thrown together. Housing also was made available to the
thousands of North African Jews (or Sephardim) who emigrated from Morocco and Algeria, hired to do the digging and
building of the reactor and reprocessing plant. European Jews
were slowly and carefully recruited from government and private businesses throughout Israel to serve as scientists and bureaucratic managers; they, too, were provided with housing in
Beersheba. There was a caste system in the desert, and the
French were on top, as they repeatedly made all too clear.
    "The French were arrogant," said one Israeli who spent part
of his career at Dimona. "They thought Jews [in Israel] were
inferior. We weren't slick and we didn't dress well—but we
were bright." Some of the French officials were openly anti-
Semitic, the Israeli recalled, and one—eventually ordered out
of Israel—was found to have collaborated with the Nazis during World War II. The French treatment of the Jews from
North Africa who had been hired as laborers was even worse,
the Israeli added: "They would speak of Jews from Algeria and
Morocco like they were stones—inferior beings. It was Nazi-
like." Even those Frenchmen who were Jewish did little to ease
the tension; many considered themselves to be of a different
class and social standing than their less sophisticated Israeli
colleagues. Ironically, the Algerian and Moroccan Jews also
were mistreated by their Israeli employers. One standing

rule was that the Moroccans and Algerians would be hired only for fifty-nine days and then dismissed, a strategem that avoided paying any of the many benefits that came with tenure (the Israeli economy was dominated by the labor movement), which was reached after two months on the job. After a few days off, the North African Jewish laborers would be rehired for another fifty-nine days. "Some socialist government," said the Israeli, with a caustic laugh. The North African Jews were "treated like slaves" by French and Israelis alike.

By mid-1960, when there were rumors of a possible French pullout, many Israelis couldn't have cared less: they'd had their fill of the French. The Israeli scientists and technicians had absorbed much of the French technical data by then—many plans were modified extensively on the job—and the reaction was, an Israeli recalled, "Go. We'll do it ourselves." Abraham Sourassi, one of the senior Israelis at Dimona—he was responsible for building the reprocessing plant—endeared himself to his countrymen by declaring, "Good riddance," upon hearing of de Gaulle's disenchantment with Dimona. "It was the typical Israeli attitude—just show us," said the former Dimona official. "We'll copy it and do it better."

The long hours, hard work, and French smugness did not diminish the excitement of being involved with Israel's most important secret. "We felt great," said one of the first Israelis hired to manage the construction in 1958. "We were pioneers." The official recalled his initial interview with Ernst Bergmann: "He tells me, 'We have a big project and we need the best brains. It's going to be something remarkable that you'll never forget.'" Bergmann also assured the young man that his new job would be good for his career—as good as serving with the Israeli Defense Force: "He said it'd be 'a feather in my cap. It's going to be modern.' So I filled out the forms. Took me three months to go through security." Those Israelis who had been members of the Communist Party (as many had been before immigrating to Israel) and those with relatives in Eastern Europe were barred from employment because of growing Israeli fears of Soviet penetration, fanned to no small degree by the growing antagonism between Moscow and Jerusalem. Israel had been racked by a series of spy scandals by the late 1950s, and the intelligence operatives in the sixty-man Soviet embassy in Tel Aviv were believed to especially target the scientific community.

Providing security for the burgeoning nuclear operation was a high priority and led Shimon Peres to insist on the creation of a new intelligence agency, initially known as the Office of Special Tasks. Its director, handpicked by Peres, was a tall, quiet former military intelligence officer named Binyamin Blumberg. The Office of Special Tasks, bureaucratically placed inside the defense ministry, would become one of the most successful intelligence agencies in modern history—and, after Blumberg's resignation more than twenty years later, be responsible for one of Israel's worst mistakes, the recruitment of Jonathan Pollard. Blumberg's sole mission in the late 1950s was protecting Dimona, and he made it a point to be involved in the details. One Israeli responsible for recruiting scientists told of having an excellent prospect rejected by Dimona's security office because of distant relatives in Eastern Europe. He appealed to Blumberg, who had the power to overturn any bureaucratic rule: "I had to beg Blumberg to get him hired. We needed him desperately. He did it—but he said it had to be 'on my life.'"

By early 1960, the reactor at Dimona was taking shape, and many Israeli nuclear physicists and technicians were summoned back from France, where they had spent years in training at Saclay and Marcoule. The top scientists were provided with double pay and subsidized seven-room apartments in Beersheba, space unheard of in those years in Israel. Those who stayed long enough eventually were given possession of the apartments, worth at least $50,000, and permitted to sell them at their leisure.

As the pace and intensity of construction grew, Beersheba inevitably became an international city. The French presence was palpable, as upward of 2,500 French men, women, and children made their life in the Negev. There were special French schools for the children, and the streets were full of French autos. All of this was duly reported by foreign diplomats and military attachés assigned to various embassies in Tel Aviv. There were constantly recurring rumors of the bomb, but the

cover stories—usually revolving around seawater desalinization or agricultural research—somehow held.

Ian Smart was a young British diplomat on his first foreign
assignment in the late 1950s, as third secretary of his country's
small embassy in Tel Aviv. He would go on to become an international expert in nonproliferation, but in those years he was
merely curious—and suspicious. "There was a lot of talk by the
end of 1960 about Dimona," he recalled years later, "prompted,
for one thing, by the sheer progress of the site. It was already
very apparent on the skyline. And from the road you could see
the cooling tower base of the [reactor] dome and the beginning
of the rib structure. Secondly, there was the French presence in
Beersheba. There was an apartment block they used with a lot
of Renault Dauphins about—all carrying French registration."
The Israeli government, when officially asked about the activities at Dimona, told the British embassy a series of stories. One
early claim, recalls Smart, was that the area was a desert grass-
lands research institute. Smart himself heard a second explanation while driving with a group of Israeli Defense Force troops
in the Negev. Smart pointed out the cooling tower and an officer replied, "Ah yes. That's the new manganese-processing
plant."

Throughout the last year of his stay, Smart adds, "I was re-
porting the 'suspicion' that this looked like a nuclear reactor.
But how do you get more than a suspicion without putting a
U-2 over it?"

The Eisenhower administration, as Smart could not know, was
in its third year of U-2 overflights of Dimona by 1960, and expanding its coverage. Art Lundahl, Dino Brugioni, and their
colleagues in the U-2 shop at the CIA were now requesting
systematic overflights of the French nuclear test site near Reg-
gane, Algeria, in the Sahara. The French had successfully
tested their first nuclear bomb in February 1960; it had a yield
of more than sixty kilotons, three times larger than the first
American test at Los Alamos. And the CIA knew that an Israeli
scientific team had been at the test site as observers. There was
another concern: Israeli scientists also had been tracked to a
nearby French chemical and biological weapons (CBW) testing

area in the Sahara. "I wondered," Brugioni recalled, "were the Israelis looking at CBW as a stopgap until they got the bomb? We thought they may have a CBW capability." All of this was immediately shared with the Eisenhower White House, Brugioni said.

The Israelis and French continued to monitor the U-2 overflights, but they also continued to operate with the most stringent secrecy at Dimona—as if no outsider understood what was going on.

French workers at Dimona were forbidden to write directly to relatives and friends in France and elsewhere, but sent mail to a phony post office box in Latin America. Mail from France to Israel was routed the same way. The sophisticated equipment for the reactor and processing plant was assembled by the French Atomic Energy Commission in a clandestine workshop in a Paris suburb and transported by truck, rail, and ship.

The heaviest equipment, such as the reactor tank, was described to French customs officials as components of a seawater desalinization plant bound for Latin America. Israel also needed an illicit shipment of heavy water—it was impractical to rely on the heavy-water process invented by the Weizmann Institute, which was too slow—and turned, as did most of the world's nuclear powers, to the Norwegians, who before World War II had invented an electrolysis method for producing large quantities of heavy water. Norway remained among the international leaders in the export of heavy water in the 1950s, and its sales to the French Atomic Energy Commission had only one condition—that the heavy water not be transferred to a third country. That stipulation was ignored as the French Air Force secretly flew as much as four tons of the water—stored in oversized barrels—to Israel sometime in 1960.* A French cover

---

* Details of this and many other areas of French cooperation with Israel were initially reported by Pierre Pean, a French journalist, in his richly documented 1982 book *Les Deux Bombes* (Fayard), which was not published in the United States. The essential facts in Pean's book were verified by the author of this book in subsequent interviews with French and Israeli officials. Those officials raised questions, however, about the motives of some of those who had aided Pean. Many of the French companies, they said, that had been involved in the construction of Dimona in the early 1960s were working under contract for Iraq, with the approval of the French Atomic Energy Commission, at the time of the bombing of Osirak in 1981. It was the subsequent politi-

firm, the Research Company for Financing and Enterprise, eventually was set up to handle the extensive contacts and negotiations with the Israeli government and various Israeli subcontractors who would actually build Dimona. There was no problem of security among the subcontractors; all contracts were funneled through Peres and his colleagues in Mapai. The largest Israeli engineering company at Dimona, Solel Bone Ltd., of Haifa, was closely associated with the Mapai Party; Israelis involved in the early stages of construction at Dimona acknowledged that there was an extensive, and traditional, system of diverting contract funds to the party.

All of this cost money, and the huge expense of Dimona was a constant source of dissent inside the Israeli government, which was in a struggle to match Egypt in the rapid arms buildup in the Middle East. Egypt acquired its first Soviet advanced fighter plane, the MiG-21, in 1960, and Israel continued to purchase the most advanced warplanes available from the French. Both countries obtained bombers from their international patrons, and both were continuing research into ballistic missile delivery systems. By 1961, however, Egypt's military expenditures had reached nearly $340 million, twice as much as Israel was spending.

The perennial critics of Israel's nuclear program, who included Levi Eshkol, the finance minister, and Pinhas Sapir, minister of commerce and industry—the two men dominated the Israeli budget process for more than fifteen years—saw the Egyptian arms buildup as the most compelling argument against investing money at Dimona.

Just how much Israel was spending on the bomb in these years is impossible to estimate accurately, and Israel's 1957 contract with the French for the construction at Dimona has never been made public. One rough estimate, published by the Israeli press in December 1960, put the cost of the reactor alone at $130 million. A detailed study of overall nuclear start-up costs was published in 1983 by Thomas W. Graham, a nonproliferation

---

cal and economic anger at the Israelis that led a few private and public officials to cooperate fully with Pean and provide him with documentation of the French role at Dimona.

expert and former U.S. Arms Control and Disarmament
Agency (ACDA) official. Graham concluded that France had
spent between $10 billion and $15 billion to assemble its secure
strike capability, including thermonuclear weapons, with as
much as half spent on delivery systems. India similarly would
have to invest as much as 10 to 23 percent of its annual defense
budget in the nuclear area, Graham wrote, if it were to achieve
status as a full-scale nuclear power.

Israel's strategic goal was to achieve nothing less than a secure strike capacity, with themonuclear weapons and missile
and aircraft delivery systems capable of reaching targets in the
Soviet Union. The cost of those ambitions was heightened by
the fact that so much of the facility at Dimona, including its
chemical reprocessing plant, was being built underground.
The difficulties of working below the surface could only sky-
rocket the already high costs of ventilation, waste disposal, and
worker safety. Other significant cost factors included the obligation to pay workers well in union-dominated Israel, a reliance on foreign nationals such as the French, and the extensive
security needed to protect a secret facility. Israel's ultimate
commitment undoubtedly amounted to many billions of dollars.

Ben-Gurion understood that getting Dimona complete
would be possible only if it were not being financed out of the
Israeli budget. The solution was to begin secret fund-raising
for the bomb abroad. Israel already was receiving, according to
American intelligence estimates, hundreds of millions a year in
overall gifts and contributions from American Jews alone.
Sometime in 1960, Shimon Peres decided to form a special
group of trusted and discreet donors that became known, according to Israeli sources, as the Committee of Thirty. Certain
wealthy Jews around the world, including Baron Edmund de
Rothschild of Paris and Abraham Feinberg of New York, were
asked to quietly raise money for what Peres called the "special
weapons" program, and they did so. Years later, Peres would
brag to an interviewer that "not one penny [for Dimona] came
from the government budget. The project was financed from
contributions I raised from Jewish millionaires who understood the importance of the issue. We collected forty million

dollars." Peres also said that he "brought Jewish millionaires to Dimona. I told them what would be here." Former Israeli government officials confirmed that at least one group of foreign contributors was permitted to visit Dimona in 1968, after its completion.

The $40 million raised by Peres would not be nearly enough, however. Israeli officials estimated that by the mid-1960s Israel was spending not scores of millions but hundreds of millions of dollars annually on its nuclear program, with the Peres operation producing a small percentage of the funds and the government underwriting the rest. Ben-Gurion's insistence on continuing to invest that kind of money in the bomb remained a severe source of conflict inside his cabinet and the Mapai Party.

There were reasons other than financial for objecting to the bomb. Old-fashioned military men such as Yigal Allon, who had led troops during the War of Independence; Yitzhak Rabin, the army chief of operations who was destined to be chief of staff; and Ariel Sharon, the Israeli general and commando leader, believed that Israel's essential advantage over the Arabs was the quality and training of its military personnel. To these men, nuclear weapons were nothing more than a great equalizer: an Egypt equipped with the bomb was far more dangerous to Israel than an Egypt limited to conventional arms, even in huge quantities. If Israel possessed nuclear weapons, their analysis continued, it would be impossible to deny them to Egypt or other nations in the Middle East.*

Another compelling argument against Dimona was made by the nation's industrial managers throughout the early 1960s, as the reactor and chemical reprocessing plant—nearing completion—continued to necessitate the recruitment of additional scientists and technicians. Israel was, in essence, facing what amounted to a domestic brain drain. By the late 1960s, senior

---

* Moshe Dayan, as one of the few military men who supported the bomb in these early years, was an anomaly. American nonproliferation experts eventually came to understand that there was a correlation between the attitude of military officers toward the bomb and a national commitment to going nuclear. Many senior military officers in both Israel and India objected bitterly to the nuclear weapons arsenal in its early development. However, once the bomb joined the military arsenal, as it did in India in the late 1970s and in Israel a few years earlier, dissent ceased.

officials of the ministry of commerce and industry were publicly critical of the reduced level of industrial research in the
nation. Government funding for such research had been drasti-
cally cut back, and industry was lagging increasingly behind
science. Scientific innovations still took place, but there were
few engineering companies capable of turning those ideas into
profitable goods that manufacturers could put into production.

Officials who worked at Dimona in those years acknowledged the predatory hiring practices, with the nation's chemical industry being a prime target. "We raided every place in the
country," one former official recalled with pride. "We depleted
Israel's industrial system." The only facility off-limits was the
small research reactor at Nahal Soreq, near the Weizmann Institute. At its height, the former official said, fifteen hundred
Israeli scientists, many with doctorates, worked at Dimona.

The first overt sign of de Gaulle's unease over France's nuclear
commitment to Israel came in May 1960, when Maurice Couve
de Murville, the French foreign minister, informed the Israeli
ambassador that France wanted Israel to make a public announcement about the reactor at Dimona and also agree to submit it to international inspection, similar to the inspection of
Nahal Soreq. Without such acts, Couve de Murville said,
France would not supply raw uranium to the reactor. Ben-
Gurion decided to fly to France for a summit meeting. The two
leaders got along well: de Gaulle would later characterize Ben-
Gurion in his memoirs as "one of the greatest statesmen of our
time. . . . From the very first moment, I felt sympathetic admiration for this courageous fighter and champion. His personality symbolized Israel, which he has ruled since the day he
presided over her creation and struggle." Ben-Gurion, in turn,
found de Gaulle to be a "lively, humane man with a sense of
humor, very alert, and much kindness."

Bertrand Goldschmidt's personal notes of the meeting, provided to the author, show that de Gaulle, embroiled in Algeria,
was worried about the potential for international scandal if
France's involvement with Dimona became publicly known.
De Gaulle explained, according to the notes, that "if France
was the only country to help Israel, while neither the United

States, Britain, or the Soviet Union has helped anyone else [get the bomb], she would put herself in an impossible international situation." There was a second worry: "No doubt if Israel had the atomic bomb, Egypt would be receiving one as well."

The critical concern for de Gaulle was Dimona's underground chemical reprocessing plant, then being built according to French specifications: he did not want to be responsible for making the Israeli bomb inevitable. French help in building the plant would have to cease. Ben-Gurion gave his view of the Arab threat, but de Gaulle insisted that the Israeli prime minister was "exaggerating the danger of destruction that threatens you. In no way will we allow you to be massacred. . . . We will defend you. We will not let Israel fall." De Gaulle offered to sell Israel more fighter aircraft.

De Gaulle came away from his meeting convinced, as he wrote in his memoirs, that he had ordered all work to stop on the reprocessing plant: "I put an end to abusive practices of collaboration established on the military level, after the Suez expedition, between Tel Aviv and Paris, and which introduced Israelis permanently to all levels of staff and French services. Thus in particular there was a stop to the aid provided by us near Beersheba, for a plant to transform uranium into plutonium from which some fine day atom bombs could arise." De Gaulle's order, if issued, was ignored. Saint-Gobain's work on the underground reprocessing plant was delayed for more than two years, but in 1962 a new French contractor arrived and finished the job.

Ben-Gurion was pleased with de Gaulle's promises of continued military aid, but he was not willing to trade an Israeli bomb for French warplanes. Over the next few months, Shimon Peres was able to work out a compromise in talks with Couve de Murville that centered on what amounted to an Israeli lie, one that would dominate Israel's public stance on nuclear arms for decades. The Israelis assured France that they had no intention of manufacturing an atomic bomb and would not do any reprocessing of plutonium. A compromise of sorts was reached: French companies would continue to supply the uranium ore and reactor parts that already had been ordered and not demand any foreign inspection. Israel would make public the existence of its nuclear reactor and continue its construction at Dimona without any official French government help.

With the friendly summit behind him, Ben-Gurion did nothing to change the status quo at Dimona. Neither did de Gaulle or the French government. The privately owned French construction firms and their employees maintained a vigorous presence at Dimona until 1966 and continued to be well paid under the existing contracts.

6

Going Public

By December 1960, John W. Finney had been a reporter for three years in the Washington bureau of the *New York Times*, covering nuclear issues and the Atomic Energy Commission (AEC). Finney, hired away from United Press International by bureau chief James A. Reston, was considered a solid addition to the news staff—but he had yet to bust a big one.

Finney's story came late that month and was, as Finney recalled, "handed to me on a platter."

The messenger was the *Times*'s redoubtable Arthur Krock, then the patriarch of Washington columnists, who approached Finney's desk late one afternoon. Krock was known to young bureau reporters such as Finney for his remoteness and for his daily long lunches with senior government officials at the private Metropolitan Club, a few blocks from the White House.

"Mr. Finney," Krock said, "I think if you call John McCone, he'll have a story for you." John A. McCone, a very wealthy Republican businessman from California, was chairman of the AEC, and Finney had established good rapport with him. Finney immediately understood the situation: "They were looking to plant a story. I was the right person and Krock was the intermediary." Finney made the call and was promptly invited to McCone's office.

"McCone was mad, sputtering mad," Finney recalled. "He started talking and saying, 'They lied to us.'"

Who?

"The Israelis. They told us it was a textile plant."* There was new intelligence, McCone said, revealing that the Israelis had secretly built a nuclear reactor in the Negev with French help; McCone wanted Finney to take the story public. Finney's subsequent article, published December 19 on page one in the *Times*, told the American people what Art Lundahl and Dino Brugioni had been reporting to the White House for more than two years: that Israel, with the aid of the French, was building a nuclear reactor to produce plutonium. "Israel had made no public announcement about the reactor, nor has she privately informed the United States of her plan," Finney wrote, faithfully reflecting what McCone told him. "There is an ill-concealed feeling of annoyance among officials that the United States has been left in the dark by two of its international friends, France and Israel."

Finney's story also noted that McCone had "questioned" Israel about the new information but then added: "Mr. McCone refused to go into details." It was standard operating procedure for official Washington: Finney got the story and McCone was able to duck responsibility for giving it to him.

McCone's leak to Finney would be his parting shot as AEC commissioner; a few days later he announced his resignation on *Meet the Press*, the NBC Sunday television interview show. The Finney story was being written that same day. Finney was

---

* There is no evidence that the Israeli government ever claimed to Washington that the construction at Dimona was a textile plant. Those American and European diplomats who inquired invariably were informed that Dimona was a research facility (usually for agriculture) or a chemical plant. McCone's comment to Finney became widely accepted as fact, nonetheless, and prompted a whimsical column by Art Buchwald in the *New York Herald Tribune* on January 10, 1961. Buchwald told of an Israeli cab driver who six months earlier had driven an American diplomat to Dimona in search of a suit, at wholesale prices, from the textile plant. The technicians at Dimona decided to let him in and pretend that "nothing was going on." When the diplomat inquired about buying a suit, he was told: " 'Perhaps you would like something in cobalt blue? Or maybe a nice uranium brown? How about a cosmic gray, double-breasted, with pinstriped particles?' " The diplomat was measured for his suit behind a six-foot wall of lead. Another scientist "rushed in with a Geiger counter, a slide rule, and two robot arms. The head of the plant took a pad and said: 'Shimshon, call off the customer's measurements.' Shimshon yelled out: 'Ten, nine, eight, seven, six, five, four, three, two, one, oi!' " There were more measurements: " 'Waist U-235; relatively good chest; there is a hexagonal prism in the left shoulder; the right sleeve needs reactor.' " As the diplomat left, Buchwald wrote, he was told: " 'Please, kind sir, do not tell your friends about us because we have too much work now, and if we take any more orders the plant will explode.' "

convinced, as McCone wanted him to be, that the commissioner's anger stemmed from recently acquired knowledge, some new intelligence about the Israelis. "McCone left me with the impression," Finney recalled, "that they'd suddenly appreciated that the Israelis were lying to them."

Finney paid a higher price than he realized for his big story; the Eisenhower administration was using him and the *New York Times* to accomplish what its senior officials were publicly apprehensive about doing themselves—taking on the Israelis over Dimona. McCone, as he did not indicate to Finney, had been briefed regularly on the Israeli nuclear program after replacing Lewis Strauss as AEC commissioner in July 1958; there is no evidence that Strauss, who also received regular briefings on Dimona from Art Lundahl and Dino Brugioni, personally shared his knowledge with McCone. But Lundahl and Brugioni did. McCone, as AEC chairman, was a member of the U.S. Intelligence Advisory Committee, the top-level group at the time, and was, according to Walter N. Elder, a former CIA official who was McCone's long-time aide, "in on the action from the beginning. He sat at the table."

What made McCone (who died in early 1991 after a long, incapacitating illness) join the administration in suddenly reacting to intelligence that had been around for years? Walt Elder, who wrote the still-classified history of McCone's CIA tenure, described McCone as being committed to the concept of nuclear nonproliferation and also aware of the convenient fact that Eisenhower was a month away from ending his eight-year reign in the White House. There could be no better time to act. "He figured, 'I'm through and this is my duty—to let the public know about this,' " said Elder. Another issue, he added, was McCone's frustration at the constant Israeli lying about Dimona: "There was an impetus to do them in."

By December 1960, work at Dimona had progressed to the point where the reactor dome had become visible from nearby roads in the Negev, and thus was more susceptible to being photographed by military attachés. By this time, too, the U-2 program was in disarray: its decline began in May 1960, when

Gary Francis Powers was shot down over the Soviet Union. Premier Nikita Khrushchev's rage at the incident, which caught the White House in a series of lies, ruined Eisenhower's Paris summit meeting scheduled for a few weeks later and led him to order an end to all reconnaissance flights over Russia. Arthur Lundahl recalled those months as being "full of finger-pointing and turbulence." The Powers fiasco did not diminish the fact that Eisenhower and Khrushchev had made steady progress over the previous year in drafting a comprehensive treaty banning all nuclear tests; such testing was suspended by both nations until September 1961. That success had led to an overall heightened sensitivity about nuclear proliferation, and also may have played a role in the sudden concern over Dimona. Another factor may have been timing: with the administration coming to an end, there was no longer any compelling reason to worry about domestic pressure from Jewish lobbying groups.

Whatever the reason, even before McCone's summoning of John Finney, there was a coordinated effort at the top levels of government to make Israel acknowledge what it was doing at Dimona. Such unanimity of purpose and widespread access to sensitive intelligence about Dimona wouldn't happen again—ever.

By the date of McCone's appearance on *Meet the Press,* Washington had been awash for at least ten days with new information about Dimona and a new desire to do something about it. Even Christian A. Herter, the usually detached and preoccupied secretary of state, was in on it. Armin H. Meyer, a senior foreign service officer soon to be posted as ambassador to Lebanon, recalled his surprise in early December at finding Herter seemingly upset upon being given a photograph of the reactor, as taken from a highway. Herter, the under secretary who had been given the top job after the death of John Foster Dulles in May 1959, had gone so far as to call in Avraham Harman, the Israeli ambassador, for an explanation. "I remember being amazed that he felt he could take on the Israelis," Meyer said. "It was the only time I really saw him burn. Something must have happened in the nuclear field that gave him the safety to raise the issue. He felt he was on sacred ground."*

Herter, in fact, had done some independent checking of his own. Shortly after receiving the intelligence, he asked an aide to approach the French and find out whether they indeed were helping the Israelis. The aide, Philip J. Farley, had been around —he'd served since 1956 as a special assistant to John Foster Dulles for arms control—and knew that a direct approach would be "pointless." Farley quietly raised the issue with a deputy to the French ambassador and came away convinced, as he reported to Herter, that the fears about a French connection were warranted. The ambassador's deputy "said all the right things," Farley recalled, referring to his pro forma denials, "but the way he acted . . ." The next step was a discussion with the ambassador, who insisted that Dimona was "merely a research reactor." Farley was enough of an expert to know that the reactor at Dimona was obviously too large for pure research, and, after a discussion in the National Security Council, Herter was instructed by the White House to give a formal diplomatic protest (known as a demarche) to the French. As luck would have it, Couve de Murville, the French foreign minister, was in Washington for a meeting. He was approached, Farley recalled, but assured the State Department that the Israeli reactor was benign and that any plutonium generated in its operation would be returned to France for safekeeping. "He just plain lied to us," said Farley, still indignant in an interview thirty years later. At the time, of course, Farley added, he and his colleagues in the bureaucracy did not begin to realize the extent of Couve de Murville's dissembling; they had no idea that it was France that had made the Israeli bomb possible.

The summoning of Israeli Ambassador Harman had taken place on December 9; within days, the administration had esca-

* Herter had stunned America's European allies during his April 1959 confirmation hearings by declaring that he could not "conceive of any President engaging in all-out nuclear war unless we were in danger of all-out devastation ourselves." The statement, while undoubtedly correct, played into the hands of de Gaulle's ambitions for the *force de frappe*. The historian Richard J. Barnet, writing about Herter's statement in 1983, commented: "In a sentence the new secretary had blown away the solemn assurances of a decade."

lated the question of what was going on at Dimona to a near-crisis level. House and Senate members of the Joint Committee on Atomic Energy were summoned urgently from Christmas recess to a secret briefing on Dimona by CIA and State Department officials. CIA Director Allen Dulles also arranged for President-elect John F. Kennedy be be briefed. It seems clear that none of this—the demarche to the French, the briefing of the joint committee, and the briefing of the President-elect—could have taken place without the explicit approval of Dwight Eisenhower.

Washington also was sharing its concern with its allies, and it was that communication that moved the diplomatic concern about Dimona onto the front pages. The story broke in the world's press on December 16, when the London *Daily Express*, a tabloid, published a major story saying that "British and American intelligence authorities believe that the Israelis are well on the way to building their first experimental nuclear bomb." The dispatch was written by Chapman Pincher, known for his close ties to the British intelligence and nuclear communities. Pincher had indeed gotten a tip from a senior figure in British atomic weapons research, whose concern was that an Israeli bomb would necessarily be "dirty"—that is, generate a lot of radioactive fallout. Pincher, in a telephone interview, said that his next step was to call an old contact in Mossad and verify the story. "I had a very good connection to Mossad," Pincher said. "I had good Jewish friends here [in London]. They did make use of me for quite a long time—feeding me anti-Palestinian information." Pincher's relationship with Mossad was predicated on the understanding that, as he recalled, "if they ever fed me a bum steer, I'd blow them out of the water."

McCone's leak to John Finney, his strong statements on *Meet the Press*, and his later actions in the Kennedy administration—he replaced Allen Dulles as CIA director in the fall of 1961—would get him labeled by some as anti-Semitic. There was no known basis for such allegations, however: McCone, as he would demonstrate anew as CIA director, was dead set against any nuclear proliferation and repeatedly railed against the

French as well as the Israelis. He also was offended by the
Israeli and French lying about their collaboration in the Negev,
and he viewed Washington's acquiescence in those lies with
contempt. Myron B. Kratzer, the AEC's director of international affairs in December 1960, recalled being telephoned a few
hours before McCone's farewell appearance on *Meet the Press* by
a State Department colleague and told to urge McCone to
downplay the Israeli issue. Kratzer relayed the request, and
McCone blew up. "He said to me," Kratzer recalls, " 'I haven't
lived all these years to go out of office telling anything less than
the truth.' "* One of McCone's goals, Kratzer says, was to force
the Israelis to accept international inspection of Dimona.

In Israel, Deputy Minister of Defense Shimon Peres, fore-
warned by Ambassador Harman and perhaps by Mossad, began working up the cover story. There was a widespread
suspicion in the prime minister's office that the truth about
Dimona had been leaked to the British press by some of
the men around de Gaulle; the French had continued to urge
the Israelis to make public the existence of the reactor since the
June summit meeting between de Gaulle and Ben-Gurion. Betrayal by an ally was, for the Israelis, always the expected; Peres's immediate goal was to keep his and Ben-Gurion's dream
on track. The stakes were high: any extended publicity about
Dimona threatened one of Israel's most significant international successes—the purchase from Norway the year before of
twenty tons of heavy water, to be used, Israel had assured the
Norwegians, to fuel what was said to be an experimental nuclear power station at Dimona. Norway had been given a
pledge of peaceful use and the right to inspect the heavy water,
which it would do only once in the next thirty-two years. The
twenty-ton purchase of heavy water was obviously much more
than required to fuel a twenty-four-megawatt reactor; a Nor-

* McCone, perhaps anticipating a return to public life, did play the game nonetheless, saying on television that there was only "informal and unofficial information"
about Dimona. He also said he did not know whether any of the nuclear powers
(France, England, the United States, and the Soviet Union) had aided Israel. McCone's
discretion was made easier, of course, by the knowledge of the Pincher dispatch and
the fact that the *New York Times* was a day away from publishing John Finney's much
more complete story.

wegian complaint, with its resulting publicity, would be devastating in the wake of the worldwide protests over Dimona.

On December 20, Peres met with those defense ministry staff aides who knew of Dimona and summarized the various cover stories that would become David Ben-Gurion's public stance on the issue: the reactor at Dimona was part of a long-range program for development of the Negev desert and existed only for peaceful purposes. Those who called for inspection of the reactor, Peres said, "are the same people who advocate the internationalization of Jerusalem."*

On the next day, Ben-Gurion publicly described to the full membership of the Knesset what was being built, in the name of Israel, in the Negev: a twenty-four-megawatt reactor "dedicated entirely to peaceful purposes." There was another facility on the grounds of Dimona, the prime minister added: "a scientific institute for arid zone research." When completed, Ben-Gurion said, the entire facility "will be open to students from other countries." It was the first time members of Israel's parliament had been officially told about the reactor construction. Asked specifically about the published reports in Europe and the United States, Ben-Gurion casually denied them as "either a deliberate or unconscious untruth."

Ben-Gurion was treating the Knesset as he always did when it came to issues of state security: as a useless deliberative body that debated and talked instead of taking action. He and his colleagues simply did not believe that the talkative Knesset had a prominent role to play when it came to security issues. They were not contemptuous of the Knesset, whose deliberations on

---

* Ben-Gurion and his immediate associates were prepared to say whatever was necessary for what they believed to be the good of the state. In his biography of Ben-Gurion, Michael Bar-Zohar tells of the prime minister's determination to shield his and the Israeli Army's responsibility for the brutal 1953 slaying of seventy Jordanians in the border village of Kibiya. The retaliatory raid had been led by Ariel Sharon. A statement was issued in Ben-Gurion's name blaming the atrocity on the inhabitants of nearby Jewish border settlements. Asked by a confidant to explain his action, Ben-Gurion cited a passage from Victor Hugo's *Les Misérables* in which a nun lies to a policeman about the whereabouts of an escaped prisoner. The nun committed no sin in lying, Ben-Gurion argued, "because her lie was designed to save human life. A lie like that is measured by a different yardstick." Moshe Sharett, Ben-Gurion's longtime rival, subsequently was depicted by Bar-Zohar as being "astounded" by the lie: "I would have resigned if it had fallen to me to step before a microphone and broadcast a fictitious account of what happened to the people of Israel and to the whole world."

other issues were accepted with respect, but saw themselves as
pragmatists who—unlike the Knesset—believed in acting first,
and then talking. Knesset members, for their part, accepted
Ben-Gurion's view that it would be inappropriate to assert
their legislative rights in a debate over Dimona. Not one member dared to ask the obvious question: if the reactor at Dimona
were nothing more than a peaceful research tool, as Ben-Gurion publicly insisted, why did it need to be swathed in such
secrecy? The Knesset was only too eager to accept any government statement denying the intent to produce nuclear weapons.

Even Ernst David Bergmann's categorical denial of any plan
to make the bomb was accepted without challenge, although
Bergmann's total involvement with the bomb was widely
known. Bergmann was in the embarrassing position of still
serving as chairman and sole member of the Israeli Atomic
Energy Commission, although there had been no commissioners for him to chair for years. The six other members all had
left their posts by the mid-1950s; the departures have repeatedly
been cited by scholars and in American intelligence files as
evidence of serious disagreement inside the Israeli scientific
community over Bergmann's plans for Dimona. For the most
part, they were not. The commission members moved en masse
to the physics department at the Weizmann Institute, according to Israeli sources, because senior government officials hostile to nuclear development, including Levi Eshkol and Pinhas
Lavon, then the defense minister, refused to allocate research
funds for them. Two of the former commissioners would
emerge in the 1960s as critics of the nuclear programs; others,
such as Amos Deshalit, Israel's most eminent nuclear physicist,
ended up being closely involved with Dimona.

The Israeli statements were not challenged in subsequent
days and weeks by the Eisenhower administration, which, having triggered the first public discussion of the Israeli bomb,
immediately retreated in the face of Israeli's shameless denials.
In a statement released to the press on the day after Ben-Gurion's speech, the White House joined with the Knesset in accepting the Israeli cover story for Dimona at face value: "The
government of Israel has given assurances that its new reactor

. . . is dedicated solely for research purposes to develop scientific knowledge and thus to serve the needs of industry, agriculture, health and science. . . . Israel states it will welcome visits by students and scientists of friendly countries to the reactor upon its completion." The statement, personally approved by the President, added, "It is gratifying to note that as made public the Israel atomic energy program does not represent cause for special concern."

The administration's retreat continued on the next day: it was now concerned with limiting the worldwide criticism directed at Israel. A private State Department circular sent on December 22 to American embassies around the world, written in cablese, noted that the government "believes Israel atomic energy program as made public does not represent cause for special concern." Officials of the department, who had been involved in the initial decision earlier in the month to pressure Israel, were now said, according to the circular, which was released under the Freedom of Information Act, to be "considerably disturbed by large amount of info re USG [United States Government] interest in Israel's atomic program which has leaked into American and world press. Effort has been to create more excitement than facts as revealed by Israelis warrant. Department will do what it can in Washington and hopes addressee posts can assist in stilling atmosphere." The notion of "stilling atmosphere" would define America's enduring policy toward the Israeli bomb.

There was one final protest, in secret. On January 6, 1961, Christian Herter gave his farewell briefing as secretary of state to a closed session of the Senate Foreign Relations Committee (the transcript was declassified in 1984). Dimona came up, and Herter was discussing the "disturbing" new element in the Middle East when Senator Bourke B. Hickenlooper, the conservative Republican from Iowa, interrupted testily. "I think the Israelis have just lied to us like horse thieves on this thing," Hickenlooper said. "They have completely distorted, misrepresented, and falsified the facts in the past. I think it is very serious . . . to have them perform in this manner in connection with this very definite production reactor facility which they have been secretly building, and which they have consistently, and with a completely straight face, denied to us they were building." Hickenlooper knew what he was talking about: at the time he was chairman of the Joint Committee on Atomic Energy.

The powerful senator also knew that he was just blowing off steam in a secret hearing. No one in the lame-duck Eisenhower administration was going to do anything more to take on Israel. "I'm not going to ask you as secretary of state to answer," Hickenlooper added limply. "I hope I am wrong."

Dimona would be left for the New Frontier of John F. Kennedy.

7

Dual Loyalty

Lewis Strauss, John McCone's predecessor as chairman of the Atomic Energy Commission, was the epitome of the 1950s Cold Warrior, an American booster who was adamantly opposed to the spread of nuclear weapons. Strauss certainly knew as much about Dimona as anybody in the intelligence community by the time he left the AEC in 1958. There is no evidence, however, that he raised questions about the Israeli weapons program while in government; nor was he known to have ever discussed Dimona after leaving office. He most certainly did not tell McCone, a devout Roman Catholic, about it.

Strauss chose not to talk about the Israeli nuclear program because, as a Jew with deep feelings about the Holocaust, he approved of it. His strong private feelings about Israel and its need for security were in sharp contrast to his public image of a thoroughly assimilated Jew who offended many—and amused others—by insisting that his name be pronounced "Straws."

A conservative investment banker from Virginia who rose to admiral in the Navy Reserves during World War II, Strauss viewed America's nuclear arsenal as essential to survival against the Soviet Union; those who disagreed with him were not merely wrong, they were Communist dupes. He had left his Wall Street firm after the war to serve until 1950 as one of the original members of the Atomic Energy Commission, an independent federal agency set up to be custodian of America's nuclear materials, just as the Army's Manhattan Engineering District had been administratively in charge of Oppenheimer's secret work in Los Alamos. Strauss and his five fellow commissioners now found themselves the proprietors of all fissionable materials; they also were responsible for operating the nation's nuclear reactors and developing atomic bombs. Civilian control of the nuclear arsenal was so total that the commission initially did not tell the military either the number or the yield of the bombs being manufactured, creating havoc with the Joint Chiefs of Staff's early nuclear war planning. (The Department of Energy is in charge of nuclear weapons production today.)

Strauss quickly emerged as the strongman of the commission, and he became even more powerful in 1953 when Eisenhower asked him to return to the AEC as its chairman. Strauss supported loyalty oaths for citizens with access to nuclear information. He was insistent on continued nuclear testing and publicly took issue with those who claimed that fallout from the tests was dangerous to human health. He also fought against attempts by the Eisenhower administration to negotiate a nuclear test ban treaty or any other nuclear arms agreement with the Soviet Union. Strauss sided with those in the government and Congress who sought to prevent the passing of weapons information to the European allies in fear that the Soviet bloc would gain access to it.

At the same time, he championed Atoms for Peace, the Eisenhower administration program that called for America's allies to be provided with American nuclear technology and nuclear fuel—under international safeguards—to promote the peaceful use of atomic energy. The assumption, which turned out to be dreadfully wrong, was that smaller nations, once supplied with the enriched uranium or plutonium needed to drive a nuclear power plant, would have no incentive or desire to develop nuclear weapons. Strauss was, not surprisingly, a proponent of private enterprise and worked hard to ensure that industry—and not the government—would be permitted to build and operate nuclear power plants.

The AEC commissioner became best known to most Americans, however, for his dislike of J. Robert Oppenheimer, who had sparked a furor in the early 1950s by calling on the United States to abate the arms race by forgoing the hydrogen bomb. In 1954, Strauss led a bitter and successful fight to strip Oppenheimer of his security clearance; the hearings, which eventually centered on Oppenheimer's loyalty and integrity, captivated the nation. Strauss's activities against Oppenheimer

were not always in the open; evidence subsequently was revealed showing that Strauss had directed the FBI to monitor
Oppenheimer's movements and tap his telephone, including
calls to his attorney, in an effort to make sure that the clearance
would be denied.

Strauss's tactics and his prickly public demeanor ensured
that he would never be well liked, despite his playing a major
role in American nuclear policy until his death in 1974, at age
seventy-seven. Even close associates viewed him as aloof, arrogant, and calculating; many others viewed his demand that he
be called "Straws" as a sign that he was defensive about being
Jewish. None of this seemed to matter to Dwight Eisenhower,
who trusted his judgment and would later describe him as
among the "towering governmental figures" of Western civili-
zation. Eisenhower offered him a series of top jobs after Strauss
decided in 1958 to leave the AEC—as secretary of state and
White House chief of staff, both of which Strauss refused—and
finally got him to agree to become secretary of commerce. The
1959 confirmation hearings were a disaster—Strauss was caught
being less than candid with the Senate Commerce Committee
—and led to a humiliating rejection. He was the only cabinet
nominee not to be confirmed during Eisenhower's two terms,
and only the eighth such rejection in American history.

Strauss remained undaunted in his hostility to the Soviet
Union after leaving public life, telling a congressional panel
during hearings on the Kennedy administration's proposed nuclear test ban, "I'm not sure that the reduction of [U.S.–USSR]
tension is necessarily a good thing." He also continued to advocate the use of atomic energy, and in 1964 made a visit to Israel
—apparently his first—to consult with the government on a
proposed nuclear-powered water desalinization plant.

At some point in his AEC career, Strauss, who attended most
of the international conferences on the peaceful uses of the
atom, met and befriended his Israeli counterpart, Ernst David
Bergmann. It was a relationship shared with few; neither
Strauss's biographer nor his son, Lewis, who has had access to
all of his father's personal papers, knew that the two had met.

The friendship with Bergmann provides the strongest evidence of Strauss's sympathy for the Israeli nuclear weapons

program. In the fall of 1966, Strauss used his influence to get Bergmann a two-month appointment as a visiting fellow at the prestigious Institute for Advanced Studies in Princeton. Strauss, who never graduated from college, had joined the institute's board of trustees during World War II, and he continued to be one of its major contributors and fund-raisers. The institute rarely dealt with chemists—its fellows are physicists and mathematicians—but the rules were bent for Strauss. Bergmann was a bitter man at that point; he had been forced to resign his posts at the defense ministry and as head of the Israeli Atomic Energy Commission after his continued objections to Prime Minister Levi Eshkol's decision—in part because of pressure from President Lyndon B. Johnson—to delay full-scale nuclear weapons production.

"Strauss had nudged me about Bergmann," recalled Carl Kaysen, then the institute's newly appointed director. "He told me he was a very distinguished scientist." It was only after Bergmann arrived, Kaysen added, that he learned who he was and what he did. Bergmann wasn't very busy, and "he would come by and talk to me. It became clear that he and Strauss were close, and also clear that he was working on [the Israeli nuclear] weapons program. He was very relaxed about it." It was also obvious that Bergmann was telling Kaysen all that he had told Strauss. Kaysen, a distinguished political economist who had been deputy assistant to the President for national security affairs, wasn't surprised to learn that Israel was interested in nuclear bombs, but it was a jolt to realize that Strauss —seemingly so ambivalent about his Jewishness and so opposed to any spread of nuclear weapons technology—privately was in favor of a nuclear-armed Israel.

Perhaps because Strauss's political life was so mired in turbulence, the public and the press never had a chance to get more than a glimpse of his private feelings about being Jewish and his guilt about not doing more in the 1930s to save Jews caught up in the Holocaust.

There was really no secret about his Jewishness—Strauss had been a leader since 1938 of Congregation Emanu-El, the largest and most prominent Reform synagogue in New York City. In

1957, Eisenhower had briefly toyed with the idea of naming him secretary of defense, but decided that his Jewishness would cause too many problems with the Arab nations in the Middle East. Yet Strauss's activities on behalf of a Jewish homeland apparently were not known, not even to his close associates in the Atomic Energy Commission. In his memoirs, published in 1962, Strauss wrote bitterly about the Nazi Holocaust and those —including himself—who did not do enough: "The years from 1933 to the outbreak of World War II will ever be a nightmare to me, and the puny efforts I made to alleviate the tragedies were utter failures, save in a few individual cases—pitifully few."

In 1933, Strauss had been asked by the American Jewish Committee to attend an international conference in London on the Jewish plight. There he met Dr. Chaim Weizmann and listened as the conferees agreed that an "astronomical sum" of money from the United States must be raised to help resettle what could be millions of Jews. Strauss, then fervently opposed to a Jewish state in Palestine, was the only delegate to raise his voice in dissent during the conference, a position he came to regret. Six years later, Strauss would spend much time and effort in an unsuccessful attempt to convince the British government to donate a large chunk of colonial Africa for resettlement by European refugees, Jews and non-Jews alike. With the Nazi blitzkrieg only months away, money was no longer an object: Strauss and his American colleagues, who included Bernard Baruch, the financier, were agreed that as much as $300 million could be raised.* It was too late; Strauss's strong feelings about that failure—and the failure of world leadership— are explicit in his memoir: "The tidal wave of war swept over the continents and across the ocean and a world in shock closed

* The goal was to convince the British to cede a tract of land in Kenya, Tanganyika (now Tanzania), or northern Rhodesia (now Zimbabwe). Strauss carried a letter to London from Baruch in the late summer of 1939 noting that the land to be ceded in Africa could be "cleaned up with modern equipment. The world has not always been as clean as it is now. Our own country was full of morasses. Panama and Cuba were cleaned up, and Africa can be cleaned up, too. . . . [I]n this new land there would be a place for tens of millions and they would be the best, the strongest and the most courageous peoples. . . ." Missing from the Baruch-Strauss proposal is any thought or concern about the Africans who lived in the areas to be ceded. Any such resettlement would have inevitably resulted in internal conflict similar to that raging then—and now—between the Israelis and those Palestinians who were ousted from their homelands by the Zionist movement.

its eyes, figuratively and literally, to the plight of the unfortu-
nate beings who were engulfed."*

Like many Jews, Strauss remained hostile to Zionism all of
his life, but he won the confidence of his colleagues in the Israeli Atomic Energy Commission by publicly joining them in
prayer in Geneva during the 1955 United Nations Conference
on the Peaceful Uses of Atomic Energy, at the time the largest
international scientific conference ever held. More than fifteen
hundred delegates from seventy nations, including Israel,
whose delegation was led by Ernst Bergmann, took part.
Moshe Sharett, then foreign minister, received a full report—as
he noted in a diary entry for September 18, 1955—from a deputy, who characteristically thought it important to tell Sharett
that at least three hundred of the delegates were Jewish. Despite that large number, Sharett wrote, when the Jewish community of Geneva arranged for a special Friday-night service,
"present only were the Jewish delegation [to the conference]
and the head of the U.S. delegation, Admiral Strauss."

* Neither Strauss nor the CIA's Dino Brugioni knew it at the time, of course, but
reconnaissance aircraft of the Mediterranean Allied Air Force and the Fifteenth U.S.
Air Force repeatedly overflew and photographed the Nazi crematoriums at Auschwitz-
Birkenau in Poland in the last year of the war, where twelve thousand Jews and gypsies
were being murdered daily by 1944. The death camps were about five miles from an
I.G. Farben synthetic oil and rubber complex that was bombed four times in World
War II. In 1978, Brugioni and Robert Poirier, a CIA colleague, noticed that the camps
were in direct alignment with the reconnaissance path for the Farben complex. Brugioni knew from his own experiences that reconnaissance cameras were always turned
on well before the target was reached. Were there aerial photos of the camps buried in
Pentagon World War II archives? In a subsequent essay, Brugioni wrote: "We found
that the extermination complex had been photographed at least thirty times. Analyzing
the photographs, we could see the four large complexes of gas chamber and crematoriums. . . . Bodies were being buried in trenches or burned in large open pits. Some of
the photos showed victims being marched to their deaths, while others showed prison-
ers being processed for slave labour." The photographs were invaluable as a historical
record—the Nazis had forbidden any photography while the camps were in operation
—and President Jimmy Carter personally presented a monograph based on them to the
President's Commission on the Holocaust. During the war, Brugioni added, there was
no historical or social background that would have enabled Air Force photo interpreters, intent on targeting the I.G. Farben plant, to understand what they were seeing:
"Anytime a line of people near a building were seen in a picture, it was usually labeled
'mess hall.' " There were other factors that prevented a close study of the camp photographs at the time, insisted Brugioni, most significantly the intense intelligence needs
of the June 1944 D-Day invasion of Europe, which resulted in heavy workloads for all
Allied photo interpreters. Allied warplanes also were attempting to break the back of
the Luftwaffe in late 1944 by heavy raids on all of the synthetic fuel plants in Germany,
Brugioni said, creating yet another demand for photo interpretation and bomb damage
assessment.

Strauss, nonetheless, worked hard while in Washington at reining in his intense feelings about being Jewish and about the Holocaust, although many of his former subordinates from the AEC remarked in interviews about his unrelenting hostility to Germans and his reluctance to deal with Germans on any issue. Yet the longtime AEC official Myron Kratzer, who is also Jewish, did not find out until Strauss had left the AEC that the former chairman followed the tradition of fasting during Yom Kippur, the holiest Jewish holiday. Strauss had been asked by Eisenhower after his retirement to head the American delegation to an international meeting in Vienna, and on Yom Kippur, Kratzer recalled, "Strauss did not show up. He simply closed himself in his room on that day."

Strauss's background and his strong feelings about the Holocaust cannot be disregarded in analyzing why he did not tell anyone—especially John McCone—about Dimona. Fair or not, the issue of "dual loyalty"—exemplified by Strauss's actions—has been a very real concern to the American intelligence community since the creation of Israel in 1948. American Jews, for example, were routinely barred for many years from dealing with Israeli issues inside CIA headquarters; none of the early station chiefs or agents assigned to Israel was Jewish. One Jew who served decades later in a high position in the CIA angrily acknowledged that when he arrived, "every fucking Jew in the CIA was in accounting or legal." The official wasn't quite right, but even those few Jews who did get to the top, such as Edward W. Proctor, who served as deputy director for intelligence in the mid-1970s, were not given access to all of the sensitive files in connection with Israel. Jews also were excluded from Hebrew language training (at one time called "special Arabic") in the National Security Agency; such training, of course, is a prerequisite for being assigned to NSA field stations that intercept Israeli communications. There was a flat ban in the Navy communications intelligence agency (known as the Naval Security Group) on the assignment of a Jew to a Middle East issue.

There was—and still is—a widespread belief among American foreign service officers that any diplomatic reporting critical of Israel would somehow be delivered within days to the Israeli embassy in Washington. In 1963 the Kennedy administration informally agreed with Israel that neither country would spy on or conduct espionage activities against the other. The agreement was sought by American officials, a former Kennedy aide recalled, in an attempt to limit the extent of Israeli penetration of America.

The truth is that Jews and non-Jews alike looked the other way when it came to Israel's nuclear capability. The notion of dual loyalty solely as a Jewish problem is far too narrow; the Jewish survivors who became Israelis, with their incredible travails and sufferings during World War II, had and still have enormous appeal to Americans of all backgrounds. The primary effect of "dual loyalty" has been a form of self-censorship that has kept the United States government from dealing rationally and coherently with the strategic and political issues raised by a nuclear-armed Israel. The issue is not whether rules or laws have been broken, but that very few officials who supported Israel, Jewish or not, have used their position to try to obtain a complete and accurate picture of the Israeli nuclear program. And no one tried to stop it. Those few government bureaucrats in the nonproliferation field who even tried to learn all there was to learn about Dimona were often accused of being "zealots"—and thus not fully trustworthy.

Yet, being Jewish inevitably raised questions, even among the most fair-minded of men. Dino Brugioni briefed Strauss regularly on U-2 nuclear intelligence, but found him inscrutable when it came to information on the Israeli nuclear reactor: "I never knew what he was thinking; never understood him. I'd get the reaction 'That's all right.' " Brugioni had his own reasons for wondering about Strauss. He knew there was evidence inside the CIA suggesting that American and European Jews had been directly involved in the financing and construction of Dimona from the start. "There was a fervor, especially among New York Jews," Brugioni added. "The attitude was 'You had to protect Israel,' and anybody [in the intelligence community] who did not suffered."

In interviews for this book with senior officials of the American nuclear weapons program—men similar to Lewis Strauss, who spent part or all of their life making bombs—none expressed any doubt about Israel's nuclear ambitions. Most told of close personal friendships with Israeli physicists who were working on the Israeli weapons program. No one with the sophistication and expertise of Lewis Strauss could have had any question about the significance of a secret reactor in the Negev. His widow, Alice, still spry in 1991 at the age of eighty-eight, acknowledged that her husband, who was very closemouthed about his work, "would have approved of Israel trying to defend itself. No question of that." Strauss also had to know that a Jewish nuclear physicist named Raymond Fox had created high-level consternation by emigrating to Israel in 1957 from California, where he had access to weapons design information at the Lawrence Livermore National Laboratory, the nuclear research facility operated by the University of California for the Atomic Energy Commission. Fox's secrets could be invaluable to the Israelis at Dimona.

Strauss's failure to discuss Dimona with John McCone may have been done in the belief that he had an obligation to ensure that what happened to the Jews of Europe under Hitler could not happen again. Perhaps he thought he was atoning for what he did not do, or could not do, to help the Jews of Europe before World War II. Similar choices were made over the next thirty years by Jews and non-Jews in the American government, who looked the other way when it came to Dimona. Were they guilty of a double standard, as Dino Brugioni and others in the intelligence community suggest? Did Lewis Strauss, who so eagerly assumed the worst when it came to the loyalty of men such as J. Robert Oppenheimer, fail to fulfill the obligations of his office in terms of the known intelligence on Dimona and his obligation to tell his successor about it?

Many American Jews, perhaps understandably, believe the question of "dual loyalty" is an issue that should never be raised in public. They fear that any discussion of Jewish support for Israel at the expense of the United States would feed anti-Semitism; the fear seems to be that non-Jews are convinced that any Jewish support for Israel precludes primary loyalty to the United States. A second issue, in terms of American Jewish

support for Israel, is that any public accounting of Israel's nuclear capacity would trigger renewed fears among Arab nations of a worldwide Jewish conspiracy and a redoubling of
Arab efforts to get the bomb.

Weighing against those concerns are several questions. Can
the world afford to pretend that Israel is not a nuclear power
because to do otherwise would raise difficult issues? Can any
international agreement to limit the spread of nuclear weapons
be enforced if Israel's bombs are not fully accounted for? Can
the Arab nations truly be expected to ignore Israel's possession
of atomic weapons simply because the weapons are not publicized? Should Israel, because of its widespread and emotional
support in America, be held to a different moral standard than
Pakistan or North Korea or South Africa?

Many senior nonproliferation officials in the American government were convinced by the early 1990s that the Middle
East remained the one place where nuclear weapons might be
used. "Israel has a well-thought-out nuclear strategy and, if suf-
ficiently threatened, they will use it," said one expert who has
been involved in government studies on the nuclear issue in
the Middle East for two decades.

Some of Strauss's former subordinates in the AEC find it difficult to believe that his Jewishness would have been the reason
that Strauss would or would not tell John McCone about
Dimona. Algie A. Wells, who was director of international affairs for the AEC in mid-1958, at the time McCone replaced
Strauss, suggested that there were far more trivial reasons for
Strauss to have ignored his statutory responsibility as AEC
chairman: "Why would Strauss have told McCone? The men
weren't close. They both had colossal egos. I can't imagine
them being buddy-buddy and having a drink together."

In Wells's view, whether Strauss did or did not tell McCone
wasn't that important. Wells had been in Israel in 1958, he recalled, and learned then—as had any government official who
chose to do so—that Israel was building a nuclear reactor. If
McCone was surprised to learn about the reactor in late 1960,
added Wells, "he shouldn't have been."

8

A Presidential Struggle

Abraham Feinberg shared Lewis Strauss's belief in operating behind the scenes on behalf of Israel, but Feinberg operated in a way Strauss could not—with single-mindedness and abandon. Feinberg, a New Yorker who made his fortune in the hosiery and apparel business, had helped bankroll Harry S. Truman's seemingly doomed 1948 presidential campaign; by the presidential campaign of 1960 he was perhaps the most important Jewish fund-raiser for the Democratic Party. There was nothing subtle in his message: the dollars he collected were meant to ensure continued Democratic Party support for Israel.

Feinberg also had been a "player"—to use his word—who shared the early dreams of his good friend Ernst David Bergmann of a nuclear-armed Israel. He served publicly as president of the Israel Bond Organization, while privately helping to raise some of the many millions of dollars needed to build the controversial reactor and reprocessing plant at Dimona. Feinberg accepted the fact that the expanding and expensive operations at Dimona had to be financed outside of the normal Israeli budget process; there were too many critics of the nuclear program inside and outside Israel to raise money any other way. The unwanted publicity at the end of the Eisenhower administration had only added to Ben-Gurion's and Shimon Peres's determination to protect the secret. Feinberg was more than just a fund-raiser in all this; he became an inside advocate for Ben-Gurion and Peres as President Kennedy, who brought in John McCone as director of central intelligence in September 1961, established himself as firmly opposed to the Israeli bomb. There was a particularly close association with

Peres: "He came to me often for money. If he gave the assignment to me, I helped him."

Feinberg remains proud of his support for Israel and its secret weapons program. His most pitched battle on behalf of Israel came in the early days of the Kennedy administration when he successfully helped fight off the initial Kennedy insistence that an American inspection team be permitted full and unfettered access to Dimona. Feinberg's success was rooted in the American political process. "My path to power," he explains, "was cooperation in terms of what they needed—campaign money."

Feinberg's first taste of political power had come in the waning days of the Truman campaign against Thomas E. Dewey, the New York Republican governor who was seemingly running away with the 1948 election. "From the beginning of my political affiliation with Truman," he explained, "I felt it was the duty of every Jew to help Israel." Feinberg, as a member of a Democratic campaign finance committee, was invited to a White House meeting with the President, who had won the worldwide admiration of Jews for his decision to recognize the State of Israel earlier in the year. "If I had to bet money," Feinberg recalled Truman saying, "I'd bet on myself—if I could go across the country by train." At least $100,000 would be needed, the President said. Feinberg told Truman's aides that he would be able to guarantee the money by the end of the day, and subsequently he arranged for Truman's whistle-stop train campaign to be met by local Jewish leaders at each stop "to be refueled"—that is, provided with additional contributions as needed.

Among Feinberg's prize possessions is a seven-page handwritten letter of thanks and praise from Truman. Feinberg estimates that he and his Jewish colleagues raised "in the neighborhood of $400,000" during the 1948 whistle-stop campaign. Truman understood the rules and at some later point discussed naming Feinberg ambassador to Israel. Feinberg declined: "I told him no Jew should be ambassador to Israel until the peace was solved."

Feinberg's account of his bankrolling of Harry Truman is

found in none of the contemporary histories of that period,* and—like some of his later special fund-raising activities for Dimona—cannot be fully verified. Strong evidence is available, however, that Feinberg's role was as pivotal as he suggests. For example, Clark Clifford, the eminent Washington attorney who was a Truman aide and poker-playing crony, has a vivid recollection of a crucial Feinberg intervention during the whistle-stop campaign. Clifford was not involved in Democratic Party fund-raising, but he did know that midway through the train trip, the presidential campaign was out of money. Keeping the campaign alive, he recalled, was "as difficult a task as anybody ever had. We couldn't find anyone who thought we'd win." Disaster loomed in Oklahoma City when one of the radio networks—this was the pre-television era—informed the campaign that it would not nationally broadcast a much-touted Truman foreign policy speech unless "it was paid for in advance. This put us in shock," Clifford added. "It would have been embarrassing beyond measure." Something like $60,000 in cash was needed—immediately. "Truman thought about who he could turn to," continued Clifford. "The fellow he later spoke about who came through for him was Abe Feinberg. I always gave credit to Abe for saving that particular program and saving us that embarrassment. He really came through."

Feinberg was also active in fund-raising for Adlai E. Stevenson, the losing Democratic candidate in 1952 and 1956, and was a strong backer of Senator Stuart Symington, Democrat of Missouri, for the Democratic presidential nomination. (Symington would emerge later as an ardent supporter of a nuclear-armed Israel and, paradoxically, as author of key Senate legislation to limit the spread of such weapons.) He played no role in John Kennedy's primary campaign for the Democratic nomination: like many Jews, Feinberg was convinced that Kennedy's father was anti-Semitic. Joseph P. Kennedy, a self-made millionaire and prominent Catholic, had fought against going to war with Germany while serving as Franklin D. Roosevelt's ambassador to England before World War II. A few weeks after Kennedy's

---

* Campaign historians were not the only ones who missed the Feinberg story; none of the contemporary daily press or television journalists covering events in 1948 wrote about the financial ties between Feinberg and the Truman campaign.

nomination by the Democrats, however, Feinberg was contacted by Governor Abraham Ribicoff of Connecticut, who had
been Kennedy's floor manager during the Democratic conven-
tion. "I was the only Jew for him," Ribicoff recalled. "And I
realized that Jews were for anybody but Jack Kennedy. I told
Kennedy I was going to get in touch with Abe Feinberg, who I
thought was a key Jew. I arranged a meeting [with Kennedy] in
Feinberg's apartment in the Hotel Pierre and we invited all the
leading Jews." About twenty prominent businessmen and fi-
nanciers showed up.*

It was a rough session. Kennedy had just returned from a
brief vacation at the family compound at Hyannis Port, Massachusetts, and it was a prominent Bostonian, Dewey D. Stone,
who set the tone with the first question, as recalled by Feinberg: "Jack, everybody knows the reputation of your father
concerning Jews and Hitler. And everybody knows that the
apple doesn't fall far from the tree." Kennedy's response was to
the point: "You know, my mother was part of that tree, too."
Ribicoff, who would join Kennedy's cabinet, understood the
message: "The sins of the father shouldn't fall on the son."
Fortunately for Kennedy, that message was enough for the
men at Feinberg's apartment. Kennedy had gone upstairs to a
separate room with Ribicoff to await their judgment, Feinberg
recalled. The group agreed on an initial contribution of
$500,000 to the presidential campaign, with more to come. "I
called him [Kennedy] right away," said Feinberg. "His voice
broke. He got emotional" with gratitude.

Kennedy was anything but grateful the next morning in
describing the session to Charles L. Bartlett, a newspaper columnist and close friend. He had driven to Bartlett's home in
northwest Washington and dragged his friend on a walk, where
he recounted a much different version of the meeting the night

* Kennedy's social friends and colleagues agreed that Kennedy, like many wealthy
Irish Catholics of his time, had gone through prep school at Choate and Harvard
College with few close Jewish friends. One especially close schoolboy friend, according
to Arthur M. Schlesinger, Jr., the presidential biographer, was Alan J. Lerner, with
whom Kennedy traveled widely as a youth. There were few other Jewish childhood
friends, as Benjamin C. Bradlee, Jr., the longtime editor of the *Washington Post* and close
Kennedy friend, acknowledged: "I don't remember a whole lot of Jewish buddies."
That changed quickly once Kennedy got into national politics after World War II.

before. "As an American citizen he was outraged," Bartlett recalled, "to have a Zionist group come to him and say: 'We know your campaign is in trouble. We're willing to pay your bills if you'll let us have control of your Middle East policy.'" Kennedy, as a presidential candidate, also resented the crudity with which he'd been approached. "They wanted control," he angrily told Bartlett.

Bartlett further recalled Kennedy promising to himself that "if he ever did get to be President, he was going to do something about it"—a candidate's perennial need for money and resulting vulnerability to the demands of those who contributed. Kennedy, in fact, kept that promise before the end of his first year in office, appointing a bipartisan commission in October to recommend ways to broaden "the financial base of our presidential campaigns." In a statement that was far more heartfelt than the public or the press could perceive, he criticized the current method of financing campaigns as "highly undesirable" and "not healthy" because it made candidates "dependent on large financial contributions of those with special interests." Presidential elections, Kennedy declared, were "the supreme test of the democratic process" in the United States. Kennedy was ahead of his time, however: the campaign financing proposals went nowhere.*

It is impossible to reconcile the differing accounts of Kennedy's attitude toward the meeting in Feinberg's apartment in the Hotel Pierre. But the fact remains that despite Kennedy's tough words to Bartlett, Abe Feinberg's influence inside the White House was established by the end of Kennedy's first year in office, and the young President did little to diminish it over the next two years. One factor obviously was political: a higher percentage of Jews (81 percent) voted for Kennedy in 1960 than did Roman Catholics (73 percent); it was the Jewish vote that provided Kennedy's narrow plurality of 114,563 votes over

* The commission, headed by Alexander Heard, then dean of the Graduate School at the University of North Carolina, recommended, among other things, the use of federal tax credits to encourage political contributions by individuals. The goal was to broaden the base of a candidate's financial support and reduce dependence on special-interest groups and the wealthy. In 1962, Kennedy submitted five draft bills to reform presidential campaign financing to Congress; none survived. Kennedy tried again in 1963, submitting two more draft bills to Congress; again neither survived.

Nixon. Feinberg got a specific reward after the election: his
lawyer brother, Wilfred, was given a federal judgeship by the
President.* "Feinberg only wanted one thing—to put his
brother on the federal bench," Ribicoff recalled. "I sat in on the
meeting with Kennedy and recommended that he do it. The
President said, 'Look, Abe, when all is said and done, the only
Jew who was for me [early in the campaign] was Abe Feinberg.' "

The issue of Jewish political power and the Israeli bomb was
complicated during these years by the fact that John Kennedy
was intellectually and emotionally committed to a halt in the
spread of nuclear weapons. Carl Kaysen, who moved from the
Harvard faculty to the National Security Council in 1961, recalled: "There were two subjects that you could get the President started on and he'd talk for hours. One was the gold
standard, the other was nonproliferation." The political expe-
diencies that forced him to be ambivalent about Dimona had to
be frustrating. Kennedy eventually agreed to a series of face-
saving American inspections of the Israeli nuclear facilities,
although the label "inspection" hardly does justice to what the
Israelis would permit.

Kennedy's complicated feelings about Jewish political power
and the Israeli issue were summarized in his appointment of
former campaign aide Myer (Mike) Feldman as the presidential
point man for Jewish and Israeli affairs. The President viewed
Feldman, whose strong support for Israel was widely known,
as a necessary evil whose highly visible White House position
was a political debt that had to be paid. Feldman recalled being
summoned by the President the day after the inauguration and

* Wilfred Feinberg, a legal scholar who had been editor in chief of the *Columbia Law
Review,* served from 1961 to 1966 as a federal judge in the Southern District of New York.
In 1966, President Lyndon Johnson, anxious to do something for his good friend Abe
Feinberg, promoted Wilfred to the United States Court of Appeals for the Second
Circuit. To do so, he had to override the recommendation of Senator Robert F. Kennedy of New York, the late President's younger brother, who had resigned as attorney
general to run, successfully, for the Senate. Robert Kennedy pushed for the nomination of Edward Weinfeld, widely considered to be the most distinguished jurist on the
lower federal court, but Kennedy understood that he could never match Abe
Feinberg's influence with Johnson. "It was pure politics," recalled Peter B. Edelman,
then a senior Kennedy aide, "but not one of those cases where politics produced a poor
judge." Wilfred Feinberg served with distinction and went on to become chief judge of
the Court of Appeals for the Second Circuit in 1980.

authorized to monitor all of the State Department and White House cable traffic on the Middle East: "I said, 'Mr. President, I come with a strong bias toward Israel.' He told me, 'That's why I want you to look at them.' " Feldman's special relationship and his special access created havoc inside the White House, as Kennedy had to know it would. The President's most senior advisers, most acutely McGeorge Bundy, the national security adviser, desperately sought to cut Feldman out of the flow of Middle East paperwork; the result often was bureaucratic chaos. "The White House staff under Kennedy was not harmonious," acknowledged Kaysen, who is Jewish. "Bundy was very suspicious of Feldman, and anxious about me and Bob Komer"—another Jewish National Security Council staff member, assigned to monitor South Asia. "He worried about us handling Israeli issues."* Robert W. Komer, who would later run the pacification program in South Vietnam for Lyndon Johnson, recalled the tension: "Mac Bundy had a standing rule. He sent nothing to Feldman, because Feldman was getting involved in issues in which he had no business. It was hard to tell the difference between what Feldman said and what the Israeli ambassador said."

The White House staff aides might well have been taking their cues on treating Feldman from their young President. Kennedy, having provided special access for Feldman, couldn't resist making wisecracks behind his back. Charles Bartlett recalled Kennedy interrupting a pleasant moment in Hyannis Port by pointedly remarking—it was a Saturday morning, the traditional time for synagogue services—"I imagine Mike's having a meeting of the Zionists in the cabinet room." An equally cynical view of Feldman was publicly expressed by Robert Kennedy in an interview published in 1988 by the John F. Kennedy Library. Speaking of Feldman, Kennedy noted that

---

* Jerome B. Wiesner, the President's science adviser, who also was Jewish, had a different concern: he was totally cut out of the intelligence about Dimona and "assumed" that Ben-Gurion had requested that he not deal with that issue in the White House. Wiesner, who played a major role on disarmament issues for the Kennedy administration, had served as a board member of the Weizmann Institute and repeatedly ran into Ben-Gurion on visits to Israel. "Ben-Gurion would always ask me two questions," Wiesner recalled: "Can computers think? And should we build a nuclear weapon? I'd always say no." That answer, Wiesner thought, marked him as a liberal in Ben-Gurion's eyes and limited his access.

his older brother, the President, had valued Feldman's work but added: "His major interest was Israel rather than the United States."

Feldman had no illusions about the backbiting inside the White House, but his obvious influence made it all tolerable: he continued to operate as Kennedy's special envoy to the Israeli government on a variety of sensitive issues, including nuclear weapons. He had been allowed to visit Dimona in 1962 and knew firsthand, as those around the President only suspected, that Israel was intent on building the bomb.

Israel's bomb, and what to do about it, became a White House fixation, part of the secret presidential agenda that would remain hidden for the next thirty years. None of the prominent John F. Kennedy presidential biographies, including those written by insiders Arthur Schlesinger and Theodore C. Sorensen, who was the President's special counsel and chief speechwriter, say anything about a nuclear-armed Israel or even mention Abe Feinberg. The U-2 intelligence collected by the CIA's Arthur Lundahl and Dino Brugioni continued to be treated as higher than top-secret, leaving a huge gap in knowledge between the bureaucracy and the men at the top. There were inevitably farcical results.

Shortly after Kennedy's inauguration, the State Department appointed William R. Crawford, a young foreign service officer, as director of Israeli affairs. Early on, Crawford recalled, the Air Force attaché in Israel managed to snap yet another long-range photograph of the reactor dome at Dimona. "It was as if there was no previous information," Crawford said. "As if the whole thing was a total surprise to the White House, intelligence community, and so forth." Meetings were held on the critical new intelligence. "This was very hot stuff. We decided that this was not what Israel was telling us."

Crawford was asked to draft a letter for the President to Ben-Gurion. The letter emphasized that America's worldwide position on nonproliferation would "be compromised if a state regarded as being dependent on us, as is Israel, pursues an independent course." Other key points, Crawford said, "were a demand for inspection and the right to convey the results to

Nasser." The idea was to reassure the Egyptian president that Dimona was not a weapons plant and to prevent Egypt from beginning its own nuclear research. The inspection of Dimona was to be carried out by an independent team of experts from the International Atomic Energy Agency (IAEA), the nuclear safeguarding agency based in Vienna; Israel had agreed in principle to permit the IAEA to replace the United States in the twice-a-year monitoring of its small research reactor at Nahal Soreq. "I drafted it very carefully," Crawford recalled. "It was the most important letter of my life at this point in my career." The letter was forwarded to the office of George Ball, then the under secretary of state, rewritten,* and dispatched. "In due course," recalled Crawford, "in comes a long, long reply from Ben-Gurion, pages and pages." Ben-Gurion's letter to Kennedy has not been made public, either by the United States or by Israel, but Crawford, nearly thirty years later, had no trouble recalling its tone. "It was very hard to see what he was saying. It seemed evasive; didn't say he was going the nuclear route: 'We're a tiny nation surrounded by enemies,' et cetera, et cetera. There may have been an allusion to a nuclear umbrella —language like 'Were we able to rely on the United States,' et cetera." In that first exchange, Crawford said, Ben-Gurion did not agree to the IAEA inspection of Dimona.

Israel's bomb program, and the continuing exchange of letters about it, would complicate, and eventually poison, Kennedy's relationship with David Ben-Gurion. The Israeli prime minister had been rebuffed in seeking a state visit to Washington but, with the aid of Abe Feinberg, contrived a May 1961 visit to the United States. The specific occasion was an evening convocation in his honor at Brandeis University near Boston. Feinberg managed to get the President to agree to a private meeting with Ben-Gurion at the Waldorf-Astoria Hotel in New York. A nervous Kennedy asked Abe Feinberg to sit in. Feinberg refused,

* Ball's office held on to the letter for days, Crawford said, eventually provoking a complaint from the White House. Crawford asked a friend on Ball's staff to check into it and was told that "Mr. Ball wants me to understand that this letter sounds as if it had been translated from the original in Sanskrit." When Ball's rewritten version finally emerged, Crawford said, it had the same message but "in JFK prose." Crawford was impressed.

but agreed to make the introductions. Ben-Gurion similarly was anxious about the session, in fear that the continued American pressure over Israel's nuclear weapons project would lead to an unwanted flare-up. Dimona already was on politically shaky ground among the various factions inside Israel, and a flap between Ben-Gurion and Kennedy on the issue could be devastating to the concept of a nuclear-armed Israel. This concern had prompted the Israeli government to assign physicist Amos Deshalit to accompany two equally distinguished American physicists, I. I. Rabi of Columbia University and Eugene Wigner of Princeton, to visit the still-incomplete reactor at Dimona sometime early in 1961. Neither reported seeing evidence of a weapons facility.*

The meeting with Kennedy was a major disappointment for the Israeli prime minister, and not only because of the nuclear issue. "He looked to me like a twenty-five-year-old boy," Ben-Gurion later told his biographer. "I asked myself: 'How can a man so young be elected President?' At first, I did not take him seriously." (Soviet Premier Nikita Khrushchev, who met Kennedy a month later at the Vienna summit, also was struck by Kennedy's youth and inexperience.) No public record of the Kennedy–Ben-Gurion meeting has been released, and it is not reliably known what transpired on the nuclear issue. Ben-Gurion later recalled that he once again asserted that Dimona was being constructed solely for research purposes. Kennedy brought up the Rabi-Wigner visit to Dimona and expressed satisfaction with their conviction that the reactor was designed for peaceful purposes. Ben-Gurion was relieved: "For the time being, at least, the reactor had been saved."

Another important summit issue was Egypt. Kennedy was

---

* Wigner, who won the Nobel Prize for physics in 1963, was visiting Israel when he was asked—seemingly spontaneously—by the Israelis to visit Dimona. He "vaguely" recalled, he said in telephone interviews in 1989 and 1991, being accompanied by Rabi, a 1944 Nobel laureate. "We didn't see much of it," Wigner, who was born in 1902, added. "I thought it was practically completed." Israeli scientists already may have begun some experimental work, he said: "They played with it." Wigner, who had joined with Albert Einstein in urging the United States to begin building the atom bomb before World War II, cautioned the author that his memory had faded with age. Rabi, a longtime consultant on technical and scientific issues to the United States government, died in 1988; neither his wife, friends, nor officials in charge of Columbia University's oral history project dealing with his career had information about his visit to Dimona.

intent on improving relations with the Nasser government, and the President outlined his new policy. Ben-Gurion renewed a standing Israeli request for the sale of U.S. Hawk surface-to-air missiles: the Hawk was needed to match the arrival of Soviet-built MiG fighters in Egypt. Kennedy promised to look into it.

The most memorable moment for Ben-Gurion came when he was leaving the hotel room. Kennedy suddenly walked him back inside to tell him "something important." It was a political message: "I know that I was elected by the votes of American Jews. I owe them my victory. Tell me, is there something I ought to do?" Ben-Gurion had not come to New York to haggle with the President about Jewish votes. "You must do whatever is good for the free world," he responded. He later told his aides: "To me, he looks like a politician." Ben-Gurion, known to his associates as B.G., made similar complaints to Abe Feinberg. "There's no way of describing the relationship between Jack Kennedy and Ben-Gurion," Feinberg said, "because there's no way B.G. was dealing with JFK as an equal, at least as far as B.G. was concerned. He had the typical attitude of an old-fashioned Jew toward the young. He disrespected him as a youth." There was an additional factor: Joseph Kennedy. "B.G. could be vicious, and he had such a hatred of the old man."

Ben-Gurion's complaints about Kennedy and the continuing pressure about Dimona unquestionably were also linked to an all-important agenda that was remaining on track. In April, a Norwegian official named Jens C. Hauge had spent two weeks conducting Norway's first—and only—inspection of the heavy water that had been sold to Israel. The inspection, closely monitored by Ernst Bergmann, couldn't have gone better. Dimona was not yet in operation, and the water, still in its original shipping barrels, was safely stored near the small and totally innocent Nahal Soreq research reactor at Rehovot. Hauge's report to the Norwegian foreign ministry was astonishing in its uncritical acceptance of all of Bergmann's assertions. "As far as I know," Hauge wrote, "Israel has not attempted to keep secret the fact that they are building a reactor. . . . Professor Bergmann at an earlier point had given information to his colleagues in the U.S. about the reactor, but Israel had not kept America officially informed about the reactor. This was possibly the background for the uproar that took place in America about the reactor." At another point, Hauge quoted Bergmann as explaining that Norway's heavy water would be used to power a twenty-four-megawatt "research reactor" that would be a model for a planned much larger power reactor. In a second memorandum to the foreign ministry, Hauge added: "Israel is interested in keeping the location of reactor building quiet and wants any commotion about it ended."

Two months after the visit with Kennedy, in July 1961, Ben-Gurion and his top advisers attended the widely publicized launching in the Negev of Israel's first rocket, known as Shavit II.* Such military events normally were kept secret, but Mapai Party leaders—with general elections scheduled for mid-August—decided to go public after receiving reports that Egypt was planning to fire some of its rockets on July 23, the ninth anniversary of the coup that had eventually brought Nasser to power. The multistage, solid-propellant Shavit II, which soared fifty miles into the upper atmosphere, was said to be designed to measure upper atmospheric winds as part of a series of experiments for the Israeli Atomic Energy Commission. Ernst Bergmann subsequently told a scientific journal: "We are not particularly interested in the prestige of space, but in the scientific aspects of it." The American intelligence community —and Israel's Arab enemies—got the message: it was only a matter of time and money before Israeli developed a missile system capable of delivering nuclear warheads. Bergmann had created another light bulb for his nuclear lamp.

Kennedy, despite his remarks to Ben-Gurion, was far from persuaded by the inspections by Rabi and Wigner that Dimona was anything but a nuclear weapons production facility. A nu-

---

* There was no Shavit I, Shimon Peres told a political rally on the night of the launch, because of the possibility that the name would be corrupted to Shavit Aleph, since aleph is the first letter of the Hebrew alphabet. Aleph also was an electoral symbol for the Mapai Party. If the rocket had been named Shavit I, Peres said, "we would be accused of making propaganda."

clear-armed Israel seemed to be looming, and it could threaten
Middle East stability as well as the President's strong desire for
a treaty with the Soviet Union to ban the testing of nuclear
weapons in the atmosphere. And there was no indication that
Ben-Gurion, who was admitting nothing, would back off. The
Israeli prime minister, in subsequent private communications
to the White House, began to refer to the President as "young
man"; Kennedy made clear to associates that he found the letters to be offensive.

The President's apprehension about the Israeli bomb undoubtedly was a factor in his surprising appointment of John
McCone to replace Allen Dulles as CIA director in the wake of
the Bay of Pigs debacle. There was every political reason not to
appoint him: McCone not only was a prominent Republican
but had spoken out against the White House's much-desired
test ban treaty with the Soviet Union. Arthur Schlesinger
writes that Kennedy, obviously sensitive about his preference,
invited McCone to a private two-hour meeting "on the pretext
of asking his views on nuclear testing." There is no public
record of what the two men discussed, although Ben-Gurion's
latest annoying letter had arrived only days before and the Soviet Union had announced the resumption of nuclear testing,
ending the informal U.S.–USSR moratorium. In any case,
McCone subsequently told Walt Elder, his executive assistant
in the CIA, that Kennedy had complained to him about the fact
that he was "getting all sorts of conflicting advice on the whole
range of nuclear issues," including the Israeli bomb. Kennedy
asked McCone to prepare a written analysis of the issue and
report back within a few weeks. McCone did so and, upon his
return, as he told Elder, the President tossed the report aside—
"Give it to the staff"—and offered him the CIA job. He also
asked McCone to keep word of his pending appointment
"quiet. Those liberal bastards in the basement [on Bundy's National Security Council staff] will complain about it."

Foreseen or not, Kennedy had found a soulmate. McCone
had his own policy goals, and they meshed closely with the
young President's, said Elder: "McCone was most adamant
about American nuclear superiority, but his trinity included
the Catholic Church and nonproliferation." A nuclear-armed

Israel did not fit into that vision: "He thought an Israeli bomb would lead to escalation and then you could just cross off oil from the Middle East for years." There were other virtues, of course, that appealed to Kennedy: McCone would join the administration with enormous credibility with the press, with the Congress, and especially with Dwight Eisenhower, who was quietly going about life in retirement in Gettysburg, Pennsylvania. "Kennedy never took a major foreign policy move without checking it out with Eisenhower," recalled Elder, who, when he retired from the CIA in 1983, was executive secretary of the National Foreign Intelligence Board. "He was terrified of having Ike on the other side."

In one of their first meetings after McCone took the job, Kennedy complained about the most recent of Ben-Gurion's letters, which continued to shrug off the issue of international inspection of Dimona, the White House's key demand that had been initially articulated by Bill Crawford. Ben-Gurion's letter was "a waffle," Walt Elder recalled. "It wasn't strong. Kennedy talked to McCone about it and McCone said, 'Write him a stiff note. Mention the United States' international obligations, and our suspicions of the French. Lay it on the line.' " The President followed McCone's advice and received what he perceived as yet another rude response: "Ben-Gurion in effect said, 'Bug off, this is none of your business,' " said Elder, who spent years after McCone left the CIA preparing and indexing all of his still-classified personal files.* At that point, McCone insisted to the President that he could "take care of it. The attachés and the State Department can't do it," Elder recalled McCone telling the President, referring to the need to get an answer to the most important question about Dimona: was there an underground chemical reprocessing plant at Dimona? "Turn it over to me." Kennedy did so, and McCone began a two-track operation.

The first step was another series of U-2 missions; its far more

---

* McCone, said Elder, ended up being very close to Kennedy: "He saw him literally whenever he wanted. He would call the White House and say, 'I'm on my way to see the President.' " After such meetings, McCone would immediately dictate a detailed memorandum to the file, which was eventually made available to Elder for further action and safekeeping.

risky and ambitious counterpart was an attempt to infiltrate spies into Dimona and, with luck, into the suspected reprocessing plant. "It was one hell of an operation," Elder said. "Even the station chiefs [in Israel and elsewhere in the Middle East] didn't know of it. We ran it right out of McCone's office." McCone's orders were, in retrospect, almost cavalier, his former executive assistant said: McCone, recognizing that the Israelis were keeping close watch over the American intelligence officers inside their country, told his men, "We can't do our job without leaving traces. Do the best job you can." Running American intelligence operatives inside Israel posed an extraordinary risk, as McCone and Kennedy had to know: any exposure would have led to a violent domestic backlash inside America. It also could end the debate about what Israel was, or was not, doing at Dimona.

The operation was not compromised—but it also didn't work. The CIA's on-the-ground agents, obviously recruited from a foreign country, were unable to get inside. "I could not say we had an agent who physically saw a bomb inside Dimona," Elder acknowledged.

The U-2 once again proved that photographs—even sensational ones—weren't enough. By December 1961, CIA officials had set up a new agency, the National Photo Interpretation Center (NPIC), with Arthur Lundahl in charge, and assigned it the mission of providing more sophisticated photo intelligence. NPIC came through early with a huge photographic mosaic of Israel, capturing not only Dimona but all other possible nuclear facilities. "It was as big as two French doors," Elder recalled. "Kennedy loved it." The only problem was that the new set of photographs did little to move the basic issue: there was no way to see underground in Dimona. "McCone said that based on his evidence," Elder said, "there is no external evidence of a nuclear capability. There's no evidence of a weapons plant." McCone was still skeptical, Elder added, telling the President, "Given their [the Israelis'] attitude toward inspection, you can't trust them."

Dimona remained a major impediment to another of Kennedy's early foreign policy ambitions—rapprochement with

Nasser's Egypt. Increased economic aid and a series of private
letters had led to a warming of relations by mid-1962, and senior
Egyptian officials were reassuring the White House that they
also desired improved relations, within the context of
nonalignment. Nasser, badly rattled by the prospect of a nuclear Israel, had responded to the December 1960 relevations
about Dimona by publicly insisting that Egypt would never
permit Israel to be its superior; if necessary, he said, Egypt
would attack and "destroy the base of aggression even at the
price of four million casualties." The question of Dimona was
repeatedly raised at Arab League conferences on defense and
foreign ministry issues during 1961, with no resolution—except
for a shared Arab determination to build up conventional arms.
The Kennedy administration reassured the Egyptians that it
would continue to press until it obtained IAEA inspection
rights to Dimona, and would provide a summary—with Israel's
agreement—of the findings to Nasser.

But securing inspection rights remained impossible. Ben-Gurion had no intention of permitting a legitimate inspection—
for obvious reasons. His first line of defense was straightforward: political pressure, in the person of Abe Feinberg. "I
fought the strongest battle of my career to keep them from a
full inspection," Feinberg recalled. "I violently intervened not
once but half a dozen times." He had been tipped off about the
inspection demands by Myer Feldman and relayed his political
complaints through him; he said he never discussed the matter
directly with the President. The message was anything but
subtle: insisting on an inspection of Dimona would result in
less support in the 1964 presidential campaign. This message,
Feinberg said, was given directly to Robert S. McNamara, the
secretary of state, and Paul H. Nitze, then a senior defense
aide: "I met with them together and said, 'You've got to keep
your nose out of it.' "

Nitze, in a subsequent interview, did not recall that meeting,
but he did remember a later one-on-one confrontation with
Feinberg over Dimona. The Israelis wanted to purchase advanced U.S. fighter aircraft: "I said no, unless they come clean
about Dimona. Then suddenly this fellow Feinberg comes into
my office and says right out, 'You can't do that to us.' I said,

'I've already done it.' Feinberg said, 'I'll see to it that you get overruled.' I remember throwing him out of the office."

Three days later, Nitze added, "I got a call from McNamara. He said he'd been instructed to tell me to change my mind and release the planes. And I did." Nitze hesitated a moment and added: "Feinberg had the power and brought it to bear. I was surprised McNamara did this." McNamara, subsequently asked about the incident, would only say cryptically: "I can understand why Israel wanted a nuclear bomb. There is a basic problem there. The existence of Israel has been a question mark in history, and that's the essential issue."

In the end, however, Feinberg and Ben-Gurion could not overcome the continued presidential pressure for inspection of Dimona. Ben-Gurion's categorical public denial of any weapons intent at Dimona had left the Israeli government few options: refusing access would undercut the government's credibility and also lend credence to the newly emerging anti-nuclear community inside Israel. In late 1961 a group of prominent Israeli scholars and scientists—including two former members of Bergmann's Atomic Energy Commission—had privately banded together to form the Committee for the Denuclearization of the Middle East. The new group's agenda was straightforward: to stop Israel's search for the nuclear option and to defuse the secrecy surrounding the activities at Dimona. In April 1962, the committee went public, stating that it considered the development of nuclear weapons "to constitute a danger to Israel and to peace in the Middle East." It urged United Nations intervention "to prevent military nuclear production." Others, who knew precisely what was going on at Dimona, were equally critical: Pinhas Lavon, former defense minister, eager to build housing for the constant stream of refugees, sarcastically complained to a Dimona official in the early 1960s, "We're taking five hundred million dollars away from settling the Galilee [in northern Israel] and instead we build a bomb."

The most important factor, clearly, in Ben-Gurion's decision to permit the inspections was the Kennedy administration's decision in mid-1962 to authorize the sale of Hawk surface-to-air missiles to Israel. The United States had provided Israel with specialized military training and sensitive electronic gear in the past, but sale of the Hawk—considered an advanced defensive weapon—was a major departure from past policy of selling no weaponry to Israel, and, as Israel had to hope, could lead to future sales of offensive American arms. The administration had spent months secretly reviewing and analyzing the Hawk sale and carefully laying the political groundwork in an attempt to avoid a political explosion in the Middle East. Armin Meyer, now the deputy assistant secretary of state for Near East and South Asian affairs, recalled that a special presidential message about Israel was sent in June to a regional meeting in Athens of American ambassadors serving in the Middle East, in which Kennedy reported that "it was necessary for him to do something special for Israel." The President solicited the group's advice on four options, all of which, Meyer recalled, "would have adverse effects in the Arab world." The ambassadors chose the Hawk sale as "least damaging" to American interests, and it was agreed that Egypt and other Arab nations would be informed in advance.

What Kennedy did not tell his ambassadors was that inspection rights to Dimona were at stake. That message was personally relayed to Ben-Gurion by Myer Feldman, who was dispatched in August to inform the Israeli government of the sale and what Jack Kennedy wanted in return. Feldman, asked about his mission, said that it would be "too strong" to suggest that the inspection of Dimona was a "quid pro quo" in return for the Hawks. "It was more like," explained Feldman, " 'We're going to show you how accommodating we are. This is what we want.' Israel said, 'This is a good friend and we're going to let you in.' " Feldman himself was taken on a private tour of the reactor at Dimona that week.

There was one major concession by Washington. Dimona did not have to be inspected by the International Atomic Energy Agency. Ben-Gurion had insisted in his private exchanges with Kennedy that such inspections would violate Israel's sovereignty. The White House eventually agreed to send a specially assembled American inspection team into Dimona. That agreement was further softened by a second concession that, in essence, guaranteed that the whole procedure would be little more than a whitewash, as the President and his senior advisers had to understand: the American inspection team would have to schedule its visits well in advance, and with the full acquiescence of Israel. There would be no spot checks permitted.

Ben-Gurion took no chances: the American inspectors—most of them experts in nuclear reprocessing—would be provided with a Potemkin Village and never know it.

The Israeli scheme, based on plans supplied by the French, was simple: a false control room was constructed at Dimona, complete with false control panels and computer-driven measuring devices that seemed to be gauging the thermal output of a twenty-four-megawatt reactor (as Israel claimed Dimona to be) in full operation. There were extensive practice sessions in the fake control room, as Israeli technicians sought to avoid any slips when the Americans arrived. The goal was to convince the inspectors that no chemical reprocessing plant existed or was possible. One big fear was that the Americans would seek to inspect the reactor core physically, and presumably discover that Dimona was utilizing large amounts of heavy water— much of it illicitly obtained from France and Norway—and obviously operating the reactor at far greater output than the acknowledged twenty-four megawatts. It was agreed that the inspection team would not be permitted to enter the core "for safety reasons." In Abe Feinberg's view, Kennedy's unyielding demand for an inspection had left Israel with no option: "It was part of my job to tip them off that Kennedy was insisting on this. So they gave him a scam job."

The American team, following a pattern that would be repeated until the inspections came to an end in 1969, spent days at Dimona, climbing through the various excavations—many facilities had yet to be constructed—but finding nothing. They did not question the fact that the reactor core was off-limits and gave no sign that they were in any way suspicious of the control room. The Israelis even stationed a few engineers in a concealed area in the control room to monitor the machinery and make sure that nothing untoward took place.

Another aspect of the cover-up was made much easier by the fact that none of the Americans spoke or understood Hebrew.

One former Israeli official recalled that his job was to interpret for the American team. "I was part of the cover-up team. One of the engineers would start talking too much" in front of the Americans, the official said, and he would tell him, in seemingly conversational Hebrew, " 'Listen, you mother-fucker, don't answer that question.' The Americans would think I was translating."

The Americans were led by Floyd L. Culler, Jr., a leading expert in the science of nuclear reprocessing who was then deputy director of the Chemical Technology Division at the Oak Ridge National Laboratory in Tennessee, where the first uranium for American nuclear weapons had been enriched. At the time, Culler said, he reported to the White House that the reactor he and his colleagues inspected was nothing more than a "standard reactor. All the elements were counted and tagged." Culler, who retired in 1989 as president of the Electrical Power Research Institute in Palo Alto, California, seemed surprised but not shocked upon being informed that his team had been duped by a false control room. "It's possible to make a system appear that it's controlling something when it's not," he explained, adding that simulated control rooms have been widely and effectively used for training purposes in reactor systems worldwide. Culler was far more disturbed to learn that by 1960 the CIA's photo interpretation team had concluded that a site was being excavated at Dimona for a chemical reprocessing plant and had even attempted to measure the amount of dirt being scooped. Such intelligence had not been provided to him, he said, and should have been.

Culler shrugged off the Israeli cheating as inevitable, but not necessary. "It's not possible to make archaeological findings about what was going on just by seeing footprints," he explained. "No one really has that much wisdom." He viewed his inspection as "part of the game of wearing away, of finding ways to not reach the point of taking action" against Israel's nuclear weapons program. He is not at all convinced today, he said, that Israel was wrong to develop its own independent deterrent.

"They were terrified that they'd be bombed," Culler recalled. After the first inspection in 1962, he said, "I was asked by an Israeli to raise the question" of an American nuclear umbrella upon his return to Washington. Culler wrote his secret report on the inspection during stopovers in Athens and Rome, and dutifully included an account of the Israeli concern. The CIA "got to me as soon as I got off the plane" in Washington, he added, and he was rushed into a debriefing. There was no further talk of nuclear umbrellas on subsequent inspections, and Culler eventually came to ask himself the following rhetorical question: Would the United States initiate nuclear war to protect any country in the Middle East, or India, or Pakistan, or Argentina? "We were all in a bind," Culler said. "We have to be careful in assigning blame. It may be a story, but there is no right or wrong."

The constant bargaining over Dimona was a factor in aborting an ambitious Kennedy administration initiative to resolve the Palestinian refugee issue. Like all American Presidents since 1948, Kennedy came into office with a belief that he could find a way to bring long-term peace to the Middle East. As a House and Senate member, Kennedy had always been a public supporter of Israel, but he had repeatedly expressed understanding of the aspirations of Arab nationalism and sympathy for the plight of the Palestinian refugees. For example, in a February 1958 speech before a Jewish group, he declared that the refugee question "must be resolved through negotiations, resettlement, and outside international assistance. But to recognize the problem is quite different from saying that the problem is insoluble short of the destruction of Israel . . . or must be solved by Israel alone."

State Department Arabists were pleasantly surprised early in 1961 to get word from the White House, according to Armin Meyer, that "just because 90 percent of the Jewish vote had gone for Kennedy, it didn't mean he was in their pocket." Kennedy asked for innovative ideas, and the department suggested that another try be made to resolve the Palestinian refugee problem in the West Bank and Gaza Strip stemming from Israel's victory in the 1948–49 Arab-Israeli War. The United Nations had approved Resolution 194 after the war, directing that the refugees had to be given the option of returning to Israel if they wished to do so.

The State Department came up with a new twist, in which individual refugees would be asked in a confidential questionnaire if they wanted to return to a former home in Israel. Those who ruled out a return would be compensated by Israel for the seizure of their property and be given a chance to emigrate to another Arab country or anywhere else in the world. There had been bitter protests by Arabs during the Eisenhower years over the failure to implement the United Nations resolution. State Department studies on the resettlement issue showed that no more than 70,000 to 100,000 Palestinians would opt to return to their seized Israeli homesteads over ten years, a number that was deemed to be manageable. The Israelis also would be given veto power over every returning Palestinian, in an attempt to minimize the security risk.

Kennedy had discussed his Arab initiative with a far from enthusiastic Ben-Gurion in their May 1961 New York meeting. A few weeks later, President Kennedy authorized a major— and highly secret—State Department effort to implement the new variant of Resolution 194; over the next eighteen months, said Armin Meyer, a workable compromise was accepted by the Arab states and endorsed by the White House. Meyer, who served as ambassador to Jordan, Iran, and Japan before retiring from the Foreign Service in 1972, is convinced today that Ben-Gurion's decision not to torpedo the resettlement project was based on his belief that the Arabs would never accept direct negotiations on any issue with Israel; any discussion of repatriation, in their eyes, would be tantamount to formal recognition. When the expected last-minute Arab rejections did not come, Meyer said, "Israel panicked," and provoked a wave of intense political pressure from American Jews upon the White House. In the end, President Kennedy—already in a war with Ben-Gurion over Dimona—backed down, bitterly disappointing his State Department supporters by doing so.* The

* There were many in the State Department, however, who understood from the outset that the resettlement plan had little chance. "We were struggling with bigger issues at the time," explained Phillips Talbot, then Armin Meyer's boss as the assistant secretary of state for Near East and South Asian affairs. "It was not at the top of my

Palestinians would remain stateless refugees in their squalid homes in the Gaza Strip and West Bank. "I think we could have been spared all this terrorism business and other miseries," said Meyer, "if we had gone ahead with that project at that time."

But, at that time, getting Dimona inspected seemed more important.

priority list." Talbot recalled President Kennedy's comment after an early briefing: "Phil, that's a great plan with only one flaw—you've never had to run for election."

9

Years of Pressure

John Kennedy, profoundly committed to the principle of nonproliferation, continued throughout 1962 to pressure Ben-Gurion about international inspection and continued to receive the prime minister's bland and irritating assurances that Israel had no intention of becoming an atomic power. The President was far too politically astute not to understand, as he angrily told his friend Charles Bartlett, that the Israeli "sons of bitches lie to me constantly about their nuclear capability." One solution was to help get Ben-Gurion, then embattled in the most serious crisis of his political career, out of office.

A few days after Christmas 1962, Kennedy made what amounted to a direct move against the prime minister's leadership. He invited Foreign Minister Golda Meir, one of Ben-Gurion's leading critics inside the cabinet and the Mapai Party, to his Palm Beach, Florida, home for a seventy-minute private talk. Meir made no secret of the fact that she resented Ben-Gurion for permitting his acolytes, Shimon Peres and Moshe Dayan, to operate behind the back of the foreign ministry; she and other party members who had been born in Eastern Europe, such as Levi Eshkol, the treasury minister, were convinced that Ben-Gurion chose to rely on young men such as Peres and Dayan only because they would be more reluctant to stand up to him.

The declassified memorandum on the Kennedy-Meir meeting contains no specific mention of nuclear weapons (some paragraphs were deleted for national security reasons), but there is little doubt that Kennedy pointedly raised the issue. The memorandum further shows that Kennedy made an extraordinary private commitment to Israel's defense. "We are asking the cooperation of Israel in the same way that we are cooperating with Israel to help meet its needs," Kennedy told Meir. "Israel doubtless thinks of itself as deeply endangered. . . . Our position in these matters may seem to be asking Israel to neglect its interests. The reason we do it is not that we are unfriendly to Israel; but in order to help more effectively. I think it is quite clear that in case of an invasion the United States would come to the support of Israel. We have that capacity and it is growing." It was language no Israeli had ever heard from Dwight Eisenhower.

Moments later, according to the memorandum, Kennedy—anticipating the chronic crisis that would be created by the refugees of the West Bank and Gaza Strip—expressed his regret that the Arab resettlement plan had failed and said his administration would not give up trying to find some solution to the refugee situation. He added that the United States "is really interested in Israel. . . . What we want from Israel arises because our relationship is a two-way street. Israel's security in the long run depends in part on what it does with the Arabs, but also on us."

Kennedy's commitment to Golda Meir, along with his decision to sell the Hawk missiles, amounted to a turning point in American foreign policy toward Israel—one little noted even today. The Kennedy offer might have been enough, if Israel's goal had been to forge a military partnership with the United States. But Israel's needs were far more basic.

John McCone remained agitated about the Israeli bomb and the failure of his agency to determine whether a chemical reprocessing plant was buried underground at Dimona. He also was more outspoken than any other Kennedy insider on the issue; at a 1962 Washington dinner party he publicly reprimanded Charles Lucet, a senior French foreign ministry official, for France's role in the Israeli bomb. Lucet, who had served as deputy ambassador in Washington in the late 1950s (and would become ambassador in 1965), was seated near McCone, who at one point abruptly asked: "So, Mr. Lucet, your country is building a reprocessing plant for the Israelis?" Lucet replied with what was France's public position on the issue: "No, we are building a reactor." McCone then turned his back on Lucet and did not speak to him for the rest of the evening; it was, given France's high standing with the President and his wife, who were both Francophiles, a pointed rebuff.*

Kennedy was constantly raising the nuclear issue in his discussions with senior Israelis—and constantly getting boilerplate answers. In early April 1963, Shimon Peres flew to the capital to meet at the White House on the still-pending Hawk sale, and was directly asked by the President about Israeli intentions. An Israeli nuclear bomb, Kennedy said, "would create a very perilous situation. That's why we have been diligent about keeping an eye on your effort in the atomic field. What can you tell me about that?" Peres's answer was a fabrication that would become the official Israeli response for years to come: "I can tell you forthrightly that we will not introduce atomic weapons into the region. We certainly won't be the first to do so. We have no interest in that. On the contrary, our interest is in de-escalating the armament tension, even in total disarmament."

The administration's lack of specific information about Israeli intentions was complicated by the fact, as the President had to know, that many senior members of Congress supported the concept of a nuclear-armed Israel. A few days before his meeting with the President, Peres had discussed nuclear weapons with Senator Stuart Symington, a Kennedy supporter and ranking member of the Senate Armed Services Committee, and had been told, as Peres told his biographer: "Don't be a bunch of fools. Don't stop making atomic bombs. And don't listen to the administration. Do whatever you think best."

Israel was doing just that. The physical plant at Dimona continued to mature. The reactor went critical—that is, began a sustained chain reaction—sometime in 1962 with no significant problems, and was capable of being operated at more than seventy megawatts, far greater than the twenty-four megawatts

---

* Lucet was offended by McCone's action and, upon his return to Paris, relayed the incident to Bertrand Goldschmidt. "He asked me if we could separate France from responsibility for the [Israeli] bomb," Goldschmidt recalled with a laugh. "I said, 'No. Not only did we take the girl when she was a virgin, but we made her pregnant.' "

publicly acknowledged by the Ben-Gurion government. Running the plant hotter would create more plutonium by-product to be reprocessed, and a larger nuclear weapons stockpile than any outsider could anticipate. Later that year, the private French construction companies at Dimona, always eager for business, began once again to work on the vital chemical reprocessing plant underground at Dimona—despite de Gaulle's insistence that France would have nothing more to do with the Israeli bomb. The French would build at a furious pace for the next three years, at high pay, finishing the reprocessing plant and the elaborate waste treatment and safety facilities that were essential. French technicians and engineers, who had begun drifting away, were back in force in Beersheba, whose population was growing steadily (it reached seventy thousand by 1970).

Israeli and French scientists continued to cooperate at the French nuclear test site in the Sahara, as the experiments became more weapons-oriented. By late 1961, the French had begun a series of underground tests and were perfecting a series of miniaturized warheads for use in aircraft and, eventually, missiles. There were further tests in the early 1960s of a more advanced Shavit rocket system, with no more public announcements; CIA analysts assumed that the long-range rocket was meant for military use. And in 1963 Israel paid $100 million to the privately owned Dassault Company of France, then one of the world's most successful missile and aircraft firms, for the joint development and manufacture of twenty-five medium-range Israeli missiles. It was anticipated that the missile, to be known to the American intelligence community as the Jericho I, would be able to deliver a miniaturized nuclear warhead to targets three hundred miles away.

By spring of 1963, Kennedy's relationship with Ben-Gurion remained at an impasse over Dimona, and the correspondence between the two became increasingly sour. None of those letters has been made public.* Ben-Gurion's responses were being

* The Kennedy exchanges with Ben-Gurion also have not been released to U.S. government officials with full clearances who have attempted to write classified histories of the period. "The culminate result" of such rigid security, one former American

drafted by Yuval Neeman, a physicist and defense ministry intelligence officer who was directly involved in the nuclear weapons program. "It was not a friendly exchange," Neeman recalled. "Kennedy was writing like a bully. It was brutal."

The President made sure that the Israeli prime minister paid for his defiance. In late April, Egypt, Syria, and Iraq united to form the short-lived Arab Federation; such unity was Ben-Gurion's recurring nightmare. He instinctively turned to Washington, and proposed in a letter to the President that the United States and Soviet Union join forces to publicly declare the territorial integrity and security of every Middle Eastern state. "If you can spare an hour or two for a discussion with me on the situation and possible solutions," Ben-Gurion asked, "I am prepared to fly to Washington at your convenience and without any publicity." Kennedy rejected Ben-Gurion's offer of a state visit and expressed "real reservations," according to Ben-Gurion's biography, about any joint statement on the issue with the Soviets. Five days later, a disappointed Ben-Gurion sent a second note to Kennedy: "Mr. President, my people have the right to exist . . . and this existence is in danger." He requested that the United States sign a security treaty with Israel. Again the answer was no, and it was clear to the Mapai Party that Ben-Gurion's leadership and his intractability about Dimona were serious liabilities in Washington. Golda Meir acknowledged to Ben-Gurion's biographer, "We knew about these approaches. . . . We said nothing, even though we wondered."

A few weeks later, on June 16, 1963, Ben-Gurion abruptly resigned as prime minister and defense minister, ending his fifteen-year reign as Israel's most influential public official.

The many accounts of Ben-Gurion's resignation have accurately described the resurgence of scandal, public distrust, and polarization that marked his last years. The Lavon Affair, stemming from the series of pre–Suez War sabotage activities inside Egypt, had come by the early 1960s to dominate much of the public agenda inside Israel, as new revelations came to light

---

official lamented, "is a very poorly informed bureaucracy—even if there are people willing to buck the system and ask taboo questions."

suggesting that low-level officials in the defense ministry might
have falsified documents and given misleading testimony in an
effort to accuse Pinhas Lavon, the former defense minister, of
authorizing the operation. Lavon, still one of the most influential members of the Mapai Party, was serving as head of the
Histadrut, the powerful federation of labor unions (85 percent
of the work force in Israel belonged to unions) that also controlled a large segment of Israeli industry. Lavon asked Ben-
Gurion for exoneration. Ben-Gurion refused, and Lavon took
his case to the Knesset's foreign affairs and defense committee.
Once at the Knesset, he charged that Ben-Gurion, Peres, and
Dayan had undermined civilian authority over the military;
then he made sure that his allegations were leaked to the press.
With those actions, Lavon broke two cardinal rules of Israeli
politics: he discussed defense matters in public and he failed to
keep the party dispute behind closed doors. The next step was
a cabinet-level committee, set up at Levi Eshkol's instigation,
that was to recommend procedures for investigating the Lavon
allegations. But the committee, instead of dealing with the pro-
cedural issue, cleared Lavon of authorizing the failed operation
in Egypt.

Ben-Gurion accused the committee of overstepping its mandate, resigned once again, and called for a new government in
an unsuccessful effort to annul the decision. Many of those who
opposed Ben-Gurion, especially Levi Eshkol and Pinhas Sapir,
also opposed Lavon's violation of political norms and successfully moved for his dismissal from the Histadrut job. The primary goal of the Mapai Party leaders at that moment was to get
the tiresome affair behind them before the Israeli citizenry, distressed by the continuing discussion of so many government
secrets, became convinced that Mapai was unable to manage
the country effectively. Ben-Gurion, arguing that someone had
lied, continued to insist, however, that a judicial inquiry be
convened. The public came to see him as a stubborn old man
who was trying to keep the issue alive; the affair tarnished his
reputation and made what seemed to be his dictatorial methods
of running the government more vulnerable than ever. The
clear victors in the scandal were Eshkol, Sapir, and Golda
Meir, who emerged with higher public standing and with re-

newed determination not to permit Ben-Gurion to bypass
them in favor of Dayan and Peres. Dayan and Peres joined
Ben-Gurion as losers: Dayan never became prime minister, and
Peres waited twenty years for the job.

A second public scandal surfaced in 1962 and 1963 when it was
reported that Egypt had developed—with support from some
West German scientists—what were alleged to be advanced
missiles capable of hitting Israel. Golda Meir and her supporters took a hard line on the Egyptian–West German activities,
warning that the coalition posed a danger to Israel's national
security. Ben-Gurion was far more skeptical of the threat posed
by Egypt's dalliance with West German scientists and, in his
public statements, emphasized the contribution that West Germany had made to Israeli security. What the public did not
know was that Ben-Gurion had just completed a successful,
and secret, negotiation with West German Chancellor Konrad
Adenauer for modern weaponry, including small arms, helicopters, and spare parts. For Ben-Gurion, there now was "another Germany," profoundly different from the Germany of
Hitler's time and far more willing than France and America to
keep Israel armed. Ben-Gurion's point of view was ignored in
the wake of press hysteria over the German aid to Egypt, with
newspaper talk of German "death rays" and renewed "final
solutions"—all of which turned out to be exaggerated. The
public campaign over the West German help for Egypt soon
evolved into a wave of criticism and scorn for Ben-Gurion and
his notion of "another Germany." Ben-Gurion's colleagues in
the Mapai Party—especially Golda Meir, who, like many Israelis, wanted nothing to do with Germans—joined in the
attack.*

The controversy over Lavon and West Germany appeared to

* The German issue was a never-ending and emotional one for a nation led by
survivors of the Holocaust; any diplomatic contact resulted in a crisis. There had been
street riots in front of the Knesset in 1952 to protest the initial Israeli–West German
talks over compensation for the loss of Jewish lives and property in the Holocaust.
Cash-starved Israel eventually accepted more than $800 million in reparations. Ten-
sions remained, despite the flow of money: an Israeli violinist was later stabbed on the
street after performing the music of Richard Strauss in public. In June 1959, a furor
over the sale of Israeli munitions to West Germany resulted in another brief resignation by Ben-Gurion and yet another call for new elections. The Mapai Party held on to
its Knesset majority, and Ben-Gurion, confidence vote in hand, returned to office.

be more than enough to convince Ben-Gurion to leave public life and return once again to his kibbutz in the desert. Tired and distracted after years of leadership, the Old Man was looking forward to writing his memoirs and telling his version of the history of Israel and Zionism. There was no way for the Israeli public, surfeited with accounts of Lavon and the German scandal, to suspect that there was yet another factor in Ben-Gurion's demise: his increasingly bitter impasse with Kennedy over a nuclear-armed Israel.

Levi Eshkol, the new prime minister, was, like Ben-Gurion, a product of Eastern Europe (he was born in 1895) who turned to Palestine and Zionism at an early age. There were few other similarities. Eshkol was far more democratic, both in politics and in personality; the notion of compromise—so foreign to Ben-Gurion—returned to the leadership of the government and the Mapai Party. Eshkol moved quickly to lighten government control of the press and also set up an independent broadcasting authority to ease the government's monitoring and censorship of the state-run television network—reforms that Ben-Gurion had bitterly resisted. Most significantly, Eshkol had spent the last eleven years as finance minister, much of it in a struggle against funding for Dimona, and was far less committed emotionally than Ben-Gurion to the concept that hundreds of millions of dollars should be spent each year on nuclear activity to the detriment of what he and his supporters saw as Israel's most immediate need—better weapons and training for the army and air force.

Kennedy, confronted with intelligence reports showing that Israel, far from slowing down its nuclear program during his presidency, had been expanding it, wasted little time in urging nuclear restraint on the new Israeli government; private presidential messages reiterating the need for international inspection of Dimona began arriving shortly after Eshkol took office. The President's belief in arms control had been strengthened in the early fall of 1963 by the positive American response to the Senate ratification of the Limited Test Ban Treaty, which banned nuclear testing in the atmosphere, underwater, and in outer space.* Continued political support for nuclear disarmament meant less reason to fear the Jewish lobby. Israel's Jericho I missile was another factor in the continued White House pressure on Eshkol. American experts considered the Jericho's guidance system to be highly unstable and inaccurate, suggesting—so the analysts concluded—that only one type of warhead made sense.

Kennedy's persistent pressure on Israel stemmed from his belief that Israel had not yet developed any nuclear weapons; that it was not yet a proliferator. There is evidence that once Israel actually began manufacturing bombs—as the French had done —the President was prepared to be as pragmatic as he needed to be. While Kennedy remained resolutely opposed to a nuclear Israel to the end, he did change his mind about de Gaulle's bombs. Daniel Ellsberg, who would later make public the Pentagon Papers on the Vietnam War, was involved in high-level nuclear weapons issues in 1963 as a deputy in the Pentagon's Office of International Strategic Affairs. He recalled seeing one morning a "Top Secret, Eyes Only" memorandum from McGeorge Bundy to the President summarizing a change in policy toward the French: "We would, after all," Ellsberg recalled Bundy's memorandum stating, "cooperate with the French and allow them to use the Nevada test site for underground testing." At the time, the French had refused to sign the Limited Test Ban Treaty, and de Gaulle had announced that France would continue to test its bombs in the atmosphere.** Kennedy's obvious goal was to bring France in line

---

* Arthur Schlesinger described in *A Thousand Days* how Kennedy, "almost by accident," raised the nuclear test ban during a speech in Billings, Montana. The President casually praised Senator Mike J. Mansfield, the majority leader from Montana, for his support for the treaty. "To his surprise," wrote Schlesinger, "this allusion produced strong and sustained applause. Heartened, he [Kennedy] set forth his hope of lessening the 'chance of a military collision between those two great nuclear powers which together have the power to kill three hundred million people in the short space of a day.' The Billings response encouraged him to make the pursuit of peace increasingly the theme of his trip."

** The French had been cut out from any postwar nuclear cooperation by the 1946 Atomic Energy Act, which prohibited the transfer of American nuclear weapons information to any other country. In 1958, President Eisenhower recommended, and Congress approved, an amendment to the 1946 act that permitted the United States to exchange nuclear design information and fissionable materials with the British; France, of course, was enraged by the exclusion. (Britain ended up completely dependent on

with the test ban treaty, whether officially signed or not. The
Bundy memorandum remained fixed in Ellsberg's memory: it
was dated November 22, 1963, the day of Kennedy's assassination in Dallas, Texas.

Kennedy's successor, Lyndon Johnson, like many Vice Presidents, had been left in the dark on sensitive national security
issues by the President and his top aides. "Johnson went ber-
serk upon being briefed in by the Agency," a former high-level
American intelligence official recalled. "He didn't know anything about the problem and he cursed Kennedy for cutting
him out."*

Johnson's ties to Israel were strong long before he became
President. Two of his closest advisers, lawyers Abe Fortas
(later named to the Supreme Court) and Edwin L. Weisl, Sr.,
while not particularly religious, felt deeply about the security
of Israel. Johnson also had known of Abe Feinberg and his
fund-raising skills since the Truman years; Feinberg was
among those who had raised money for Johnson's successful
1948 campaign for the Senate.

---

the United States by the early 1960s for its strategic nuclear delivery vehicles, a status
that existed into the early 1990s.) The Kennedy administration continued to antagonize
the French on nuclear issues. Secretary of Defense Robert McNamara, distressed at
France's nuclear independence and its continued testing in the Sahara, went on a
public campaign in 1962 against the *force de frappe*. In a famous spring commencement
address at the University of Michigan (in which he announced that the United States
was moving away in its targeting from massive retaliation to limited nuclear war),
McNamara criticized "weak national nuclear forces" as being "dangerous, expensive,
prone to obsolescence, and lacking in credibility as a deterrent." Instead, he insisted,
the nations of Europe should buy American arms and rockets to build up their conventional forces and let the United States handle the issue of nuclear deterrence. He had
delivered essentially the same message a few weeks earlier in Athens, enraging not only
de Gaulle, but America's NATO allies. ". . . [A]ll the allies are angry," British Prime
Minister Harold Macmillan wrote in his diary, "with the American proposal that we
should buy rockets to the tune of umpteen million dollars, the warheads to be under
American control. This is not a European rocket. It's a racket of the American industry. . . . It's rather sad, because the Americans (who are naive and inexperienced) are
up against centuries of diplomatic skill and finesse." Continued U.S. opposition to the
force de frappe was one reason for de Gaulle's 1966 decision to remove France from
NATO's military organization and evict NATO headquarters and all allied military
facilities from French territory.

* Johnson similarly had been excluded from the intense meetings and discussions
during the Cuban missile crisis the year before, and it was left to John McCone to tell
the Vice President about the issue just hours before it was to be made public. "Johnson
was pissed," McCone later told Walt Elder, and, "harrumphing and belching," threatened not to support the President on the issue if the Senate leadership did not. McCone
assured the Vice President that the Senate was indeed backing the President, and the
placated Vice President reversed course.

There was a much deeper link, however, that had nothing to
do with campaign funds: Johnson had visited the Nazi concentration camp at Dachau while on a congressional fact-finding
trip at the end of World War II. His wife, Lady Bird, told a
Texas historian years after Johnson's death that he had returned "just shaken, bursting with overpowering revulsion and
incredulous horror at what he had seen. Hearing about it is one
thing, being there is another." There are no photographs of the
visit, but Johnson's congressional archives contain a full set of
U.S. Army photos taken two days after the liberation of the
death camp on April 30, 1945.

Johnson's sensitivity to the plight of European Jews had begun even before World War II when, as a young congressman
from Texas, he was urged by Jewish supporters in his home
district to cut through Washington's red tape and get asylum in
America for German refugees running for their lives. Once the
refugees got into the country, Johnson had worked hard to
keep them in, and his congressional files show that Erich Leinsdorf, the eminent conductor, was among those whose deportation Johnson had prevented. Leinsdorf had made a stunning
American debut with New York's Metropolitan Opera in 1938,
but was scheduled to be deported late in the year when his six-
month visa was up. Deportation to Austria after the Nazi An-
schluss in Vienna meant slow death in a concentration camp.
Johnson won the respect and the financial backing of the Jewish community in Texas by taking on the Leinsdorf case, and
others, and finding a way to circumvent the rules.*

President Johnson stayed loyal to his old friends. Five weeks
after assuming office, he dedicated a newly constructed Austin
synagogue, Agudas Achim, as a favor to James Novy, a longtime Texas political ally and Zionist leader who was chairman
of the building committee. He was the first American President to do so, yet only a few newspapers took note of the event.
In his introduction, Novy, once the Southwest regional chair-

* Jews in Europe found it extremely difficult in the 1930s to get visas for the United
States, although American immigration quotas went unfilled. Between 1933 and 1938, for
example, only 27,000 German Jews were granted entry visas to the United States, far
less than the 129,875 permissible under the quotas. More on Johnson's early role in
support of Jews can be found in "Prologue: LBJ's Foreign Affairs Background," an
unpublished 1989 University of Texas doctoral thesis by Louis S. Gomolak.

man of the Zionist Organization of America, looked at the President and said, "We can't ever thank him enough for all those Jews he got out of Germany during the days of Hitler." Lady Bird Johnson later explained: "Jews have been woven into the warp and woof of all his years."

Lyndon Johnson was quickly consumed by the Vietnam War, and what he saw as the struggle of a small democratic nation against the forces of Communism. But Israel likewise was perceived as a besieged democracy standing up to the Soviet Union and its clients in the Arab world. Johnson's strong emotional ties to Israel and his belief that Soviet arms were altering the balance of power in the Middle East drove him to become the first American President to supply Israel with offensive weapons and the first publicly to commit America to its defense. The American Jewish community eventually would be torn apart by Johnson's continued prosecution of the Vietnam War, with many Jewish leaders insisting that Johnson's steadfast support of Israel entitled him to loyalty on Vietnam, while others continued to oppose the war on principle.

In the early years of his presidency, however, Johnson echoed Kennedy's policy by urging Israel to submit Dimona to International Atomic Energy Agency (IAEA) inspection. His support for nonproliferation and his desire to end the Cold War were motivated by his belief that only by a relaxing of international tensions could he achieve his ultimate goal—the extension of the New Deal to all Americans. A nuclear Israel was unacceptable: it could mean a nuclear Egypt, increased Soviet involvement in the Middle East, and perhaps war.

10

The Samson Option

Levi Eshkol's goal was to find a middle ground between the White House, with its insistence on international inspections, and the pro-nuclear faction of the Mapai Party, led by David Ben-Gurion, who, from retirement, turned his insistence on an Israeli nuclear arsenal into a political Last Hurrah.

The prime minister's dilemma was not whether to go nuclear, but when and at what cost, in terms of the competing need to equip and train the conventional units of the army, navy, and air force.

The debate over the nuclear option had surfaced in the nation's newspapers, in deliberately innocuous language, long before Eshkol took office. In mid-1962, for example, Shimon Peres and former army chief of staff Moshe Dayan, then Ben-Gurion's minister of agriculture, took advantage of the funeral of a prominent Zionist military leader to warn their peers that Israel's existence was linked to the "technological achievements of the 1970s" and investment in "equipment of the future." In April 1963, Dayan wrote an article for *Maariv*, the afternoon newspaper, urging the Israeli arms industry to keep pace with Egyptian President Gamal Abdel Nasser's effort to build nuclear weapons. "In the era of rockets with conventional and unconventional warheads," Dayan wrote, "we must diligently develop those weapons so that we don't lag."

Ben-Gurion was even more explicit in an interview with columnist C. L. Sulzberger of the *New York Times* five months after leaving office. Sulzberger quoted Ben-Gurion's concern about a rocket-armed Egypt and added: "As a result he [Ben-Gurion] hints grimly that in its nearby Dimona reactor Israel itself may

be experimenting with military atomics." Nuclear energy cannot be ruled out, the ex–prime minister was quoted as saying,
"because Nasser won't give up. Nor will he risk war again
until he's sure he can win. That means atomic weapons—and
he has a large desert in which to test. We can't test here."
Sulzberger's column was published on Saturday, November 16,
1963. It got to Ben-Gurion in a hurry, for on that same day he
wrote a letter to the editor of the *New York Times* denying that
he in any way had suggested or hinted of nuclear weapons
during the interview with Sulzberger.

The Eshkol government, under pressure first from President
Kennedy and then from Johnson, worked at keeping the lid on,
and had no qualms about stretching the truth to do so. In December 1963, Shimon Yiftach, director of scientific programs
for the defense ministry, publicly told a group of Israeli science
writers that, as they had assumed, the advanced reactor at
Dimona would produce plutonium as a by-product. However,
Yiftach insisted that the Israeli government had no plans to
build a separate plant for chemically reprocessing plutonium.
Yiftach, who had been trained at the Argonne National Laboratory in Illinois, was then one of Israel's leading experts in the
chemistry of plutonium and knew that French construction
companies had started up once again on the underground
reprocessing plant at Dimona.

Eshkol's apprehension about committing Israel to the mass
production of nuclear weapons did not impede the steady progress at Dimona. By mid-1964, the reactor had been in operation for almost two years and the reprocessing plant, with its
remote-controlled laboratories and computer-driven machinery, was essentially completed and ready to begin producing
weapons-grade plutonium from the reactor's spent uranium
fuel rods. Israel's nuclear facilities eventually would include a
weapons assembly plant in Haifa, to the north, and a well-
fortified nuclear storage igloo at the Tel Nof fighter base near
Rehovot. Extreme security is a way of life inside the nuclear
complex, and especially at Dimona, which is under the constant watch of Israeli troops, electronic detection systems, and
radar screens linked to a missile battery. All aircraft, including

those belonging to the Israeli Air Force, are forbidden to overfly the facility—and do so at perilous risk.*

Well-placed Israeli sources say that the physicists and technicians at Dimona conducted at least one successful low-yield
nuclear test sometime in the mid-1960s at an underground cav-
ern near the Israeli-Egyptian border in the Negev desert. Such
detonations, known in the weapons community as "zero yield,"
produce a fission yield that is low, but discernible, and are considered to be a perfectly reliable measurement of the overall
weapons assembly system.** The test was said to have shaken
parts of the Sinai.

In early 1965, completion of the underground reprocessing
plant removed the last barrier to Israel's nuclear ambitions; it
also heightened the ongoing debate inside the government over
the issue. Completion of the reprocessing plant also made it
even more essential that Floyd Culler's annual visits to Dimona
continue to produce nothing, and the Israeli cover-up was constantly being improved and embellished by Binyamin
Blumberg and his colleagues in the Office of Special Tasks.
(International inspections by the IAEA were, of course, considered and rejected in the Kennedy years.) In the mid-1960s,
Dimona's managers came up with a new method of hiding its
underground world. Members of the Israeli Defense Force's
269th General Staff Reconnaissance Unit, the most elite undercover group in the nation, were ordered to the nuclear facility a
few weeks before the arrival of a Culler inspection and told to
bring with them, one former 269th member recalled, "eight
semitrailers loaded with grass. It was sod—all for camouflage,"

---

* During the 1967 Six-Day War, an Israeli Mirage III was shot down when its pilot,
either confused or dealing with equipment problems, ventured into Dimona's airspace.
In February 1973, a Libyan airliner flew off course over the Sinai because of a naviga-
tional error and also, after ignoring or failing to see signals to land, was destroyed by
fighter planes of the Israeli Air Force, killing 108 of the 113 people aboard. Israel
claimed, without evidence, that the plane was headed for Dimona.

** Theodore B. Taylor, a physicist who designed weapons for the American nuclear
program, has written that such low-yield events are, in fact, "more stringent" than full-
yield tests because any failings or imperfections in the weapons design show up more
readily at very low yield than at high yield. Taylor, in a 1988 paper presented to an
arms control seminar in London, noted that low-yield tests are reliable enough to be
useful to countries with considerable weapons testing experience. "But," he added,
"they can also be useful to countries starting nuclear weapons development, if they
want to test without detection."

he added. "Our job for ten days is to cover the walks and bunkers with dirt, sod, and bushes. When the delegation comes,
I'm standing watering grass that looks like it's been there for
years." The scene remains vivid in his memory, the former
officer said, because he'd never before seen sod.*

There is no evidence that the American intelligence community, and President Johnson, had any idea how close Israel was
to joining the nuclear club; the available documents show that
the President's men somehow managed to convince themselves
that by continuing to focus on IAEA inspection as the solution,
all of the nagging questions about Dimona and Israeli nuclear
proliferation would go away.** Eshkol was invited for a state
visit in June 1964—the first visit to Washington by an Israeli
prime minister—and declassified presidential documents on file
at the LBJ Library at the University of Texas show that the
White House believed that Eshkol could be induced by the
promise of American arms to open up Dimona to the International Atomic Energy Agency. The President's men were, in
essence, operating in self-inflicted darkness when it came to
Dimona: they were convinced that Israel had the technical skill
to build a bomb and install it on a warhead, but no one seemed
to know whether Israel seriously intended to do so or not. It
was as if the White House believed there really were two atoms, one of which was peaceful.

* The CIA's photo interpreters, recalled Dino Brugioni, were far from fooled by the
sudden appearance of seemingly new grass. "It was a foolish move on their [the Israe-
lis] part and confirmed what we knew," he said. "You could see what they were doing
in the aerial photos. They planted sod, trees, and bushes. Nothing grows in Beersheba
like that. I mean, why in hell would you plant that stuff there and not around their
homes? It just spotlights activity."

** Washington may have gotten the wrong signal when the Eshkol government,
after extended negotiations, finally went forward in April 1965 with an American request to shift responsibility for inspection of the Nahal Soreq reactor to the IAEA.
American teams had conducted the inspection two times a year until then, without
incident, under the original 1955 agreement that had set up the small research reactor—
which, unlike Dimona, was constantly being used for medical and scientific research
by the staff of the Weizmann Institute. The American request was consistent with the
Johnson administration's policy of strengthening IAEA safeguards by insisting that all
countries participating in the Atoms for Peace program submit to international, and
not American, inspection. Another factor in the switch to international safeguards, a
former nonproliferation official explained, was the widespread belief that the bilateral
American inspections were weak. In return for the Israeli acquiescence, the United
States agreed to provide forty more kilograms of enriched uranium, under safeguards,
for Nahal Soreq's research program.

McGeorge Bundy, the national security adviser, who had been involved with the Israeli weapons question since early 1961, professed to Johnson not to have any intelligence about Israel's nuclear intentions, according to the White House documents, in a memorandum summarizing the potential threat to Israel posed by Egypt's missile systems. Both nations could make missiles, Bundy told the President on May 18, two weeks before the Eshkol visit, but "the difference was that the Israelis could make nuclear warheads to put on their missiles, while the UAR [United Arab Republic] couldn't. The real issue was whether Israel was going for a nuclear capability." It's inconceivable that Bundy and his colleagues did not know what Israel was doing with a secret nuclear reactor in the Negev.

Eshkol wanted to buy American M-48 tanks, and was delighted when Johnson agreed before their summit meeting to use the prestige of his office to persuade West Germany to sell Israel the M-48 out of its NATO stockpiles. Such a purchase, even if circuitous, would be a first for offensive weapons, and would open the American arms pipeline. The Johnson men had a fallback in case Eshkol did not agree to international inspections, as many must have expected he would not: they wanted Israel's permission to brief Arab nations on the results of the annual Floyd Culler inspections.

Eshkol's mission in coming to America was to get what he could—in the way of U.S. arms and commitments—without making any real concessions on Dimona, which, of course, he could not. He had told the White House prior to his arrival that he would continue to accept the Culler inspections of Dimona, but he wanted nothing to do with the International Atomic Energy Agency. Israel offered the public argument, as did other putatively nonnuclear nations, that it should not be forced to place its national laboratories under IAEA aegis until all of the world's nuclear powers did so. China and France were not parties to the agreement. There was a second issue, equally contrived: the contention that the IAEA, like the United Nations, had systematically discriminated against Israel in favor of the Arab nations. There were perhaps some inside Israel who profoundly believed that such discrimination existed, but it had nothing to do with the reason the IAEA was not welcome. Eshkol also drew the line at any briefing of the Arabs.

The White House staff had to anticipate hard bargaining on the Arab and IAEA issues; Eshkol's delegation included Peres, who was violently opposed to international inspection and to the sharing of anything about Dimona with the Arab world. Nonetheless, NSC aide Robert Komer, in his pre-summit memorandum to Johnson, suggested that the President try to change Eshkol's mind on both issues. "We hope you'll personally tell Eshkol they should bite the bullet now," he said of the IAEA inspections. "Without in any way implying that Israel is going nuclear, one has to admit that a functioning . . . reactor plus an oncoming missile delivery system add up to an inescapable conclusion that Israel is at least putting itself in a position to go nuclear. This could have the gravest repercussions on U.S.–Israeli relations, and the earlier we try to halt it the better chance we have. This is why your raising a to-do . . . even if unsuccessful, will at least put Israel firmly on notice that we may be back at it again."

Turning to the relaying of information about Dimona to the Arabs, Komer wrote, "We're firmly convinced that Israel's apparent desire to keep the Arabs guessing is highly dangerous. To appear to be going nuclear without really doing so is to invite trouble. It might spark Nasser into a foolish preemptive move."

Komer, who served for years with the CIA before joining Bundy's National Security Council staff, had few illusions at the time about what was going on underground at Dimona. He vividly recalled discussing the Israeli nuclear bomb project with John McCone, his boss: "We knew the program was continuing. They never told us they would stop."

His recommendations to the President, as he had to know, had no chance of being accepted by the Israelis, nor could they even serve as a negotiating device. Raising a "to-do" to put Israel "firmly on notice" was not going to stop the bomb.

A declassified summary of the June 1 Johnson-Eshkol conversation shows that Johnson indeed did follow his staff's advice to the letter, as if he, too, believed that Washington could negotiate Israel out of its nuclear arsenal. Johnson was emphatic in telling Eshkol that international inspection of Dimona would calm the Arabs and slow the Middle East missile race. "The President pointed out that the Arabs will inevitably tie Israeli missiles to Israel's nuclear potential," the official memorandum of conversation said. "This is why we see IAEA control as in Israel's interest. We should like to remind the Prime Minister that we are violently against nuclear proliferation."

The President also reminded Eshkol that the Soviet Union was becoming more of a factor in the Middle East, and an Israeli reassurance on Dimona could go a long way toward keeping the Russians out. Komer summarized the issue for the President on the day after the Eshkol meeting: "Peres said yesterday Israel wasn't worried so much about present UAR missiles but about better stuff Soviets might give Nasser. This is our whole point too—if Nasser thinks Israel is getting better missiles than he has, and is not reassured on Dimona, he'll be forced to pay Soviet price to get missiles. Therefore, you urge Eshkol to agree both to Dimona reassurances, and to IAEA controls. These two acts would help diminish Nasser's incentive to get exotic weapons help from the USSR. Eshkol's argument, 'Why reassure an enemy?' is short-sighted."

Komer added, "All in all, we understand why Israel, being under the gun, is more fearful of its future than Washington. But Israel can count on us. All we ask in return is that Israel recognize our Arab interests and our common aim of keeping the Soviets out of the Middle East."

Israel, of course, was willing to play along in any way to get more American arms. But it would never "count" on America to protect its future. Komer's comment referred to the main message of the June 1 summit meeting, one that echoed the assurances that John Kennedy had privately given Golda Meir two years earlier: the United States would become Israel's supplier of arms as long as Israel did not produce nuclear weapons. It was this proposal, not found in any of the declassified documents in the Johnson Library, that drove the June 1 summit meeting. The White House's offer soon became known to David Ben-Gurion and Ernst David Bergmann, who viewed any such commitment by the Eshkol government, according to a former Israeli official, "as compromising the security of Israel."

Johnson's pleas about IAEA inspection and the sharing of information with the Arabs went nowhere, but his promise of continued arms support became a factor in what emerged by the fall of 1964 as a major strategic issue for the State of Israel: when to begin the mass production of a nuclear arsenal. Eshkol obviously was far from a pacifist; he had, for example, no ambivalence about continuing Israel's ongoing chemical and biological weapons programs. "Maybe he looks now to you as a moderate, but he was—like all our leaders then—a pragmatic son of a bitch," a former aide recalled with pride. "This was a man who grew up in a generation that saw the Holocaust, the Communists in Russia, the Arabs—all wanting to destroy Jews."

Eshkol's only doubts about Dimona were practical ones: Dimona was costing upward of $500 million a year, more than 10 percent of the Israeli military budget. It was money not being spent elsewhere, the former aide added: "Eshkol would say, 'I don't have the money for it. How many children will go without shoes? How many students will not go to university? And there's no threat. None of our neighbors are going nuclear. Why should we go nuclear?' "

Eshkol's questions led to a series of high-level and highly secret conferences on the bomb in late 1964 and early 1965 at the Midrasha, a Mossad retreat outside Tel Aviv. The meetings were attended by senior officials of the leading Israeli political parties, as well as many defense experts. "The issue was not whether to go nuclear or not," one participant recalled. "But when."

Dimona's supporters had convinced most of the leadership that only nuclear weapons could provide the absolute and final deterrent to the Arab threat, and only nuclear weapons could convince the Arabs—who were bolstered by rapidly growing Soviet economic and military aid—that they must renounce all plans for military conquest of Israel and agree to a peace settlement. With a nuclear arsenal there would be no more Masadas

in Israel's history, a reference to the decision of more than nine
hundred Jewish defenders—known as the Zealots—to commit
suicide in A.D. 73 rather than endure defeat at the hands of the
Romans.

In its place, argued the nuclear advocates, would be the Samson Option. Samson, according to the Bible, had been captured
by the Philistines after a bloody fight and put on display, with
his eyes torn out, for public entertainment in Dagon's Temple
in Gaza. He asked God to give him back his strength for the
last time and cried out, "Let my soul die with the Philistines."
With that, he pushed apart the temple pillars, bringing down
the roof and killing himself and his enemies. For Israel's nuclear advocates, the Samson Option became another way of
saying "Never again."*

The basic argument against the nuclear arsenal went beyond
its impact on the readiness of the military: these were years of
huge economic growth and business expansion inside Israel,
and Dimona still was absorbing far too much skilled manpower, in the view of many industrial managers—whose constant complaints to government officials on that issue went
nowhere. Dimona continued to distort the economy and limit
development. There was, for example, no private computer industry in Israel by the late 1960s, although American intelligence officials had rated Israel for years as an international
leader—with Japan and the United States—in the ability to
design and program computer software.

The long-range social and military costs of Dimona were
most certainly the concerns of Yitzhak Rabin, the new army

* In a 1976 essay in *Commentary*, Norman Podhoretz accurately summarized the pro-
nuclear argument in describing what Israel would do if abandoned by the United
States and overrun by Arabs: "The Israelis would fight . . . with conventional weapons for as long as they could, and if the tide were turning decisively against them, and
if help in the form of resupply from the United States or any other guarantors were
not forthcoming, it is safe to predict that they would fight with nuclear weapons in the
end. . . . It used to be said that the Israelis had a Masada complex . . . but if the
Israelis are to be understood in terms of a 'complex' involving suicide rather than
surrender and rooted in a relevant precedent of Jewish history, the example of Samson,
whose suicide brought about the destruction of his enemies, would be more appropriate than Masada, where in committing suicide the Zealots killed only themselves and
took no Romans with them." Podhoretz, asked years later about his essay, said that his
conclusions about the Samson Option were just that—his conclusions, and not based
on any specific information from Israelis or anyone else about Israel's nuclear capability.

chief of staff, and Yigal Allon, a close Eshkol adviser and former commander of the irregular Palmach forces before the 1948
War of Independence. Less compelling to the military men was
the moral argument against the bomb raised by some on the
left and in academia: that the Jewish people, victims of the
Holocaust, had an obligation to prevent the degeneration of
the Arab-Israeli dispute into a war of mass destruction. Those
who held that view did not underestimate the danger of a conventional arms race, but believed that, as Simha Flapan, their
passionate spokesman, wrote, "the qualitative advantages of
Israel—social cohesion and organization, education and technical skills, intelligence and moral incentive—can be brought
into play only in a conventional war fought by men."

A major complication in the debate, seemingly, was the Arab
and Israeli press, which routinely published exaggerated accounts of each side's weapons of mass destruction. In Israel,
there were alarmist accounts of Soviet and Chinese support for
an Egyptian nuclear bomb. Egypt, in turn, publicly suggested
that it had received a Soviet commitment to come to its aid in
case of an Israeli nuclear attack, and President Gamal Nasser
warned in an interview that "preventive war" was the "only
answer" to a nuclear-armed Israel. It was a period, Simha
Flapan later wrote, when both Israel and Egypt "were trapped
in a vicious circle of tension and suspicion and were doing
everything possible to make them a self-fulfilling prophecy."

The officials at the top in Israel understood the difference
between public perceptions and private realities. Before the
Midrasha conference, for example, Binyamin Blumberg prepared an analysis estimating that the Arab world would not be
able to develop sophisticated nuclear weapons for twenty-five
years—until 1990. The paper was important to Eshkol, who, as
he told the conference, was considering three postures: a ready-
to-go bomb in the basement; the nuclear option, with the
weapons parts manufactured but not assembled; and further
research. "He said," an Israeli recalled, " 'We're not in a
hurry. It'll take the Arabs twenty-five years.' " Eshkol's choice
was to merely continue research and use that added time to
"jump a stage"—to bypass the crude plutonium weapon detonated by the United States at Nagasaki and go directly to

more efficient warhead designs. There was a second compelling argument, along with the issue of money, for temporarily limiting the work at Dimona to research: Israel as yet had no long-range aircraft or missiles in place that were capable of accurately delivering a bomb to targets inside the Soviet Union, which was always Israel's primary nuclear target; no Arab nation would dare wage war against Israel, so the Israeli leadership thought, without Soviet backing.

Levi Eshkol parlayed the Midrasha decision into a strategic asset: he told Washington that he would defer a decision on the nuclear arsenal in return for a commitment to supply offensive arms that would match the quality of arms being supplied to Egypt by the Soviet Union. It was more than good enough for Johnson, who was losing interest with each passing year in waging political war with Israel over the bomb. The President rewarded Eshkol's pledge of a delay by authorizing the sale to Israel in 1966 of forty-eight advanced A-4E Skyhawk tactical fighters, capable of carrying a payload of eight thousand pounds. Johnson's refusal to ask more of the Israelis on the nuclear issue was eased by the strong evidence of renewed Soviet economic and military commitments in the Middle East: Moscow was moving to encourage Arab socialism and unity. For Johnson, this meant that the Cold War was moving to the Arab world, with Israel serving as a surrogate for America.

Eshkol's decision to put a hold on the nuclear issue enraged Ben-Gurion, still smarting over the Mapai Party's handling of the Lavon Affair; Ben-Gurion eventually would publicly compare Eshkol to Neville Chamberlain, the British prime minister who attempted to appease Adolf Hitler before World War II. In June 1965, Ben-Gurion, talking darkly of Eshkol's "endangering the nation's security," dramatically resigned from the Mapai Party and created a new party, known as Rafi (an acronym for the Israel Workers' List). He was joined by a reluctant but loyal Peres, who became Rafi's power broker, and the restless Dayan, who had recently resigned as agricultural minister. Ben-Gurion's hope was that Rafi could capture as many as twenty-five seats in the 120-member Knesset and emerge as a major power broker in Israeli politics.

Ben-Gurion and his followers changed forever the political structure of Israel. Rafi would now become an opposition party, and play the role that had traditionally belonged to right-wing groups. Ben-Gurion's immediate reason for splitting with the Mapai leadership was his continued anger over Lavon, but the Rafi Party, under Peres's leadership, stood for a more aggressive position across the spectrum of defense issues, and especially on nuclear weapons. Ernst Bergmann was another founding member of Rafi, and once again had Ben-Gurion's ear: "Ben-Gurion was quoting Bergmann all the time," recalled an Israeli, about the dangers of not initiating the production of a nuclear arsenal. The issue emerged as a dominant one in the 1965 elections, although it was played out in code language. Israeli newspapers were full of criticism from Peres and Ben-Gurion over what was referred to in Hebrew as *ha'a-noseh ha'adin*, "the sensitive topic," or *b'chia ledorot*, "a lament for generations"; the Rafi leaders also constantly criticized what they euphemistically called Eshkol's "big mistake," language understood by many inside Israel as referring to Eshkol's hesitations about opening a nuclear weapons assembly line at Dimona. None of this was reported by American or other newspapers: the foreign correspondents in Israel apparently did not understand what really was at stake.* Neither did the American intelligence community.

It was an ugly election, with insults and accusations from all parties. One prominent lawyer with close ties to Golda Meir referred publicly to Ben-Gurion as a "coward" and Rafi as a "neo-Fascist group." Many Israelis understood, in a way that no outsider could, that the debate was not only about defense policy or the bomb, but about Ben-Gurion's profound belief that Israel could survive only by relying on the state—and not on the traditional volunteerism of the Zionist movement. In Ben-Gurion's view, the kibbutzim, the Mapai Party, the

---

* John Finney of the *New York Times* did a little better with the Floyd Culler inspections. Finney, who remained on the nuclear beat for the *Times*, reported on June 28, 1966, that the American team had arrived at "the same tentative conclusion as a year ago, that the reactor is not being used at this time for producing plutonium for weapons." The reporter wisely cautioned, however, that the team's conclusion "was tentative because it is difficult to establish in once-a-year inspections that none of the reactor fuel rods have been removed for extracting the plutonium. . . ."

Hagannah of the 1948 war—all populated by volunteers who believed in the cause—had to give way to the more impersonal institutions of universal military service, universal public education, and promotion on the basis of competence and merit rather than party affiliation. Many aspects of this debate coalesced—at least for his critics—in Ben-Gurion's unwavering support of the nuclear arsenal. Some of his opponents in the 1965 election viewed Dimona as nothing more than a collection of competent scientists and bureaucrats, with unclear ideological affiliations, who had created a powerful weapon away from public scrutiny and approval. For many, the election was perhaps a last-ditch struggle between an Israel that continued to utilize the willing spirit of dedicated volunteers and an Israel that relied on the use of science, objective knowledge, and the state.

Ben-Gurion and his Rafi Party were sorely disappointed by the election, winning only ten seats in the Knesset, not enough to provide Ben-Gurion with a power base. The election amounted to a brutal referendum on his dream of returning to power, and the end of his role in the public policy of Israel.*

The election also was interpreted by Levi Eshkol as a referendum on his handling of the nuclear issue; Dimona would remain a standby operation. The country seemingly had rejected the efficient "can do" approach of Ben-Gurion, Dayan, and Peres in favor of the social-democratic and volunteerist goals of the Meir-Eshkol wing of Mapai. It was a low point for Ben-Gurion and his followers.

By the spring of 1966, Ernst David Bergmann had had enough: he resigned under pressure as director of the commissionerless Israeli Atomic Energy Commission, as well as from his two high-level defense science posts. Many in the Eshkol cabinet viewed his departure as long overdue, and it showed; Bergmann was angered and hurt when a ministry of defense official came to his apartment within an hour of his resignation

---

* Ben-Gurion was an inveterate diarist and spent many hours in his later years—he died in early 1974—assembling his papers and helping his biographer, Michael Bar-Zohar. Myer Feldman recalls being accompanied on one of his last scheduled meetings with Ben-Gurion by Teddy Kollek, the mayor of Jerusalem and longtime associate of the Old Man. The two men stood waiting as Ben-Gurion scribbled away in his notebook. "I said to Kollek, 'What's he doing?' " Feldman recalled. Kollek replied, with a smile, "Oh, he's falsifying history."

to retrieve his government car. Eshkol moved quickly to make the Bergmann portfolio less independent: bureaucratic responsibility for the AEC was shifted from the defense ministry to the prime minister's personal staff, and Eshkol himself became chairman of an expanded and revitalized commission. Decisions about the future of nuclear weapons in Israel would now be made by the highest political authority. A pouting Bergmann retreated, with the aid of Lewis Strauss, to the Institute of Advanced Studies at Princeton University, but not before granting an interview to *Maariv*, the popular Israeli newspaper. The *New York Times* account of that interview provides a classic example of the public doubletalk and doublethink that then surrounded the nuclear issue in Israel and the American press: "The scientist [Bergmann] suggested that the Eshkol Government was less sympathetic to long-term scientific planning than former Premier David Ben-Gurion, with whom Professor Bergmann was closely associated. He spoke of the lack of funds for research and the risk of dependence on foreign sources."

Nonetheless, the nuclear weapons issue, even if depicted as "long-term scientific planning," had moved into the open inside Israel. In the United States, where all foreign policy was rapidly becoming consumed by the Vietnam War, Israel's nuclear option continued to be an issue solely for government insiders, who weren't talking.

11

Playing the Game

The ambivalence and hypocrisy at the top of the American government about a nuclear-armed Israel inevitably was mirrored by the bureaucracy. By the middle 1960s, the game was fixed: President Johnson and his advisers would pretend that the American inspections amounted to proof that Israel was not building the bomb, leaving unblemished America's newly reaffirmed support for nuclear nonproliferation.

The men and women analyzing intelligence data and writing reports for their higher-ups understood, as Arthur Lundahl and Dino Brugioni had learned earlier, that there was little to be gained by relaying information that those at the top did not want to know. Nonetheless, the information was there.

There was much known, for example, about the Israeli Jericho missiles, rapidly being assembled by Dassault. "We had a direct line to God," a middle-level CIA technical analyst recalled. "We had everything—not only from the French but also from the Israelis. We stole some and we had spies. I was able to draw a scale model of the system. I even designed three warheads for it—nuclear, chemical, and HE [high explosive]—as a game. We were predicting what they could do." What Israel could do, the former CIA official said, was successfully target and fire a nuclear warhead. The problem arose in conveying the intelligence. "I was never able to get anything officially published" by the CIA for distribution throughout the government, he said. "Everybody knew" about the Israeli missile, he added, "but nobody would talk about it." The official said he decided to bootleg a copy of the intelligence report—risking his job by doing so—to senior officials in the Pentagon and State Department. "I remember briefing a DIA [Defense Intelligence Agency] admiral. He wasn't ready to believe it. I got him turned around, but he retired and no one else cared."

Even James Jesus Angleton, the CIA's director of counter-intelligence, who also was responsible for liaison with Israel, had his problems when it came to the Israeli bomb. The moody Angleton was legendary—and feared—for his insistence on secrecy and his paranoia about Soviet penetration of the Agency. He was a master of backchannel and "eyes only" reports, and his increasing inability to deal with the real world eventually led to his firing in late 1974, but his glaring faults in counter-intelligence apparently did not spill over to Israel.* Former Agency officials, who, in prior interviews with me, had been unsparing in their criticism of Angleton's bizarre methods in counterintelligence, acknowledged that he had performed correctly and proficiently in his handling of Israel. Angleton had worked closely with members of the Jewish resistance in Italy while serving with the Office of Strategic Services (OSS) at the end of World War II; it was a dramatic period when thousands of Jewish refugees and concentration camp survivors were being illicitly funneled from Europe into Palestine, then under British control.

One of Angleton's closest colleagues was Meir (Meme) Deshalit, a resistance leader and Israeli intelligence official who had been posted to Washington in 1948. Deshalit was the older brother of Amos Deshalit, the physicist who had done much to develop Israel's nuclear arsenal before dying of cancer in 1969. Angleton shared Meir Deshalit's view of the Soviet and Arab

---

* The first prominent public mention of Angleton's role in counterintelligence came in a major front-page exposé by the author in the *New York Times* of December 22, 1974. The story linked Angleton and his office to Operation CHAOS, the massive and illegal spying by the CIA on antiwar dissidents in America. Angleton, in a telephone conversation with me before the story was published, suggested that he could provide better stories, dealing with Communist penetration of the antiwar movement and CIA operatives in the Soviet Union, if the domestic spying story was not published. On the day of its publication, a Sunday, as I later wrote in the *Times*, Angleton telephoned me very early at home and complained that Cecily, his wife of thirty-one years, had learned only by reading my story that her husband was not a postal employee, as Angleton claimed he had told her. He added: "And now she's left me." The call shook me up; the upset in his voice seemed real. I mumbled something about a newsman's responsibility to the truth, hung up, and telephoned an old friend who had served in the CIA with Angleton. He laughingly told me that Cecily of course had known from the beginning what her husband did for a living, and had left him three years earlier to move to Arizona, only to return.

PLAYING THE GAME 145

threat to Israel; his personal contacts and strong feelings made him the logical choice to handle liaison between the CIA and the Israeli government. His was one of the most important assignments in the 1950s and early 1960s, the height of the Cold War, because of the continuing flow of Soviet and Eastern European refugees into Israel. Angleton and his Israeli counterparts ran the "rat lines," as the Jewish refugee link became known. It was the Jewish refugee operations, as many in the CIA understood, that provided the West in the early postwar years with its most important insights into the Soviet bloc. Some of the programs were financed off the shelf by CIA contingency funds, as part of KK MOUNTAIN.

Angleton's love for Israel and his shared views on the Arab and Soviet question, however, did not keep him from investigating, as a counterintelligence officer, any Israeli or American Jew he suspected of trafficking in classified information. One of the big question marks was nuclear technology. The CIA knew from its analysis of the fallout of the ongoing French nuclear tests in the Sahara that the increasingly modernized and miniaturized French warheads were based on United States design. A former American nuclear intelligence official recalled that he and his colleagues "were driven crazy" by the suspicion that Israel's quid pro quo for the French help at Dimona included access to design information purloined from the government's nuclear laboratories at Los Alamos and Livermore, California.

No evidence of such a link was found, but intelligence community investigators were surprised to discover at the end of the CHAOS inquiry a cache of Angleton's personal files, secured with black tape, that revealed what obviously had been a long-running—and highly questionable—study of American Jews in the government. The files showed that Angleton had constructed what amounted to a matrix of the position and Jewishness of senior officials in the CIA and elsewhere who had access to classified information of use to Israel. Someone in a sensitive position who was very active in Jewish affairs in his personal life, or perhaps had family members who were Zionists, scored high on what amounted to a Jewishness index.

One government investigator, talking about the Angleton files in a 1991 interview, recalled his surprise at discovering that

even going to synagogue was a basis for suspicion. "I remembered the First Amendment," the investigator added sardoni-
cally. "You know, Freedom of Religion." The Angleton matrix
suggested that at some point a suspect who measured high
enough on the Jewishness scale was subjected to a full-bore
field investigation. "Was there simply a background check, or
was there physical or electronic surveillance?" the investigator
asked rhetorically. "I don't know. I was angry but at the same
time thought it wasn't irrational because a lot of Jews were
giving help to Israel." In the end, the Angleton files were not
investigated further or even brought to the attention of the
House or Senate intelligence committees: "We decided not to
do anything with it."

Samuel Halpern, a Jew who served for years as executive
assistant to the director of the CIA's clandestine services, was
under constant investigation by Angleton. Halpern's position,
the highest reached by any Jew in the clandestine service, gave
him access to the name and background of every foreigner who
had ever been recruited by the CIA. His father, Hanoch, was a
Pole who had become active in Zionism before World War II
and, after emigrating to Palestine, had worked closely with
Ben-Gurion and Moshe Sharett, among others, after the State
of Israel was formed in 1948. "Jim looked at me real hard,"
Halpern recalled with a laugh, "but I told him, 'I'm not going
to muck up your desk.' The Israelis never approached me. Why
should they when I'm sitting on the third floor [of the CIA] and
Jim's on the second?"

Angleton did more than just collect information on American Jews. He also was a sponsor, through the CHAOS program,
of a highly secret CIA operation involving the Agency's purchase of a Washington trash collection company. The firm,
known in the CIA as a proprietary, had contracts to pick up
garbage at various Third World embassies, including the Israeli
embassy. Another of its stops was the downtown Washington
offices of B'nai B'rith, the powerful Jewish social and volunteer
organization with worldwide activities. The trash would be
systematically sorted and analyzed for any possible intelligence.

·   ·   ·

Angleton's close personal ties with the Deshalit family and others in Israel made it inevitable that he would learn about the construction in the Negev. One senior official recalled that Angleton's first intelligence report on Israel's plans to build the bomb was filed routinely in the late 1950s, and not by backchannel, and thus could be made available to those who needed to know inside the CIA's Directorate of Operations, the unit responsible for clandestine action. "I have no idea who his sources were," the senior official said. "He probably never told the director." Over the next few years Angleton continued to produce intelligence on Dimona, also based on information supplied by his personal contacts, but never learned—or, at least, never reported—the extent to which Israel was deceiving Washington about its nuclear weapons progress.

Angleton, of course, had been given periodic briefings in the late 1950s and early 1960s by Lundahl or Brugioni on the intelligence collected by the U-2 overflights of the Negev, but never evinced much interest. His forte was human intelligence, or HUMINT, as the intelligence community calls it, and not technical intelligence, such as the U-2 imagery. "He was a real funny guy," Brugioni recalled. "I'd meet with him, brief him; he'd ask a few questions, you'd leave—and never know what he's holding. Sometimes he'd have his office real dark and have a light only on you. He was a real spook."

For all of his mystique and freedom to operate, Angleton, too, was stymied by the Israeli bomb. His reports on Dimona, buttressed by the U-2 data, did not even result in an official CIA estimate that Israel was going nuclear. Such formal estimates, which are distributed to the President and other key government officials, were the responsibility of analysts in the CIA's Office of National Estimates (ONE). "Jim kept saying, 'Yes, they've got it,' and the analysts would say, 'I don't believe it,' " one former intelligence official recalled. The analysts simply did not think Angleton's HUMINT sources were reliable, the official said, adding that tension and second-guessing over human intelligence sources were a way of life in the CIA. By 1965, an extensive dossier of HUMINT reports on Dimona had built up, the official said, and the nuclear issue was again raised with the

ONE analysts: "They told me that even if Israel did have the bomb, they'd never use it."

The intelligence official, recalling the issue in an interview, got angry again at the analysts: "They were so stupid. You'd have to put the bomb under their noses before they'd believe it. They didn't have any understanding of Israel; didn't know what made them think. They were so stupid."

It is not known how many CIA analyses on the Israeli bomb were produced in the early 1960s by the Office of National Estimates, but the one memorandum that does exist was astonishingly inept about Israeli attitudes. The paper, entitled "Consequences of Israeli Acquisition of Nuclear Capability," was dated March 6, 1963, and was made available nearly twenty years later at the John F. Kennedy Library without any deletions. The national estimate concluded that Israel, once having attained a nuclear capability, "would use all the means at its command to persuade the U.S. to acquiesce in, and even to support, its possession. . . . Israel could be expected to use the argument that this possession entitled it to participate in all international negotiations respecting nuclear questions and disarmament." The staggering flaw in the CIA analysis was its basic assumption: that Israel would make public or otherwise let its nuclear capability become officially known. The reality was precisely the opposite: Israel had no intention of going public with the bomb in fear of American and worldwide Jewish disapproval that would result in international reprobation and diminished financial support from the Diaspora.

Such flawed intelligence analyses went a long way toward keeping the men at the top officially ignorant of what no one wanted to know. In public, the Johnson administration, as were its predecessors, was firmly opposed to the spread of nuclear weapons anywhere in the world; official acknowledgment of an Israeli bomb would have presented Washington with an unwanted dilemma—either sanction Israel or be accused of a nuclear double standard.

Israel was not considered a nuclear weapons state on October 18, 1964, when China exploded its long-awaited first nuclear bomb. President Johnson, three weeks away from his over-

whelming election triumph over Senator Barry Goldwater of
Arizona, the Republican presidential candidate, reaffirmed his
commitment to nonproliferation in a nationally televised
speech: "Until this week, only four powers [the United States,
the Soviet Union, Great Britain, and France] had entered the
dangerous world of nuclear explosions. Whatever their differences, all four are sober and serious states, with long experience as major powers in the modern world. Communist China
has no such experience. . . . [Its] expensive and demanding
effort tempts other states to equal folly," the President said.
"Nuclear spread is dangerous to all mankind. . . . [W]e must
continue to work against it, and we will."*

The President may have believed his impassioned words, but
not all of his senior advisers did. Six weeks later, McGeorge
Bundy, Robert McNamara, and Secretary of State Dean Rusk
discussed what they considered the administration's real policy
options at a secret meeting on nonproliferation. Among those
taking careful notes was Glenn T. Seaborg, chairman of the
Atomic Energy Commission, who recounted the session in his
little-noted 1987 memoir, *Stemming the Tide:*

"Rusk said he thought a basic question was whether we really should have a nonproliferation policy prescribing that no
countries beyond the present five might acquire nuclear weapons. Were we clear that this should be a major objective of U.S.
policy? For example, might we not want to be in a position
where India or Japan would be able to respond with nuclear
weapons to a Chinese threat? Rusk mentioned the possibility of
having an Asian group of nuclear weapons countries, pointing
out that the real issue was among Asian countries and not between northern countries and the Asians.

"McNamara thought it would take decades for India or Japan to have any appreciable deterrent. Nevertheless, he

---

* Johnson also reassured the nation that his administration had not been surprised
by the Chinese test. The President perhaps did not know it at the time of his talk, but
the American intelligence community was aghast to learn from air sampling that the
Chinese bomb had been fueled by enriched uranium, and not, as predicted by the CIA,
by far-easier-to-produce plutonium. The American guess had been that China would
chemically reprocess plutonium from the spent uranium rods in a reactor, as at
Dimona. Confronted with evidence to the contrary, some in the CIA believed that
China might have stolen or otherwise misappropriated the enriched uranium for its
bomb.

thought the question Rusk had raised should be studied. He pointed out that adoption of a nonproliferation policy by the United States might require us to guarantee the security of nations that renounced nuclear weapons.

"I [Seaborg] expressed doubt that a policy condoning further proliferation should be considered, saying that, once a process of making exceptions was started, we would lose control and that this would inevitably lead to serious trouble. . . .

"Bundy warned about the need to keep very quiet the fact that we were discussing the basic questions of whether U.S. policy should be nonproliferation, because everyone assumed that this was our policy. Any intimation to the contrary would be very disturbing throughout the world. McNamara added that we had to the stop the leaks that come out of meetings like this. He agreed with Bundy that the fact that the U.S. commitment to nonproliferation was being questioned simply must not be allowed to leak."*

One senior American who resisted the persuasive talk about expanding the nuclear club was John McCone, the increasingly frustrated CIA director. McCone sorely felt the loss of John Kennedy; his relationship with Lyndon Johnson was much less intimate and his advice not always welcome. McCone's solution to the Chinese bomb (and to the problems with North Vietnam) was to send in the Air Force. "McCone just raised hell" about the Chinese bomb, recalled Walt Elder. "He wanted permission to fly U-2s over the test site and was turned down." The CIA director wasn't daunted: he next floated "the idea of what if we got in and took out the Chinese capability?" Daniel Ellsberg recalled similar talk at high levels in the Pentagon: "We were saying, in essence, that if we could have stopped the

---

* Rusk carried his fight to other bureaucratic forums, with the focus on a nuclear India. Daniel Ellsberg recalled being told by his Pentagon superiors after the Chinese test in 1964 that Rusk's position was that "India needed a nuclear weapon as a deterrent and there was no reason for them not to have it." Rusk's basic approach, Ellsberg added, was "Why shouldn't our friends have nuclear weapons now that our enemies have them?" It should be noted that there was no mention of this extraordinary debate in McGeorge Bundy's seemingly comprehensive history of the atom bomb, *Danger and Survival,* published in 1988. India's drive for the bomb, wrote Bundy, "remains a doubtful prize in that something about this apocalyptically destructive standard of greatness is not truly Indian." Bundy could have added that there were a few Americans in high Washington positions in 1964 who had no doubt then that India's desire for the bomb was quite truly Indian.

Russian bomb, we would have saved the world a lot of trouble. It's too bad the Soviets got the bomb." One thought was to use unmarked bombers to strike at the Chinese, thus avoiding identification. Cooler heads prevailed, Ellsberg recalled: "The mission just looked too big to be plausibly denied."

McCone resigned as CIA director in 1965, despite his support for Johnson's continuing escalations in Vietnam. He explained to a colleague: "When I cannot get the President to read my reports, then it's time to go." McCone knew that Floyd Culler's inspections were accomplishing little; he also understood what Israel's continuing refusal to permit full-fledged international inspections meant. But, said Elder, the CIA director found that Johnson "didn't understand the implications" of the inspection issue and didn't want to hear about it. By the end of McCone's tenure, Elder added, he believed Lyndon Johnson as President had three basic concerns: "His standing in polls. 'Can I sell it to Congress?' And 'How can I get out of Vietnam?' "

There was yet another concern: Johnson's understanding that good nonproliferation policies made for bad politics. The President needed no one to remind him that any serious move to squeeze the Israelis on their nuclear weapons program would lead to a firestorm of protest from American Jews, many of whose leaders had consistently supported his presidency and the Vietnam War. He got another reminder of the political danger of nonproliferation from a special panel on that subject he convened a few weeks after the Chinese test. The distinguished panel, headed by Roswell L. Gilpatric, who had served John Kennedy as deputy secretary of defense, returned on January 21, 1965—the day after Johnson's inauguration—with a report that amounted to an indictment of past and present policy.* It warned that the world was "fast approaching a point of no return" in opportunities for controlling the spread of nuclear weapons and urged the President, "as a matter of great urgency, [to] substantially increase the scope and intensity of our effort if we are to have any hope of success." The report

* Panel members included the retired Allen Dulles, the former secretary of state Dean Acheson, the former defense secretary Robert A. Lovett, the former White House science adviser George B. Kistiakowsky, and IBM chairman Arthur K. Watson.

also advocated the establishment of nuclear-free zones in Latin America, Africa, and the Middle East, including Israel and Egypt. Most significantly, it suggested that the President should reconsider—in terms of nonproliferation—a controversial American plan to create a multilateral force (MLF) that would give NATO members, including the West Germans, a joint finger on the nuclear trigger. The raising of any question about the MLF issue was especially sensitive, for the Soviet Union was insisting that any proposed nonproliferation treaty prohibit a separate European nuclear force, which it viewed as nothing more than a vehicle for providing the West Germans with the bomb.

At a White House meeting with the President, individual members of the panel listed a sweeping series of priorities—including encouraging France to turn its *force de frappe* into a NATO nuclear missile battery—that prompted the President to note caustically, according to Glenn Seaborg, that implementation of the committee's report would be "a very pleasant undertaking." Johnson and his aides at the meeting, who included McGeorge Bundy and Dean Rusk, warned Gilpatric and the committee members not to discuss the report with any outsiders or even to acknowledge that a written document had been presented to the White House (the Gilpatric report remains highly classified today). Seaborg, who attended the meeting, noted in his memoir that Rusk, when asked by the President for his views, depicted the report as being "as explosive as a nuclear weapon." Its premature release, Rusk added, "could start the ball rolling in an undesirable manner"—in terms of the MLF and future negotiations on a nonproliferation treaty. The report went nowhere, despite the President's promise of further consultations with Gilpatric.

Political disaster, from the White House's point of view, struck in June, when newly elected Senator Robert Kennedy based his maiden Senate floor speech on many of the until then unknown and ignored recommendations of Gilpatric's panel. Kennedy, often invoking his dead brother, urged the President to rise above the immediate issues and begin dealing with nuclear proliferation: "Upon the success of this effort depends the only future our children will have. The need to halt the spread of nuclear weapons must be a central priority of American policy." Kennedy specifically called for Johnson to immediately open worldwide negotiations for a comprehensive test ban treaty; such talks, he proposed, should include Communist China, one of North Vietnam's allies, and he indirectly criticized Johnson for his preoccupation with Vietnam by stating: "We cannot allow the demands of day-to-day policy to obstruct our efforts to solve the problems of nuclear spread. We cannot wait for peace in the Southeast—which will not come until nuclear weapons spread beyond recall."* Johnson, of course, was made apoplectic by what he was convinced was Gilpatric's leaking of the report to Kennedy and responded by deleting material on nonproliferation from a speech he was scheduled to deliver the day after the Kennedy speech. Over the next months, Glenn Seaborg recalled, there was nothing more heard about the Gilpatric report from the White House, and nonproliferation continued to be treated as a topic fit only for the arms controllers in the Arms Control and Disarmament Agency (ACDA), whose advice—no matter how prudent—rarely carried weight with the White House. President Johnson held out for two years before agreeing in secret talks with the Soviets to drop the MLF, clearing the way for the 1968 Nonproliferation Treaty and giving the government's arms controllers an important victory.

In the mid-1960s, the Soviet Union had begun to step up its military and economic aid programs in the Middle East, and Israel was increasingly seen by the Johnson White House as a regional American bulwark. It was inevitable that high-level interest in the perennial and profitless issue of international inspection for Dimona began to wane in 1967—as the A-4E Skyhawks began arriving in Israel, as the routine Floyd Culler inspections proceeded, and as America got more and more enmeshed in the Southeast Asian war.

---

* Kennedy also warned that Israel and India "already possess weapons-grade fissionable material, and could fabricate an atomic device within a few months." Further Israeli progress on the bomb, he added, "would certainly impel the Egyptians to intensify their present efforts." The senator's remarks caused a sensation in Israel, but were little noted elsewhere. The *New York Times*'s page-one account of the Kennedy speech included no mention of Israel.

There were strong public clues, nonetheless, that Israel never stopped planning to build its bombs. In mid-1966, the Israeli government delayed in accepting nearly $60 million in possible American aid for the construction of a much-needed nuclear desalinization and power plant because the aid was contingent on an Israeli commitment to permit IAEA inspection of Dimona. Johnson and Eshkol had announced a preliminary agreement to build the plant in 1964, amid much fanfare, and subsequent studies showed the facility could produce two hundred megawatts of power and 100 million gallons of desalted water daily. Continued American insistence on IAEA inspections made the Israelis walk away, without any explicit explanation, from the project. The proposed desalinization plant was studied for the next decade, but the American conditions were never accepted, and the plant was never built. The pro-nuclear advocates in the Rafi Party, including Peres and Bergmann, urged Israel to refuse American aid for the plant and publicly accused the United States of attempting to violate Israeli sovereignty by linking its support to Dimona's IAEA inspection.

Privately, Peres and Bergmann—still influential, although out of office—suspected that the United States had a hidden agenda in its support of the nuclear desalinization plant: to divert Israeli funds, manpower, and resources from Israel's nuclear arsenal, in the hope that Israel would at some point be forced to make a choice between nuclear weapons and nuclear energy.

A second clue came in July 1966, during a debate in the Knesset on the most recent inspection of Dimona by Floyd Culler, whose conclusion—that there was still no evidence of a bomb facility—had again been made available by American officials to John Finney of the *New York Times* and, so some Israelis thought, also to Egypt. During the debate, Shimon Peres told of his recent participation at an international conference on nuclear weapons where, he said, the Middle East was discussed: "I found that there is unfortunately no possibility of limiting the spread of nuclear weapons in the near future—not because of Israel, but because big powers are not agreeing among themselves. . . . I was glad to discover that most experts on the subject do not believe it possible to envisage nuclear disarmament for the Middle East in isolation from the conventional arms race. . . ."* Peres was, in essence, defending Israel's decision not to give in to Washington's IAEA inspection demands on the ground that the Arabs had conventional superiority. The same argument—Warsaw Pact tank and troop superiority —had been used a few years earlier by the United States and its allies to justify the deployment of nuclear missiles in Europe.

By the late 1960s, much of the United States' primary analysis of nuclear intelligence had been shifted from the CIA to the design and engineering laboratories for nuclear weapons at Los Alamos and Sandia and, later, Livermore, where intelligence units dealing with the Soviet Union and China had been set up after World War II. The growing danger of proliferation became starkly clear during the Kennedy administration, when a group of scientists awaiting clearance before beginning work at Los Alamos successfully designed a nuclear bomb from the open literature. The laboratories' primary targets continued to be the reactors and research centers in the Soviet Union and China, but the intelligence units eventually began monitoring the transfer of nuclear technology and those countries that were viewed as "nth" nations, as near-nuclear countries came to be known. "We had tremendous data" that went beyond satellite photography and intercepted communications, a closely involved official said. "We had people who had worked inside plants in the USSR and China. We were even able to do mock-ups of their weapons system—go from the warhead back through the plant. As part of the drill, I was required to summarize who's got the bomb and who was next, in near-term capability." Israel was always at the top of his list, the official recalled, followed by South Africa. "We were watching the relationship between France and Israel and between Israel and South Africa," he added. "Those were the links."

* Peres misstated the conference's findings. His Knesset statement was initially reported in *Israel and Nuclear Weapons*, by Fuad Jabber, published in 1971 by the International Institute for Strategic Studies (IISS) in London. Jabber wrote that the conference, known as the International Assembly on Nuclear Weapons and sponsored in part by the IISS, had, in fact, issued a call for "a serious effort" to negotiate a nuclear-free zone in the Middle East. The assembly took place June 23–26, 1966, in Toronto, Canada.

His assignment also included monitoring the flow of uranium ore into Israel from supplier nations such as Argentina and South Africa. Such ore, known as yellowcake, served as the raw fuel for the heavy-water reactor at Dimona; by the mid-1960s, its sale was a highly competitive and profitable business whose transfer in lots under ten tons was not monitored by the IAEA in Vienna. The first known shipment of ore from South Africa to Israel had arrived in 1963 and, since it totaled ten tons, was duly reported. In subsequent years, however, clandestine shipments of South African yellowcake began to arrive at Dimona, often escorted by a special operations unit of the Israeli Defense Force. Israel's goal was to prevent outsiders from learning that the reactor was operating at two to three times greater capacity than publicly acknowledged, utilizing that much more uranium ore—and therefore capable of reprocessing greater amounts of plutonium. At least some of those later clandestine shipments from South Africa became known in the late 1960s to the intelligence officers in Los Alamos and Sandia, who were carefully watching—by satellites and other means—most of the major uranium mines in the world. But after Israel's overwhelming victory in the 1967 Six-Day War, the intelligence about Dimona and its nuclear potential became highly compartmentalized, as the White House decided to side more openly with Israel in the Middle East, and thus much harder to access. "We knew about the yellowcake," the official recalled, "but we weren't allowed to keep a file on it. It simply wasn't part of the record. Anytime we began to follow it, somebody in the system would say, 'That's not relevant.'"

The U-2 was still flying, but Lundahl and Brugioni had gone on to new assignments in photo interpretation and were no longer directly involved in Israeli nuclear matters. Far more intelligence was being collected by America's CORONA and GAMBIT satellite systems, which, after much trial and error, had by the mid-1960s begun consistently to produce high-resolution photography from their orbital perches in outer space. Any interesting intelligence on Israel was now being routed to Livermore and Los Alamos through the CIA's Office of Science and Technology, headed by Carl E. Duckett, to which Lundahl's National Photo Interpretation Center was now reporting.

Duckett, a college dropout, had been recruited to the Agency in 1963 from the Army's Missile Command headquarters at the Redstone Arsenal in Alabama. As a civilian Army expert on Soviet missile systems, he had been regularly consulted in prior years by Lundahl and Brugioni on U-2 photo intelligence, but had been told nothing about the findings on Dimona. That process reversed once Duckett joined the CIA, where he got his own special access to the Israeli intelligence. In the beginning, Brugioni recalled, there were long meetings in the late afternoon, usually over a few drinks, at which Duckett and his colleagues would openly discuss the day's findings. Eventually those faded away. Duckett was a quick study, Brugioni said: "By the mid-1960s, it was all his baby." Lundahl and Brugioni soon came to understand that Duckett was no longer sharing all of his information about the Israeli bomb—the U-2's spy flights were no longer as important, and there was no longer any need for them to know. It was the end of an era.

The screening out of Lundahl and Brugioni was perhaps more of a loss than Duckett and his colleagues in the Office of Science and Technology could understand: those two were the institutional memory of the U-2 intelligence on Dimona—almost none of which had been reduced to writing prior to 1960. "Duckett knew very little about what went on before," Brugioni said. "He never asked me and I never told him. Lundahl always said, 'This is very, very sensitive.'" In subsequent years, even the most senior officials of the American government would learn little about the pre-1960 U-2 flights over Dimona; the lack of written history meant that there was nothing in the files. It was the first of many disconnects that would come to dominate the processing of U.S. intelligence on Dimona.

12

The Ambassador

Walworth Barbour, the American ambassador to Israel, was a compelling presence to the Israelis—a tall, shy, hugely overweight diplomat with a gluttonous appetite and acute emphysema. He constantly sprayed his throat with a vaporizer, wore yellowing white suits with brown-and-white shoes, and walked with a shambling gait, an outsized Sydney Greenstreet. Barbour spoke no Hebrew and by the end of his stay in Israel still had little to do with the people of the country, rarely attending educational, cultural, or social events. And yet he was beloved by Israel's leadership, and had been since his appointment in 1961 by John F. Kennedy; he remained on the job for the next twelve years. Only three American ambassadors ever served longer in one post.* A lifelong bachelor, Barbour retired quietly in 1973, along with his spinster sister, to the family home in Gloucester, Massachusetts, taking with him an extensive knowledge of Israel's nuclear capability.

Barbour's long assignment as ambassador was not a testament to his intelligence and competence, which were exceptional, but to his understanding of when and when not to accept every Israeli assertion at face value and his willingness to operate the American embassy as a subsidiary, if necessary, of the Israeli foreign ministry. The ambassador often reminded his questioning subordinates that he was not a servant of the Department of State or its secretary, but a President's man

* The State Department's historical office lists George P. Marsh, minister to Italy from 1861 to 1882; Edwin V. Morgan, ambassador to Brazil from 1912 to 1933; and Claude G. Bowers, ambassador to Chile from 1939 to 1953.

with a personal mandate in an important embassy—a function-
ary who would stand aside when ordered to do so, and permit
the White House and the Israeli ambassador to Washington to
run the real policy behind his back.

A graduate of Exeter and Harvard, Barbour was unfailingly
courteous and correct to his subordinates, and in his first six
years as ambassador, when some of the most accurate reporting
on Dimona was forwarded to Washington, rarely interfered
with the job of those working in his embassy. But the field
reports had no impact; they simply disappeared into the bureaucratic maze. Barbour did nothing to keep them alive, and
after the 1967 Six-Day War ordered his staff—over the objection
of one key aide—to stop reporting on nuclear weapons in
Israel. Barbour's assignment at that moment was to insulate
Lyndon Johnson and his men from those facts that would com-
pel action, and he did his President's bidding. He was the best,
and the worst, of American diplomacy.

Barbour's important role in the history of U.S.–Israeli relations—and his knowledge of Israel's nuclear capability—was
hidden by his insistence on a low profile. He was a virtual
nonperson to the American correspondents assigned to Israel;
he rarely met with them, unlike most ambassadors, and he
never spoke on the record. His name occurs only six times in
the *New York Times Index* for the years 1961 to 1966, a period of
political turmoil in which the United States, after intense diplomatic activity, emerged as Israel's chief arms supplier. His
reclusiveness was legendary in his embassy, a five-story building located near the beach at Tel Aviv. Barbour's daily pattern
was inviolate, and interrupted only by international crises or
the visits of the traveling secretary of state and senior White
House advisers: he was chauffered to the embassy's basement
garage around nine in the morning, rode an elevator to his top-
floor office, stayed there until noon, rode the elevator down to
the garage, and returned home. There were afternoon rounds
of golf, weather permitting, dips in his pool, and an occasional
evening of bridge. When Barbour did entertain—he did so less
frequently over the years—his guests often included prominent
visiting Jews, such as Abe Feinberg and Victor Rothschild of

London.* Such events, Barbour once explained to William N. Dale, who arrived in 1964 as deputy chief of mission, were his way of fulfilling a direct assignment from Lyndon Johnson: "I'm here under orders from Johnson, who told me, 'I don't care a thing about what happens to Israel, but your job is to keep the Jews off my back.' Everything I do is designed to keep Jews off the President's back," Barbour added. "To keep them happy." He told another newcomer to the embassy, upon being asked why he did not respond to messages from the State Department, "I go back to Washington every year to see the President and I get my orders directly from him—not from those pipsqueaks [at State]." Barbour also was phobic about using a newly installed State Department telephone scrambler system, designed to protect conversations from being intercepted. "If they can talk to you over a secure telephone line," he told an aide, "then you have to do what they want." He repeatedly urged Bill Dale to send embassy reports by mail, especially if the intelligence was adverse to Israeli interests, because "Israel has friends all over the State Department" and would intercept the information.

Most junior members of the embassy staff had no contact with the ambassador and could go for months or longer without even seeing him; Barbour's weekly staff meetings were only for senior subordinates. One personal aide recalled being asked by Barbour in 1967, six years after he became ambassador, whether it was possible to cash a check in the embassy. "He had never been on the second floor," the aide added, where the cashier's office was located. Still, many subordinates viewed him with awe. "He was the finest man I've ever known in the government," said John L. Hadden, who served as CIA station chief in Tel Aviv in the mid-1960s. "He was a real professional. He was Boston Back Bay and friendship was not in the books with him. Respect is a better word. He didn't bother with

* His sister, Ellen, served as embassy hostess during her extended annual visits to Israel. Barbour kept photographs of Ellen and one other woman on his desk; a personal aide recalled Barbour explaining, when queried, that the other woman was someone he'd known in Cairo, where he was serving as political officer during World War II. "What happened to her?" "I asked her to marry me and she said no," Barbour replied. The young aide was astonished: "She said no and he kept her picture there twenty years later."

friends." Barbour's closest associates were not his fellow Americans, but senior officials of the Israeli government, including Golda Meir, who became prime minister in 1969, and Major General Aharon Yariv, director of military intelligence from 1964 to 1972.

Of course, no senior Israeli official would talk to an outsider about nuclear weapons, and Barbour, in the end, shared that taboo.

Yet it was Barbour's men who reported before the June 1967 war that Israel had completed its basic weapons design and was capable of manufacturing warheads for deployment on missiles. Israel also may have had a crudely manufactured bomb or two ready to go, but—as the embassy could not know—no decision had been made by Prime Minister Eshkol to begin mass production.

Spying on Dimona was not the responsibility of the Central Intelligence Agency, as in most foreign countries, but left to the U.S. Army, Air Force, and Navy attachés assigned to the embassy; the Agency's espionage functions included the monitoring of Soviet activities and the providing of special cameras, film, and free bottles of wine to any officer who wanted to picnic on the weekend with his family in the Negev. The 1963 restrictions on the CIA's operations inside Israel, American officials acknowledged, were a sop aimed at avoiding any undue embarrassment for the Israeli government, whose extensive penetration of the United States government needed to be curbed. "We were helpful to the Israelis" in terms of supplying essential intelligence, explains a senior American diplomat, "but we knew that if we weren't—they'd get it anyway." The few espionage attempts organized by the CIA before 1963 had gone nowhere, in part because of the nature of Israel's close-knit society but also because of Israel's ability to monitor the activities of the Americans assigned to Israel. All of the U.S. embassy contacts with Israeli citizens and government officials were—and continue to be—funneled through a special liaison office of the Israeli foreign ministry. It was understood that American intelligence and military officials who tried to evade the liaison system would be carefully watched. Given the difficulty of operating clandestinely inside Israel, the function of the CIA station chief was reduced to writing political assessments and staying in close touch with his counterparts in Mossad and in military intelligence, Aman. Israel, with its steady stream of Soviet and Eastern European Jewish refugees, remained the most important country for collecting intelligence on the Soviet Union, but those operations were left to James Angleton and his men in Washington. It was sometimes hard for a newcomer, like John McCone, to keep things straight.

McCone was still eager to have his agency prove what he knew to be true: that a chemical reprocessing plant did exist underground at Dimona. Peter C. Jessup, the CIA station chief in the early 1960s, recalled being peremptorily ordered to fly to Rome early in McCone's tenure, where the director—then on a grand tour of CIA facilities in Europe—was scheduled to see the pope. The trip, in the days before jet travel, had taken many hours, but McCone had only a moment to spare. "He was in a great hurry," Jessup recalled, "and told me that President Kennedy thinks the most serious problem facing us is the proliferation of nuclear weapons." McCone wanted the questions about Israel put to rest, and urged the station chief to put "his staff" to work. At the time, the bemused Jessup added, his "staff" at the CIA station consisted of two aides.

Despite the difficulties, the men in the U.S. embassy—wanting, like most people, to do their job as well as possible—kept on trying to find out what they could about Dimona. Getting close was fun and a little dangerous—one American officer was chastised by Barbour after being caught by the Israelis with a butterfly net outside Dimona's barbed-wire fence—but occasionally added something useful to the intelligence. Colonel Carmelo V. Alba was the U.S. Army's military attaché to Israel in the mid-1960s and, like the other attachés from Western embassies, spent many weekends cruising in the Negev with his long-range telescopic camera. "All I was doing was taking pictures," Alba recalled. He did so at least once a month, shipping the film off to Washington, with no reaction—until one of his photographs showed "evidence of activity at Dimona. Smoke was coming out of the dome," Alba added. "Finally, the CIA got excited."

Dimona had gone critical, and the embassy continued its watch. John Hadden, who began his tour as CIA station chief in 1963, sent Alba one weekend to Beersheba to do a census of French names on the mailboxes of the city's apartment complexes.* A constant goal was to try to determine who was doing what at Dimona. Barbour did not interfere with the hunt; William Dale, as the second-highest-ranking American diplomat, was given wide latitude in the day-to-day management of the embassy, and he encouraged his staff to find out what it could. The embassy's scientific attaché was a physicist named Robert T. Webber, who shared Dale's interest in Dimona. Webber, who had earned a doctorate in physics at Yale University, worked closely with John Hadden—in clear violation of a State Department decree forbidding scientific attachés to engage in intelligence work.** Webber also relied on the intelligence gathered by Mel Alba and encouraged the Army colonel to collaborate with his British and Canadian counterparts in collecting more.

It was a hunt, and the men in the embassy got a break sometime in 1966 from an unlikely source—an American Jew living in Israel. Dale and the rest of the embassy staff stayed on good terms—as American diplomats do all over the world—with the many American citizens who chose to live abroad. Americans in Israel were routinely invited to embassy parties and picnics,

* Alba got Hadden in trouble with the Israeli foreign office by inadvertently putting Hadden's American license plates on a jeep before taking one of his weekend jaunts to the Negev. All diplomatic cars in Israel were required to have special license plates, and the embassy mechanics routinely removed the American license plates from the private cars of newly arrived diplomatic personnel and placed them on the walls for decoration. Alba had asked the embassy car pool for a black jeep. It arrived with no plates, and the colonel, in a hurry, ordered the mechanic to grab a set at random from the walls and throw them on. The plates turned out to be Hadden's. The jeep, of course, was monitored by the Israelis, leading to a stiff protest: why was the CIA station chief sneaking around in the Negev?

** "We were very strict," recalled Herman Pollack, then the director of the State Department Bureau of International Scientific and Technological Affairs. "No intelligence work by science attachés. He was supposed to keep his hands very clean." Hadden, who retired from the Agency a few years after returning from Israel, acknowledged with a laugh that he "never paid any attention to organizational charts and titles. Life seemed to be better run if people worked together to accomplish joint goals that made sense."

as well as to screenings of American movies. Dale and his wife had become especially friendly with Dr. Max Ben, a Princeton-trained pharmacologist who was helping the Israelis set up a pharmacology institute under United Nations auspices. "One morning," Dale recalled, "Max came into the embassy and said, 'I have a story to tell you. I've been down to Dimona and I was shown the nuclear facilities. I'm convinced that Israel is making nuclear warheads.' " Ben, contacted later, vividly recalled his trip to Dimona. He had become a close friend and confidant of Ernst Bergmann's while in Israel, and it was that friendship, he claimed, that led to the invitation to take a firsthand look at the reactor. Though he had studied physics at Princeton, Ben found the visit to be "exciting" but confusing: "A lot of it I didn't understand." What troubled him, however, was not any concern about proliferation, but his belief that the United States was not helping Israel in its serious pursuit of the bomb: "I thought we ought to do something about it—to give them an assist." He talked to Dale and then agreed to discuss what he knew on a more sophisticated level with Bob Webber. Dale arranged the meeting. Ben explained years later that his purpose in taking up the issue with Dale and Webber had not been to inform on Israel's nuclear progress, as Dale obviously assumed, but to try to pass word of the accomplishments at Dimona to Washington. "My goal," he recalled, "was to see how the U.S. could help Israel. I tried to walk a line."

Dale felt he had enough to report. He brought Webber and others into the embassy's most secure room—a lead-sealed facility known as the "bubble"—and the group drafted a highly classified dispatch to Washington summarizing their intelligence. Its essential message, Dale recalled, was: "Israel is getting ready to start putting warheads into missiles so they can be quickly assembled into weapons for delivery by plane." The paper had to be approved by the ambassador, who was approached with trepidation. "Barbour harrumphed," Dale recalled, "and said, 'Well, I suppose it's time. Go ahead, they deserve it. Let it go.' " Dale forwarded it with a sense of accomplishment. It was, Dale thought, the embassy's most definitive report by far on Dimona.

"So what happened?" asked Dale. "Not a damn thing. Nobody responded." Webber eventually was replaced as science attaché by someone much less interested in Dimona, and Colonel Alba was reassigned as an aide to the Joint Chiefs of Staff.

Adding to the frustration, Dale said, was the fact that more revealing information about Israeli intentions was provided early the next year by another American Jew. The embassy was entertaining a group of American government officials who were en route from India after attending a regional meeting of American economic and commercial attachés. There was a party set up in Tel Aviv with Israeli trade officials. On the next day, Eugene M. Braderman, then a deputy assistant secretary of state for commercial affairs, approached Dale, "looking ashen. He said, 'One of the Israelis at the party told me that my primary duty, as an American Jew, was to help the United States government accept Israeli nuclear weapons.' Braderman was very agitated," Dale added. "He said to me: 'I'm an American first, not a Jew first.' He told me to do whatever was right with the information.'"* By that point, Dale understood that Braderman's story had nowhere to go. "I didn't do anything with it," he said. "I knew it'd not do any good."

There were other issues, of course, for the embassy. Israel decided in early June 1967 to preempt the increasing Arab buildup in the Sinai and go to war. A year of steady tension had culminated two weeks before in an Egyptian blockade of the Israeli port city of Elat. An increasingly confident Nasser had sent his troops to occupy Sharm el Sheikh on the southern tip of the Sinai Peninsula, blocking the access of Israeli shipping to the Strait of Tiran, which leads from the Red Sea to the Gulf of Aqaba and then to Elat.

Israel considered the Egyptian move to be an act of war, but —under pressure from the Johnson administration not to attack—the Eshkol government wavered. The prime minister, confronted by a public that wanted to initiate war with the Arabs, was viciously criticized for his indecisiveness and lack of military experience. To maintain political control—intelli-

---

* Braderman, now retired and living in Washington, recalled the 1967 visit to Israel and said it was "possible that I'd said something like that" to Bill Dale. He added that Dale's recollection certainly reflected his general view of the issue of Jewish loyalty.

gence reports reached the White House of military coup plotting—Eshkol was forced in late May to turn to his political enemies, including Moshe Dayan and Menachem Begin, and form a government of national unity. For Begin, now a minister without portfolio, the appointment meant that he was serving in the Israeli government for the first time in his political career. Dayan's nomination as defense minister had to be much more difficult for Eshkol; it amounted, in essence, to an acknowledgment that he was unable to lead the nation in wartime. Dayan, with his romantic image, was as admired among the population as the hesitating Eshkol was not. Dayan came to the defense portfolio with enormous political strength, raising the possibility that the hard-line pro-nuclear Rafi Party of David Ben-Gurion would once again be dominant in Israeli military affairs.

The army, led by Chief of Staff Yitzhak Rabin, was ready. Israel struck first on June 5 and achieved its stunning victory in six days, humiliating the Soviet-supplied Arabs and seizing Egypt's Sinai Peninsula, the Gaza Strip, Jordan's West Bank, and Syria's Golan Heights, and, most stirring of all, fulfilling a two-thousand-year-old dream by bringing the Old City of Jerusalem under Jewish control. But Israel suddenly found itself in control of one million more Palestinians.

Wally Barbour spent much of the war in the Israeli war room, and he shared the jubilation throughout the nation—and in much of America—over the stunning Israeli victory. There was no pretense of objectivity in his reporting to Washington; his views and those of the Israeli leadership were identical. For example, Barbour urged that Washington downplay the Israeli Air Force's rocket and strafing attack on the USS *Liberty*, a naval intelligence ship, on the third day of the war. The *Liberty*, flying the American flag, had been monitoring Middle East communications traffic in international waters off the coast of Israel and had been identified as an American ship before the attack, which resulted in a death toll of thirty-four with 171 men wounded. The incident triggered resentment throughout the United States government. Barbour, however, was anything but angered. A declassified cable on file in the LBJ Library shows that hours after the incident he reported that Israel did not intend to admit to the incident and added: "Urge strongly that we too avoid publicity. [*Liberty*'s] proximity to scene could feed Arab suspicions of U.S.–Israel collusion. . . . Israelis obviously shocked by error and tender sincere apologies."*

At war's end, Bill Dale was summoned by Barbour and told of a change in policy regarding the collection of intelligence about Dimona. Dale was to inform the embassy's military attachés, Barbour said, that they were no longer to report on Dimona and no longer to undercut the Israelis by conducting operations with their British or Canadian counterparts. "Israel is going to be our main ally," Barbour told Dale, "and we can't dilute it by working with others." There was a second message, Dale recalled: "Barbour said, 'Arab oil is not as important as Israel is to us. Therefore, I'm going to side with Israel in all of my reporting.' And maybe he was right," added Dale. "From that time on, it was a different Wally Barbour."**

Dale objected to the policy change, "and our relationship soured." Barbour subsequently attempted to amend a favorable fitness report he had turned in on Dale's behalf; Dale remains convinced that his disagreement over Dimona set back his career (he was named ambassador to the Central African Republic in 1973 and retired from the Foreign Service in 1975). Dale did, however, file one more embassy intelligence report on Dimona. In the fall of 1967, Henry A. Kissinger, then a Harvard University professor and a consultant on Vietnam to the Johnson administration, showed up in Tel Aviv to teach for a week at the Israeli Defense College. At the end of the course,

* The Johnson Library documents also show that Clark Clifford, a key presidential adviser and later secretary of defense, complained about the government's initially tepid response at a National Security Council meeting the next day: "My concern is that we're not tough enough. Handle as if Arabs or USSR had done it." It was "inconceivable," Clifford added, according to the NSC notes, that Israel destroyed the *Liberty* by error, as it claimed.
** It was a different CIA, too. A former senior intelligence officer recalled that "a big change took place" inside the Agency after the Six-Day War. "All of a sudden a lot of people were saying the Israelis were wonderful," the former official added. "Israeli intelligence became untouchable, and the professional suspicion you should have about another intelligence service—even a friendly one—disappeared." This became especially true in the Nixon administration; Nixon and Henry A. Kissinger, his national security adviser, became renowned inside the CIA for preferring Mossad's intelligence assessments on the Middle East to those supplied by the Agency.

Kissinger went to Dale's office in the embassy and announced
that he needed to send an urgent, top-secret message to the
White House. "He wrote it in longhand," Dale recalled, "and
gave it to me to send." It was a warning about Dimona, and
Dale vividly recalled its conclusion: "As a result of my course
here, I am convinced Israel is making nuclear warheads." Dale
also vividly recalled a Kissinger warning to him: " 'I'll have
your ass if this gets out.' Those were my first words from Kissinger."

After leaving Israel, Dale gave a series of perfunctory end-of-
the-tour debriefings in Washington to W. Walt Rostow, Johnson's national security adviser, and other senior government
officials; not surprisingly, he said, "Nobody asked me about the
Israeli bomb." In his next post, with the State Department's
Policy Planning Council, he again tried to raise questions about
Dimona, with similar results. One of his early assignments on
the council, the State Department's in-house think tank, was to
do a paper on nonproliferation. He wanted to include a chapter
on Dimona, but was refused permission to discuss that issue
with members of Congress or members of the Atomic Energy
Commission. When he protested, said Dale, a senior State Department official, declaring that the Israeli bomb "was the most
sensitive foreign policy issue in the United States," threatened
to discuss his conduct with the secretary of state. His final paper, Dale said, did not mention Dimona.

With Barbour staying on and on, the Israeli bomb disappeared
after 1967 as a significant issue in the American embassy.
Dimona became a nonplace and the Israeli bomb a nonbomb.
Sometime that year the Israelis invited Arnold Kramish, an
American expert on nuclear fuel cycles, to visit the reactor. "I
made a mistake," recalled Kramish, who was then visiting
Israel as a fellow at London's International Institute of Strategic Studies. "I paid a courtesy call on Barbour. He said I
couldn't go—it would imply U.S. recognition of Dimona."
Kramish had read about the American inspections in the *New
York Times* and raised the obvious argument: "I'm not even an
official visitor." The ambassador didn't budge, and Kramish
decided not to challenge his dubious theory: "I didn't go."

Joseph O. Zurhellen, Jr., Bill Dale's replacement as deputy chief of mission, followed the ambassador's cue and was also much less interested in the subject. "Barbour was not well versed in anything technical—words such as 'reprocessing plant,' et cetera," Zurhellen explained. "Of course, he knew something screwy had gone on in Dimona. The French had pulled wool over our eyes, and so had the Israelis." But, Zurhellen added, the embassy's view was that much of the international concern about Dimona had been deliberately fostered by Israel. "A strong element of their policy is to convince others they have the bomb. It's disinformation." Anyway, he added, "the nuclear issue was not on our mind. We had a war of attrition." Zurhellen was referring to the steadily escalating air and artillery battles in the late 1960s and early 1970s between Israel and Egypt, whose army and air force had been dramatically reinforced by the Soviet Union after the Six-Day War.

After the inauguration of President Richard M. Nixon in January 1969, Barbour was even less than uninterested in Dimona—he exorcised the issue. A senior American intelligence officer recalled summoning a group of staff aides to provide Barbour, then in Washington, with a special briefing on the Israeli nuclear weapons program. "Barbour listened to it all," said the intelligence official, "and then said, 'Gentlemen, I don't believe a word of it.' " The official was astonished: he had given the same briefing in Israel to Barbour without challenge a few months before. He privately took Barbour aside. "Mr. Ambassador," he recalled saying, "you know it's true." Barbour replied: "If I acknowledge this, then I have to go to the President. And if he admitted it, he'd have to do something about it. The President didn't send me there to give him problems. He does not want to be told any bad news."

Barbour had many good reasons for not wanting to tell President Nixon bad news. His emphysema was getting worse. He was increasingly phobic about death, Zurhellen said, and kept an oxygen tent near his bed. The ambassador also continued his easygoing work habits; Zurhellen recalled only two occasions in their five years together when Barbour stayed at the embassy after his usual noon departure time.

The overweight ambassador had a huge scare early in the

Nixon presidency upon being informed that he had been selected to serve in the Foreign Service's most prestigious ambas-
sadorial post—in Moscow. The appointment, as were all such
assignments, was contingent upon medical approval, but, said
Zurhellen, Barbour hadn't had a State Department physical in
years, and knew he'd never pass one. "We'd finessed it by having a local Israeli physician write a note every two years saying, 'You're capable of carrying out your mission.' I drafted the
answer, thanking State for its confidence, but saying that 'in
seven years here I have carved out a unique situation.' " Barbour was allowed to stay on the job.

In 1970, Barbour made one of his rare public appearances,
sharing a podium with Prime Minister Golda Meir at the opening of an American school in Tel Aviv. The ambassador congratulated Meir for attending and said, "I wish I knew how to
influence the premier to do what I ask her to do." She replied:
"I will now reveal the secret to you—you must only ask me to
do what I want to do."

When it came to Dimona, Barbour did what Israel wanted—
without asking. His support for Israel was profound and heartfelt; nonetheless, many of his former colleagues in the Foreign
Service were confounded and distressed when on April 3, 1974,
a year after retirement, he agreed to become a board member of
the American branch of Bank Leumi, the Israeli state bank.
There was nothing illegal in doing so, but many State Department officials consider such appointments to pose an obvious
conflict of interest. Barbour, characteristically, couldn't have
cared less about what his peers thought, and he remained on
the board until his death.

13

An Israeli Decision

In early December 1967, Yigal Allon, the 1948 war hero and advocate of West Bank resettlement, was given a private look at Israel's nuclear future. It moved him to tears. He and a group of aides had been invited to inspect the early work on Israel's first nuclear missile field, under construction at an obscure site known on the map as Hirbat Zachariah, in the foothills of the Judean Mountains west of Jerusalem. The expertly concealed shelters, not identified for years by the American intelligence community, were to be burrowed into the ground at the end of an unmarked road lined with closed-circuit cameras.

The shelters represented the best of Israeli technology and ingenuity. They were being built by Tahal, the government-owned water planning corporation, which was then negotiating with the shah of Iran to build a forty-two-inch oil pipeline to relay Iranian crude to the Israeli port cities of Elat and Ashdod. The smooth barrels through which the missiles would be launched had been imported into the country marked as lengths of pipeline.* Israel was many years away from anything amounting to a nuclear missile capability—the first field test of the Jericho I had been held, with mixed results, only a few months before. The missile, jointly being developed with France's Dassault Company, had guidance problems: it wasn't yet capable of going where it was aimed.

Nonetheless, those first shelters represented, as Allon clearly understood, a new kind of military security for the nation. "Al-

---

* A Tahal representative was appointed in 1966 by Prime Minister Eshkol to the expanded and revamped Israeli Atomic Energy Commission, to serve on the new power and water subcommittee. Missile tubing also may have been shipped to Israel described as water mains.

lon got all excited," one Israeli observer recalled. "Here's a
man who had fought in 1948 with only a British submachine
gun, and now—twenty years later—here is Israel building nuclear missiles. We're a people," added the observer, "who have
come back from the dead. In one generation we have become
the warriors—the Sparta of our time."

Allon couldn't resist boasting about what he had seen. A few
days later, he stunned his cabinet colleagues by warning Egypt
in a public speech at Haifa that Israel would reply in kind to
any Egyptian attack on a population center using advanced
weapons. "Every weapon Egypt can produce or purchase with
the aid of a great power," he said, "we can match, sometimes
with and sometimes without the aid of a big power." As a
member of the prime minister's select committee on national
security issues, Allon had great credibility. But no Israeli official had ever publicly acknowledged the existence of a nuclear
missile system, and Allon's cryptic assertions were privately
attacked by other government officials as a breach of security
and publicly criticized in the press for creating a panic.

Israel's missile program, code-named Project 700, had been envisioned years earlier by Ernst David Bergmann as the final,
costly step toward the Samson Option. One former Israeli government official recalled seeing figures indicating that the overall long-range price of Project 700, if fully authorized by the
prime minister's national security committee, would be $850
million—more than was budgeted for all Israeli defense expenditures in 1967. The staggering price of the missiles was more
than matched by other elements of the nuclear system, and the
overall cost of the nuclear program continued to be the major
barrier to the bomb and the biggest hurdle for the official who
emerged in the late 1960s with responsibility for Israel's nuclear
future, Defense Minister Moshe Dayan.

Allon's visit to Zachariah had had a strategic purpose: he was
being proselytized by Dayan, who, with his black eye patch
and flair for the dramatic, had emerged from the Six-Day War
as an international hero. The war's aftermath also gave Dayan
and his pro-nuclear colleagues a renewed opportunity to publicly condemn the major target of their prospective bombs—the

Soviet Union. Dayan was among the first in the Eshkol cabinet to predict that the Soviets, searching for any foothold they could get in their ideological struggle with the United States, would fill the power vacuum in the Middle East and become the major threat to Israel. In early July, Dayan warned in an interview with the *Frankfurter Allgemeine* newspaper of West Germany that if the Soviets chose to unite with the Arabs against Israel, he would not "hesitate an instant to advise his government to fight and defeat the Russians just like the Arabs. . . . Israel need be intimidated by no one."

Dayan was articulating the sense of isolation that had worked its way into the top levels of the Israeli leadership, in a way not felt since the 1956 Suez Crisis. Charles de Gaulle had responded to the war by accusing Israel of being the aggressor and canceling all of France's arms sales to Israel, abrogating twelve years of close French support for Israel. De Gaulle also delayed the pending shipment of fifty previously purchased Mirage III jet fighters. He even claimed to newsmen that he had not known of Dassault's contract with Israel until the first field test in 1967 of the Jericho I (although the French firm would continue to work with Israelis on the missile program for another year).

The Soviets and their satellites in the Eastern bloc, with the exception of Romania, had gone further: all diplomatic relations with Israel were severed. The Soviets also immediately began rearming their Arab clients. President Nikolai V. Podgorny made a triumphant state visit to Cairo in late June and was greeted by hundreds of thousands of cheering Egyptians. Planeloads of Soviet arms began arriving shortly thereafter, initiating an extensive and rapid buildup of the depleted Egyptian war stores, all of which would be renewed within a year. Moscow eventually sent Soviet advisers and high-performance MiG fighters to Egypt; in return, the Russians were granted preferential treatment at four Mediterranean harbors as well as virtual control of seven Egyptian air bases. The Soviets were similarly generous in their support for Syria and Iraq, the other losers (along with Jordan) in the Six-Day War.

Israeli intelligence intercepted high-level communications between Cairo, Damascus, and Moscow that were replete with boastful talk about the next war in the Middle East, and little discussion of the last one. The Soviet fleet was suddenly being deployed in greater force in the Mediterranean, with two or three ships—obviously attempting to intercept Israeli communications—parked off the Israeli coast. There was no response to these provocations, as seen by the Israelis, from the world's other great superpower, the United States.

In late August 1967, the Arab nations, buoyed by the Soviet support and guided by Soviet advice, gathered for the first postwar summit at Khartoum and agreed on what became known as the "three no's"—no peace, no negotiations, and no recognition.

Dayan's drive for the bomb was heightened by his conviction that Israel could not depend on America to deter a Soviet attack. In 1966, he had spent time as a journalist in South Vietnam and come away "very much worried," as he later told NSC adviser Walt Rostow, about "the steadiness of the United States in honoring its commitments." In a crisis, Israel either would or would not—as in Suez—be supported by Washington, depending on the White House's assessment of its international and regional interests. Dayan believed Moscow similarly would be willing to come to the aid of the Arabs not because of a deep concern for the Middle East, but to protect its prestige and international interests. Whatever their motives, Dayan was convinced that the superpowers would dictate events in the Middle East unless Israel took steps to arm itself fully. Israel's survival, in Dayan's view, was now dependent on its ability to mass-produce nuclear weapons and target them at the Soviet Union—just as the French goal was to target its *force de frappe* at Moscow.

Dayan's mission in late 1967 and early 1968 was to convince his fellow cabinet members that if the Soviets could be persuaded that the Israeli threat was credible, they might decide that there was no Middle East war worth fighting. A credible Israeli bomb also would deter the Soviets from taking any steps in the Middle East that would jeopardize Israel's survival—such as agreeing to supply an Arab nation with a nuclear weapon. In Dayan's scenario, Israeli intelligence agents would secretly inform their Soviet counterparts as soon as Dimona's assembly line went into full production. And when Israel developed its first bomb in a suitcase, Moscow also would be told —and reminded that there was no way to stop Mossad from smuggling a nuclear weapon across the border by automobile or into a Soviet port by boat. As for the rest of the world, including the United States, there would still be studied ambiguity on the question of whether Israel had the bomb. The argument for an Israeli "bomb in the basement" was born.

Dayan got a boost in his lobbying sometime in the last few months of 1967 when the Israelis learned from American intelligence that the Soviet Union had added four major Israeli cities —Tel Aviv, Haifa, Beersheba, and Ashdod—to its nuclear targeting list. This most sensitive information was apparently obtained unofficially, according to a former member of Prime Minister Eshkol's staff: "We got it in a nonkosher way," the Israeli explained, without amplification.*

A second boost was supplied by Henry Kissinger, then New York Governor Nelson A. Rockefeller's foreign policy adviser in the campaign for the Republican nomination. Kissinger met privately in February 1968 with a group of Israeli scholars at the Jerusalem home of Major General Elad Peled, director of Israel's Defense College, where Kissinger had taught the year before. His message, according to Shlomo Aronson, an academic who has written on Israeli nuclear policy, was electrifying: the United States would not "lift a finger for Israel" if the Soviets chose directly to intervene by, "say, a Soviet missile attack against the Israeli Air Force bases in Sinai." Aronson, who attended the meeting, quoted Kissinger as making three declarations: "The main aim of any American President is to prevent World War III. Second, that no American President would risk World War III because of territories occupied by Israel. Three, the Russians know this."

By early 1968, it was obvious that the overwhelming victory

---

* American intelligence officials subsequently told me that the United States did not obtain a physical copy of the Soviet nuclear targeting list until the early 1970s. Some human intelligence about Soviet targets did exist, however, and it was that information, known only to a few in the CIA and elsewhere, that conceivably could have been passed along to the Israelis.

in the Six-Day War had solved none of Israel's basic political and military problems in the Middle East. Yitzhak Rabin, the army chief of staff, flew to Washington in mid-December 1967 and said as much in a meeting with General Earle G. Wheeler, chairman of the Joint Chiefs of Staff. "Rabin opened the conversation by stating that Israel finds itself in the peculiar position of having won the war, but not the peace," Wheeler noted in a memorandum for the record, later declassified and put on file in the LBJ Library. "Israel was in a less favorable position now than prior to 5 June [when the war began]. The Soviets do not want a peaceful settlement," Rabin told Wheeler. "[T]heir objective is to maintain a climate of tension, whereby they can continue to foster an increasing Arab dependence on Soviet power and influence . . . with a view toward maintaining Soviet access to port and air terminal facilities and, ultimately, control of Arab oil."

America's Jewish community responded to the dramatic June victory with showers of money and increased visits; tourism was booming in late 1967, and so was the Israeli economy. Israel's success, as Ambassador Walworth Barbour told his doubting staff in the American embassy in Tel Aviv, had cemented its relationship to Washington. Yet for Dayan and many of his supporters at Dimona and elsewhere, America had proved its basic unreliability as an ally a month before the Six-Day War when it failed to respond to Nasser's closing of the Strait of Tiran and blockade of Elat. Israeli foreign ministry documents showed that Dwight Eisenhower had promised in writing after the Suez debacle in 1956 that the United States would use force, if necessary, to keep the strait open. Israel called on Johnson to keep that commitment after Nasser's blockade and felt betrayed upon learning that the State Department considered Eisenhower's commitment to have expired when Eisenhower left office in early 1961. Only a treaty ratified by the U.S. Senate was binding on subsequent administrations, the Israelis were told. Washington, without knowing it, was playing into the hands of Moshe Dayan and his nuclear ambitions.

. . .

But Israel was not yet a full nuclear power: no senior official had authorized the reactor and reprocessing plant to begin systematically turning out plutonium. Financial fears continued to haunt the leadership. One Israeli official recalled seeing estimates indicating that by the early 1970s a full-scale nuclear weapons program, including warheads and missiles, would be chewing up more than 10 percent of Israel's overall budget—nearly $1 billion. Pinhas Sapir, renowned among Israel's leadership as the economic boss of the newly formed Labor Party,* was a strong believer in government loans and investments to promote economic development; dollars for Dimona never made much sense to him. In his view, an Israeli bomb would only lead to conflicts with the United States and a lessened flow of American contributions.

Dayan, one Israeli official recalled, made a critical decision early in 1968. He telephoned Sapir and asked him to spend a day with him, just as he had done with Allon. The two men went to Dimona. "He showed him the whole thing, from A to Z," the Israeli said. "Nobody had seen the whole [reprocessing] facility. Sapir was like a cat with sour cream. He came back and said to Allon, who was still resisting a full nuclear commitment: 'Have you seen it all? I've seen it and you don't know shit.** There will be no more Auschwitzes.' "

Sometime early in 1968, Dimona finally was ordered into full-scale production and began turning out four or five warheads a year—there were more than twenty-five bombs in the arsenal by the Yom Kippur War in September 1973. There is no evidence that the Israeli cabinet ever made a formal decision about Dimona. Nonetheless, production of the first assembly line bomb, whether officially sanctioned or not, was quickly known to the top layer of national security officials and widely applauded. An Israeli recalled that champagne was broken out at

* In 1965, Mapai and Achdut Avodah had agreed to join forces to run as a bloc for seats in the Knesset. After the Six-Day War, the two parties merged with Rafi to create the Labor Party. The next year, Mapam decided to join forces with the unified Labor Party and stand for election on the same ticket, but did not formally join the party.

** It should be noted that there is no such expression in Hebrew as "You don't know shit." The Israeli who used that phrase in an interview was fluent in idiomatic English and, in his translation, was trying to describe the essence and import of Sapir's comment to Allon.

Dimona, and in some government offices in Tel Aviv and Jerusalem, at word that the first bomb had been assembled. It was
widely believed, the Israeli added, that the first warhead had
the following phrase welded, in Hebrew and English, onto its
exterior: NEVER AGAIN.

One former Israeli government official explained the bureaucratic procedure behind the decision to open Dimona's assembly line by saying, with a shrug and a smile, that Moshe Dayan
had unilaterally decided that he had received the support of the
key money men and had all the authority he needed—as defense minister—to turn Israel into a nuclear power. A similar
suggestion was made at the time to Dr. Max Ben, Ernst
Bergmann's American friend, by Amos Deshalit. "We were
talking about Dayan," recalled Ben, "and Amos said, 'He's the
guy who's acting on his own.' "*

With the decision finally taken, the bureaucracy closed
ranks, as Israelis always do in matters of state security. The
first necessity was the acquisition of uranium ore—lots of it.
Mossad knew that there were hundreds of tons of ore sitting in
a warehouse near Antwerp, Belgium, available for purchase in
Europe, but that option theoretically did not exist: such sales
in Europe were controlled by Euratom, the Common Market
nuclear agency, and it was inconceivable that approval would
be forthcoming for a large sale to Israel. Dimona was, after all,
under no international supervision. Even if such a sale could be
arranged, no one in Israel was willing to let the world know
that Dimona, ostensibly a twenty-four-megawatt reactor capable of consuming no more than twenty-four tons of ore in a
year, was purchasing an eight-year supply of uranium. Mossad's solution was to approach one of its agents in West Ger-

---

* In April 1976, *Time* magazine reported that shortly after the Six-Day War, Dayan
"had secretly ordered the start of construction" on a reprocessing plant. Prime Minister Eshkol then decided, said the magazine, that "they could only rubber-stamp a
project already under way." The article, despite its confusion about the reprocessing
plant, which was already finished by 1967, provided the world with its first hard information about the Israeli weapons program. The story carried no byline, apparently
because it was reported by David Halevy, who, as an Israeli citizen, was subject to
government censorship. Halevy, a former intelligence and army officer, was known for
good contacts inside the Israeli government and intelligence community; it was widely
believed inside the Israeli government, which officially denied the story, that his basic
source was Moshe Dayan.

many in March 1968 and ask him to make the purchase of the uranium—for $4 million—allegedly on behalf of an Italian chemical company in Milan. The sale was approved by Euratom in October, and the uranium was shipped out of Antwerp aboard a vessel renamed the *Scheersberg A*. The *Scheersberg A* had been purchased, with Mossad funds, by another Israeli agent-in-place in Turkey. Once at sea, according to published accounts that were confirmed by Israeli officials, the uranium ore was transferred to an Israeli freighter guarded by gunboats and taken to Israel. The disappearance of the huge shipment of uranium ore was known, of course, within months to Euratom; it wasn't much longer before U.S. and European intelligence agencies were reporting internally that the Israelis were involved. It took nine years, nonetheless, before word of the uranium hijacking reached the press, and the affair eventually became the subject of a 1978 book, *The Plumbat Affair*. Israel's response to the book and to the earlier newspaper accounts was to continue to deny that it had a nuclear capability. No one, except for a few public-interest advocates and a few reporters, seemed to care.

14

A Presidential Gift

After the Six-Day War, and despite Israeli complaints about the increased Soviet threat in the Middle East, the Johnson administration turned out once again to be a fitful ally in Israel's eyes, as the President—anxious to avoid a break with the Arab world—joined de Gaulle and embargoed all arms deliveries to Israel for 135 days. America did so, bitter Israelis noted, while the Soviets continued to resupply their allies. Johnson also publicly eschewed any firm commitment to defend Israel in a crisis. He was asked by CBS newsman Dan Rather at an end-of-the-year press conference whether the United States had "the same kind of unwavering commitment to defend Israel against invasion as we have in South Vietnam." His answer satisfied few Israelis: "We have made clear our very definite interest in Israel, and our desire to preserve peace in that area of the world by many means. But we do not have a mutual security treaty with them, as we do in Southeast Asia."

Nonetheless, Prime Minister Eshkol was eager to make a second state visit to Washington in January 1968 to plead for the sale of F-4 jet fighters to balance the Soviet introduction of MiGs into Egypt. The F-4 was the most advanced fighter in the American arsenal, and the Pentagon and State Department argued that Israel did not need such aircraft to maintain a military advantage against the Egyptians, whose MiG-21s had a much more limited range and bombing capacity. Introducing the top-of-the-line F-4s into the Middle East would be an unwarranted and unnecessary escalation; Israel would remain superior with the previously supplied A-4 Skyhawk bombers.

But Johnson, or some of his senior staff, apparently still

hadn't given up on persuading Israel to accept the Nonproliferation Treaty (NPT) and were willing to trade fifty F-4s for it.
In a pre-summit memorandum for Johnson on January 5, 1968,
Walt Rostow discussed two lists—"What We Want" and "What
We'll Give." The want list included the Rostow reminder "We
think we have an acceptable NPT. We believe this will serve
Israel's long-range security. We expect Israel to sign." The give
list included twenty-seven more Skyhawks and a promise to
"cut lead time if Israel needs Phantoms."

Rostow's suggestion that it would be possible to link the
Phantom sale to the NPT was farcical, given Israel's commitment to Dimona and the ample U.S. intelligence—much of it
supplied by Wally Barbour's embassy in Tel Aviv—about that
commitment. Many years later, in an interview, Rostow acknowledged that he had had few doubts about Israel's nuclear
goals: "If you were to ask me what I thought in the sixties, I
thought they were moving to put themselves in a position to
have a bomb. Everybody and his brother knew what Israel was
doing."

There was a similar lack of realism in the White House's
approach to the broader Middle East picture, as summarized in
Rostow's January 5 memorandum: "[W]e can't support an
Israel that sits tight. . . . The Arabs need hope of Israeli concessions—on refugees, Jerusalem, letting new refugees return
to the West Bank, avoiding permanent moves in occupied
lands." The issues would stay the same for at least the next
twenty-three years.

Rostow had to know that the Israeli military had gone on a
virtual rampage at the end of the Six-Day War in the newly
occupied areas of Jerusalem, the West Bank and Golan Heights,
ransacking and destroying Arab homes in an obvious attempt
to drive Palestinians and other Arabs off their land and into
Jordan and Syria. More than one hundred Arab homes were
demolished in the Old City of Jerusalem on the first night after
the war by Israeli troops, operating under floodlights with bulldozers. Teddy Kollek, Jerusalem's mayor, explained in a 1978
memoir why such speed was necessary: "My overpowering
feeling was: do it now; it may be impossible to do it later, and it
must be done." Bulldozers and dynamite were used with espe-

cial ferocity throughout the West Bank; the village of Qalqiliya, west of Nablus, had 850 of its 2,000 homes destroyed during three days of Israel occupation. Moshe Dayan later accused the Israeli soldiers of taking "punitive" action in the village and ordered cement and other goods to be provided to the villagers for rebuilding.

There was a brief period after the war in which many senior Israelis, among them Dayan and David Ben-Gurion, openly questioned the wisdom of holding on to the occupied lands.* They saw the war as offering Israel a chance to trade land for lasting peace; Jews, Ben-Gurion often said to his followers, made lousy rulers. "Sinai? . . . Gaza? The West Bank? Let them all go," Ben-Gurion told an American reporter. "Peace is more important than real estate. We do not need territories." Levi Eshkol expressed his own doubts to the visiting Abe Feinberg a few weeks after the war, saying in Yiddish, "What am I going to do with a million Arabs? They fuck like rabbits."

Competing against those practical concerns were the religious and philosophical views of many Revisionist Zionists who believed, along with Menachem Begin and his mentor, the late Vladimir Jabotinsky, that Israel's expansion into the West Bank was not an issue of politics, but a historical necessity; the West Bank was the birthplace of the Jewish people, and the area, part of Eretz Israel, had not been occupied during the war

---

* James Critchfield, a longtime CIA official who was chief of the Near East Division in 1967, recalled that Dayan and Zvi Zamir, then head of Mossad, joined forces with him and James Angleton at the end of the Six-Day War in a brief and ill-fated attempt to stop the abuse in the West Bank and elsewhere. The goal, said Critchfield, was to reach a quick accord on trading land for peace before the Israelis began settling the occupied territories. Dayan and Zamir were convinced that such a step would be "a disastrous development," said Critchfield. "We had to reverse it immediately, or it'd be a *fait accompli.*" The goal was to start negotiations with Jordan's King Hussein, who had entered the war reluctantly and late, and was eager to negotiate an end to Israeli attacks on his country and his palace. "We started talking and we were making progress," said Critchfield. "I'd kept Mac Bundy [who had returned briefly to the White House as Johnson's special national security assistant for the Middle East] informed and he'd approved it. Twelve days after the end of the war, I thought we ought to remind Mac that we were doing it." A White House meeting was arranged with Bundy and Nicholas D. Katzenbach, then the under secretary of state. "We were told to knock it off," Critchfield said. "They thought it was not well prepared. Angleton argued that if we do not act now with Dayan's and Zamir's support, there will be settlements in the West Bank. As we walked out, Mac said to me, 'I'd forgotten how passionable Angleton could be. We were at Yale together.' " Katzenbach subsequently said he had no recollection of the meeting. Critchfield, who retired from the Agency in 1974, wasn't surprised at the loss of memory: "They made a dumb act, and wanted to forget it."

but "liberated." The Revisionists' position emerged as the government's policy over the years. The Israeli intransigence over return of the territories, coupled with the rearmed Arabs' desire for revenge, doomed United Nations Resolution 242, which called for Israeli withdrawal from the occupied territories in return for Arab commitments of territorial integrity and peace. It had been unanimously approved by the United Nations Security Council in late November 1967.

Things couldn't have gone worse, from the Israeli point of view, at the Johnson-Eshkol summit meeting in early 1968 at the President's ranch in Texas. Eshkol and his advisers, including Ephraim (Effy) Evron, the Israeli ambassador to Washington, who was a Johnson favorite, had sat through a day of briefings at which a series of Senate and Defense Department officials argued against selling F-4s to Israel. "Johnson was stiffing them on the Nonproliferation Treaty," recalled Harry C. McPherson, one of the President's advisers. "Finally he gets up and said, 'Let's all go piss.' So we all go into a huge bathroom and piss. As Johnson's leaving he sees Effy looking hangdog. 'What's the matter, Effy?' Effy said, 'We're not going to get our F-4s.' 'Oh goddam, Effy,' Johnson said, 'you're going to get the F-4s. But I'm going to get something out of Eshkol. But don't tell him.' "

McPherson and Evron thought that Johnson's comment amounted to a commitment, but what Johnson wanted to get, Israel could not give. One of Dayan's followers recalled the despair over the seemingly relentless American pressure for IAEA inspections: "We realized we were out there alone."

Dayan's men were too pessimistic. Israel had the best friend it could have—the President. Within weeks of the summit meeting with Eshkol, Johnson was presented with a CIA estimate concluding—for the first time—that Israel had manufactured at least four nuclear warheads. He ordered CIA Director Richard M. Helms to bury the report, and Helms obeyed the order, as he always did.

The CIA estimate was not a result of any intelligence breakthrough, explained Carl Duckett, who, by 1968, had become the Agency's assistant director for science and technology, but arose out of a dinner he had with Edward Teller, the eminent nuclear physicist who had devoted much of his life to weapons building. Duckett had briefed Teller in the past and, as he acknowledged, stood in awe of him. Teller had arranged for the private dinner to deliver a pointed message, Duckett recalled: "He was convinced that Israel now had several weapons ready to go." Teller explained that he had just returned from Israel— he had a sister living in Tel Aviv and was a frequent visitor there—where he had many contacts in the Israeli scientific and defense community. "He'd talked to a lot of his old friends," Duckett said, "and he was concerned." Teller was careful to say that he had no specific information about Israeli nuclear weapons. But it was his understanding, Teller told Duckett, that the Agency was waiting for an Israeli test before making any final assessment about Israeli nuclear capability. If so, the CIA was making a mistake. "The Israelis have it and they aren't going to test it," Duckett recalled Teller explaining. "They might be wrong by a few kilotons [on the yield of an untested bomb], but so what?"

Duckett was as impressed as Teller wanted him to be: "It was the most single convincing piece of evidence I got the whole time I was in the CIA."* He reported the conversation to Helms the next morning: "I can tell you that everybody was very concerned." The Office of Science and Technology had just distributed a top-secret estimate on nonproliferation, and Duckett decided that an update, known inside the intelligence community as a "Memo to Holders," would be dispatched. "It was very brief," Duckett recalled. "The conclusion was that they [the Israelis] had nuclear weapons."

Another factor in that conclusion was the widespread belief inside the Agency that the Israelis were somehow behind the reported disappearance of some two hundred pounds of weapons-grade uranium from the Nuclear Materials and Equipment Corporation (NUMEC), a privately owned nuclear enriching

---

* Duckett acknowledged that his faith in Teller was shaken more than a little, however, a few years later when Teller arranged another meeting to confide that he was convinced that the Soviet Union would conduct a first strike with thermonuclear weapons across the United States on July 4, 1976—the two hundredth anniversary of American independence.

plant in Apollo, Pennsylvania. The company's owner, Zalman Mordecai Shapiro, a devout Jew with close ties to Israel, insisted that the uranium loss—first reported by Shapiro in 1965 —was routine, an inevitable by-product of the difficult task of enrichment. Duckett and many others in the intelligence community thought otherwise. Duckett acknowledged that he had no evidence that Shapiro's uranium had been diverted to Israel, but "made an assumption" that it had while preparing the updated Israeli estimate. "Assuming a crude device, Israel could have made four weapons with the Shapiro material," Duckett said, and the initial draft of the Memo to Holders revealed that there was new evidence suggesting that Israel had three to four nuclear weapons.

Without the Teller report and the suspicions about Shapiro, Duckett acknowledged, the CIA didn't have much to go on. The Agency had been unable to determine whether Israel had built, as suspected, an underground chemical reprocessing plant at Dimona. The Agency also had not been able to penetrate any of the military commands or intelligence services of Israel. And no Israeli had defected to the United States with nuclear information. The National Security Agency and its electronic eavesdropping also had not been much help, Duckett said, although it had provided early evidence suggesting that some Israeli Air Force pilots had practiced bomb runs in a manner that made sense only if nuclear weapons were to be dropped.

Thin as its evidence was, Duckett was now willing to state in a top-secret written report that Israel was a nuclear power. The revised estimate was more than a little bit sensitive, Duckett knew, and he cleared it first with Dick Helms. The CIA director told Duckett not to publish the estimate in any form and also declared that he himself would be the messenger with bad tidings. Helms walked the Duckett information into the Oval Office and gave it to the President. Johnson exploded, as Helms later recounted to Duckett, and demanded that the document be buried: "Don't tell anyone else, even [Secretary of State] Dean Rusk and [Defense Secretary] Robert McNamara." Helms did as he was told, but not without trepidation: "Helms knew that he would get in trouble with Rusk and McNamara if they learned that he had withheld it."*

Johnson's purpose in chasing Helms—and his intelligence— away was clear: he did not want to know what the CIA was trying to tell him, for once he accepted that information, he would have to act on it. By 1968, the President had no intention of doing anything to stop the Israeli bomb, as Helms, Duckett, Walworth Barbour, William Dale, and a very few others in the U.S. government came to understand.

Moshe Dayan's unilateral action to push Dimona into full-scale production carried what should have been a huge risk—a nu- clear-armed Israel would find it impossible to sign the Non- proliferation Treaty, and Israel thus would not get its F-4s from the Johnson administration. The pressure from the Wash- ington bureaucracy on that issue remained intense, especially at the Pentagon, where Clark Clifford, who had replaced Rob- ert McNamara as secretary of defense at the end of January, and his senior aides were adamant. Clifford and his colleagues had no idea where their President really stood on the question of Israel and the NPT. In October 1968, one month before the presidential election, Johnson formally approved the F-4 sale in principle, but left the bargaining over delivery dates and other details to be negotiated. Paul C. Warnke, the assistant secretary of defense for international security affairs, recalled thinking there still was "an outside chance" Israel could be forced to sign the NPT in exchange for immediate delivery. "It was worth doing," he added, as a sign of a more even-handed ap- proach to the Middle East.

Warnke called in Yitzhak Rabin, newly named as Israel's am-

---

* Helms, despite his public image as a suave spymaster, was more of a bureaucrat than most newsmen and government officials in Washington could imagine. One of Helms's senior deputies recalled the occasion in the last year of the Johnson adminis- tration when an angry President ordered a twenty-four-hour halt to all CIA intelli- gence collection and reporting on Vietnam. The President's goal was to prevent a leak, and his assumption seemed to be that if he could stop the voluminous traffic to and from the CIA, he would do just that. Of course, shutting off the communications link had its obvious perils, and the senior CIA staff were sure that Helms would ignore, or override, the irrational presidential order. Not so. Although he most certainly knew better, Helms followed orders and stopped the traffic. "You don't question what a President can do," the CIA director told his dispirited aides.

bassador to Washington, and began asking some tough questions about the bomb—direct questions that, obviously, had
never before been posed to him by a high-level American official. "I was trying to find out what they had," recalled Warnke,
"and then stop it." The discomfited Rabin asked Warnke for a
definition of a nuclear weapon: "I said," added Warnke, " 'It's if
you've got a delivery device in one room and the nuclear warhead in another room.' " The ambassador then asked: "Do you
have a nuclear weapon unless you say you do?" A Warnke aide,
Harry H. Schwartz, also was at the meeting and recalled an
even tougher Warnke remark. "Mr. Ambassador," Schwartz
quoted Warnke as saying, "we are shocked at the manner in
which you are dealing with us. . . . You, our close ally, are
building nuclear bombs in Israel behind our back." Rabin denied it, said Schwartz.

The ambassador, of course, was enraged by the encounter,
which he subsequently claimed had nothing to do with nuclear
weapons. In his memoirs, published in 1979, Rabin depicted the
basic issue as Warnke's insistence that the United States, as a
condition of the F-4 sale, be permitted to have on-site supervision of every Israeli arms manufacturing plant and every defense installation engaged in research and development. "To
say I was appalled would be a gross understatement," Rabin
wrote. "I sat there stupefied, feeling the blood rising to my
face." He left the meeting, he added, and began passing "broad
hints" to Israel's supporters in Congress and elsewhere to generate support for the F-4 sale.

Rabin did more than just pass hints. He and Major General
Mordecai Hod, the Israeli Air Force's chief of staff, went to see
one of the few Americans who could get the President to
change his mind—Abe Feinberg. "They were agitated," Feinberg recalled. "Needed to see me right away. 'Everything
you've done about the Phantoms is going down the drain. Clifford is insisting on the NPT.' " Feinberg had met privately a
few weeks earlier with Johnson and Walter Rostow and heard
the President declare that there would be "no conditions" to
the F-4 sale. "So I picked up the telephone," he said, "called the
White House, and asked for Rostow." The national security
adviser was having dinner at Clifford's house, and Feinberg,

who was well known to the White House switchboard opera-
tors, was patched through. "Walt gets on the telephone," continued Feinberg, "and I say, 'Walt, you and I and the President
were together and Johnson said no conditions.' Walt agrees. I
say, 'When you get back to the table, tell that to Clifford.' "

Clifford, who did not recount the incident in his 1991 memoir, *Counsel to the President,* telephoned the President and got the
message. Paul Warnke arrived at a later meeting of his staff, all
of whom favored tying the F-4 sale to Israeli acceptance of the
NPT, and dramatically drew his hand across his neck. The
NPT was out. Harry Schwartz recalled Warnke's account of
the Clifford-Johnson dialogue: "Clifford called Johnson and
LBJ said, 'Sell them anything they want.'

" 'Mr. President, I don't want to live in a world where the
Israelis have nuclear weapons.'

" 'Don't bother me with this anymore.' And he hangs up."
Johnson had given essentially that same message at the beginning of the year to Dick Helms'.

In his memoirs, President Johnson recounted with pride the
formal White House ceremony in which the United States,
the Soviet Union, and more than fifty other nations signed the
NPT. The treaty, he wrote, was "the most difficult and most
important . . . of all the agreements reached with Moscow"
during his presidency. Why, then, did he make it possible for
Israel to flout the NPT and keep its F-4s? Johnson's decision
had nothing to do with domestic politics or the heavy lobbying
on the issue from Israel's supporters in the Congress: his
abrupt conversation with Clark Clifford took place after Nixon
had won the 1968 Presidential elections. There's also no evidence that Johnson felt he was in debt to the Israeli government for its support of his policies in Vietnam; American Jews,
despite that support, were overwhelmingly hostile to the war.
"A bunch of rabbis came here one day in 1967 to tell me that I
ought not to send a single screwdriver to Vietnam," the President complained to Israeli Foreign Minister Abba Eban in late
1968, "but on the other hand, [the U.S.] should push all our
aircraft carriers through the Strait of Tiran to help Israel."
There is no ready explanation for Johnson's refusal to deal

with the Israeli nuclear bomb. His decision not to stop the F-4 sale had given Israel, as Johnson had to know, a high-performance aircraft capable of carrying a nuclear weapon on a one-way mission to Moscow. It was, perhaps, nothing more than his farewell gift to the Israeli people and his way of repaying the loyalty of Abe Feinberg.

There is no question that Feinberg enjoyed the greatest presidential access and influence in his twenty years as a Jewish fund-raiser and lobbyist with Lyndon Johnson. Documents at the Johnson Library show that even the most senior members of the National Security Council understood that any issue raised by Feinberg had to be answered. In late October 1968, for example, Rostow was given a memorandum by a White House aide about Israeli press coverage of the "NPT-Phantom problem . . . just to give you a factual basis for your continued dealings with Feinberg. . . ." By 1968, the government of Israel had rewarded Feinberg for his services by permitting him to become the major owner of the nation's Coca-Cola franchise. It would quickly become a multimillion-dollar profit center.*

Feinberg's role as a fund-raiser was nonpareil in the Johnson White House: his cash was, on occasion, supplied directly to Walter W. Jenkins, the President's most trusted personal aide, and his fellow political operatives in the White House—and not to the Democratic Party. There were others in the Jewish political establishment, men such as Arthur B. Krim, the New York attorney and president of United Artists, who raised large amounts of money specifically for the Democratic Party. Feinberg's status was different, recalled Myer Feldman, Johnson's aide for Jewish affairs: "Abe only raised cash—where it went only he knows."

Feinberg acknowledged that he had a special cache: "A lot of people were afraid publicly to give as much as they could, so

---

* Israel had rewarded other financial supporters with similarly lucrative business deals. In 1959, for example, Tricontinenal Pipelines, Ltd., an international investment group controlled by Baron Edmund de Rothschild, was given the concession to operate a sixteen-inch oil pipeline between Elat and Haifa, via Ashdod. The contract, signed by then Finance Minister Levi Eshkol on behalf of Israel, committed the state to ship at least 1.5 million tons of oil through the pipeline for the next fifteen years. Edmund de Rothschild was, according to Abe Feinberg, another major contributor to Dimona's start-up costs.

they arranged sub rosa cash payments. It had to be done laboriously—man-to-man. Raising money is a very humiliating process," he added. "People you don't respect piss all over you." Feinberg's special status became clear to some in the White House after the press revealed on October 14, 1964, that Walter Jenkins had been arrested a week earlier in the bathroom of a Washington YMCA on homosexual solicitation charges. The arrest took place three weeks before the 1964 presidential election. Johnson, in New York when word of the arrest—which he had attempted to suppress—became public, insisted that he and others in the White House distance themselves from the potentially scandalous incident. There was one immediate problem: at least $250,000 in cash that had been raised by Feinberg was in Jenkins's safe and needed to be removed. Johnson telephoned Feldman and ordered him and Bill Moyers, another trusted aide and sometime speechwriter, to clean out Jenkins's safe. Feldman was not surprised by the assignment: "Jenkins is the only person who knew everything that was going on. He took shorthand notes—reams of notes—ever since Johnson came into the Congress." Feldman also knew that Jenkins was especially trusted on national security issues. What he and Moyers did not know was that they would find the Feinberg money. "Bill said, 'What do we do with this?' I said, 'I don't know. You handle it.' " The cash was in a briefcase.

Moyers, asked about the incident in early 1991, said his memory was vague, but acknowledged that "circumstances did lead me to believe" that Jenkins had a private cache of money in his safe. "I think there was a private fund. There was a lot of cash washed around in Washington in those days." Asked specifically whether the cash was meant for the Democratic campaign, Moyers said, "I don't know and I don't know what happened to it. Anybody who smelled of money was always routed to Walter. He was the contact man for the contributors and he took his secrets to the grave with him."

Moyers, now a prominent television personality, recalled the time in the Johnson White House when "a guy from North Carolina came to see me. He'd been routed from Walter—who wasn't in—to me. He had a leather satchel and left it in my office. I ran out and told my secretary to find him." The man was grabbed just as he was leaving the West Entrance, but refused to take back the briefcase. "He said," Moyers recounted, " 'Oh no, I left it for Jenkins and Moyers.' I told her to take it to Mildred [Walter Jenkins's secretary]."

President Johnson, Moyers added, "was an equal opportunity taker. He'd take from friends and adversaries just because he thought that's the way the system worked. No decisions were made on the basis of cash," Moyers added, "but cash did give you access." Asked about Feinberg, Moyers said, "I always thought Abe Feinberg had a lot of impact on Johnson; he had a big role to play."

Harry Schwartz, Paul Warnke's deputy, who died in early 1991, had a special reason to be frustrated by the Johnson administration's inability to get Israel to sign the NPT. He had been stunned a year earlier when a group of Israeli military attachés had come into his Pentagon office and asked for a Low Altitude Bombing System (LABS) for nuclear weapons. The computerized bombing system provided time for an aircraft to drop its weapons and roll away to avoid the blast effects. "I just laughed at them," recalled Schwartz. The Israelis cited the buildup of the Egyptian Army across the Sinai Canal and insisted that the LABS was needed only to "lob" high-explosive bombs onto the Egyptian emplacements. "I told them," said Schwartz, "that any American who sells you a bombsight for that purpose is crazy, and I'm not crazy."

There was a friendly private lunch early in the Nixon administration with Ambassador Rabin, well after Israel began receiving the F-4s. Schwartz decided to bring up the Israeli bomb, which Israel was still publicly insisting was only an option: "I think what you should do is what you're doing now. Don't ever haul one out, because your little government will disappear. The Soviets almost assuredly have your country targeted."

"Mr. Schwartz," calmly replied Rabin after a moment, "do you think we are crazy?"

15

The Tunnel

Israelis have done their best work from below.

The huge underground laboratories at Dimona had their precedent in the Jewish struggle after World War II against the British mandatory power in Palestine. The British authorities had angered David Ben-Gurion and his followers by insisting that they adhere to the strict limits on Jewish immigration to Palestine that were set in 1939, after three years of Arab revolts. The British ruling had meant then that hundreds of thousands of Eastern European Jews were unable to escape the Holocaust. And now those who had somehow managed to survive were again being denied a chance to come legally to Palestine. Many were faced with a desperate dilemma: either return to what was left of their prewar homes and prewar life or remain in the dispirited and overcrowded displaced persons (DP) camps scattered across Europe.

The heavily outnumbered and outgunned members of the Hagannah, the Jewish underground, began the inevitable guerrilla war against the British troops with little other than their guile and determination. One of the war's most imaginative operations involved what seemed to be yet another farming kibbutz that was set up in 1946 about fifteen miles outside Tel Aviv, adjacent to a large British military base. The kibbutz's administrative building was constructed, seemingly at random, within a half mile of the base.

"The whole thing was a fraud," recalled Abe Feinberg, who had been recruited by Ben-Gurion the year before to help raise money for that and other guerrilla operations. The function of the kibbutz was not farming, but to provide cover for an elaborate and secret underground plant that was turning out bullets for the Sten submachine gun, the basic weapon of the Hagannah. Metal for the bullets had been shipped into Israel disguised as lipstick tubes, and it cleared British customs without challenge.

The underground facility had been "scooped out," said Feinberg, in twenty-seven days. The men and women who worked underground alternated that work with farming; those who completed a shift in the arms factory were ordered to muddy their shoes and sit under sunlamps so they could appear to the British and others as if they had been innocently tending crops or looking after the kibbutz's cows and sheep. Over the next two years, British soldiers and officers were constant—and unsuspecting—customers of the kibbutz's bakery and laundry, which cheerfully offered their services to the military. Feinberg recalled that a few of the British soldiers even made a point of coming to the kibbutz's Friday-night Shabbat dinners. Today the underground bullet factory is known as the Ayalon Museum, a popular attraction for Israeli schoolchildren.

Located a few hundred feet from the reactor, Dimona's chemical reprocessing plant looked, on the surface, very much like an ordinary administration building—a nondescript two-story windowless facility, eighty by two hundred feet, containing a workers' canteen and shower rooms, a few offices, some warehouse space, and an air filtration plant. The building had thickly reinforced walls, not an unusual safety feature, given its location. Once inside, there was no hint of what had been dug out below, apparently to the same dimensions, to a depth of eighty feet: a six-level highly automated chemical reprocessing plant. A bank of elevators on the top floor was routinely bricked over before foreign visitors, such as the American inspection teams headed by Floyd Culler, were permitted to enter the building. (Culler noted in his official reports during the 1960s that his team had seen evidence of freshly plastered and painted walls inside Dimona.) No outsider is ever known to have entered the reprocessing plant, whose long-suspected existence was not established until 1986, when the London *Sunday Times* published an extraordinary inside account based on extensive interviews with a thirty-one-year-old Moroccan Jew named Mordecai Vanunu.

Vanunu began working as a technican at Dimona in August 1977 and spent much of the next eight years assigned to various tasks inside the reprocessing plant, formally known as Machon 2 (*machon* means "facility" or "institute" in Hebrew) and informally known as the Tunnel. The reprocessing plant, which was handling materials that were exceedingly "hot"—that is, highly radioactive—was the most sensitive area at Dimona; only 150 of Dimona's 2,700 employes worked there. A special pass was needed to enter the plant, and all movement inside, even to and from the bathroom, was—in theory—to be closely monitored. Vanunu, once at work in the Tunnel, found that the stringent security existed in theory only. Constantly in trouble for his public pro-Arab views, he had been laid off in mid-1985 as part of a government-wide cutback. Vanunu appealed through his union, powerful as are all unions in Israel, and won back his job. It was at that point that he smuggled a camera into the reprocessing plant during an overnight shift and wandered around undetected for some forty minutes, taking fifty-seven color photographs. A few weeks later he was fired after calling for the formation of a Palestinian state during an Arab rally. Even then, again with help from his union, Vanunu was able to negotiate a settlement from Dimona's management that gave him severance pay and a letter attesting to his good record.

A combination of factors—disenchantment with his life, distress at the treatment of Arabs in Israel, and what he had learned inside Dimona—drove him to exile in Australia and eventually to the London *Sunday Times*. The newspaper's editors and reporters were appropriately skeptical of Vanunu's account of the goings-on inside Dimona, but the photographs he had taken proved to be critical in finally establishing his credibility. However, even as he talked to the *Sunday Times*, he was being closely monitored by the Israeli government, whose operatives have long-standing ties to the London newspaper world. Copies of some of Vanunu's sensational photographs had been made available in London—before publication of the *Sunday Times* story—to an Israeli intelligence agent masquerad-

ing as an American newspaper reporter. The photographs
were sent by courier to the office of Prime Minister Shimon
Peres, who ordered Mossad to get Vanunu out of London and
into Israeli custody. No kidnapping could take place in England for diplomatic reasons. Instead, the lonely Vanunu was
enticed by a Mossad agent named Cindy Hanin Bentov (a
pseudonym) to leave for Rome a few days before publication of
the story. Once in Rome, Vanunu has told family members, he
was taken by taxi to an apartment, where he was drugged and
returned to Israel by ship to stand trial. He was sentenced in
March 1988 to eighteen years in a maximum-security prison.

Vanunu's *Times* interview and his photographs of many of
the production units in the Tunnel, or Machon 2, provided the
American intelligence community with the first extensive evidence of Israeli capability to manufacture fusion, or thermonuclear, weapons. American intelligence also obtained a copy of
many of the *Sunday Times*'s interview notes with Vanunu; those
notes, some of which were also made available to the author,
provided much more specific detail of the inner workings of
Dimona than was published. Senior American officials, including men and women who have worked in nuclear weapons
production and nuclear intelligence, uniformly agreed that the
unpublished Vanunu notes are highly credible. One intelligence official who has been analyzing Israel's nuclear capability
since the late 1960s depicted Vanunu's information, which includes a breakdown of the specific function of each unit inside
the Tunnel, as stunning: "The scope of this is much more extensive than we thought. This is an enormous operation."

The most exhaustive analysis of the Vanunu statements and
photographs was conducted by the Z Division, a special intelligence unit at the Livermore Laboratories whose experts are
considered to be the final word on proliferation issues. It is
responsible for analyzing foreign nuclear weapons, with emphasis on Soviet weaponry. "Z Division's only debate was over
the numbers," recalled a former White House nonproliferation
official. Vanunu told the *Sunday Times* that he believed the Israeli nuclear stockpile totaled more than two hundred warheads, an astonishingly high number—the CIA and Defense
Intelligence Agency were estimating into the early 1980s that

Israel had only between twenty-four and thirty warheads. "On the basis of what Z Division knew," added the White House aide, "it could not relate those kinds of numbers to what they could see" in the Vanunu photographs.

There was no evidence in the Vanunu materials of additional cooling capacity for Dimona's reactor, whose output would have had to have been dramatically increased to produce enough plutonium for two hundred warheads. Vanunu, however, in a portion of his interview not published and not made available to Z Division, explained that a new cooling unit had been installed at the reactor while he was employed at Dimona.* American nonproliferation experts had independently learned in the last year of the Carter administration of the boost in Dimona's cooling capacity, further evidence of Vanunu's credibility as well as proof that the reactor was capable of operating at a higher level and producing more plutonium.

Of extreme interest to the United States were Vanunu's photographs of what apparently were full-sized models of Israeli nuclear weapons.** Copies of those photos were provided to weapons designers at the Los Alamos and Livermore laboratories for evaluation and analysis, and the designers, working from the photographs, constructed replicas of the Israeli weapons, as had been done with Soviet weapons in the past. They concluded that Israel was capable of manufacturing one of the most sophisticated weapons in the nuclear arsenal—a low-yield neutron bomb. Such weapons, which first came into the American stockpile in the mid-1970s, utilize enhanced radiation and minimal blast to kill anything living within a limited range

---

* Vanunu described the cooling unit to Frank Barnaby, a nuclear physicist and former employee of Britain's nuclear weapons installation at Aldermaston. Barnaby spent two days with Vanunu, at the request of the *Sunday Times*, in a continuing effort to verify his account. He concluded, the *Sunday Times* said, that Vanunu's account "is totally convincing." After leaving government service, Barnaby became director of the Stockholm International Peace Research Institute (SIPRI), an arms control study group funded by the Swedish government.

** Mock-ups are commonly used for training purposes and military briefings in the American nuclear weapons complex, for the obvious reason that no one would want to work next to a fully operational nuclear warhead filled with highly enriched materials. The mock-ups are accurate replicas, in terms of external design and size, of a normal warhead, and American nonproliferation experts assumed that the Israelis' models were carefully prepared.

200 THE SAMSON OPTION

with limited damage to property. The weapon actually is a two-stage thermonuclear device that utilizes tritium and deuterium (both by-products of hydrogen), and not lithium deuteride, to maximize the release of neutrons.

The Vanunu information also helped American intelligence experts date the progress of the Israeli nuclear arsenal. Vanunu revealed, for example, that Unit 92 in the Tunnel had been painstakingly removing tritium from heavy water since the 1960s, indicating that physicists at Dimona—following Levi Eshkol's 1965 plea for advanced research—had been attempting from the earliest days of Dimona's production to manufacture "boosted" fission weapons. The United States began experimenting in the early 1950s with boosting, which dramatically increases the yield, or destructiveness, of a single-stage fission device. Boosting is a process in which small quantities (a few grams) of tritium and deuterium are inserted directly into a plutonium warhead and designed to flood the warhead with additional neutrons at the moment of fission—in essence, jump-starting the weapon at the moment of critical mass—producing a bigger kick, or yield, with smaller amounts of plutonium. Vanunu also told the *Sunday Times* of returning from a vacation in 1980—his first trip abroad since emigrating with his family to Israel in 1963—and being assigned then to work at a new production plant for lithium 6, another essential element of the hydrogen bomb. In 1984, he further reported, a new facility (Unit 93) for large-scale production of tritium was opened. Lithium is irradiated in the reactor, then moved to Unit 93, where it is heated to release tritium in a gas form, along with helium and hydrogen. The gases are then driven under high pressure through an asbestos palladium column and separated. The helium is stored in powdered uranium and can again be released by heating. The opening of Unit 93 suggests that full-scale production of neutron weapons began then, for up to twenty grams of tritium are used in each neutron warhead.

As described by Vanunu (and confirmed by the author in later interviews with Israeli officials), Dimona includes the reactor and at least eight other buildings, or Machons, the most important of which is the chemical reprocessing plant. Each building apparently is self-contained. Machon 1 is the large silver-domed reactor, sixty feet in diameter, that can be clearly seen from the nearby highway. The uranium fuel rods remain for three months in the reactor, which is cooled and moderated by heavy water. The heavy water is itself cooled by ordinary water flowing through a heat exchanger, creating steam, which in a nuclear power plant would drive a turbine and create electricity. Instead, the steam in Machon 1 is vented into the atmosphere, creating a radioactive cloud.* Machon 2 is the chemical reprocessing plant. Machon 3 converts lithium 6 into a solid for insertion into a nuclear warhead and also processes natural uranium for the reactor. Machon 4 contains a waste treatment plant for the radioactive residue from the chemical reprocessing plant in Machon 2. Machon 5 coats the uranium rods (shipped from Machon 3) with aluminum to be consumed in the reactor. The rods, once stacked in the core of the reactor, provide the fuel needed to sustain a chain reaction—and capture weapons-grade isotopes of plutonium. Machon 6 provides basic services and power for Dimona. Machon 8 contains a laboratory for testing samples and experimenting on new manufacturing processes; it also is the site of Special Unit 840, where Israeli scientists have developed a gas centrifuge method of enriching uranium for weapons use. There also is a laser-isotope-reprocessing facility for the enrichment of uranium in Machon 9. Depleted uranium—that is, uranium with very little or no uranium 235 left—is chemically isolated in Machon 10 for eventual shipment to the Israeli Defense Force or sale to arms manufacturers in Europe and elsewhere for use in bullets, armor plating, and artillery and bomb shells. The shells, buttressed by the heavy uranium, which is much denser than lead, can easily penetrate thick armor plating and are a staple in modern arsenals.** (There was no Machon 7 in the years he worked at

---

* Vanunu said that the steam, contaminated to varying degrees by leaks and corrosion, was vented only on those days when the prevailing wind was blowing toward the Jordanian border, about twenty-five miles to the east. It was one of those ventings, apparently, that was photographed by Army Colonel Carmelo Alba in 1965, providing the CIA with the first concrete evidence that Dimona was operational.
** The American forces who fought in Desert Storm, the 1991 war against Iraq, were equipped with uranium-tipped bullets and antitank munitions. Some of the American tanks also were equipped with uranium armor plating for added defense against Iraqi attacks.

Dimona, Vanunu told the *Sunday Times,* and he did not know what, if anything, had taken place there.)

Dimona's most essential facility, of course, is the reprocessing plant in Machon 2, where Vanunu spent most of his career. It is here that plutonium, a by-product of the fission process in the reactor, is extracted by chemical means from the spent uranium rods. The residual uranium is then reprocessed and reconstituted for use in new fuel rods. There are at least thirty-nine separate units in the six underground levels of the Tunnel, the most important of which is the production hall where the spent uranium rods undergo reprocessing. Before reprocessing can begin, however, the rods must be cooled for weeks in water-filled tanks, reducing radioactivity by a factor of several thousand. Even then, the radioactive rods are still lethal and are always handled by remote control and from behind lead shielding. The Tunnel's production hall dominates levels one through four below ground; work there is monitored by a large control room that includes an observation area known to technicians as "Golda's Balcony," a reference to Golda Meir's frequent visits after she became prime minister in 1969. The end result of the chemical processing, according to Vanunu, is a weekly average of nine "buttons" of pure plutonium whose combined weight is 1.2 kilograms.

The plutonium is fabricated by machine in a secure area on level five, the only floor in the Tunnel to which Vanunu was denied access. He eventually obtained a key and found a series of separate rooms—isolated for safety reasons—where the weapons-grade plutonium, now in metal form, is stored inside sealed glove boxes filled with argon, an inert gas. The glove boxes are designed so that workers can stand outside the "hot" area and manipulate remote-controlled robotic devices by hand to mold the plutonium pellets into microscopically thin hemispheres for insertion into a nuclear warhead. Other chemicals used in the Israeli nuclear arsenal, including lithium compounds and beryllium, also are machine-fabricated on the fifth level. Such milling involves exquisite machinery: any microscopic flaw in the interior surface of a bomb core can cause a significant reduction in the yield, or lead to a nonevent. The allowable tolerances are difficult for an outsider to comprehend: the hemisphere of an American-made plutonium war-head, for example, is permitted to deviate from prescribed thickness by less than five ten-thousandths of an inch, about one-sixth the diameter of a human hair.

Once completed, the weapons parts are moved by convoys of unmarked cars, under armed guard, to another facility to the north—not known to Vanunu—for assembly into warheads. Is-raeli officials subsequently told me that the final stage of war-head production takes place at a defense plant north of Haifa operated by Rafael, the top-secret Israeli research and manufac-turing agency that is responsible for Israel's most sensitive weaponry.

The Tunnel remained in operation around the clock for thirty-four weeks a year, according to Vanunu, and was shut down from July to November for routine maintenance and re-pair. American nuclear experts consulted about Vanunu's story describe the methods used to reprocess the spent uranium at Dimona as essentially routine; the industrial solvents and solu-tions used by the Israelis are the same as those relied upon at the Savannah River Plant in Aiken, South Carolina, where state-of-the-art heavy-water-production reactors have operated since the mid-1950s.

What was surprising, however, was the scope of the Israeli operation. If Vanunu's information about the rate of plutonium reprocessing is correct—a steady production rate of 1.2 kilo-grams weekly—the reactor would be producing enough en-riched materials for four to a dozen or more bombs a year, depending on warhead design. The reactor also would have to be operating at about 120 to 150 megawatts, more than five times its officially stated output, and consuming nearly one hun-dred tons of uranium ore a year.* Some American experts be-

* The nuclear fuel cycle is so precise that scientists can compute how much ura-nium was consumed by Dimona at a given reactor output. According to Vanunu, the average flow rate of dissolved uranium and plutonium through the chemical reproces-sing plant was 20.9 liters per hour with a uranium concentration of 450 grams per liter and a plutonium concentration of 170 to 180 milligrams per liter (or 0.39 milligrams of plutonium per gram of uranium). Vanunu said, however, that the actual flow rate in the Tunnel normally exceeded the standard flow rate by 150 to 175 percent, which corresponds to the reprocessing of as much as thirty-seven kilograms of weapons-grade plutonium a year, assuming eight months of continuous operation. Nuclear technicians have further noted that Vanunu claimed that the spent uranium fuel processed at

lieve that Vanunu's statistics, whose essential accuracy is not in dispute, may reflect peak output, and not what is known as the normal flow rate. If so, Dimona could be producing sixteen to twenty kilograms of weapons-grade plutonium per year, enough for four or five warheads.

What especially impressed American experts about Dimona's reprocessing plant was its location—underground—and its sophistication. "You have to understand," an American explained, "Machon 2 is very sophisticated because it's so hot. There's an extraordinary level of radioactivity. You need three-foot lead walls, all automated; people in suits; robotics. You're going to have a hell of a time keeping it undetected. So you go very deep." That, in turn, drives up the price of ventilation shafts, air intakes, and fan systems, as well as all ordinary construction costs.

Going underground also posed enormous engineering risks that could be met only by superb master planning and expert intelligence. For example, the construction teams that initially built the U.S. Atomic Energy Commission's Savannah River Plant in South Carolina decided to put the thick, lead-shielded doors that protected the work force on custom-made coasters with specially engineered automated motors for opening and closing. "We didn't move the doors often enough," the American added, "and the coasters flattened. The doors were too heavy and we had misjudged the physics. We had to stop the process to remove them. We didn't test this beforehand because we didn't think of it."

The possibility exists, the official said, that the Israelis determined from the outset that they could avoid such problems by finding out what had gone right—and wrong—from the Americans who built the Savannah River Plant. "This is not highly

Dimona contained a smaller concentration of plutonium—about 0.30 milligrams per gram instead of 0.39 milligrams per gram—suggesting that as much as 125 metric tons of uranium was needed to operate the reactor, far more than officially estimated. It is impossible to even roughly determine the amount of plutonium that has been produced at Dimona without knowing the power output and operating history of the reactor. That information remains a closely guarded state secret in Israel. The general accuracy and scientific validity of Vanunu's statistical data added to his credibility with American intelligence officials.

classified information—it's dumb-shit stuff that has to be done. That kind of intelligence is crucial to not having to reinvent the wheel. Anything you can learn about what the other guy has learned just leaps you forward." This, presumably, was one of the missions of Binyamin Blumberg and his Office of Special Tasks, which became known in the mid-1970s as the Science Liaison Bureau, or LAKAM. Blumberg's agents were operating all over the world, collecting available technical information and also setting up front companies in Europe and Latin America for the purchase from the United States of high-tech equipment whose export to Israel would not be permitted.

Another area of great sensitivity involved the science of robotics, whose most important early use in the United States came in the hot weapons laboratories where humans could not work. The precision involved in machining the thin plutonium hemispheres and placing them around the gases needed to create boosted nuclear weapons was achieved only after enormous strides had been made in the use of remote control. It was not an accident that Aharon Katzir (formerly Katchalsky), who became, like Ernst Bergmann, an intellectual force inside the Israeli Atomic Energy Commission, was world-renowned for his research into robotics at the Weizmann Institute. Katzir was even featured with some of his research apparatus on the cover of the December 3, 1966, issue of the *Saturday Review;* the article was entitled "Man's First Robot with Muscles." It reported on Katzir's pioneering work in converting chemical energy into the energy of motion. Katzir's team at the Weizmann Institute also was concentrating on the development of artificial muscle tissue for use in robots. His research was heavily funded by the U.S. Air Force's Office of Scientific Research; the Air Force's primary interest was in utilizing robotics in outer-space research. The Air Force had no idea that it was also helping to underwrite research for the Israeli nuclear arsenal; nor did it know that Katzir's main work was being done at Dimona, and not at the Weizmann Institute.

Vanunu's revelations staunchly reaffirmed the recurring suspicions of many in the American intelligence community that Israel either had covertly tested its advanced thermonuclear weapons, all of which needed to be miniaturized to fit into bombs and missile warheads, or somehow had managed to obtain illicitly the results of American testing. "We'd go through ten to twelve underground tests [at the American underground range in Nevada] just to come up with the data," one weapons expert recalled. "How could they spend that kind of money [for the underground reprocessing plant] without having tested? You'd have to be so certain of your intelligence. You just can't afford to be wrong."

Despite such comments, there remains no actual evidence that Israel needed outside help for its nuclear weaponry. Dr. George A. Cowan, who spent more than twenty years designing nuclear weapons at Los Alamos, acknowledged that there always was a close association with Israeli physicists from the Weizmann Institute. "They've visited the labs [Los Alamos and Livermore] and probably are treated more openly than other visitors here, but there's too much emphasis to the notion that there's a secret that somebody has to tell them," Cowan said. "The Israelis are smart enough to do their own research. The need for secret information is largely promoted by spy novelists. There's very much less to it than most people believe." Like many of the scientists in the American nuclear laboratories, Cowan has a close Israeli friend who was involved with Dimona: "He never asked me anything over the years about the bomb and wouldn't have." Similarly, physicist Hans Bethe, the Nobel laureate who helped design the first American nuclear and thermonuclear weapons, recalled three visits to the Weizmann Institute during which his hosts would "take me anywhere and discuss anything with me. They knew I was interested in nuclear power reactors," he added, "and yet they never offered to take me to Dimona. I found that significant."

If there was any solace for the American intelligence community in the wake of the startling Vanunu disclosures, which gave Washington the most specific evidence of an Israeli reprocessing plant, it was in the conviction that the extraordinary degree of master planning that had to take place at Dimona was little appreciated by senior officials in the Israeli chain of command. "It's unlikely," said one expert, "that the top people in the government of Israel truly understood" what was taking place at Dimona—just as America's intelligence experts had failed to understand.

The American experts got that one right, at least. Shimon Peres has confided to friends that during the early construction of Dimona he often signed requisition orders and other technical documents on behalf of the Ben-Gurion government without knowing precisely what he had approved.

16

Prelude to War

Israel's development as a full-blown nuclear power by 1969 could not have come at a more fortuitous time, in terms of the American presidency. Richard Nixon and Henry Kissinger approached inauguration day on January 20, 1969, convinced that Israel's nuclear ambitions were justified and understandable. Once in office, they went a step further: they endorsed Israel's nuclear ambitions.

The two American leaders also shared a contempt for the 1968 Nonproliferation Treaty, which had been so ardently endorsed in public by Lyndon Johnson. Nixon, midway in his campaign against Vice President Hubert H. Humphrey, dismayed the arms control community by urging the Senate to delay ratification of the NPT until after the election. He went further a few days later, telling newsmen in Charlotte, North Carolina, that he specifically was concerned about the NPT's failure to permit the transfer of "defensive nuclear weapons," such as mines or antiballistic missile systems, to non-nuclear powers. Government arms controllers were hugely relieved in early February 1969 when Nixon formally requested the Senate to take up the treaty and then stated at a news conference that he would do all he could to urge France and West Germany—known to have reservations—to sign it: "I will make it clear that I believe that ratification of the treaty by all governments, nuclear and non-nuclear, is in the interest of peace and in the interest of reducing the possibility of nuclear proliferation."

In the secrecy of their offices, however, as only a few in the government knew, Nixon and Kissinger had simultaneously issued a presidential order to the bureaucracy undercutting all that was said in public. The classified document, formally known as National Security Decision Memorandum (NSDM) No. 6, stated that "there should be no efforts by the United States government to pressure other nations, particularly the Federal Government of Germany, to follow suit [and ratify the NPT]. The government, in its public posture, should reflect a tone of optimism that other countries will sign or ratify, while clearly disassociating itself [in private] from any plan to bring pressure on these countries to sign or ratify."

"It was a major change in American policy," recalled Morton H. Halperin, then Kissinger's closest aide on the National Security Council staff. "Henry believed that it was good to spread nuclear weapons around the world. I heard him say that if he were the Israelis, he would get nuclear weapons. He did not believe that the United States should try and talk them out of it." Kissinger also told his staff in the first months of 1969 that Japan, as well as Israel, would be better off with the bomb than without it. He was convinced, said Halperin, that nuclear weapons were essential to the national security of both nations. Kissinger's view was essentially pragmatic, added Halperin: most of the major powers would eventually obtain nuclear weapons, and the United States could benefit the most by helping them to do so rather than by participating in futile exercises in morality, such as the Nonproliferation Treaty.

Kissinger's support for Israel's nuclear weapons program, as spelled out during his 1968 meeting at General Elad Peled's home, was widely known to the Israeli leadership. If an overt sign of the administration's stand was needed, it came quickly, with the decision in 1969 to end the Floyd Culler inspections of Dimona. The inspections, begun in 1962, had long been considered by the American arms control community to be important in principle but in practice to have marginal utility; they dragged on without change, nonetheless, through the Johnson years. Israel resented the inspections as an intrusion on its sovereignty; there also was fear that Culler or one of his team might actually stumble onto something useful, especially as Dimona began gearing up in the late 1960s for the full-scale production of warheads.

Culler's inspection in 1969 seemed to some Americans to be

especially pointless, in the wake of President Johnson's last-minute decision to allow Israel to purchase its much-desired F-4s without insisting—as the State Department and Pentagon wanted—on Israeli ratification of the NPT in exchange. "Culler's team came on a Saturday and spent only a few hours," recalled the late Joseph Zurhellen, then senior deputy to Ambassador Wally Barbour in Tel Aviv. "You just can't walk in and take a guided tour. You've got to do an awful lot to determine what's been done to a reactor." Zurhellen had no illusions about what was going on at Dimona: "The French had pulled the wool over our eyes and so had the Israelis." His point, in a memorandum he forwarded to Washington, was essentially one of public relations: the Israelis "could claim that our inspection showed Dimona to be clean, when in fact it showed nothing at all." Such complaints had been voiced before.

But now Washington found it convenient to end the charade, and the inspections ended. They were never to be reinstated, as the Nixon administration made a judgment that would become American policy for the next two decades: Israel had gone nuclear, and there was nothing that the United States could—or wanted to—do about it.

The new policy soon worked its way through the bureaucracy, which reacted as the bureaucracy always did: it followed orders —with varying degrees of resentment. Charles N. Van Doren, who was deputy general counsel of the Arms Control and Disarmament Agency in the Nixon administration, was convinced that Israel was the "Achilles heel" of America's NPT policy: "We were winking at it." Van Doren, who persevered for nineteen years in the arms control bureaucracy, recalled he had repeatedly tried under Nixon and Kissinger "to get the NPT on the agenda for talks on the Middle East, but I was told there was too much on the table." He understood the underlying reason, of course: "An order had gone out that no nuclear information on Israeli proliferation was to be put out. It was very frustrating."*

---

* In November 1969, Kissinger and Nixon decided that "budgetary constraints" made it impossible for the United States to underwrite the much-discussed Israeli ambitions for a nuclear desalting plant. Israeli officials subsequently explained the

The Nixon and Kissinger tolerance for a nuclear Israel also was reflected by the media. In July 1970, Carl Duckett's intelligence report on Israel's nuclear arsenal, which had been initially suppressed in 1968 by Lyndon Johnson and later by Richard Helms, the CIA director, finally made its way onto the front page of the *New York Times*—and nobody cared. The *Times* story, written by Washington correspondent Hedrick Smith, provided the American public with its first account of the CIA's assessment of the Israeli nuclear arsenal, beginning with its lead sentence: "For at least two years the United States Government has been conducting its Middle East policy on the assumption that Israel either possesses an atomic bomb or has component parts available for quick assembly." The Smith story also described Israel's progress in developing its Jericho I missile system and revealed that a manufacturing plant had been set up near Tel Aviv for the production of solid propellants and engines for the missiles. Smith recalled trying for two years to get the article published in the *Times*, and failing because "I just didn't have it hard enough." He was given a boost that July by Senator Stuart Symington, the Missouri Democrat, who acknowledged on a Sunday television interview show that there was "no question that Israel is doing its best to develop nuclear weapons." The Symington peg helped Smith get the story published a few days later; the reporter, experienced in covering diplomatic affairs, awaited the attention he was sure the article would attract from others in the media and the Congress. Nothing happened. "I was astonished," Smith said. "Nobody could get near it. The networks didn't go for it." Neither did any of the *Times*'s newspaper competitors, who found it impossible to confirm the story. "I had a sense of being way out in front of the field," said Smith. The reporter did hear from the Israeli embassy in Washington; there was a subsequent meeting with a "very upset" Ambassador Yitzhak Rabin.

---

decision not in terms of costs, but as stemming from a concern that the nuclear-powered plant would become too much of a target for Arab terrorism in the wake of the Six-Day War and the renewed War of Attrition with Egypt. Nonetheless, the White House's decision, promulgated as NSDM 32, signed on behalf of the President by Kissinger, effectively ended the dispute over the Johnson administration's insistence on linking financial support for the plant to an Israeli commitment to permit inspection by the IAEA.

"He repeated the standard line that Israel would not be the first to use it," said Smith, who recalled asking Rabin if he was specifically denying the story: "Rabin would not answer."

By mid-1971, the White House's permissive attitude toward the Israeli bomb made it possible for even those officials responsible for monitoring the shipment of sensitive materials to look the other way. Glenn R. Cella, a foreign service officer, was assigned that summer to handle political-military affairs on the State Department's Israeli desk; he also was named the department's representative on the Middle East Task Force, an interagency group whose main mission was to monitor American arms transfer policies. Cella, who had served in Morocco, Algeria, and Egypt, began asking about the Israeli bomb and quickly learned of Duckett's suppressed estimate. He also learned that if there was going to be any pressure on Israel to stop its nuclear weapons program, it would not come from the task force or the State Department. Israel was then pushing for the immediate shipment of more F-4s, and the State Department's Bureau of Intelligence and Research (INR) had been ordered to make a study of the military balance in the region. The study, when completed, made no mention of Israeli nuclear capability, to Cella's dismay. "I thought we ought to face up to the fact that they had it," Cella said, "but nobody was allowed to talk about it."

A few months later, Cella was notified that an Israeli request for the sale of krytrons had been routinely approved by his Pentagon counterpart on the task force. Krytrons, the inquisitive Cella was informed, were sensitive electronic timing devices used to trigger strobe lights. "I remember calling up [the Pentagon task force member] and being told, in essence, that you could buy this thing in a Hechinger's [a popular Washington chain of hardware stores]," recalled Cella. "I wasn't told it was a central part in nuclear weaponry. Then I learned krytrons triggered nuclear bombs." The high-speed device, whose export usually is closely monitored, is essential for the precise detonation of the chemical explosives that cause implosion in a nuclear weapon—facts that should have been known to the Pentagon official.

Cella stayed on the Middle East desk for two years and

quickly became marked, he said, as an Arabist—"which I resented." He'd learned his lesson, however. A year later the U.S. budget somehow included funds earmarked for the supply of two supercomputers to the Weizmann Institute. The computers' function, Cella knew, included nuclear simulation. "It was clear what they were for," he said, "but I didn't even try to fight it."

The atmosphere wasn't much better at CIA headquarters. Richard Helms, the consummate bureaucrat, continued to please his superiors by stifling significant intelligence about the Israeli bomb. He'd also come to a personal conclusion about Israeli intelligence, repeatedly telling his deputies and aides that he was convinced Israel was funneling American satellite information to the Soviet Union. "The CIA got a copy of the Israeli [intelligence] requirements list in late 1972," Carl Duckett explained. "The Israelis were asking their contacts [in America] for overhead [satellite] intelligence. Helms was convinced the Israelis were doing it on behalf of the Soviets. He thought Israel was an open pipeline for pumping intelligence to Moscow." There was, of course, a much more direct explanation, one that Duckett and Helms could not envision in the early 1970s: Israel wanted the satellite imagery of the Soviet Union because of its own nuclear targeting needs.*

The men and women in the bureaucracy understood, as did Helms, that the Israeli nuclear issue was taboo. "The issue had never been dealt with at the working level in State," explained David E. Long, a State Department Near East expert. Those State Department and Pentagon staff officers who in the early 1970s wanted to learn more about Israel's nuclear weapons could not, Long added, because such intelligence carried the highest order of classification: "Whenever you moved an inch

---

* Helms had no knowledge of science and found it difficult to testify as CIA director on technical nuclear issues before the Joint Atomic Energy Commission, as his position required. To his credit, Duckett said, Helms asked for help, and a series of educational briefings was arranged, amid great secrecy, in his office. At the first session, Helms was asked by his instructor, one of the Agency's leading experts in nuclear fission, whether he'd ever studied physics in high school. The answer was no. "Okay," said the instructor, "we're going to start with the table of elements." Helms eventually spent a day with Duckett and other government officials at the nuclear underground test center in Nevada. After serving nearly eight years as the head of the CIA, he was appointed ambassador to Iran by Richard Nixon in early 1973.

in that direction, you had to decide whether you wanted to make a crusade or get on with your job." On the other hand, Long said that he and others were constantly being informally questioned about Israel's nuclear arms by diplomats from the Middle East: "My response was to say that we don't know anything and here is what the Israelis say." Long recalled once being asked by a superior to put that response in writing, in a formal diplomatic note to a Middle Eastern nation. He refused. "I backed away and argued that we just should say 'No comment,'" he recalled. "I thought that delivering a deliberately false impression went beyond subterfuge. I wasn't a crusader. I just asked that someone else deliver the note. And they did." Curtis F. Jones similarly spent his career as a Middle East expert in the Foreign Service; his final assignment from 1971 to 1975 was as director of Near East, North African, and South Asian affairs for the Bureau of Intelligence and Research. "Stopping Israeli nuclear weapons was never an issue for the U.S. government, for as long as I was there," Jones said. "We never sat down and talked about it."

The easing of the pressure from Washington removed any constraints on Dimona and the Israeli leadership, which correctly interpreted the end of the Culler inspections as an American carte blanche. The technicians and scientists at Dimona began operating in the early 1970s exactly as their American and Soviet counterparts had done in the first days of the Cold War— the Israelis made as many bombs as possible.*

By 1973, according to former Israeli government officials, the Israeli nuclear arsenal totaled at least twenty warheads, with three or more missile launchers in place and operational at

---

* Between 1945 and 1985 the United States manufactured an estimated sixty thousand nuclear warheads for 116 weapons systems, an average production rate of four per day. These ranged from huge thermonuclear city busters to an atomic warhead for a jeep-mounted bazooka. In a 1985 essay, three critics of the American arsenal, Robert S. Norris, Thomas B. Cochran, and William M. Arkin, concluded: "Bureaucratic competition and inertia have led to nuclear warheads for every conceivable military mission, arm of service, and geographic theater—all compounded by a technological momentum that overwhelmed what should have been a more sober analysis of what was enough for deterrence. The result is a gigantic nuclear weapons system—laboratories, production facilities, forces, and so on—that has become self-perpetuating, conducting its business out of public view and with little accountability."

Hirbat Zachariah; Israel also had an unknown number of mobile Jericho I missile launchers that had been manufactured as part of Project 700. The missiles had been capable since 1971 of hitting targets in southern Russia, including Tbilisi, near the Soviet oil fields, and Baku, off the coast of the Caspian Sea, as well as Arab capitals. There also was a squadron of nuclear-capable F-4 fighters on twenty-four-hour alert in underground revetments at the Tel Nof air base near Rehovot. The specially trained F-4 pilots were the elite of the Israeli Air Force and were forbidden to discuss their mission with any outsider. The long-range F-4s were capable of flying one-way to Moscow with a nuclear bomb; the daring pilots would have to be resupplied by an airborne tanker to make it home.

By this time, Dimona had solved many of the basic problems of weapons miniaturization; the smaller warheads provided Israeli weapons designers with an array of options that included the development of low-yield tactical weapons for battlefield use. The United States had done its part by approving the sale of long-range 175mm and 203mm cannons to the Israeli Defense Force in the early 1970s; those weapons, capable of striking targets twenty-five miles away, also became part of the Israeli nuclear option. American intelligence later learned that Israel had experimented by fusing together two long-range artillery barrels to produce a cannon capable of hurling a shell more than forty-five miles.

The Israelis also had contracted with Dr. Gerald Bull, a controversial Canadian arms designer, for the supply of specially configured artillery shells whose range was extended as much as 25 percent.* There were some American weapons experts

* Bull was killed outside his home in Brussels in March 1990 by assassins widely suspected of working on behalf of the Israelis. At the time of his death, Bull had accomplished for Iraq's artillery what he had done for the Israelis. There was high-level Israeli concern over Bull's success in constructing a "supergun" for the Iraqis—a weapon, as the Israelis knew only too well, that provided Iraq with the ability to threaten Israel with long-range chemical, biological, or conventional high-explosive shells. Bull's initial contracts with Israel phased out in the mid-1970s; his firm, the Space Research Corporation (SRC), later did business with South Africa and China from an eight-thousand-acre compound straddling the Vermont-Canadian border. Bull's partners in SRC during much of the 1970s included the Arthur D. Little Company, a highly respected management research firm. Four executives from Arthur D. Little were on the SRC board of directors. The mysterious Bull spent six months in a federal jail after pleading guilty in 1980 to one count of selling cannons, shells, and a

who understood what Israel's real goal had to be, given the
inaccuracy of an artillery shell fired at such long range. "If
you're going forty-five miles and precision is three percent of
range," explained one expert, "what would you hit with an HE
[high explosive] shell? Nothing much. You'd need a nuclear
weapon." This American, who was a senior official at one of
the U.S. Army's weapons testing facilities, had visited Israel in
1973 and had been told of the intended use of the long-range
cannons, information he dutifully reported to U.S. intelligence. There also were suggestions, added the American, that
Israel had targeted Damascus, Syria's capital, with the special
cannons during the Yom Kippur War. Washington got the message. A senior State Department intelligence official recalled
widespread concern in the early 1970s over the ambitious Israeli
artillery program. "Our supposition was that they'd developed
a miniaturized [nuclear] artillery shell and wanted to test it,"
the official said.

As the Israeli weapons program prospered, there was a new
element of caution inside the Israeli government and the military commands. The political struggles and infighting were put
aside as the new weapon became standardized for battlefield
use. There was doctrine to write and training to get done. The
Israeli leadership had to work out procedures for the actual use
of the bomb; at one early stage it was agreed that no nuclear
weapon could be armed and fired without authorization from
the prime minister, minister of defense, and army chief of staff.
The rules of engagement subsequently were modified to include the head of the Israeli Air Force; the air force's warheads
were reportedly maintained in preassembled units in special
secure boxes that could be opened only with three keys, to be
supplied by representatives of the top civilian and military
leadership. Other fail-safe mechanisms, if any, could not be
learned. "The day we had enough bombs to feel comfortable,"
one Israeli military officer explained, "we stopped talking
about it. People realized the moment that the bomb was upon
us that we'd become targets, too."

---

radar van to South Africa without a license—although he insisted until his death that
his activities on behalf of South Africa had been sanctioned by the American intelligence community.

The increased security of the early 1970s had one immediate casualty: Minister of Defense Moshe Dayan. Dayan's standing among his peers in the military and the upper echelons of the Israeli government was far lower than among the public; he was considered overrated as a military leader and suspect because of his incessant womanizing and his financial wheeling and dealing—there was categorical evidence, never officially acted upon, of his appropriation of excavated antiquities for personal use, in direct violation of Israeli law.* The main complaint about Dayan, however, was over his propensity to talk: one close army associate declared that "he had the biggest mouth in the world." The Israeli added: "The feeling was that he was a loose cannon at a time when Israel was in a very precarious situation. We wanted the Arabs to know what we had"—without explicitly saying too much. Dayan, with his public statements and leaks to the press, blurred that tactic. There was another problem, the Israeli added: "Dayan went to bed with everything that moved"—not that unusual a trait among aggressive Israeli military men—"but he was totally capable of meeting a good-looking woman and telling her about Dimona. He and Peres felt like they were almost parents" of the nuclear complex. While Dayan lost no authority, it was eventually made clear to him, the Israeli said, that he was no longer welcome at Dimona; he no longer had a military need to know anything about the Israeli nuclear program, which was being managed out of the prime minister's office.

Tragedy struck the program in May 1972, when Aharon Katzir, the innovative physicist in charge of Dimona, was killed in a Japanese Red Army terrorist attack at Lod Airport near Tel Aviv; there is no evidence that Katzir was specifically targeted. His replacement, Shalheveth Freier, was a nuclear

---

* Dayan outraged many of his countrymen after the Six-Day War, when the biblical lands of the West Bank and Gaza were once again open to Israeli academics and archaeologists, by commandeering military units to cordon off areas known to be rich in antiquities. Dayan, with the help of the troops, would then remove artifacts—many of them invaluable—for his personal gain. He eventually established an antique garden in the rear of his home in Zahala, an exclusive suburb of Tel Aviv. The minister of defense's activities led to occasional critiques in the Israeli press, but no government investigation. Americans who served as diplomats and military attachés in Israel have acknowledged the purchase of antiques from Dayan, who invariably insisted on payment in American dollars.

physicist with impeccable credentials; he had served as scientific counselor to the Israeli embassy in Paris in the critical days of the 1950s, when the Israeli-French nuclear understanding was reached. Freier also enjoyed high standing among international scientists and was particularly well known to American nuclear weapons designers, many of whom understood exactly what he did.

The researchers at Dimona and the Weizmann Institute continued to produce superb work. In 1973, two Israeli scientists caused a stir in the academic and intelligence world by receiving a West German patent for a laser process that, as they claimed, could cheaply produce as much as seven grams of uranium enriched to 60 percent U-235 in twenty-four hours. The research paid off six years later, according to Mordecai Vanunu, when Dimona opened a special Machon for the production of laser-enriched uranium.

The burgeoning nuclear bastion at Dimona may have officially remained a secret to the world, but the Israeli intelligence community discovered in the early 1970s that the Soviet KGB had penetrated the top offices of the defense ministry and intelligence establishment and was relaying the essentials of major strategic decisions to Moscow and its allies in the Middle East. The unraveling of the Soviet operation was initiated by one of the most secret units in the Israeli military, Detachment 515 (later redesignated Detachment 8200), which is in charge of signals intelligence and code-breaking—the Israeli equivalent of the U.S. National Security Agency.

One of the detachment's most senior officers was Reuven (Rudi) Yerdor, an accomplished linguist who had cracked a Soviet code—for which he later received Israel's highest defense medal—that had masked the communications between KGB headquarters in Moscow and its regional base in Cyprus. The Israelis began poring over the backlog of undeciphered Soviet message traffic and discovered that many of the major secret decisions of the Israeli defense ministry, including those dealing with nuclear weapons, were being reported to Moscow within, in some cases, twelve hours. "They went apeshit," recalled a former Israeli intelligence officer, "and set up a special team to begin an investigation." The team was headed by Shin Beth, Israel's internal security agency, and included members from Mossad and Prime Minister Meir's office. Yet it was unable to find out how the KGB, which continued its spying during the secret inquiry, was able to transmit its intelligence out of Israel. The investigators were able, however, to determine that only a small number of Israeli officials had access to all the material that had been funneled to the KGB—including at least one of Golda Meir's personal aides. A few of the suspects, including the aide, cleared themselves by passing lie detector tests; others chose not to take the test, and the matter was left unresolved, to the acute frustration of the investigators.*

There was an ironic twist to the spy scandal, for the senior leadership of the Israeli government understood from the moment of the first collaboration with the French that the Soviets not only were the primary targets of the nuclear arsenal but would be among the first to be told of its existence. By 1973, Dimona's success in miniaturization enabled its technicians to build warheads small enough to fit into a suitcase; word of the bomb in a suitcase was relayed to the Soviet Union, according to a former Israeli intelligence official, during one of what apparently was a regular series of meetings in Europe between representatives of Mossad and the KGB. The Soviets understood that no amount of surveillance could prevent Israeli agents from smuggling nuclear bombs across the border in automobiles, aircraft, or commercial ships.

Israel's leadership, especially Moshe Dayan, had nothing but contempt for the Arab combat ability in the early 1970s. In their view, Israel's main antagonist in the Middle East was and would continue to be the Soviet Union. Dimona's arsenal, known by the Kremlin to be targeted as much as possible at

---

* One of the most nagging questions of the inquiry had to do with the transmission of the intelligence. How did the KGB spies get the information out? At one point, a knowledgeable Israeli said, the investigators turned to the National Security Agency for help, but the NSA was unable to come up with an answer. Years later, an Iranian general spying for the KGB in Iran was arrested and found to be carrying an American satellite communication device, which he had used for filing his intelligence reports. "Once he was caught," the former Israeli officer added, "they said, 'Ah-ha. This explains why no messages [out of Israel] were intercepted.' The Soviets stole the American satcom device and did better with it than we did."

Soviet cities, theoretically would deter the Soviets from supporting an all-out Arab attack on Israel; the bombs also would
give pause to any Egyptian or Syrian invasion plans.

These were years of status quo for Israeli diplomacy. Israel
had a steady flow of American arms and American acquiescence in its continued control of the occupied territories,
where settlements were systematically being constructed.
Those territories, and the land they added to the national borders, had done nothing to diminish Israel's hunger for more
advanced weapons—defense spending rose by 500 percent between 1966 and 1972.

The death of Nasser in September 1970 had not altered the
basic equation in the Middle East; his successor, Anwar Sadat,
was, in the view of Prime Minister Golda Meir and her cabinet,
nothing more than yet another unyielding threat to Jews. The
new Egyptian leader had been jailed by the British authorities
during much of World War II because of his openly pro-German stance and his public endorsement of Hitler; the fact that
his actions were more anti-British than pro-German was of little solace to the Israeli leadership. Sadat, however, broke new
ground by offering the Israelis a peace agreement shortly after
taking office—the first Arab leader willing even to discuss such
a commitment. In return, the Israelis were to withdraw to the
1967 borders. The Sadat offer was rejected out of hand by Golda
Meir (only Dayan urged that it be explored); she viewed the
compromise as nothing more than a starting point for extended
negotiations.

Sadat waited for Washington to intervene. That did not happen, and the bitterly disappointed Egyptian president, in trouble at home and ridiculed by many of his Middle Eastern peers,
tried again in mid-1972 to get Washington's respect; he abruptly
ordered Soviet troops and advisers out of Egypt to demonstrate, in part, that Egypt was not pro-Communist. Nixon and
Kissinger were astonished, as was the rest of the world, at the
Soviet ouster, but they mistakenly viewed it as only reaffirmation of their policy of support for Israel. Kissinger went further and privately reviled Sadat as a fool who, by acting
unilaterally and emotionally, had thrown away an opportunity
to use the Soviet explusion as a bargaining tool. Sadat ended up

with no diplomatic gains from the West and eventually concluded that the only way he—and Egypt—would be taken seriously was to go to war with Israel.

Israel, preoccupied by the Soviet threat, saw the expulsion as diminishing any real chance of war. On paper, Israel's army and air force were more than a match for even the combined forces of the Arab Middle East. Without Soviet backing, no Arab nation would dare to initiate a fight. There would be no peace, perhaps, but there was no immediate threat to continued Israeli control of the captured territories. This message came through loud and clear in the late summer of 1973 to Kenneth B. Keating, a former Republican senator from New York who was Wally Barbour's replacement as U.S. ambassador to Israel. In August, Keating and his deputy, Nicholas A. Veliotes, paid a courtesy call on Moshe Dayan, whom they found to be not just confident, but swaggering. There had been constant talk that summer of an impending Arab attack, Veliotes recalls, and the embassy had been put on a higher alert. Dayan was asked if he was worried. His response, recalled Veliotes, was " 'Don't worry.' He described the Arab armies in the desert as 'rusty ships slowly sinking'—as if the desert were a sea. It was very arrogant." Dayan's comments were accepted without challenge at the time, said Veliotes: "We had a great belief that the Israelis knew more than we did. We also were mesmerized by 1967"— the Six-Day War.

Israel wasn't ready when Sadat attacked across the Sinai and Syria invaded the Golan Heights on Saturday, October 6, 1973 —Yom Kippur, the Day of Atonement, the holiest day of the year for a Jew. The first days were a stunning rout. Israeli soldiers were being killed as never before; some units simply fled in disarray from battle. Five hundred tanks and forty-nine aircraft, including fourteen F-4 Phantoms, were lost in the first three days. In the Sinai, Egyptian forces, equipped with missiles and electronic defenses, blasted through the Bar-Lev defense line along the eastern bank of the canal and soon had two large armies on the eastern bank. The initial Israeli counterattacks by three tank divisions were beaten off. On the Golan Heights, Syrian forces, bolstered by fourteen hundred tanks, rolled through Israeli defenses and moved to the edge of Galilee. Only a few Israeli tanks stood between the Syrians and the heavily populated Hulla Valley. Haifa was just hours away.

Many Israelis thought it was all over—that, as Moshe Dayan said, "this is the end of the Third Temple." The extent of Dayan's panic on Monday, October 8, has never been fully reported, but it is widely known among Israelis. One of Dayan's functions as defense minister was to provide the censored media and their editors-in-chief with a daily briefing on the war—in essence, to control what they wrote. One journalist, a retired army general, who attended the Monday session, recalled Dayan's assessment: "The situation is desperate. Everything is lost. We must withdraw." There was talk in a later meeting of appeals to world Jewry, distribution of antitank weapons to every citizen, and last-ditch resistance in the civilian population centers. It was Israel's darkest hour, but no withdrawal was ordered.

Instead, Israel called its first nuclear alert and began arming its nuclear arsenal. And it used that alert to blackmail Washington into a major policy change.

17

Nuclear Blackmail

Moshe Dayan's fears and Israel's gloom were turned around during a dramatic meeting on Monday, October 8, at Golda Meir's office in Tel Aviv, just a few hundred feet from "the Bor," the military's huge underground war complex. Meir's closest aides, the so-called kitchen cabinet, assembled for what turned out to be an all-night session. Among those in attendance, besides Dayan and Meir, were General David (Dado) Elazar, the army chief of staff; Yigal Allon, the deputy prime minister; Brigadier General Yisrael (Gingy) Leor, the prime minister's military aide; and Israel Galili, the influential minister without portfolio and longtime confidant of Meir.

Over the next hours, the Israeli leadership—faced with its greatest crisis—resolved to implement three critical decisions: it would rally its collapsing forces for a major counterattack; it would arm and target its nuclear arsenal in the event of total collapse and subsequent need for the Samson Option; and, finally, it would inform Washington of its unprecedented nuclear action—and unprecedented peril—and demand that the United States begin an emergency airlift of replacement arms and ammunition needed to sustain an extended all-out war effort.

The kitchen cabinet agreed that the nuclear missile launchers at Hirbat Zachariah, as many as were ready, would be made operational, along with eight specially marked F-4s that were on twenty-four-hour alert at Tel Nof, the air force base near Rehovot. The initial target list included the Egyptian and Syrian military headquarters near Cairo and Damascus. It could not be learned how many weapons were armed, although Dimona was known to have manufactured more than twenty

warheads by 1973. No weapons were targeted on the Soviet
Union, but there was little doubt that the Soviets would
quickly learn what was going on. Israeli intelligence was intercepting indecipherable signals from what were presumed to be
Soviet operatives inside the country; the encoded messages
were beamed throughout the early morning.

All of the key players are now dead, and none left any record of
what took place. (In his daily diary, published in Hebrew, General Elazar blacked out the night of October 8 and recorded
only the following phrase: "Crucial meeting.") There is widespread knowledge among the Israeli defense and political leadership of what took place at the crucial meeting, but in
subsequent years those who were there—including stenogra-
phers and advisers—have never talked publicly about it.

The only significant objections came from within the nuclear
community, some of whose senior officials—but not Freier—
were said by an Israeli source to have accused the senior officials, in essence, of panicking. Their view was that the situation had not yet been reached for weapons of last resort, which
were then code-named, appropriately, the "Temple" weapons.

One former Israeli government official who was in the prime
minister's office that night depicted the chain-smoking Meir,
who slept very little during the early stages of the war, as confused and concerned by Dayan's report of imminent collapse.
The basic decision to arm the weapons of last resort was
reached easily, he said; there were far more complicated discussions of how many warheads to arm and where they were to be
targeted. There was a separate, preliminary briefing by technical experts from Dimona, led by Shalheveth Freier, who described the weapons and targets that were available for
immediate assembly.

The senior official also described the fear that swept through
the prime minister's staff when the arming of nuclear weapons
became known: "There were a few days there when it seemed
that the end of the world was near. For those of us who lived
through the Holocaust, we knew one thing—it will never happen again." The aide learned what happened from General
Leor, Meir's military assistant: "Gingy told me about the arm-

ing of the weapons. We were very intimate." The young general, who later died of cancer, had a child on duty at the front and was, as he told the aide, "scared to death."

One Israeli assumption was that the Soviets, who would learn—as they had learned other secrets inside Israel in recent years—of the nuclear arming, would then be compelled to urge their allies in Egypt and Syria to limit their offensive and not attempt to advance beyond the pre-1967 borders. And a Soviet warning was given, according to Mohammed Heikal, editor of *Al-Ahram*, the leading Egyptian newspaper, and *éminence grise* to Nasser and Sadat. In an interview, Heikal revealed that the Soviet Union had told the senior leadership of Egypt early in the war that the "Israelis had three warheads assembled and ready." The information was given to General Mohammed Abdel Ghany el-Gamasy, the Egyptian chief of staff, by a Soviet intelligence officer who had worked closely with el-Gamasy when he served earlier as chief of military intelligence. The Soviet message also reported, Heikal recalled, that Moshe Dayan had visited the front and returned to Tel Aviv "with a scary report" that was presented to Golda Meir's equally alarmed kitchen cabinet.

There was an equally important second purpose for the arming of nuclear weapons, according to former Israeli government officials: such a drastic step would force the United States to begin an immediate and massive resupply of the Israeli military. There was widespread rage inside the Israeli cabinet at the Nixon White House—aimed especially at Henry Kissinger —over what was correctly perceived in Israel as an American strategy of delaying the resupply in an attempt to let the Arabs win some territory, and some self-respect, and thus set up the possibility of serious land-for-peace bargaining. Kissinger, just sworn in as secretary of state, would direct the negotiations.

Kissinger made no secret of his initial strategy in the war, telling James R. Schlesinger, the secretary of defense, that his goal was to "let Israel come out ahead, but bleed." Kissinger's goal was defended by some of his fellow diplomats as business as usual. "Trying to take advantage of the situation?" rhetorically asked Nicholas Veliotes. "We always do this."

In the second volume of his memoirs, *Years of Upheaval,* Kissinger made no mention of a nuclear threat, but he did describe a series of urgent telephone calls from Simcha Dinitz, the Israeli ambassador to Washington, that began at 1:45 A.M. on Tuesday, October 9—just as the all-night meeting in Golda Meir's office was breaking up (it was 8:45 A.M. in Israel). Dinitz focused on one question, wrote Kissinger: "What could we do about resupply?" The same question was asked again, in a second telephone call, at 3:00 A.M. "Unless he wanted to prove to the [Israeli] cabinet that he could get me out of bed at will," wrote Kissinger, "something was wrong." Kissinger, accompanied by Peter W. Rodman, his longtime assistant, and Dinitz, accompanied by General Mordecai Gur, the Israeli military attaché, met at 8:20 A.M. in the Map Room of the White House, where Kissinger was told of the desperate situation of the Israeli military and the need for more tanks and aircraft. "Israel stood on the threshold of a bitter war of attrition that it could not possibly win given the disparity of manpower," Kissinger said. "It had to do something decisive." At one point during the Map Room meeting, Kissinger wrote, Dinitz insisted that he and Kissinger needed to be alone. Rodman and Gur, who both could be trusted with the most sensitive information, were dismissed. Once they were alone, Dinitz's message, according to Kissinger, was merely that Golda Meir "was prepared to come to the United States personally for an hour to plead with President Nixon for urgent arms aid. . . ." It was a request that Kissinger could, and did, as he wrote, reject "out of hand and without checking with Nixon. Such a proposal could reflect only either hysteria or blackmail."

A more complete account of the Dinitz message would undoubtedly show that it was closer to blackmail, as Kissinger knew, and it worked. "By the evening of October 9," Kissinger said in his memoir, "Israel had been assured that its war losses would be made up. Relying on this assurance, it stepped up its consumption of war matériel, as we had intended."

How was Israel's warning of a potential Armageddon delivered to the United States? Neither Kissinger nor Dinitz could be reached to discuss the subject, although Dinitz's insistence on the one-on-one meeting with Kissinger—as well as Kissinger's description of the Dinitz message as "blackmail"—seems obviously linked to the nuclear issue. Word of the Israeli nuclear arming also came from the Soviets, according to a former Israeli intelligence official. The official said that Detachment 8200, the Israeli communications intelligence agency that had picked up the Soviet warning to Cairo—as acknowledged by Heikal—also intercepted on the morning of October 9 a Soviet warning to Washington about the Israeli arming of nuclear weapons. Asked why he thought the United States has never publicly mentioned such a warning, the Israeli responded: "Who in the U.S. is ready to admit that the Soviets were ahead?"

Kissinger has never talked publicly about the Israeli nuclear arming, and his closest advisers at the time, including Rodman and William G. Hyland, then handling Soviet affairs for the National Security Council, said they knew of no such information. The best source for what happened, nonetheless, is Kissinger himself, who privately acknowledged that there had been an Israeli nuclear threat both to Anwar Sadat and to Hermann F. Eilts, the American ambassador to Egypt who worked closely with Kissinger during the intense Middle East shuttle diplomacy of the mid-1970s.*

Eilts had been handpicked in October 1973 by Kissinger for the assignment to Cairo, and he arrived there at the end of the Yom Kippur War. His first detailed conversation with Kissinger about his new assignment couldn't have been more dramatic. It took took place, at Kissinger's request, at a hastily arranged breakfast in early November in Islamabad, Pakistan, where Kissinger had stopped overnight en route to a much-delayed visit to China. "Henry spoke a lot about how on the fourth day of the war [October 9] the Israelis panicked," Eilts recalled, "and that's when the judgment was made to assist them. At that point"—and in similar discussions with Kissinger over the next three years—"there was never a word about nuclear arming." There was a final meeting in late 1976,

---

* Eilts, a career diplomat, retired in 1979 after spending six years as ambassador to Egypt to become director of the Center for International Relations at Boston University.

at the end of the Ford administration—and the end of Kissinger's tenure as secretary of state—and Kissinger brought up the 1973 war again. "And then, in a sort of casual reference," Eilts said, "Henry threw in that there was concern that the Israelis might go nuclear. There had been intimations that if they didn't get military equipment, and quickly, they might go nuclear." Eilts recalled his surprise that "none of this had come out earlier." He also was surprised at the casualness of Kissinger's attitude: "It was just sort of a passing comment."

Kissinger was far less casual at the time he learned of Israel's intention. He told none of his colleagues in the cabinet about the nuclear threat, of course, but changed his mind overnight about the need to get military arms—in huge quantities—to Israel. "Israel's [ammunition] consumption rate was gauged for a seven-day war," recalled James Schlesinger—a reflection of Washington's confidence in the fighting ability of Israel's army and air force. "But Kissinger just turned around totally. He got a little hysterical" in urging an immediate and massive resupply. "Henry seemed to be more concerned than I was over the possibility of a nuclear exchange" in the Middle East, Schlesinger added. Kissinger's actions led some senior officials to conclude that Israeli use of a nuclear weapon was not out of the question. "From where we sat," Schlesinger said, "there was an assumption that Israel had a few nukes and that if there was a collapse, there was a possibility that Israel would use them." William E. Colby, then director of the CIA, shared the assumption: "We were afraid Israel might go for broke." It was believed, Colby added, that nuclear weapons would be used "only in an extreme situation."

Kissinger referred to the Israeli nuclear threat in his first extended private meeting in Cairo on November 7, 1973, with Egyptian President Anwar Sadat; it was a precursor of Kissinger's famed Middle East shuttle diplomacy that would begin the next year.* Sadat later briefed Mohammed Heikal about the

---

* During a tense moment in the shuttle diplomacy, Kissinger, in Israel, suddenly declared to Golda Meir, according to an American eyewitness: "First, I am an American; second, I am the secretary of state of the United States of America; third, I am a Jew." Meir replied without missing a beat: "That's all right, sonny, we read from right to left."

off-the-record meeting and, according to Heikal, told of a senior "American"—it could only have been Kissinger—who explained the sudden American airlift to Israel as a decision
aimed at avoiding a nuclear escalation. Sadat further quoted
Kissinger as saying, "It was serious, more serious than you can
imagine." Israel had at least three warheads and was preparing
to use them, Sadat told Heikal. (Kissinger apparently was relying on Carl Duckett's 1968 CIA estimate of Israeli warheads—
the only U.S. government estimate in existence in 1973—that
had placed the number of warheads at three or four.) The
Egyptian president, faithful to his promise of confidentiality to
Kissinger, never explicitly told Heikal where his information
came from, but Heikal had no doubt at the time or later: "The
only American with that kind of credibility, who would make
Sadat believe him [about the Israeli threat], was Henry Kissinger." Heikal subsequently wrote about the Kissinger comment, without indicating that Sadat had been his source, in *Al-
Ahram,* saying that the Nixon administration had feared during
the fighting that the Israelis "might lose their nerve and use
one of the three bombs they had in order to repel the Arab
offensive."

Sometime in this period, the American intelligence community
got what apparently was its first look, via the KH-11, at the
completed and operational missile launchers hidden in the side
of a hill at Hirbat Zachariah. The launchers were left in the
open, perhaps deliberately, making it much easier for American photo interpreters to spot them. (The Soviets also had satellite coverage in the Middle East, and presumably saw the same
missile field.) One U.S. official also recalled seeing hollowed-
out nuclear storage bunkers and huge blast doors, with railroad
tracks leading to a nearby mobile launching site.

By mid-October, the Israeli military had successfully counter-
attacked in the Golan Heights and the Sinai, ending any immediate threat—and the necessity for the nuclear alert. The
weapons were removed from their forward positions by October 14. The Egyptians, however, bolstered by a renewed airlift
of Soviet arms that began on October 10, mounted a second

offensive in the Sinai, which eventually was offset by a brilliant Israeli strike across the Suez Canal through a gap in the Egyptian lines.

With Egypt suddenly on the defensive, Soviet Premier Alexei N. Kosygin flew to Cairo on October 16 and persuaded Sadat to call for a cease-fire. Kissinger flew to Moscow on October 20 and to Tel Aviv two days later, where he received Israeli acquiesence for a cease-fire in place. In the meantime, the Egyptian Third Army was in danger of being surrounded and left essentially to the mercy of the Israeli Defense Force. The Israelis continued their offensive in Egyptian territory, moving north and west to a point within sixty miles of Cairo. The continued encirclement of the Third Army led Soviet party leader Leonid Brezhnev to increase the alert status of his airborne divisions and warn the White House that unless Israel stopped violating the cease-fire, "we should be faced with the necessity urgently to consider the question of taking appropriate steps unilaterally." The implication seemed to be that Brezhnev would send some of his troops as a blocking force behind the front lines in Egypt to prevent the Israelis from going on to Cairo.

The perceived threat came a few days after Nixon, more deeply embattled than ever over the Watergate scandals, had publicly fired Archibald Cox, the special Watergate prosecutor, and accepted the resignation of Attorney General Elliot L. Richardson and William D. Ruckelshaus, Richardson's deputy, in what became known as the "Saturday Night Massacre." The President earlier had been rocked by the indictment on corruption charges and subsequent resignation of Vice President Spiro T. Agnew. Another complication was the publicly announced Arab boycott of oil sales to the United States and the Arab decision to increase crude oil prices dramatically.

There is no evidence that the Soviets did, in fact, contemplate any significant deployment of their airborne troops, despite their high alert status. Most scholars now agree that Brezhnev's warning to the White House was aimed at forcing Washington to urge the Israelis to adhere to the cease-fire. Kissinger did pressure the Israelis (there is no evidence that Nixon, consumed by Watergate, played any significant role in the issue) on the cease-fire, but at the same time he ordered the 82nd Airborne Division and the nuclear-armed B-52s of the Strategic Air Command to go on alert. The aircraft carrier *John F. Kennedy* also was dispatched to the Mediterranean, and at least fifty B-52s were redeployed from Guam to the United States. The nation, still reeling from the continuing Watergate revelations, was stunned—and distressed—by the White House's unilateral action; there was widespread belief that the alert had been ordered primarily for domestic political purposes and not because the Soviets were ready to move into the Middle East.*

Israel responded to the American alert by going on nuclear alert for a second time in the Yom Kippur War, according to Yuval Neeman, the physicist and nuclear expert who served in later Israeli governments as minister of science and technology.

This time, the crisis resolved itself quickly, as Golda Meir ordered her army to stop all offensive action against Egypt, permitting a United Nations peacekeeping force to impose the cease-fire. At this point, however, a small undercover U.S. Navy intelligence unit, known as Task Force 157, operating in the waters of the Bosporus off Turkey, relayed data to Washington suggesting that one of the Soviet ships leaving the Black Sea en route to the Mediterranean was carrying radioactive material. The report from the Navy swept through the American intelligence community and the White House. Over the next few days, as the Soviets and many in Congress and the American media accused Nixon and Kissinger of overreacting,

---

* Many of Kissinger's senior aides and others in the government, including William Colby, defended the alert. Colby recalled that there had been a steady stream of intelligence reports suggesting that the Soviet Union was preparing some of its most highly trained paratroop units and its transport fleet for deployment to the Middle East. On the night of the alert, he said, the American intelligence community "lost the transport fleet. We were afraid it'd gone" to the Middle East with Soviet paratroopers. Another senior NSC aide confirmed Colby's account and added: "I thought they were coming" —a point of view, he added, that he successfully urged on Kissinger. The NSC aide added that neither he nor Kissinger anticipated that word of the heightened alert would become known so quickly. "We weren't trying to signal the Soviets," the aide said. "We just didn't realize that the military would begin calling back privates and corporals from leave"—making it impossible to keep the alert secret from the press. Another equally senior American official, who had access to all of the available intelligence, viewed the actions of both Washington and Moscow simply as "posturing. We were publicly threatening to go [into the Sinai] ourselves and the Soviets were countering."

descriptions of the Soviet threat, including dramatic details of
its shipment of nuclear warheads into Egypt, began appearing
in the press.

The most complete account of the alleged Soviet escalation,
as seen from the White House, was published in *Kissinger*, a 1974
biography written by Marvin and Bernard Kalb, then correspondents for CBS. Kissinger, the main source for the book,
was said on the morning after the alert to have been informed
by the CIA of "an alarming report from Egypt—that the Russians might have landed nuclear weapons there." American intelligence, the Kalbs wrote, "had kept track of a Soviet ship
carrying radioactive material and heading toward Port Said."
It was presumed, the authors wrote, that several Soviet nuclear
warheads had been provided to Egypt for deployment in Scud
missiles. "The report tended to harden Kissinger's judgment
that the Russians were going to send airborne troops to
Egypt," the Kalbs added. "Nuclear weapons could serve as
backup protection for a sizable Soviet force. On the other hand,
Kissinger could not dismiss the possibility that the Russians
were moving nuclear weapons into Egypt because they believed that the Israelis had nuclear weapons and intended to
use them against Egypt."

The only flaw in the Kissinger account, as told to the Kalbs,
is that it was not true. In fact, the Task Force 157 report had
been discounted almost immediately by the intelligence community. One high-ranking American officer, who was in
charge of a major intelligence agency at the time, said that
reconnaissance had established that the Soviets had loaded nuclear warheads on a cargo ship in a Black Sea port—but never
shipped them. "A different ship goes through," the officer explained, "and dumb little 157 flashes a message" that Soviet warheads were heading for the Mediterranean, and possibly Egypt.
"Everybody in the United States goes crazy, but it turns out to
be a totally false reading. It was a different ship" that moved
into the Black Sea. There was a direct approach to Soviet officials: "The Soviets said, 'We didn't send anything out.'" The
intelligence community concluded that there was no evidence
of a Soviet attempt to bring nuclear warheads into the battle

zone.* The evidence that did exist, in fact, as was not reported at the time, or cited later by Kissinger in his memoirs, demonstrated that the Soviets had ordered their destroyers and other vessels in the Middle East to steam to the nearest ports and off-load their nuclear weapons. There was a consensus among senior intelligence officials in the Pentagon, recalled Patrick J. Parker, then the deputy assistant secretary of defense for intelligence, that "[t]he Soviets were understandably frightened of the situation and eager to contain it."

Kissinger also made no mention of the alleged Soviet warhead shipment in the second volume of his memoirs, nor has he —or any American official—revealed that Israel issued two nuclear alerts during the crisis. He did emerge, however, from the October crisis with renewed official concern about Dimona. Some weeks afterward, Kissinger asked the CIA for a formal National Intelligence Estimate on the Israeli nuclear program; the paper, which concluded that Israel had at least ten nuclear warheads, took Carl Duckett's Office of Science and Technology months to prepare and then was submitted only to the White House.**

The Israeli government concluded by the end of the war that the American intelligence community had somehow learned—

---

* A former member of Task Force 157 acknowledged that there was no way that the unit on duty in Turkey, whose function was to photograph and monitor all Soviet ship deployments from the Black Sea, could independently establish the bona fides of its reports. The unit, he explained, was manned by specially recruited Turkish citizens who were not competent to make on-the-spot assessments, but instead relayed their tapes and other data by commercial aircraft to Washington for analysis. The conclusion that there were warheads aboard the Soviet cargo ship came from a Navy laboratory in Washington, the former 157 member said, and not from Turkey. "We never had any knowledge at all [in the field] whether anything was hot or not," he added.

** Another as yet unresolved question about the Yom Kippur War revolves around the question of nuclear deterrence: did Egypt and Syria limit their initial operations in fear of a nuclear response if they penetrated too deeply? Mohammed Heikal, for example, insisted that the Soviet reports about the Israeli nuclear arming—while taken very seriously—had no impact on the overall Egyptian military operation. Egypt's military goals, he said, had been sharply limited from the outset. There is clear evidence that Syria also set very limited goals for its military, for its army came to a literal stop—with no opposition in front of it—more than a day before Golda Meir's kitchen cabinet met in Tel Aviv to authorize the nuclear arming. The best guess at this point is that Syrian and Egyptian planners certainly were aware that any deep penetration inside the pre-1967 borders would have occasioned a massive, and perhaps nuclear, counterattack—but the fact that no such advance was planned or sought had much more to do with the myth of Israeli military invincibility than with a specific concern about the weapons at Dimona.

independently of what the Soviets or Ambassador Dinitz had revealed—of the arming of the Israeli warheads. "Somehow, and this I know for sure," a former member of Golda Meir's personal staff said, "the Americans found out about it and Mossad did an investigation as to how the U.S. found out. Golda asked Mossad to investigate how much damage it caused." There was another aspect to the inquiry, the Israeli added, based on Israel's understanding that American intelligence had discovered Soviet warheads being moved through the Black Sea: "Was there a threat? How much did they [the United States] tell us? What did the U.S. know and when did they tell us?"

The results of the Mossad inquiry could not be learned, but Golda Meir's concern about America's ability to penetrate Israel seemed to diminish as Kissinger's shuttle diplomacy got under way. There was one tantalizing public reference, however, published with little fanfare seven years later, suggesting that the United States had known independently of the nuclear alert as it took place. On March 10, 1980, journalist Jack Anderson's syndicated daily column—largely about the American oil industry's influence inside the Department of Energy—included a four-paragraph addendum entitled "Close Call." The filler item said in part: "Locked in secret Pentagon files is startling evidence that Israel maneuvered dangerously near the edge of nuclear war after the 1973 Arab assault. The secret documents claim that Israel came within hours of running out of essential arms. 'At this crucial moment, the possibility of nuclear arms was discussed with the U.S.,' declares one report. American authorities feared the Israelis might resort to nuclear weapons to assure their survival. This was the most compelling reason, according to the secret papers, that the United States rushed conventional weapons to Israel."

Further evidence of the Israeli willingness to use nuclear weapons in the 1973 war—or to threaten their use—was provided at a meeting early the next year between David Elazar and Lieutenant General Orwin C. Talbott, deputy commander of the U.S. Army's Training and Doctrine Command (TRADOC). Talbott was on an extended visit to Israel to discuss some of the lessons learned in the 1973 war and to inspect captured Arab and Soviet military equipment; there was considerable contact with Elazar, still the Israeli chief of staff. At one meeting, Talbott recalled, Elazar suddenly began talking "out of the blue" about Israel's threat to use nuclear weapons in the desperate moments of the 1973 war: "My impression at the time was that he was trying through me to let Washington know how serious the situation was—approaching the point where they were ready to use them [nuclear weapons]." Talbott understood the significance of the information and quickly filed a top-secret one-page memorandum for General Creighton W. Abrams, the Army chief of staff. "I made no copies of it and gave it to nobody else," the general, now retired, said. "I figured this was not discussable information at that time. I assumed Dado was trying to get a message to us."*

General Talbott had done his part, but his report to Creighton Abrams went nowhere. Carl Duckett, who at the time had direct responsibility for the CIA's intelligence on the Israeli nuclear arsenal, first learned of the Talbott message from the author; he also said he had never been informed of any intelligence suggesting that Israel had gone on two nuclear alerts during the Yom Kippur War.

The disconnect when it came to a nuclear-armed Israel was near-total: a CIA official assigned to Israel also had direct knowledge of the nuclear alert and did not tell his superiors what he knew, just as Henry Kissinger had told no one. The CIA official was an expert in communications intelligence and spent three years in Israel in the early 1970s as an undercover liaison officer with Detachment 8200; one of his assignments was to help the Israelis monitor the sophisticated Soviet radar and communications gear that had been supplied to the Egyptians during the War of Attrition. Israel also was operating, with the aid of equipment leased from the National Security Agency, at least three supersecret listening posts capable of

* Talbott was accompanied during the meeting with Elazar by Colonel Bruce Williams, the U.S. Army attaché in Israel. Williams similarly remembered Elazar's remarks as revelatory: "I can't recall the exact words," he said, "but the message was clear: Israel was prepared to use nuclear weapons against the Syrians if they'd broken through."

intercepting communications throughout the Middle East and as far north as southern Russia.* The intercepted intelligence was shared with the United States, and the American under- cover operative was able to learn a great deal about the opera- tions of the Israeli signals intelligence community.

After the war, the official prepared a highly classified report on some of the Israeli deception techniques that had been suc- cessfully used for, among other things, relaying bogus orders to Egyptian and Syrian forces. "I wrote a small report for Jessup" —Peter Jessup had returned for a second tour as CIA station chief in the early 1970s—"but I knew the Israelis would pick it up out of Washington if it was filed. So I was very careful in what I said. I did not mention that the conversations [with his Israeli counterparts] got to nuclear threats. I knew that the weapons available were something to be reckoned with, and they [the Israelis] told me that this had been communicated to the Egyptians. They said, 'We've developed this method of communication with each other.'"

The CIA official was rotated back to Washington after the 1973 war and was summoned by James Angleton, the counter- intelligence head, who was still handling Israeli affairs. An- gleton had seen his report on Israeli deception techniques and wanted a special debriefing. It was a bizarre experience, the CIA official recalled: "I went through two days of debriefing by one of Angleton's guys with Angleton sitting outside the room at a secretary's desk." It was clear that the room was wired so that Angleton could monitor the conversation. The aide would occasionally leave the room to check a fact or line of query with Angleton, who never made an appearance, and whose presence was limited to an occasional scraping of his chair.

"I did not talk about the nuclear issue," the CIA official ac- knowledged. "And I did not put it into any messages. I felt it was something that other people knew about—and nobody wanted to hear it from me."

* One of the joint sites, at Mount Hermon in the Golan Heights, was overrun by Syria in the first day of the war. Within fifteen minutes, according to former Israeli intelligence officers, Soviet helicopters had arrived and began dismantling the equip- ment. It was a stunning loss: there were as many as seven underground levels full of most sensitive listening and recording gear—all of which ended up in Soviet posses- sion. Israel reclaimed the destroyed facility by war's end.

The Israeli and American governments returned to the policy of see no evil, hear no evil, speak no evil. In June 1974, however, Anwar Sadat announced that his country had obtained intelligence indicating that Israel had developed tactical nuclear weapons. A week later, Shimon Peres, defense minister in a new Israeli government headed by Yitzhak Rabin, categorically denied the existence of any such weapons and accused Sadat of "gathering information of his own making." The squabble between the two countries was treated perfunctorily by the press and provoked no concern from President Gerald R. Ford or his senior aides. A National Security Council official did broach the issue, very gently, with an Israeli diplomat over lunch more than a year later. "I told him I thought my people had the perception that Israel had nuclear weapons," the aide reported in a subsequent internal memorandum. The Israeli diplomat denied the existence of any Israeli bomb and seemed to be "visibly disturbed. . . . He was not pleased with the course of the conversation, and switched the subject to music and the arts, where it remained."

Carl Duckett made a career-ending mistake in March 1976: he talked openly about Israel's nuclear weapons. On March 11, 1976, Duckett was one of a group of CIA officials who participated in an informal seminar before a group of local members of the American Institute of Aeronautics and Astronautics. Such sessions, held at an auditorium near the CIA's main headquarters building at McLean, Virginia, were standard Washington fare; any remarks were understood to be limited to unclassified materials. During a question-and-answer session, Duckett was asked about Israel's nuclear capability and replied without hesitation that Israel was estimated to have ten to twenty nuclear weapons "available for use." Within days, an account of his remarks was published in the *Washington Post*, forcing George Bush, the newly installed CIA director, to issue a public statement assuming "full responsibility" for the disclosure of the secret information. The obviously angry Bush added that he was "determined it will not happen again." Duckett was rumored to have been drinking at the time of his appearance—the assumption seemed to be that only someone drunk would be so reckless as to discuss Israel's nuclear weaponry in public—and his subsequent request for retirement was accepted by Bush.

Duckett, discussing those events years later, acknowledged that the rumors of his heavy drinking "led to a discussion with Bush and my decision to leave." The real issue, however, he insisted, was not his drinking but Bush's unwillingness to promote him to deputy CIA director.

There was one enduring legacy: the CIA would continue to know very little about the Israeli nuclear arsenal. Duckett's 1974 estimate giving Israel ten to twenty nuclear weapons would remain the official American intelligence estimate until the early 1980s—years in which Israel was exponentially increasing its nuclear warhead stockpile. Duckett acknowledged that there was no specific intelligence behind the estimate. "We were trying to think what their targets would be," he explained, and using that information to predict the number of warheads that would be manufactured. "We were speculating," he said of his staff. "Our guess was that the Israelis would not have a reason for building more bombs [than ten to twenty]—and that's why our numbers stayed fairly fixed. It was based on very little."

18

Injustice

Carl Duckett's top-secret CIA estimate in 1968 that Israel had three or four nuclear bombs was primarily based on his conviction that an American Jew named Zalman Shapiro had smuggled more than two hundred pounds of enriched uranium into Israel—enough for four bombs. The alleged smuggled uranium also was a major factor in Duckett's second estimate, in 1974, that credited Israel with at least ten bombs; it was based on the amount of uranium he believed Shapiro had diverted plus a guess that the technicians at Dimona could have chemically separated enough plutonium from the reactor to have produced six weapons or more since 1970. Just how Israel would accomplish that feat without a chemical reprocessing plant—the CIA still had no proof that such a plant existed in Israel—was not clear, but what was clear was Shapiro's culpability. To Duckett and his colleagues, especially Richard Helms, the case against Shapiro was unassailable.

In the CIA's view, Shapiro was more than just a Jew who supported Israel; he was a Jew in the nuclear-fuel-processing business who traveled regularly to Israel and was a partner with the Israeli government in some business ventures. He fit the dual-loyalty stereotype in many other ways: he was the high-achieving son of an Orthodox rabbi who emigrated from Lithuania; he was valedictorian of his high school class in Passaic, New Jersey, before attending Johns Hopkins University; he got a master's degree while going to night school; and—with the aid of a fellowship from Standard Oil of Indiana—he earned his doctorate in chemistry in 1948, at the age of twenty-eight. Shapiro, with his brilliance and capacity for hard work, was among the first scientists—and most certainly one of the first Jews—to be hired to develop submarine reactors for a newly established laboratory operated by the Westinghouse Electric Corporation for the U.S. Navy.

As his career progressed, Shapiro—who underwent rigorous national security checks while at Westinghouse—made no secret of his strong commitment to Israel; some of his family had been victims of the Nazis, and he believed in the need for an independent Jewish state. He became an active member of the Zionist Organization of America and also generously supported the American Technion Society, which raises funds and provides equipment to the Technion-Israel Institute of Technology in Haifa, Israel's most advanced school of science and engineering.

In 1957, he organized a publicly owned nuclear fuel processing firm, with at least twenty-five stockholders, in an abandoned World War II steel plant in Apollo, Pennsylvania, twenty-five miles northeast of Pittsburgh. The firm, known as the Nuclear Materials and Equipment Corporation (NUMEC), was a small company in a nuclear-fuel-processing world that was dominated by Fortune 500 firms; there was a constant struggle to get contracts. Shapiro was aggressive in the pursuit of work for his young company, and by the early 1960s NUMEC was providing nuclear services for at least nine foreign countries. There was a steady stream of foreign visitors to the factory, many at the instigation of the Department of Commerce and the State Department, which were eager to show off the government's Atoms for Peace effort. There were at least three foreign employees at NUMEC, including an Israeli metallurgist assigned to unclassified breeder reactor fuel research. There also was constant back-and-forth in those years between AEC security officials and NUMEC over the handling of classified materials, and the company was required to improve its procedures.

In 1965, after years of internal audits and reviews, an AEC inspection team determined that more than two hundred pounds of enriched uranium that had been supplied by Westinghouse and the Navy to NUMEC for processing and fabrication could not be accounted for; eventually the Joint Atomic

Energy Committee—as well as the CIA—came to suspect that Shapiro had diverted the uranium to Israel.

Shapiro would be hounded by those suspicions for the next twenty-five years—although the most significant evidence against him seemed to be his Jewishness and the fact that one of the major investors in NUMEC shared his support for Israel. A number of experienced investigators from the government and the Congress, as well as dozens of journalists, assumed that Shapiro's emotional tie to Israel was enough of a motive for him to commit nuclear espionage, a crime punishable by death under the Atomic Energy Act.

Despite more than ten years of intensive investigation involving active FBI surveillance, however, no significant evidence proving that Shapiro had diverted any uranium from his plant was ever found. Nonetheless, he remained guilty in the minds of many in the government and the press; reporters invariably included an account of Shapiro's ties to Israel and the alleged NUMEC diversion in any story about the development of nuclear arms in Israel. Some of the newspaper and book accounts did note that the charges against Shapiro were never proved; many others simply declared that it was the Shapiro uranium that gave Israel the nuclear bomb.

Zalman Shapiro did not divert uranium from his processing plant to Israel, but there is little solace for the nuclear industry in that fact: the missing uranium was not stolen at all—it ended up in the air and water of the city of Apollo as well as in the ducts, tubes, and floors of the NUMEC plant. There is little solace, too, for the American intelligence community in Shapiro's noninvolvement with nuclear diversion, for it failed to learn of Shapiro's close ties to Ernst David Bergmann and Binyamin Blumberg and the sensitive—and legitimate—mission he did conduct for his beloved Israel.

Shapiro's business was not a pretty one: many of NUMEC's contracts involved the chemical isolation and recovery of enriched uranium from the dirt and scrap generated in fabricating nuclear fuel. The scrap was chemically treated—sometimes two or three times—in an attempt to isolate the salvageable uranium. The process inherently generated some loss; small amounts of enriched uranium were constantly being flushed out in waste water or lodged in scrub brushes, air vents, filtration systems, cleaning pads, and air masks. It was the kind of work NUMEC's larger and more solidly financed competitors did not want. Other NUMEC contracts involved cleaner work, such the conversion of highly enriched uranium (93 percent U-235) from gaseous uranium hexafluoride—the form in which it was shipped from the government's huge uranium diffusion plants—into uranium oxide powder capable of being fabricated into nuclear fuel for Navy reactors. That process, too, created waste—as much as 10 to 15 percent of the uranium eventually ended up as scrap and needed to be recovered. Since working with weapons-grade material was exceedingly dangerous, NUMEC had to divide the uranium being processed into small lots—creating more opportunity for waste— to guard against the horrible possibility of setting off a chain reaction. Under the stringent AEC rules governing the reprocessing of weapons-grade uranium and plutonium, Shapiro's firm was responsible and had to pay enormous penalties for any enriched materials that could not be accounted for —as much as $10 a gram; each missing pound thus meant a loss of more than $4,500.

The term MUF, for "material unaccounted for," became a common one in the nuclear processing industry. Making the contractors pay for missing materials also was the backbone of the AEC's safeguards program; the assumption was that no reprocessing firm would divert or steal uranium if it resulted in a stiff fine.

The AEC eventually worked out complicated rules for accounting for MUF that enabled private firms such as NUMEC to estimate in their regular reports how much missing but accountable uranium was believed to be in a plant's air filtration system or buried in its waste pits. NUMEC would routinely report seemingly huge losses of enriched materials on any given contract—thirty or forty pounds was not unusual—and then estimate that 80 percent or more of the lost materials would be recovered upon cleanup. The AEC accepted such estimates as realistic, and deferred the assessments of any penalties.

The fact that nuclear waste was considered an inevitable by-product of the business, just as sawmills produce sawdust, was not really a secret—it was just one of those facts that the public did not need to know, and especially so as the nation became increasingly sensitized to the environmental costs of the nuclear industry. The enriched materials handled by the workers at NUMEC were not "hot," as commonly understood, for they had not yet been irradiated in a reactor and thus did not emit penetrating and lethal radiation. The danger facing the NUMEC employees came from breathing in or otherwise ingesting uranium, which, like all heavy metals, accumulates in bones, where it eventually impacts on bone marrow, causing leukemia. Enriched uranium, if breathed into the lungs, also could trigger lung cancer, and the NUMEC employees were constantly urged to wear face masks, although many refused to do so in the summer.

Zalman Shapiro's career-destroying problems began in 1962, when he was the low bidder for two complicated Westinghouse contracts, involving the processing of more than 2,500 pounds of enriched uranium. NUMEC was assured by Westinghouse that 60 percent or more of each hundred kilograms of uranium could successfully be processed—meaning that as much as 40 percent of the uranium would be scrap, to be separately recovered. In fact, NUMEC found that the process was far more difficult than Westinghouse had claimed for one of the contracts, and resulted in only a 35 percent yield of acceptable product. Nearly two thirds of the Westinghouse-supplied uranium ended up as scrap, much of it—so Shapiro and his associates thought—eventually buried in barrels, along with contaminated rags and other cleaning equipment, in two huge waste pits on the NUMEC grounds. The pits included contaminated waste not only from the Westinghouse contract but from other processing jobs for private companies; Shapiro had not isolated the scrap from each of his contracts, as the AEC demanded. AEC investigators subsequently became convinced that Shapiro had deliberately commingled the scrap from different contracts as a money-saving bookkeeping measure. Shapiro also angered the AEC by his reluctance—again for pocketbook reasons—to begin the time-consuming job of reprocessing the scrap to extract the missing uranium; he instead kept his employees at work on new processing contracts, for which there would be immediate payment. Stalling the AEC inspection teams, which were demanding that the missing uranium be accounted for, one way or another, became a way of life at NUMEC.

The AEC tried to resolve the complicated mess in a series of extensive negotiations in 1964 and 1965, with Shapiro constantly citing NUMEC's precarious financial condition to justify his actions. Portions of the 1963 waste pit eventually were dug up, and AEC inspectors found that the amount of enriched uranium buried there was not nearly enough to match the huge losses. The inspectors concluded that there was a MUF of 93.8 kilograms (206 pounds) of enriched uranium; they also told headquarters that because of NUMEC's "inadequate and incomplete accounting records," a diversion could not be ruled out, although there was "no evidence" that a diversion had taken place. The issue was aired at a special meeting in February 1966 of the AEC commissioners and senior staff, and, according to a declassified transcript of that meeting, the commissioners agreed that NUMEC's employees be interviewed to find out what had happened. It was further agreed that a trip would have to be taken to Capitol Hill to inform the Joint Atomic Energy Committee of the loss.

The report to Congress was a bombshell. The American nuclear community already had been rocked in October 1964 upon learning that China's first nuclear bomb had been triggered by uranium, and not plutonium, as the CIA and other intelligence agencies had widely anticipated. There was immediate suspicion that China had somehow bought on the black market—or stolen—the enriched uranium for its bomb (the CIA would not learn for another year or so that China had completed a huge diffusion plant much earlier than expected). A special study into AEC safeguards was commissioned, and it questioned the commission's heavy reliance on financial penalties as a sufficient bar against nuclear diversion. The Joint Committee's report noted that the AEC's position seemed to be that all of its responsibility "had been fulfilled . . . as long as material was paid for."

The AEC, sensitive to the diversion issue, had referred the NUMEC losses to the FBI in October 1965, but the FBI saw no basis for an investigation; its senior counterintelligence officials concluded, according to declassified documents, that "this situation up to now has been rightfully treated by AEC as an administration matter and there appears to be no basis for us to take any action. . . ." An AEC inspection team eventually interviewed more than 120 employees at NUMEC. No evidence of a diversion was established.

The CIA, nonetheless, found Shapiro's long-standing ties to Israel to be of continuing interest. Shapiro was a frequent visitor to Israel, and Israelis were among the many foreign visitors who had registered for tours of NUMEC. Shapiro also was a partner with the Israeli government in a business involving the pasteurization of food and the sterilization of medical supplies by irradiation; packages to and from NUMEC were being shipped out of and into Israel. By late 1966, although reports of Israel's progress in nuclear weaponry began to flow from the American embassy in Tel Aviv, John Hadden, the CIA station chief, was still unable to find proof that Israel had a chemical reprocessing plant at Dimona. And without such a plant, Israel would have needed an independent source of enriched uranium or plutonium to manufacture the bombs that, so Hadden's informants told him, existed.

Duckett and Helms shared Hadden's view that Shapiro had to have been the source for the Israeli progress in nuclear weaponry; the two men would spend the next few years pushing their suspicions on anybody—including Presidents Johnson and Nixon—who would listen. They were mesmerized by Shapiro's links to Israel and the fact that one of the initial stockholders in NUMEC, David Lowenthal, had helped bring illegal immigrants into Israel before 1948. Duckett even came to believe, as he later told congressional investigators, that NUMEC had been set up in 1957 by Shapiro as part of a long-range Israeli intelligence scheme to divert uranium. Duckett and Helms were supported in most of their suspicions by

George F. Murphy, assistant staff director of the Joint Atomic Energy Committee, who also was convinced that the two hundred pounds of enriched uranium could not simply have disappeared into NUMEC's refuse pits and air ducts. Murphy, who had no technical understanding of the nuclear fuel cycle, found Shapiro's alleged sloppy bookkeeping, as reported by the AEC, to be preposterous: in his view, "Shapiro was the sharpest, hardest-headed businessman I've ever known." Murphy also was appalled by what he considered to be a lack of security at NUMEC and told a congressional investigator of seeing uranium pellets scattered "all over the benches" during a visit to the Apollo plant. The possibility of a diversion to Israel seemed solid, and Shapiro was put under FBI surveillance in the late 1960s.

Shapiro, meanwhile, in a desperate effort to save his company, hired James E. Lovett, a senior AEC scientist, to take over nuclear materials accountability at NUMEC. One of Lovett's first acts was to insist that the concrete floor of the old plant be protected with stainless steel; concrete, Lovett knew, absorbed far more uranium than suspected. Shapiro and other company officials "were deluding themselves," Lovett recalled. "They honestly thought that if it came down to the end, they'd recover most" of the two hundred or more pounds of missing uranium in NUMEC's waste pits. But most of the uranium was not in the plant's waste pits; it was embedded in the concrete floor, clinging to ventilation ducts, flushed out with other plant wastes into the local waterways, and scattered in the air.

The continuing controversy over the alleged diversion became widely known inside the tight-knit nuclear community, and Shapiro suffered. "I was a smelly dead fish," he bitterly recalled. "Contracts were pulled away and given to others." In 1967, Shapiro and his partners were forced to merge their interest in NUMEC into the Atlantic Richfield Company (ARCO); Shapiro, with his special Q clearance (for atomic energy matters) still intact, continued to run the plant.

Shapiro, as the CIA and AEC never learned, did have a secret life. He had met and befriended many of Israel's senior nuclear scientists on his visits there, and was especially devoted to Ernst David Bergmann, who was head of Israel's Atomic En-

ergy Commission until 1966. "He was a genius," Shapiro said of
Bergmann. "He was a genius's genius. He worked night and
day. I don't know when he slept." Bergmann was especially
interested in a nuclear-powered water desalinization plant,
Shapiro said.

Water, of course, was the most precious of commodities in
Israel. In 1964, the country completed a 150-mile conduit,
known as the National Water Carrier, to bring water from the
north to the Negev. The system, then Israel's largest development project, linked local and regional water conduits to form
an integrated network that sought to capture all of the nation's
rainfall and channel it into reservoirs. The National Water Carrier was not completed, however, without a series of disputes
with Syria, especially over Israel's goal of bringing water south
from Lake Kinneret in Galilee. There were huge stretches in
northern Israel where water being moved to the south was in
the open, protected only by fencing; the waterway was an obvious target for terrorists. El Fatah, the Arab guerrilla group
(and later an important member of the Palestine Liberation
Organization), boasted that it would poison the water. At one
point, Israeli security officials suspected that El Fatah had attempted to cut the fence protecting the water works in what
was feared to be an effort to plant a bomb.

It was at this point that Zalman Shapiro was asked by Israel
to devise a rapid and accurate method of determining whether
water had been contaminated with toxic materials. There was a
second problem: as much as 30 percent of the water was disap-
pearing while traveling to the south, and Israeli officials were
unable to determine where and how the loss was taking place.
Shapiro acknowledged, reluctantly, that he also advised on that
issue, eventually recommending that a radioactive tracer be
added to the water in Lake Kinneret to monitor the flow. He
had decided not to discuss specifically all of his activities on
behalf of Israel during the many government and congressional
investigations into NUMEC, he said, because of the continued
threat to the Israeli water supply: "I didn't want to put any
ideas into people's minds."

In the late 1960s, Shapiro convened a series of meetings—
some in his home—of American scientists and Israelis to dis-

cuss, he said, the issue of how to protect the National Water
Carrier from potential terrorists. Some of the sessions, considered *prima facie* suspect by Duckett and his colleagues, were
monitored by the FBI. At the time, NUMEC was under contract to provide to Israel specialized small power sources,
whose function Shapiro refused to spell out, other than to acknowledge that they were linked to the security of the waterways. All of the items shipped were approved by the
Commerce Department for export, he said. "We had permits
for what we did. I never transmitted any documents to anybody," he insisted. "The meetings pertained only to the water
supply."

Shapiro would not say whether he knew—as did many
American scientists—of the work being done at Dimona. He
did acknowledge an acquaintanceship with Binyamin Blumberg, the director of Israel's Science Liaison Bureau: "I never
said I didn't know him." But he denied revealing any American
secrets or diverting any materials. "I worked my butt off to
assure the security of this country—do you think for a moment
I'd do anything to impair its security?"

Duckett and Helms remained convinced that Shapiro was
guilty of espionage. Duckett's conversation with Edward
Teller and his early-1968 estimate of Israeli nuclear capacity led
Helms to urge the FBI to renew its investigation into Shapiro's
dealings with Israel. The FBI's J. Edgar Hoover was then in
the midst of a bitter dispute with James Angleton's counter-
intelligence shop over the CIA's handling of defectors, as well
as the continuing—and illegal—CIA spying inside the United
States under a presidential mandate to determine whether the
anti–Vietnam War movement was being directed by Moscow.
Hoover chose to spar with Helms over the Shapiro issue for the
next year, according to a former congressional investigator
who has reviewed the Senate and House intelligence committees' files on Shapiro. "The CIA was saying to Hoover," the
investigator recalled, " 'You're responsible for counterintelligence in America. Investigate Shapiro, and if he's a spy, catch
him.' Hoover's answer was, 'We don't really know if anything's
been taken. Go to Israel and get inside Dimona, and if you find

it [evidence of the Shapiro uranium], let us know.' It was kind of a game," the investigator added. "The memos were hysterical—they went back and forth."

The NUMEC file remained buried, with Shapiro again working for Westinghouse, until 1975, when James H. Conran, an analyst in the Nuclear Regulation Commission (NRC), one of two new agencies that had been formed when the AEC was dissolved earlier in the year, was assigned to write a history of nuclear safeguards. He was denied access to the NUMEC file on grounds of security, and began a fervid campaign to get a briefing on NUMEC for the five NRC commissioners and their immediate staffs. He could not write his report, he said, unless he got that file.

There was another significant issue at stake: the nuclear power industry was pushing hard to get public and government support for a huge plutonium recycling industry. It seemed as if the future of nuclear power now depended on public acceptance of fast breeder reactors capable of generating more plutonium fuel than they consumed. The public policy issue was obvious: how could the world's governments prevent the diversion of plutonium for military use? Bringing up the NUMEC issue once again created a very much unwanted dilemma: either there had been a diversion, or the inherent loss of plutonium and uranium at processing facilities such as NUMEC—and there were many scattered across the nation—was far higher than publicly understood.

The advocates of nuclear power, who included many in the NRC, shuddered at the prospect of more adverse publicity about nuclear reactor safety and possible widespread contamination. Antinuclear groups were being organized around the world and had begun large, and sometimes violent, demonstrations in an effort to halt nuclear power.

Conran's insistence on determining what had happened to the missing uranium at NUMEC won him few friends, therefore, inside the NRC. A high-level briefing by Carl Duckett was arranged to discuss the possibility of a diversion. Victor Gilinsky, then an NRC commissioner, recalled Duckett's presentation as matter-of-fact: "Basically, Duckett was asked [about an Israeli bomb] and said the CIA thought Israel had nuclear weapons and the Agency thought there was a diversion. He didn't say anything that would convince you that was the case—but the issue from our point, our little world, is that he said what he did. We [the NRC commissioners] did not have responsibility for dealing with the Israelis—we take what other agencies think as a starting point." Gilinsky's contention was that the NRC had no obligation to determine whether Duckett's assertions were correct, but it agreed on the basis of what Duckett said to tighten up procedures for dealing with nuclear materials. Most of those at the Duckett briefing "were not involved in foreign affairs," Gilinsky noted. "They were protecting the notion that the NRC's procedures were adequate to protect plutonium. It was a threat to our claims that you could protect the stuff."

Duckett's briefing to the NRC and his subsequent informal talk at the CIA before the American Institute of Aeronautics and Astronautics Association, while ruinous to his career, did provoke another brief flurry of concern over NUMEC at the Ford White House—yet another investigation of Shapiro was initiated. Once again, however, the FBI could find no evidence of a diversion.

There was independent evidence, moreover, demonstrating that Shapiro's problems in operating NUMEC were not as exceptional as the AEC had publicly indicated in the mid-1960s. A continuing NRC investigation of the plant, which had been taken over in the early 1970s by Babcock & Wilcox, one of the nation's major reactor designers, concluded that another 198 pounds of enriched uranium was missing over a twenty-nine-month period beginning in April 1974. Further study showed that more than 110 pounds could be accounted for by what the NRC study called previously "unidentified and undocumented loss mechanisms"—such as the contamination of workers' clothing, losses from scrubber systems, material embedded in the flooring, and residual deposits in the processing equipment. The remaining lost uranium was attributed to "inevitable uncertainties in the measurement system and errors in the accounting system." In other words, uranium loss is hard to measure. The high volume of lost uranium raised obvious pol-

lution questions for the immediate area; the Apollo facility had
been discharging an average of 13,300 gallons of water and waste
effluents daily into the nearby Kiskiminetas River, a tributary
of the Allegheny River, which is the main source of drinking
water for several communities in the Pittsburgh area.*

In October 1977, Jody Powell, President Jimmy Carter's press
secretary, publicly announced that "four years of continuing
investigation" by the AEC, FBI, and General Accounting Office had "failed to reveal" a diversion of uranium to Israel. By
the end of the year the NUMEC case was being actively pur-
sued by the House Subcommittee on Oversight and Investigations, one of the most competent and aggressive investigative
units in the Congress, as well as the House Subcommittee on
Energy and the Environment. Carl Duckett and John Hadden,
both retired from the CIA, cooperated fully with the subcommittees; at one point, Duckett telephoned an investigator in the
middle of the night and insisted that he go to a pay telephone at
a gas station to return the call. He then urged that the investigation into Shapiro be carried forward. Hadden, meanwhile,
was repeatedly suggesting that the Israeli government had to
have a "mole"—a clandestine operative—inside the Atomic Energy Commission who had protected Shapiro in the early investigations of a possible diversion.

There was little due process for Shapiro in all of this. The
subcommittee investigators seemed to take every one of Duckett's and Hadden's claims at face value. But it is through those
claims that outsiders can begin to understand how the CIA and
the two congressional subcommittees weighed evidence and
what kind of internal checks and balances were imposed on
their investigations.

---

* An Apollo housewife, Cynthia A. Virostek, eventually began a campaign to increase public awareness of the potential pollution risk from the plant. In 1990, largely
on the strength of her protests, she was elected local councilwoman. Mrs. Virostek,
then thirty-five years old, lives with her husband and two sons five hundred feet from
the Babcock & Wilcox plant. She became involved after company officials announced in
the early 1980s that they were beginning decontamination operations. "That kind of
opened my eyes," she said. "I began asking questions about the plant and nobody gave
me answers." She then began a relentless campaign, through Freedom of Information
inquiries, to force information out into the open. A Pennsylvania health department
study eventually noted, Mrs. Virostek said, that her community was the only one in the
immediate area to have a statistically significant excess in the number of cancer deaths.

Duckett's beliefs were most directly expressed in a 1981 ABC television interview, when he said there had been a "clear consensus" inside the CIA that the "most likely case" was that Israel had become a nuclear power because of uranium supplied by Shapiro. "I certainly believe that to be the case. . . . I believe that all of my senior analysts who worked on the problem agreed with me fully," Duckett said. The subcommittee investigators had no way of knowing, of course, how little Duckett and his "senior analysts" had been able to learn about the Israeli nuclear arsenal. The subcommittees also did not know that Duckett's initial estimate of Israeli nuclear capability was primarily based on an assertion to that effect by Edward Teller, and not on any specific intelligence about the capacity of the Israeli reactor or the established existence of a chemical reprocessing plant at Dimona. There also was no specific evidence linking Shapiro to the delivery of enriched uranium to Israel. Nor did the subcommittees realize that Duckett's 1974 CIA estimate was not without its critics at the time. Intelligence officials at the Atomic Energy Commission insisted that a footnote be added to the estimate pointing out that "any information" about a diversion of uranium to Israel was unknown to the commission. "Duckett pushed real hard inside the USIB [United States Intelligence Board] to incorporate Israel and Apollo" in the special estimate, one AEC official recalled, "and it got in there."

Nonetheless, Henry R. Myers and Peter D. Stockton, the chief investigators for the congressional subcommittees, have spent nearly fifteen years relaying the Duckett and Hadden suppositions to journalists as the views of knowledgeable intelligence sources; many reporters published the beliefs of Duckett and Hadden as "facts."

For example, Myers, a specialist on energy issues for the House Subcommittee on Energy, told the author at the beginning of his research into Zalman Shapiro that there "are reasons to believe that NUMEC had been set up solely for the diversion. The reason for this," Myers explained, "is that no one's ever seen clearly where the money came from." Myers referred to David Lowenthal's role in 1948 in Israel and added: "There were reports of a secure telephone or teletype between

NUMEC and the Israeli embassy." Myers also told of sitting in
on a meeting about NUMEC between Richard Helms and a
group of legislators: "Helms said, in effect, that Shapiro was
the head of a group of people collecting information, some classified and some not, for Israel." There was a further allegation
that CIA operatives in Israel had found "traces of enriched
uranium" near Dimona that was similar to the enriched products that had been delivered for processing to Shapiro's plant.
There also was a highly suspicious meeting at the airport in
Pittsburgh between Shapiro and Jeruham Kafkafi, an Israeli
scientific attaché, who flew, so the FBI reported, from Washington to Pittsburgh for the meeting and returned immediately
to Washington. Myers described Kafkafi as "a possible Israeli
intelligence officer."

Myers continued to believe well into the early 1990s that his
statements were correct. But the fact is that David Lowenthal
was one of a number of investors in NUMEC, some of whom
were not Jewish. There was no special secure telephone or teletype at NUMEC, a fact acknowledged by Duckett and others
who have investigated the alleged diversion. Richard Helms
may indeed have been convinced that Shapiro was the head of
an Israeli spy ring, but there is no known factual basis for that
assertion. Duckett and other government investigators into
NUMEC acknowledged that there was no meaningful correlation between the uranium processed in the NUMEC plant and
the traces of enriched uranium picked up by American agents
outside Dimona. And, finally, Shapiro told the congressional
investigators—who obviously did not believe him—that his airport meeting with Kafkafi was arranged at his request because
he had not been paid for the antiterrorist equipment his company had shipped to Israel; NUMEC was owed $32,000—a fact
he found "embarrassing"—but the company needed the
money.

Duckett, in a 1991 interview, essentially recanted many of his
previous assertions. "With all the grief I've caused," he said,
referring to Shapiro's ruined career, "I know of nothing at all
to indicate that Shapiro was guilty. There's circumstantial information, but I have never attempted to make a judgment on

this. At no point did I have any vested interest in this whole process. It was a matter of trying to be sure when you had information that you passed it along. Ultimately," Duckett said, "you have no control over the information. I never met Shapiro and at no point was I interested in peddling the story."

Peter Stockton also acknowledged in a 1991 interview that he'd had continuing doubts about the credibility of Hadden. "I was never overwhelmed with him," Stockton said. He had been troubled, he said, when Hadden told one story to subcommittee investigators and legislators, and then told a different version of the same event to officials of the Government Accounting Office, which did a separate investigation of the alleged NUMEC diversion. "We were dependent on certain people," Stockton said, "who jerked us around." Yet Stockton continued to meet with reporters about NUMEC and continued to spread the same misinformation, and many journalists remain convinced that Shapiro diverted uranium for the Israeli bomb. In their book *Dangerous Liaison,* published in 1991, Andrew and Leslie Cockburn, who interviewed Stockton in 1989, depicted Shapiro's role in the Israeli acquisition of nuclear weapons as being so "delicate" that five American Presidents covered it up. "Stockton," they wrote, "found that at least one CIA official had a very clear idea of what the NUMEC affair was really all about. John Hadden. . . ."

Babcock & Wilcox shut down Zalman Shapiro's Apollo plant in 1978, when the nuclear fuels business suffered a downturn, largely because of reduced business from the Navy. Shapiro's insistence that the missing uranium had seeped into the ground or been flung into the air eventually spawned a controversy over nuclear pollution; Babcock & Wilcox, under public pressure, agreed to keep the Apollo plant open in an attempt to determine how much contamination existed. In 1989 the firm began to decontaminate the plant, an expensive process that involved the virtual dismantling of some areas. Babcock & Wilcox told the community that it would explore ways to return the site to productive use—and promised that future operations would involve no radioactive materials.

Late in 1990, Congress approved a Defense Department appropriations bill that included $30 million to be spent in an attempt to clean up the plant, with matching funds from Babcock & Wilcox. Company officials acknowledged that many sections of the plant, including its concrete floor, were so contaminated that they had to be dismantled, piece by piece, and buried at appropriate sites—after the valuable uranium was removed. Nuclear Regulatory Commission officials subsequently admitted that more than one hundred kilograms of enriched uranium—the amount allegedly diverted to Israel by Zalman Shapiro—was recovered from the decommissioned plant by 1982, with still more being recovered each year. (Such recoveries are called "inventory gains" by the NRC.) It wasn't clear how much uranium would finally be found. It also wasn't clear whether the $60 million allotted for the cleanup by the government and Babcock & Wilcox would be enough to do the job. And it wasn't clear that the site would ever be safe for occupancy.

19

The Carter Malaise

The surprising victory of Menachem Begin's Likud Party in the May 1977 national elections ended twenty-nine years of Mapai and Labor Party domination of the political process in Israel. It brought to power a government that was even more committed than Labor to the Samson Option and the necessity of an Israeli nuclear arsenal. Begin and his political followers represented a populist-nationalist view of a greater Israel with a right to permanent control of the West Bank; in their view, the mainstream Zionists, represented by men such as David Ben-Gurion, had fought three major wars with no grand strategy. Israel's military aims were seen as having been dictated by the other side, whose leaders had chosen when and on which front war would begin. Begin and his coalition were determined—as they would demonstrate with disastrous effect in the 1982 Lebanon War—to use Israeli might to redraw the political map of the Middle East.

Nuclear weapons appealed to another side of Begin's character—his fascination with dramatic military moves, as exemplified by his insistence on the bombing of Iraq's Osirak and his involvement, as a leader of Irgun, the underground Jewish terrorist organization, in the July 1946 bombing of the King David Hotel in Jerusalem.* Unlike many Israelis who had immigrated

---

* The hotel, which was the headquarters for the British military in Jerusalem, was destroyed after months of planning, following a major British sweep against the Jewish resistance movement in Palestine that resulted in many arrests and the capture of some weapons. The explosion killed eighty-two people, including forty Arabs and seventeen Jews, and led to international condemnation. The British responded a week later by hanging three suspected Irgun terrorists, and Begin, in turn, ordered the execution of two British sergeants held captive by Begin's terrorist organization; their bodies were booby-trapped and left hanging upside down, to the long-lasting horror of many Jews.

from Eastern Europe, Begin had a hatred of Communism and the Soviet Union. He and his family had fled to eastern Poland after the 1939 German blitzkrieg and, like many Zionists, were arrested by Soviet troops and expelled to a Siberian gulag, only to be released into a hastily assembled Polish contingent of the Red Army after the 1941 Nazi invasion of Russia.

By all accounts, Begin had never visited Dimona before becoming prime minister, nor was he especially well informed about it. His initial briefings on sensitive national security matters were provided by the outgoing prime minister, Yitzhak Rabin. Ari Ben-Menashe, a former Israeli signals intelligence expert then serving as a civilian official in the ministry of defense, recalled that Begin strongly endorsed Dimona's plans for the nuclear targeting of the Soviet Union. Begin went a step further, according to Ben-Menashe: "He gave orders to target more Soviet cities."* The increased targeting, Ben-Menashe said, created a heightened demand for American satellite intelligence. But Israeli military attachés and diplomats were running into a brick wall in Washington, as the Carter

---

* Ben-Menashe served more than ten years in the External Relations Department of the Israeli Defense Force, one of the most sensitive offices in Israel's intelligence community. He left the ministry in 1987, he said, to work directly for Prime Minister Yitzhak Shamir as an adviser on intelligence affairs. He was arrested in 1989 in the United States on charges of conspiring to violate the Arms Export Control Act by attempting to sell Israeli-owned C-130 military aircraft to Iran; he was acquitted in November 1990 by a federal jury in New York City. During preliminary proceedings and the trial, the Israeli government provided a series of conflicting statements about Ben-Menashe, who claimed that the illegal sale had been sanctioned by his government and the United States. Israel initially told the court that it had no knowledge of Ben-Menashe. It later accused Ben-Menashe of forging the four letters of reference that he had obtained upon leaving his job in External Relations. After acknowledging that the letters were genuine, it then depicted Ben-Menashe as nothing more than a low-level translator for the Israeli intelligence community. Ben-Menashe, in turn, accused his government of betrayal after Israel insisted to the court that he had been moonlighting as an arms salesman, and he began to talk publicly about what he alleged was his involvement in hundreds of millions of dollars' worth of authorized arms sales to Iran in the early 1980s that had been secretly endorsed by the Reagan administration. He also accused Robert M. Gates, a senior CIA official under Reagan, of direct involvement, despite Israeli protests, in the sale of arms, including chemical weapons, to Iraq from 1986 to 1989. Ben-Menashe's allegations, which have been strongly denied in Washington and Jerusalem, were still under congressional review as of summer 1991.

The author was initially contacted by Ben-Menashe in mid-1990 and began interviewing him in Washington and elsewhere in early 1991 about the Israeli nuclear arsenal and his activities inside the Israeli signals intelligence establishment. Ben-Menashe agreed—as no other Israeli would—to be directly quoted by the author on nuclear issues and other matters. In June, he left America for exile in Australia.

administration retreated from the intense relationship that had developed under Presidents Nixon and Ford. One American officer who was in charge of a military intelligence agency in the first years of the Carter presidency depicted the Israelis as being all over the Pentagon and preoccupied with intelligence on the Soviets: "They were buzzing around. They were trying to get into overhead and they also wanted to know what our [military] attachés were reporting and what our requirements were. Our establishment was like a honeycomb for them."

Begin's enthusiastic support for the targeting of the Soviet Union was not known to the American intelligence community, still obsessed with its efforts to prove that Zalman Shapiro had diverted uranium to Israel. There was no doubt inside the intelligence community that Israel had the bomb, and yet no one in Washington—not even the new administration of Jimmy Carter, the first to be seriously committed to nuclear non-proliferation—saw any reason to raise the issue.

The Israeli government, worried about a backlash from its American supporters, continued to publicly deny the existence of any nuclear weapons—even when faced with evidence to the contrary. In 1976, after Carl Duckett inadvertently revealed in Washington that the CIA estimated Israel's arsenal to total at least ten warheads, U.S. Ambassador Malcolm Toon had been summoned by Yigal Allon, the foreign minister, to discuss the issue. "[Allon] was very disturbed over this development," Toon said in a cable to the State Department, "and felt it scarcely compatible with relationship between our two countries. . . . He asked rhetorically why CIA had done it." Toon reported that he dutifully explained to Allon that Duckett's remarks were supposed to have been off-the-record. He then asked Allon whether Duckett's conclusion was accurate: "Allon looked at me, somewhat startled," Toon reported, "and said, 'It is not true.' "

Allon's bald denial rankled, and a year later, after Carter's election, Toon told a delegation of thirteen visiting American senators that he was sure Israel had the bomb. The senators, led by Abraham Ribicoff, Democrat of Connecticut, were on a fact-finding tour about the prospects for nonproliferation in the Middle East. They asked permission to inspect Dimona and were flatly told that no outsider had visited the reactor since the American inspections had ended in 1969, and none was welcome. Toon cabled the State Department about their treatment, complaining that "it was indecent for Israel to keep us out of Dimona." He vividly recalled the bureaucratic response: "Don't stir up the waters."*

The senators went much further than the State Department in attempting to paper over the fact that they had been denied entrance to the reactor. "This denial was dramatized by the press far beyond its actual significance," their subsequent public report noted. "Most of the delegation did not wish to visit Dimona because they lacked the technical expertise to make such a visit worthwhile. The delegation received no information as to whether Israel has nuclear weapons or not."

The senators were especially sensitive to the issue, for Congress had just approved an amendment to the Arms Export Control Act making it illegal to provide U.S. foreign aid funds to those nations that sold or received nuclear reprocessing or enrichment materials, equipment, or technology. The amendment, as written, had no impact on those nations, such as Israel, which had been involved in the transfer or sale of nuclear materials prior to the bill's enactment. Israel, in other words, had been grandfathered out. The legislation, sponsored by Senator Stuart Symington, also provided for the President to override the law if he determined that the termination of such aid would be damaging to American national security.** The law has been applied two times to Pakistan, and to no other nation, since its approval.

Congress and the White House were, in essence, acceding to what had become the arms control community's rationalization

* Mordecai Vanunu, in one of his many interviews with the London *Sunday Times*, told of finding a newspaper clip about the rebuff of the senators derisively taped to a wall in Machon 2, the chemical separation plant at Dimona, when he began working there in August 1977.

** Victor Gilinsky, the NRC commissioner, said he had been at a Washington dinner party shortly after the legislation was passed and listened intently as Symington made an informal speech about the importance of limiting the spread of nuclear weapons. "When he sat down," Gilinsky said, "I asked him, 'What about Israel?' 'Oh, they need it,' the senator responded. 'I've been telling Dayan for thirty years they have to have the bomb.' "

for its failure to raise questions about the Israeli bomb: Israel was no longer a proliferation problem—it had already proliferated. One ranking State Department intelligence official, whose testimony was crucial to the first Pakistani foreign aid cutoff, recalled his cynicism about the Symington legislation: "Did any of these guys [senators] who were grilling me so mercilessly about Pakistan ever ask about Israel?" A former Nuclear Regulatory Commission official, who was responsible for testimony on the NRC's position on Israeli compliance with the Symington Amendment, recalled his understanding that Congress "doesn't want to discover anything in an open hearing." Although he was personally convinced Israel had developed nuclear arms, the official said that he repeatedly testified that he had "no evidence" of such weapons existing in Israel. If there were any significant items of information that needed to be passed along, the official added, "you told them over coffee. Never at an open hearing."

America's tolerance for a nuclear-armed Israel may not have troubled the Congress or the media, but it rankled Pakistan's President Mohammad Zia ul-Haq. George H. Rathjens, a deputy early in the Carter administration to Gerard C. Smith, the President's specially appointed ambassador-at-large for non-proliferation issues, vividly recalled Zia's response when Smith raised questions about Pakistan's nuclear program: " 'Why don't you people talk to Israel?' Smith was upset," Rathjens added, "but there was no way to answer Zia—no satisfactory answer." The Israeli nuclear program "wasn't anything people [in the U.S. government] wanted to talk about or discuss," Rathjens said. "It was an embarrassment."

Cooperation between Israel and South Africa on nuclear issues began in earnest after the 1967 Six-Day War when Israel, rebuffed by Charles de Gaulle, was forced to look elsewhere for support. Pierre Pean, in *Les deux bombes*, told of the surprising encounter in Johannesburg in 1967 between a French nuclear scientist who had been at Dimona and a group of Israeli nuclear scientists who had worked ten years earlier with the French at Saclay and Marcoule. The French physicist and his colleagues had helped the Israelis learn skills that they were now passing along to the South Africans. Israel was trading its expertise in nuclear physics for the uranium ore and other strategic minerals that existed in abundance in South Africa. The South Africans needed all the technical support they could get, recalled Ari Ben-Menashe: "They weren't good at all as a nuclear state. We had to help all the way."

In 1968, Ernst David Bergmann, out of office in Israel but still influential on nuclear issues, traveled to South Africa, where he spoke publicly on the "move toward international collaboration" on nuclear issues. In a speech to the South African Institute of International Affairs in Johannesburg, Bergmann said nothing about nuclear weapons, but talked candidly about the "common problem" facing Israel and South Africa: "Neither of us has neighbors to whom we can speak and to whom we are going to be able to speak in the near future. If we are in this position of isolation, perhaps it might be best for both countries to speak to each other."

Bergmann's talk of isolation seemed prophetic as all but three black African states (Malawi, Lesotho, and Swaziland) broke diplomatic relations with Israel in the wake of the 1973 Yom Kippur War and Israel's continued insistence on holding on to the occupied territories. Many of Israel's former allies in Africa increasingly began to support Palestinian aspirations. In November 1975, the United Nations General Assembly voted seventy-two to thirty-five (with thirty-two abstentions) in favor of a resolution that defined Zionism as "a form of racism and racial discrimination." Israeli Ambassador Chaim Herzog responded by accusing the United Nations of becoming "the world center of anti-Semitism."

Israel and South Africa, two "pariah" states, had turned to each other with renewed trading and arms sales after the war; within three years, joint trade grew from $30 million to $100 million a year. South Africa's small but influential Jewish population of 118,000 were always large contributors to Israeli bond drives and charities; now they also became more vocal in their support for Israel's more conservative political parties, including Menachem Begin's Likud Party. In 1974, Defense Minister Moshe Dayan had made a secret trip to Pretoria, where, according to Ari Ben-Menashe, he discussed the possibility of an

Israeli nuclear test on South African soil. Dayan left the Israeli cabinet a few months later, when Yitzhak Rabin became prime minister, but continuity on key Israeli–South African defense and nuclear issues was assured with Rabin's appointment of Shimon Peres to the defense portfolio. Two years later, Prime Minister John Vorster, who had sided with Germany during World War II, visited Israel—the first official state visit by a South African prime minister in Israel's history.*

Peres made at least one private trip to Pretoria before the Vorster visit, just as he had made private trips to France twenty years earlier to arrange for arms and nuclear cooperation. His agenda included nuclear testing—the issue initially raised by Moshe Dayan—and he won a commitment in principle from John Vorster, according to Ben-Menashe, for a series of joint Israeli–South African tests in South Africa. Vorster's highly publicized visit to Israel resulted in a renewal of full diplomatic relations, as well as secret arms transfer agreements that would enable the two countries, working together in defiance of international opinion and United Nations sanctions, to emerge by the early 1980s as economies that were highly dependent on foreign arms sales.

Israeli sources put the number of secret military and nuclear understandings between Israel and South Africa at "six or seven" by the end of the Vorster visit. "Why?" a former Israeli official asked rhetorically. He cited four reasons. "One: to share basic resources. South Africa is a very rich country and Israel is poor. Two: the supply of raw materials. Three: testing grounds. Try to do a [nuclear] test in Israel and all hell breaks loose. In South Africa it's different. Four: there is a certain sympathy for the situation of South Africa among Israelis. They are also European settlers standing against a hostile world.

"South Africa, when it realized it wanted to go nuclear, also realized there was one country it could turn to," added the Israeli, who has firsthand knowledge of Israel's nuclear policy.

. . .

---

* The April 1976 visit was denounced by the Organization of African States (OAS) and the Cairo-based Arab League, as well as by the Soviet Union and the Netherlands.

The issue of Israel's nuclear arms remained in the background
in the first years of the Carter administration, whose major
priorities included a Middle East solution. The nuclear intelligence experts at Los Alamos and Livermore had been trying
to monitor the shipment of uranium ore from South Africa to
Israel since the early 1960s, but simply failed to see, or failed to
understand, the full scope of South Africa's continuing efforts
in nuclear technology. In 1970, Prime Minister John Vorster
informed Parliament that the nation's nuclear scientists had
developed a unique uranium enrichment process involving jet-
nozzle enrichment and a sophisticated cascade technique.
Within a few years, South Africa began construction of a pilot
plant for the production of enriched uranium, not subject to
IAEA safeguards, at a plant called Valindaba near Pretoria.*

The American intelligence community knew nothing of the
secret negotiations between Vorster and Peres, but there were
a few analysts who knew something was up between the two
nations. By the mid-1970s, one American official recalled, "[t]he
South Africans and Israel were suddenly doing things in such a
different way that it took us by surprise. They went from the
drawing board to the production [of enriched uranium]. They
leapfrogged us in production design and output and we
weren't looking in the right places." The official's point was
that the nuclear production process in the United States was so
huge and unwieldy that innovations were difficult to achieve;
any new process would be tested for years in pilot production
before being adopted in the government's main weapons assembly line near Amarillo, Texas, which is capable of producing five thousand or more warheads a year.

By the mid-1970s, South Africa considered itself in an analo-
gous position to that faced by Israel after 1967: it was fighting
an internal war against the African National Congress and the
anti-apartheid movement as well as a war of secession in
Namibia, and an external war against the growing black nationalism and emerging independence of Angola and Mozam-

---

* The plant's name, *Valindaba*, hints at its real purpose: it means "the council is
closed" or "the talking is over" in the local African Sotho dialect.

bique in the frontline states of southern Africa. In the long run, the military prospects of South Africa were bleak: the leaders of South Africa saw themselves, as did the men running Israel, to be vastly outnumbered by their enemies.

There was security, so the Afrikaners believed, in the nuclear bomb. And, like Israel, South Africa would need a weapon—a low-yield nuclear artillery shell—that could be used in case frontline defenses were breached and urban centers threatened. In August 1977, Soviet President Leonid Brezhnev privately warned the Carter administration that his nation's Cosmos satellite system had detected evidence of South African preparations for a nuclear test, or series of tests, at what was determined to be an underground site in the Kalahari. Similar warnings were sent to Britain, France, and West Germany, all participants—with the Soviets and the United States—in a 1975 conference in London that had set up the Nuclear Suppliers Group, which established a series of voluntary guidelines for limiting technical and material aid to non-nuclear nations.*

An American satellite was immediately routed over the Kalahari and saw the classic signs of preparations for an underground nuclear test—a test hole had been dug with casing around it, an observation tower had been put up, and the many cables needed for measurement were in place. Carter and Brezhnev, working together, led an international campaign of protest, and the South African government, facing the loss of diplomatic relations, backed down by the end of August. Carter publicly announced that "South Africa has informed us that they do not have and do not intend to develop nuclear explosive devices for any purpose, either peaceful or as a weapon." The President also said he had been assured that the Kalahari test site "is not designed . . . to test nuclear explosives, and

---

* Third World nations, not without reason, accused the Nuclear Suppliers Group—convened after India's 1974 nuclear test—of instituting what amounted to an international cartel to perpetuate the advanced positions of the major powers; there were further claims that the agreements violated the promise given to non-nuclear states in Article Six of the Nonproliferation Treaty, which explicitly calls on all parties to facilitate "the fullest possible exchange of equipment, materials and scientific and technological information for the peaceful uses of nuclear energy." The NPT also called for special attention to the "needs of the developing areas of the world."

that no nuclear explosive test will be taken in South Africa now or in the future."

The White House, jubilant over its first major foreign policy success, arranged for a series of elaborate briefings to the news media about the intricacies of its successful diplomacy. The reporters were not told, however, that the CIA had reported that Israeli military personnel, in civilian clothes, were all over the Kalahari test site, and being "quite open about it," as a CIA officer recalled. The press also was not told that a senior South African diplomat had privately assured the United States at the height of the crisis in early August that his military was not planning to test a long-range missile, but only "a rocket or artillery round—something like that."

The CIA would later conclude, in a formal assessment for the White House, that the strong international protests over Kalahari had deflected South Africa "at least temporarily" from carrying out its planned test. Israelis, added the CIA assessment, have "participated in certain South African nuclear research activities over the last few years. . . ."

Carter's heavily promoted diplomatic "victory in the desert" was far less significant than it appeared; a real triumph would have involved going a step further and taking on the Israeli nuclear program, and no one in the Carter White House had the stomach for that.

It was into this Washington that an Israeli with inside information about Dimona—seeking to trade that information for personal advancement—arrived late in the year. He contacted a senior official in the American nuclear intelligence community with whom he had dealt professionally in the past, and immediately revealed the fact that Israel had assembled well over one hundred nuclear warheads. There would be more than two hundred warheads, many of them low-yield devices, by the year 1980, the Israeli added. The American official, who is Jewish, understood why the Israeli was willing to talk: "He was a technical person looking for favors. This guy wanted to become a U.S. citizen." The fact that Israel had nuclear weapons, the American rationalized, was "general knowledge throughout the U.S. government. My feeling was this one individual wanted to hustle information for personal advantage. I decided to ignore it."

And so he did not forward the information to his superiors and colleagues, although he had no doubt that the information was accurate. The American said he knew of Israelis in other technical fields, apparently dismayed by the election of Begin, who had approached their American counterparts with offers to trade information and intelligence for a chance to emigrate to the United States.

There were other, and more traditional, approaches, as the relationship between Jimmy Carter and Menachem Begin became increasingly strained in the wake of Camp David, and as some Israeli officials tried—apparently without high-level approval—to get some strategic help for Israeli ambitions and put an end to America's refusal to recognize the reality of the Israeli nuclear arsenal.

Their starting point was an appropriately obscure corner of the Pentagon known as the Office of Net Assessments, whose director, Andrew W. Marshall, a former Rand Corporation analyst, has been providing secretaries of defense with an independent flow of intelligence and analysis for two decades. In the last months of the Ford administration, Marshall won acceptance of a plan to begin a strategic dialogue with Israel; one goal was to investigate a possible cooperative U.S.–Israeli defense treaty. Some of Israel's most sophisticated strategic thinkers were assigned by Prime Minister Rabin to the ad hoc group, including Avraham Tamir, an Israeli Army general who would later serve as director general of the foreign ministry. It was Tamir, one member of the Marshall group recalled, who repeatedly sought to discuss nuclear issues after Anwar Sadat's dramatic visit to Jerusalem in November 1977, the first step toward the Camp David talks.* The question was: would Marshall and his Defense Department staff discuss contingency

---

* Sadat met privately with Begin shortly after arriving in Jerusalem, and, according to Israeli officials, his first questions dealt with the Israeli nuclear arsenal. One Israeli who has seen a high-level summary of the Begin-Sadat meeting said that the Egyptian leader sought assurances that Israel would pledge not to use nuclear weapons against Egypt if a peace treaty between the two nations was signed. Begin did not reply, according to the Israeli account.

plans for joint nuclear targeting of southern Russia in case of war?

That question was supersensitive, as all involved understood —America was still officially accepting Israeli assurances it had no nuclear arms—and it was referred in writing on at least two occasions to Secretary of Defense Harold Brown for guidance. The answer, in both cases, came back quickly: there was to be no discussion of nuclear doctrine by Marshall's shop.

Brown, interviewed later about Tamir's initiative, at first dismissed it as another example of the need for military planners to make contingency plans. He then spoke hypothetically: "If such a request did come to me, it didn't take me long to think about it." He finally acknowledged that he had rejected the Israeli approach without discussing it with President Carter. The Carter administration, Brown asserted, "would not have wanted to get involved in an Israeli-Soviet conflict. The whole idea of Israel becoming our asset seems crazy to me. The Israelis would say, 'Let us help you,' and then you end up being their tool. The Israelis have their own security interests and we have our interests. They are not identical." Andrew Marshall and his colleagues in the Office of Net Assessments viewed Brown's position as—as one American put it—"a foolish constraint," but followed his instructions and, of course, told no one else in the U.S. government about the Israeli request for joint nuclear targeting.*

It was another disconnect as the American bureaucracy instinctively continued to protect its President from learning the facts about the Israeli nuclear capability—and from having to act on that knowledge. That instinct reached its height in the fall of 1979, when the Israelis and the South Africans finally pulled off their test.

---

* A senior American intelligence official recalled that the French had occasionally made similar requests to the Pentagon for joint nuclear targeting and intelligence sharing and invariably been rejected out of hand, without the issue being raised at the secretary of defense level, as was done with Avraham Tamir's proposal. "It was manifest that no one was afraid of the French," the official said, "but they were afraid of the Israelis. We all knew the French didn't have a back-door relationship" with the White House, as Israel did.

20

An Israeli Test

Just before dawn on the stormy morning of September 22, 1979, the clouds over the South Indian Ocean suddenly broke and an American satellite was able to record two distinctive bright flashes of light within a fraction of a second—probable evidence of a nuclear explosion. The nuclear detection satellite, known as VELA, had seen similar flashes of light on forty-one previous occasions, and in each case it was subsequently determined that a nuclear explosion had taken place. Most of the sightings were over Lap Nor, where the Chinese atmospheric nuclear tests took place, or in the South Pacific, site of the French tests. There were a few intelligence officials and non-proliferation experts in the Carter administration who immediately concluded that Israel and South Africa had finally conducted a nuclear test, a test that they had tried, and failed, to accomplish two years earlier.

They were right.

Former Israeli government officials, whose information on other aspects of Dimona's activities has been corroborated, said that the warhead tested that Saturday morning was a low-yield nuclear artillery shell that had been standardized for use by the Israeli Defense Force. The Israeli sources also said the event captured by the VELA satellite was not the first but the third test of a nuclear device over the Indian Ocean. At least two Israeli Navy ships had sailed to the site in advance, and a contingent of Israeli military men and nuclear experts—along with the South African Navy—was observing the tests. "We wouldn't send ships down there for one test," one Israeli said. "It was a fuck-up," he added, referring to the capture of a test by the VELA satellite. "There was a storm and we figured it would

block VELA, but there was a gap in the weather—a window—
and VELA got blinded by the flash."

The VELA satellite, as it was programmed to do, digitally relayed its sighting to the headquarters of the Air Force Technical Applications Center (AFTAC) at Patrick Air Force Base in
Cape Canaveral, Florida; it was Friday night, September 21, on
the East Coast. Once evaluated and confirmed, the intelligence
was routed, via the Defense Intelligence Agency, to the Pentagon's National Military Command Center and relayed to
America's top civilian and military leaders. The nuclear event
was estimated to have taken place off the coast of Prince Edward Island, about fifteen hundred miles southeast of the Cape
of Good Hope in South Africa, halfway to Antarctica. The
intelligence was at the top of the CIA's and DIA's Saturday-
morning briefing for President Carter and his national security
adviser, Zbigniew Brzezinski.

Gerald G. Oplinger, Brzezinski's aide for global issues, was
spending the early fall weekend at his summer house at Deep
Creek Lake, Maryland, when word of the possible test came: he
was summoned back to an urgent meeting in the White House
situation room. Oplinger had retired from the Foreign Service
and worked at the Nuclear Regulatory Commission before
joining Brzezinski's staff; he was familiar with the VELA program and knew that its previous sightings of Chinese and
French atmospheric tests had been unfailingly accurate. "Everybody showed up," Oplinger recalled, meaning that Brzezinski was at the meeting, "and we went around and asked, 'Was it
a test?' CIA and DIA said that odds were at least ninety percent
that it had been a nuclear explosion." Oplinger personally had
no doubt, as he recalled: "Common sense told me that there
was a high probability that it was what it was—it was just too
incredible."

"People just stood there, paralyzed," recalled Spurgeon M.
Keeny, Jr., deputy director of the Arms Control and Disarmament Agency (ACDA), a senior bureaucrat who had been involved in high-level scientific issues since the Eisenhower
administration. Keeny realized, he said, that he and his colleagues "needed to buy some time. Even if a test was done, we

didn't know who did it. This was a serious matter." Keeny also was troubled by the intelligence community's assurances that its assessment was 90 percent accurate. In his view, the CIA and DIA officials at the situation-room meeting surely could not know all the facts: "They were middle-level bureaucrats relaying data."

In Keeny's account, it was his idea to set up an outside panel to study the VELA data and ensure that the satellite had not made an error—one with enormous political consequences. Jerry Oplinger had a different recollection: "The meeting was going nowhere and Frank Press [the presidential science adviser] said, 'Let's convene an unbiased outside study.'" Oplinger had no illusions about what Frank Press meant: "Press kept on asking, 'What do we do if it leaks out that we've concluded it was a test?' He did not want that panel to conclude there had been a nuclear explosion." Brzezinski had little to say during the meeting, Oplinger recalled.*

Frank Press, a seismologist who had worked for years on classified nuclear detection issues, knew the VELA program far better than any of his peers in the White House. He knew that the satellites were ancient by satellite standards—some having been launched in the early 1960s—and were constantly being updated and analyzed by scientists at the Los Alamos Scientific Laboratories, who had helped design the system, to ensure that no deterioration had set in. There had been, in fact, recent concern about false alarms that could trigger a phony intelligence report. The outside panel was a natural step, one that would indeed buy some time, and one that would also add a patina of legitimacy to the delaying effort. Meanwhile, exis-

---

* Brzezinski, according to his aides, was never particularly interested in proliferation or nuclear-fuel-cycle issues. President Carter had triggered an uproar by continuing President Ford's 1976 ban on the commercial reprocessing of spent nuclear fuel for power reactors. Carter's action, based on environmental and proliferation concerns, was viewed by the American nuclear power industry as a foolish move that would stifle the sale of American reactors and equipment around the world. His NSC aides weren't convinced that Brzezinski fully understood the issue. At one stage early in the administration, Oplinger recalled being told, Brzezinski agreed to a briefing by Jessica Tuchman, Oplinger's predecessor on the NSC staff, and stood by as she described the nuclear fuel cycle, beginning with the insertion of nuclear fuel into a reactor and ending with the reprocessing of the spent fuel. "Zbig listened to all this," Oplinger related, "and then asked, 'Okay, now tell me—where does the energy come from?'" Brzezinski did not mention the VELA incident in his 1983 memoir *Power and Principle*.

tence of the VELA sighting became one of the most important secrets of the Carter administration.

The officials at the top of the troubled Carter administration knew that public revelation of the VELA sighting, with its strong inference of an illicit Israeli–South African test, would create a horrible dilemma for the President, just a few months away from the 1980 presidential campaign. Carter had draped himself in the flag of nonproliferation, and if he did not get tough with the two pariah nations, he would be criticized for hypocrisy; if he did seek sanctions, there would be political hell to pay. "When that thing up there went 'Twinkle, twinkle, little star,'" recalled Hodding Carter III, then the assistant secretary of state for public affairs, "I can remember running around on the seventh floor," where Secretary of State Cyrus R. Vance's office was located. "There was sheer panic," Carter said. "It was very much 'Oh, shit. Oh, dear. What do we do with this?'"

"We were in the worst possible position," another government official recalled. "Here we are, ready to send the SALT treaty up to the Senate, and we know there's been a violation of the [1963] test ban treaty and we can't prove it and we can't pin it on anyone. There was a very immediate strategic imperative to make this thing go away." The official, who had access to all of the available intelligence on the VELA sighting, said it was evident that the satellite had observed what "could only be a nuclear event. Our capturing it fortuitously was an embarrassment, a big political problem, and there were a lot of people who wanted to obscure the event."

The American policy in Iran was in chaos, with the ailing shah—who had been so warmly toasted two years earlier by Jimmy Carter—in Mexico and pleading for admission to the United States.* There had been a stupendous intelligence gaffe

---

* The shah was admitted for medical treatment into the United States on October 22, triggering a renewed wave of anti-American rioting in Tehran and the eventual seizure of the American embassy on November 4, beginning Jimmy Carter's hostage nightmare. During the tense discussions before the shah's arrival, recalled Nicholas Veliotes, then serving as the assistant secretary of state for Near East and South Asian affairs, the ousted leader confided that he had been negotiating with the Israelis for the purchase of long-range missiles capable of firing a nuclear warhead. "He said that the Israelis had told him not to tell us," Veliotes added. Veliotes's information, like most

just a few weeks before over a breathtaking report suggesting that a Soviet brigade had moved into Cuba, presenting a direct challenge to Carter, just as the Soviets had challenged John F. Kennedy in 1962. The intelligence leaked, and the administration, taking the hard line in public, demanded that the Soviets remove their troops. It turned out not to be a triumphant Cuban missile crisis, however, as embarrassed Carter officials were forced to acknowledge that their initial intelligence report was simply wrong: Soviet soldiers had been in Cuba since the early 1960s. Adding to the mortification was the fact that the administration was then preparing for what was sure to be a bitter fight with Senate Republicans over the U.S. government's ability to verify the June 1979 SALT II agreements. The SALT agreement plus Carter's success at Camp David were scheduled to be featured in his reelection campaign.

An Israeli bomb threatened all this and made it imperative that the American President, once again, not know what there was to know. The American bureaucracy had been in training for more than thirty years in looking the other way when it came to the Israeli nuclear program, and every part of the system instinctively sought to find a way to avoid calling the Israeli–South African test a test.

There was widespread knowledge of the test in Israel. Ari Ben-Menashe recalled seeing correspondence on the issue in his ministry of defense office shortly after Menachem Begin's election in 1977. It was widely assumed that there had been some secret diplomacy between former Defense Minister Shimon Peres and John Vorster during Peres's visit to South Africa in 1976, but just what commitments had been made were not widely known inside the Israeli government. It was also understood, Ben-Menashe said, that Peres was not going to tell Menachem Begin about it. And Begin, in turn, would not directly approach Peres, who—along with David Ben-Gurion—had treated him with contempt and ridicule throughout his career. Begin's solution was to dispatch Ezer Weizman, the newly appointed minister of defense, to South Africa.

intelligence data about Israeli nuclear intentions, was not made known to other American officials.

Weizman's mission, said Ben-Menashe, was "just to find out what was going on."

"Weizman came back," Ben-Menashe recalled, "and said, 'We've promised these guys nuclear warheads.' He recommended to Begin that they pay up and carry out the promise." Ben-Menashe said he and others in External Relations understood that Begin responded by saying, in effect, "Yes. Do it!"

Another Israeli, who also had direct access to defense ministry information about the test in South Africa, said that Weizman signed an agreement before the 1979 tests calling for the sale to South Africa of technology and equipment needed for the manufacture of low-yield 175mm and 203mm nuclear artillery shells. Weizman's order triggered an internal dispute with senior nuclear officials, the Israeli recalled, who protested the government's decision to sell the information, considered by the men running Dimona to be "the best stuff we got."*

Frank Press finally settled on Jack P. Ruina, a professor of electrical engineering at the Massachusetts Institute of Technology, to direct the outside panel and determine whether some of Israel's "best stuff" had ended up over the South Indian Ocean. It was a perfect choice, in terms of discretion: Ruina, a longtime consultant to the Pentagon on military and scientific issues, held many of the most sensitive clearances in the American military and scientific community; he had served as director in the early 1960s of the Advanced Research Project Agency (ARPA), the Pentagon's research arm, and later directed the Institute for Defense Analysis (IDA), the Pentagon's most important think tank. Ruina was an honorable and cautious man who could be counted on to follow orders and not talk to reporters, especially after his hush-hush introduction to the White House crisis. "Press called and asked me to come on

---

* After the 1973 war, the Israeli Defense Force established at least three nuclear-capable artillery battalions, each containing twelve self-propelled 175mm cannons. The battalions were considered part of Israel's strategic reserve and operated under streamlined command-and-control: nuclear shells could be fired on the direct orders of the prime minister, as relayed through the minister of defense, the Army Chief of Staff, and the chief of operations directly to the artillery battalion commander. Clearance was not required, as in normal operations, from any officer at the regional headquarters, corps, division, or brigade level. Former Israeli army officers said at least three nuclear artillery shells eventually were stockpiled for each weapon—a total of 108 warheads. Additional warheads were supplied for Israel's 203mm cannons.

down [to the White House]," Ruina recalled. "He said, 'I can't talk about it on the phone. Just come on down.'"

Within weeks, as the White House's secret continued to hold, Press and Ruina picked an ad hoc panel of eight distinguished scientists, whose integrity was beyond reproach. Ruina's key colleagues included Luis Alvarez, of the physics department at the University of California, a Nobel laureate; Wolfgang K. H. Panofsky, of Stanford University's Linear Accelerator Center; and Richard L. Garwin, of IBM's Thomas J. Watson Research Center. Panofsky and Garwin had served often as government consultants and were known for their independence.

The panel's assignment, carefully drawn up by Spurgeon Keeny and Frank Press, was weighted, to no one's surprise, toward a thorough investigation into the possibility that the VELA sighting had been a false alarm. The Ruina panel was also told to investigate the possibility that the recorded signal "was of natural origin, possibly resulting from the coincidence of two or more natural phenomena. . . ."

Ruina was clear about the limits on his assignment. "My mandate was to only look at technical data," he recalled. He and his colleagues were provided with all of the available intelligence about the VELA sighting, Ruina said, "but we didn't include any political data—like are the Israelis interested in nuclear weapons? That was not in our charter." The panel members were comfortable with their mandate: purely technical studies were a way of life for scientific consultants to the government.

Despite its explosiveness, knowledge of the VELA report remained a closely held secret for more than a month, until ABC television reporter John Scali was told by an old friend about a simulated Soviet nuclear attack on the United States that had been missed by America's early warning system. The old friend was very conservative, Scali recalled, and he thought the American failure "was an outrage." Scali, who had been the ambassador to the United Nations under Nixon, ran the story by another old friend in the Pentagon. Within hours, he was summoned to the office of a senior Defense Department official who gave him the essential facts.* He broadcast his story on the evening of October 25: the secret had held for more than a month, long enough for the White House to have its cover story ready. Its spokesmen immediately informed the news media that there was "no confirmation" of a test. Secretary of State Vance, following the company line, also told journalists there was no conclusive evidence of a test, and South Africa issued a heated denial.** "Faced with a denial by South Africa of such nuclear activity," dutifully wrote the *New York Times*, "and lacking any proof beyond the uncorroborated evidence of a single satellite, the United States Government sought to avoid a major confrontation over what it said was only the possibility that some nation had secretly exploded a nuclear device in an area of some 4,500 square miles. . . ." Vance further told the press that within hours of the first VELA signal, he had discussed the matter with Brzezinski and Defense Secretary Harold Brown.

None of the reporters knew, of course, that Harold Brown's Office of Net Assessments had already been approached two times by a senior Israeli official seeking to discuss joint U.S.–Israeli strategic targeting of the Soviet Union. Did Brown tell Cyrus Vance at the time about the nuclear approach, or, for that matter, did he report it to the President and his national security adviser? Did anyone in the U.S. government review the intelligence files on the planned 1977 South African test in the Kalahari? Did any of the senior White House officials wonder why a flotilla of South African and Israeli military ships had been tracked by the National Security Agency and other elements of the intelligence community to a site fifteen hundred miles off the coast of South Africa?†

---

* Carter, with his emphasis on nonproliferation and human rights, was less than popular at the Pentagon.
** One of the strangest denials to emerge from the controversy came from South African Vice Admiral J. C. Walters, who made public a statement suggesting that the flash could have been caused by an accident aboard a Soviet nuclear submarine. The admiral's statement, which said that Soviet involvement was "a real possibility," was reported by the *New York Times* to have been issued with the approval of Prime Minister P. W. Botha, who also was South Africa's minister of defense. The admiral offered no factual basis for his Cold War assertion, which soon sank from sight.
† Victor Gilinsky, still serving in 1979 on the Nuclear Regulatory Commission, recalled inquiring during an official briefing whether there were ships in the Indian Ocean and being told no. He learned the next day that there indeed had been ships

And, finally, did anyone notice what Prime Minister P. W. Botha had to say on September 25, 1979, three days after the test —three days in which there had been no international comment or outcry? Botha had reason to believe that his nation and its Israeli partners had pulled it off. There was a swagger in his remarks before a meeting of the Cape National Party congress as he warned, according to the *Rand Daily Mail*, that South Africa had and could produce sufficient arms to counter terrorism—an obvious reference to the African National Congress (ANC), leaders of the anti-apartheid movement. "If there are people who are thinking of doing something else," the newspaper quoted Botha as saying, "I suggest they think twice about it. They might find out we have military weapons they do not know about."

The Ruina panel members would spend months effectively poking holes in and raising legitimate questions about the reliability and integrity of the VELA satellite system. The panel chose to concentrate on what became known as the "false alarm" issue. Nuclear explosions produce two distinctly characteristic and separate flashes of light—from the initial detonation and the subsequent fireball about one third of a second later—that are recorded as double humps on a graph by the VELA satellite. The panel was troubled by the anomalies it found in the double humps as recorded on September 22 and concluded, as it stated in its final report, that the VELA sighting "contains sufficient internal inconsistency to cast serious doubt whether that signal originated from a nuclear explosion or in fact from any light sources in the proximity of the VELA satellite." The panel also could find no collateral signs of a nuclear event—seismic signals, acoustic waves, ionospheric disturbances, magnetic or electromagnetic pulses that had accompanied previous VELA reports. No significant radioactive fallout or other debris was located; there was no "smoking gun" that made the panel's conclusion ineluctable. The lack of such findings was not unusual in itself, given the low yield of the test and its isolated location; Press and the panel members knew

---

there. Gilinsky wasn't surprised when the Ruina panel concluded that no nuclear test probably had taken place: "Everyone took the bureaucratically appropriate decision."

that U.S. government seismologists had long suspected the Soviets had conducted many low-yield tests in the 1950s and 1960s that were not detected by the available American systems.

The panel eventually reported in July 1980, ten months after the event, that the flash observed by the satellite "was probably not from a nuclear explosion. Although we cannot rule out the possibility that this signal was of nuclear origin," the unclassified version of the ad hoc report said, "the panel considers it more likely that the signal was one of the zoo events [a signal of unknown cause], possibly a consequence of the impact of a small meteoroid on the satellite."

The findings outraged the nuclear scientists and professional bomb makers of Los Alamos, who had designed the VELA system. Many of these men were members of the Nuclear Intelligence Panel (NIP), the most highly classified nuclear intelligence group in the U.S. government. NIP had done its own investigation into the VELA test, and had been ordered by the White House—citing national security—not to discuss it publicly.

Its finding, openly discussed by NIP members in interviews with the author, was that a low-yield nuclear weapon most certainly had been detonated on September 22. They were dismayed by the extent of White House interference in the investigation. "If it looks like a duck, it's got to be a duck," said Harold M. Agnew, a NIP member and director of the Los Alamos laboratory from 1970 to 1979. "But that wasn't an answer Carter liked." The overriding issue, in Agnew's view, was not whether a nuclear bomb was exploded, but "Who did it?" Another panel member, Louis H. Roddis, Jr., who played a major role in America's postwar nuclear weapons development, concluded that the South African–Israeli test had taken place on a barge, or on one of the islands in the South Indian Ocean archipelago. He, too, expressed anger at Frank Press and the White House. "There was a real effort on the part of the administration to downplay it," Roddis said. "They were, indeed, concealing the facts—manipulating the facts. Everybody in New Mexico was convinced that it was a test."

The secret NIP study was directed by Donald M. Kerr, Jr., who had served in the Carter administration as acting director of the defense programs at the Department of Energy—he was the man responsible for America's nuclear bombs. "We were all insiders—not the kind of guys who'd run off at the mouth in public," he said, in explaining why his panel members did not speak out on the issue at the time. "We had no doubt it was a bomb," Kerr said, adding that in his opinion the Ruina panel's mandate was driven by politics: "to find a different explanation."

One mystery is why the Ruina panel scientists, all honorable men, would place themselves in a position where others could limit what information they could evaluate. The panel members had been assured that they would be given all of the relevant intelligence about the satellite, and yet one of the most important discoveries—uncovered by Ruina himself and known to the White House—was not made available to them.

Ruina was a director of MIT's Defense and Arms Control Studies Program and, as such, was involved in late 1979 in the preparation of a federally funded MIT report that assessed the foreign availability of critical components for the assembly of short-range ballistic missiles and compared those components with those manufactured in the United States. One of Ruina's three colleagues in preparing the report was an Israeli postgraduate student. Shortly after Ruina's involvement on the VELA sighting became known at MIT, the Israeli, who said he had worked on the Israeli nuclear missile systems, began talking to Ruina about Israel's nuclear capability. "I had the feeling he [the Israeli] knew an enormous amount," recalled George Rathjens, the former Carter administration nonproliferation official who was Ruina's close colleague at MIT. "He knew about missiles and he knew about guidance systems, and he talked freely about anything. It was almost as if he had an ordinary kind of job." Ruina, appropriately, forwarded the Israeli's information in a written report to Spurgeon Keeny at ACDA. "Some people [in the intelligence community] thought he was telling it like it was," Keeny said of the Israeli's intelligence. "The message is 'We've got a huge system that's more sophisticated than you think.' The guy said it [the September 22 flash] was a joint Israeli–South African attempt."

Keeny, confronted with the potentially explosive intelligence about what had happened and who had been involved, remained loyal to the Carter presidency and dismissed the report as nonsense. "I concluded that it was very questionable," he acknowledged. "I took it with a grain of salt." His colleagues in the White House, Keeny said, shared his view that Ruina's postgraduate student was peddling Israeli disinformation. The information was not made known to the intelligence community or to Ruina's colleagues on the panel. It stayed buried in the bureaucracy.

There were a few government experts on nonproliferation policy who were convinced that Frank Press and Spurgeon Kenny made the right choice in seeking to mitigate the impact of a South African–Israeli nuclear test. "My belief is that the conclusion of the Ruina panel was the right conclusion for that time," one nonproliferation official said. "What do you do? Look at the issues involved—apartheid, Camp David, NPT, human rights, dealing with the Indians [on nuclear proliferation], stopping reprocessing worldwide. You would have do something strong, especially to Israel, but there was a large segment of the population that Carter couldn't alienate."

The American intelligence community had done far better in its reporting on the South African test—the CIA insisted in internal estimates throughout 1979 and 1980 that there had been a test—but it basically remained in the dark about the sophistication of the Israeli nuclear program. In 1980, the Agency published another Special National Intelligence Estimate (SNIE) on Israeli capability and came up with essentially the same numbers as Carl Duckett had produced in 1974. Israel, the CIA said, had manufactured at least twenty and as many as thirty nuclear warheads. The new estimate, however, was much more comprehensive than previous studies. The CIA was able to report that the Israelis had upgraded the reactor to increase its output and also improved the reactor's cooling capacity—clear signs that a greater amount of plutonium for nuclear weapons was being generated. There was no longer any doubt, the estimate said, that Israel had completed construction of a chemical reprocessing plant—but just where and how was not known. "It was the first serious estimate," one Carter administration official said, "and it enabled the people in the field to really look out for what Israel had." Even so, the CIA report seriously underestimated the number of Israeli warheads and the sophistication of its nuclear operation. Sometimes facts were strained to keep the numbers low. The KH-11, with its brilliant photography, had captured an Israeli nuclear missile storage site and the experts at the National Photographic Interpretation Center (NPIC) had been able to count ten items that were subsequently confirmed as nuclear warheads. No one had ever seen an Israeli warhead before, and the intelligence community chose to take the fact that only ten warheads were seen, one official recalled, "as confirmation of our guesses. We thought the pictures were extraordinary, but decided that they didn't add anything new. It was consistent with our numbers."

The 1980 CIA estimate had been ordered by Deputy Under Secretary of State Joseph S. Nye, Jr., who emerged as the Carter administration's key—and highly progressive—adviser on nonproliferation policy. Nye acknowledged that coping with the Israeli bomb was a low priority under Jimmy Carter. "There wasn't much that could be done," Nye said. "The Israelis had already done it. It was not something you could make a demarche [diplomatic protest] about. The question is: do you make a big hullaballoo about it?"

The answer was no.

21

Israel's Nuclear Spy

For many Americans, Jonathan Jay Pollard is the American Jew who spied for Israel out of misguided loyalty, a man who believed that his documents and information would make Israel more secure in its war against international terrorism. When arrested in November 1985, he claimed he had been turning over secret documents—many of which, he maintained, should have been provided to Israel by the United States—for only fourteen months. The Israeli government apologized for its spying and insisted that the recruitment of Pollard was an aberration, an unauthorized "rogue" operation. Pollard is now serving a life sentence for espionage.

Pollard indeed spied for Israel out of misguided loyalty—and for money—but none of the other widely held beliefs about the case is true. He was Israel's first nuclear spy.

Pollard, who began working in 1979 as a civilian employee of U.S. Navy intelligence, offered to supply Israel with intelligence as early as 1980, but was not recruited as an operative until the fall of 1981, three years earlier than he and the Israeli government have admitted. He was then working as an intelligence specialist with the Navy's Field Operations Intelligence Office. At the height of his activity, in 1984 and 1985, one of his main assignments was the gathering of American intelligence relevant to Israel's nuclear targeting of the oil fields and Soviet military installations in southern Russia, a fact that was hidden from Justice Department investigators and prosecutors by Israeli officials.

Pollard has insisted in all of his Justice Department interrogations that his spying did not begin until July 1984, after a social meeting with Israeli Air Force Colonel Aviem Sella, one of his heroes, who had been involved in Israel's 1981 bombing of the Iraqi nuclear reactor at Osirak. In fact, Sella was one of the Israeli Air Force's leading nuclear bombing and targeting experts and was specifically assigned to serve as Pollard's handler. The nuclear targeting data supplied by Pollard included top-secret American intelligence on the location of Soviet military targets, as well as specific data on the Soviet means for protecting those targets, by concealment or hardening of the sites. Pollard also gave the Israelis American intelligence on Soviet air defenses, especially the feared SA-5 surface-to-air missile system, which was so effective against U.S. B-52s in the Vietnam War. Pollard eventually even turned over a copy of the U.S. intelligence community's annual review of the Soviet strategic arms system, known as the 11-38 and considered—because of its appendices dealing with satellite photography, communication intercepts, radar intelligence, and agent reports—to be one of the most sensitive documents in the U.S. government. Pollard also provided Israel with the codes for American diplomatic communications, enabling Israel's signals intelligence agency to intercept cables and backchannel messages to and from the office of Samuel W. Lewis, the well-informed U.S. ambassador who had been assigned to Israel in 1977. In all, according to federal prosecutors, Pollard provided Israel with eighteen hundred documents—an estimated 500,000 pages—before his arrest.

The top political officials of Israel, including Shimon Peres, Yitzhak Rabin, and Yitzhak Shamir, understood that there was a high-level source inside the United States. In fact, some of the most important Pollard documents were retyped and sanitized by Israeli intelligence officials and then made available to the Soviet Union as a gesture of Israeli goodwill, at the specific instructions of Yitzhak Shamir, a longtime advocate of closer Israeli-Soviet ties. All of this was successfully hidden by the Israeli government after Pollard's arrest and subsequent plea bargain. Israel still continues to depict the Pollard affair as a rogue operation that was conducted without high-level involvement.

The Pollard story actually begins with the U.S.–Israeli meetings that took place inside the Reagan White House in September 1981, three months after the raid on Osirak. Ariel Sharon, newly named by Menachem Begin as minister of defense, had come to Washington with Begin to present a far-reaching agenda for U.S.–Israeli strategic cooperation. Israel would become America's military partner—and military arm—in the Middle East and the Persian Gulf, and serve as a depository for pre-positioned arms and ammunition for American armed forces. The Israelis' most eagerly awaited meeting took place in the cabinet room with President Reagan and his top advisers, including Defense Secretary Caspar Weinberger, Secretary of State Alexander Haig, and National Security Adviser Richard Allen.

Sam Lewis, as the U.S. ambassador to Israel, also was at the meeting. "Begin said, 'Mr. President, we share the same view of the Communist menace. We should formalize our relationship. I suggest a formal alliance.' Reagan said yes," Lewis recounted. "Everyone else was shocked. Begin then said, 'Mr. President, I'd like to ask Minister Sharon to outline to you our ideas.' Sharon then gave a half-hour outline about how the American and Israeli strategic interest should be established. Even Al Haig [a strong supporter of Israel] was turning green. Dick Allen and the rest of the White House staff were also turning green. Cap [Weinberger] turned purple. I thought he'd explode."

Sharon's plan, as outlined at the cabinet-room meeting, also called for joint use of airfields and Navy ports. One significant aspect was shared intelligence, including formal Israeli access to the KH-11 satellite, desperately sought by Israel—as most of the Americans at the cabinet-room meeting did not understand —for its nuclear targeting of the Soviet Union.

At the end of Sharon's presentation, Begin turned to the President, whose reactions were not discernible, and said, according to Lewis, " 'Why don't we ask our two defense ministers to work it out.' I thought Cap would faint."

Over the next few months, Weinberger proceeded to "entangle" Sharon in a negotiation, Lewis recalled, that "turned out a mouse." There would be no joint U.S.–Israeli bases in the Middle East, and Israel would not get the access it wanted to American satellite intelligence. Sharon also was told that Israel would not be permitted a receiving station in Tel Aviv for the real-time KH-11 photography.

Sharon initially resisted any curtailing of his strategic plan, and he was ready to fight for it, but Begin, Lewis explained, was eager "to formalize an alliance with the United States— especially after the Carter years." Sharon eventually was forced to accept the watered-down American version, which he vehemently opposed and then had to defend publicly before the Knesset. He remained loyal to his prime minister and did his bidding. There were bigger fish to fry.

Over the next few months, Sharon found a way to carry out his strategic goals without the help of Washington. He led Israel, with the support of Begin, into an invasion of Lebanon in an effort to destroy the Palestine Liberation Organization and use Israel's military dominance to change the political structure of the Middle East. Israel would carry the fight, under Sharon's plan, to the outskirts of Beirut, serving as an anti-Syrian blocking force while its Lebanese Christian allies, the Phalangists, cleaned out the city of PLO followers. But the Phalangists failed to move, and the Israeli Air Force was called upon to begin the bombing of Beirut. Instead of victory, there was impasse, as five hundred Israeli soldiers were killed along with more than ten thousand Palestinians and Lebanese, some in the shocking massacre at the Palestinian refugee camps in Sabra and Shatila.

Before carrying out this plan, Sharon needed to control Israel's intelligence services and its "Temple" weapons—the nuclear arsenal. Men loyal to him and his strategic goals were put into key positions. One of the first of the Old Guard to be shoved out was Binyamin Blumberg, who had served since the 1950s as head of the Office of Special Tasks, widely known in the early 1980s by its Hebrew acronym, LAKAM. The new head of LAKAM was a Sharon crony and long-time clandestine operative named Rafael (Rafi) Eitan, who was then also serving as Begin's special assistant for counterterrorism. He would keep both jobs. The ambitious Eitan, known throughout Israel as "Rafi the stinker,"* had participated in the 1960 kidnapping of Adolf Eichmann in Buenos Aires and was a veteran of many operations inside the Arab world. He had been forced to resign, nonetheless, from Mossad years earlier, and was bitter about his stunted career and the failure of Mossad and Israel's other intelligence agencies to cooperate with his counterterrorism office.

Sharon did not hide his political agenda, but publicly spelled it out on many occasions after leaving the Israeli Army in 1973. His major goals included the overthrow of King Hussein of Jordan and the transformation of that country into a Palestinian state, to which Palestinian refugees would be "transferred" —or driven. A few weeks after his return from Washington in the early fall of 1981, Sharon called together the senior officer corps of the Israeli Defense Force and told them for the first time about his specific plans to put his political agenda into effect—Israel was going to invade Lebanon. One officer who was present recalled that he and others were dismayed to hear Sharon "talk about the need to go to Lebanon and destroy the 'capital of terrorism.'" He talked of the long reach of the IDF and the need—"not in such words," the officer said—"to change regimes in the Arab world." The Israeli officer, a former intelligence specialist, further recalled Sharon's talk about the "need to change the structure of Israeli intelligence."

"I was sitting with a bunch of brigadiers [generals]," the officer added, "and I said, 'He's going to take us to war in the Middle East.' There was nervous laughter all around."

There was one more distinct element in the Sharon briefing: "He returned [from Washington] anti-American, in a way I'd never detected before. He gave us his impression of Washington. He said, 'Americans treat us like an aircraft carrier—a floating base. They don't understand our real significance: we're not one aircraft carrier. We are twenty aircraft carriers. We are much more important than they think. We can take the Middle East with us whenever we go.'" It was a strange and

---

* Eitan's nickname arose from his habit of refusing to change his socks while fighting in Israel's War of Independence in 1948.

unsettling performance, the officer thought, punctuated by Sharon's threat to "court-martial" anyone who publicly discussed what he had said.

On December 15, Sharon, in a speech read by Aharon Yariv (Sharon was not present) at a conference at the Institute of Strategic Studies at Tel Aviv University, suggested that the United States was indirectly responsible for the growing threat posed by Moscow in the Middle East: "Soviet advances in the region have been made possible during the seventies because of the U.S. strategic passivity in those years and the freedom of action the Soviet Union has enjoyed. . . ." The increased Soviet freedom of maneuver in the Middle East and Africa, he added, "endangers the stability of the region and vital interest of the free world. I want to stress this point with all possible emphasis. The great danger to the free world in the eighties would be to continue [to] indulge in the wishful thinking and the inaction which have characterized Western attitudes to Soviet gradual expansion during the last two decades."

Sharon called for Israel to broaden its national security interests "to include, beyond the Middle East and Red Sea, states like Turkey, Iran, and Pakistan, and regions such as the Persian Gulf and central and northern Africa." The new minister of defense was telling his nation that Israel's national security now depended on its ability to influence events in a huge area that stretched from Kenya in the south to Turkey, and from Mauritania in the west to Pakistan.

There was one sure way to meet the new and expanded Soviet threat: increase Israeli reliance on its nuclear arsenal. But that could not be accomplished without KH-11 satellite information and other intelligence from the United States.

As Sharon was beginning to redesign Israel's strategic posture, Washington finally got some hard intelligence on the Israeli nuclear arsenal. It was a "walk-in," an Israeli scientist or technician who had worked at Dimona and who, as Mordecai Vanunu would do five years later, had taken some photographs of the underground storage bunkers there. "It was our first look inside," one senior intelligence official recalled. "What got our attention was the fact that he was inside a storage facility." The photographs showed Israeli warheads individually stored in heavy lead compartments, very similar to those used in American nuclear storage igloos: "We actually saw the weapons lined up there."

The men handling the defector were experts in weapons production and knew they were seeing the real thing—thermonuclear warheads. The defector told them that Israel had more than one hundred weapons in storage. "Our thought was 'Holy shit!' " one involved American recalled. " 'How could we have been so wrong?' We always said, 'So the Israelis got ten warheads? Okay. So what? Anybody can build those.' All of a sudden we learned they'd become sophisticated. It blew everybody's mind. Why do you need a thermonuclear device? We know twenty KTs [kilotons] will take out Cairo. [Israel] was more advanced and better than any of our people had presumed it could be—clean bombs, better warheads. The White House was briefed, but not in terms that I gave you because it was a real black eye for the [intelligence] community."

The defector also provided specific data about warhead size and delivery systems—"we got lots of paper"—that convinced the Americans that the Israelis were capable of delivering a nuclear warhead with accuracy. It was clear from the defector's data, the American said, that the Israelis "can do anything we or the Soviets can do."

There was the usual disconnect, as there had been with all Israeli nuclear information since the late 1950s, and the defector's data was not shared with the State Department's proliferation experts nor with any of the analysts of Z Division at Livermore, who were seen as liberals. "You bet your ass it was kept away from the people at Z Division," the Reagan administration official said. "We were paranoid that they'd get it anyway." The defector's information was left dangling, and those Americans who should have known the extent and nature of Israel's nuclear capability did not.

Jonathan Pollard was an unhappy child in South Bend, Indiana. The son of a professor at Notre Dame University, he was tormented and beaten in grade school for being Jewish. He told an interviewer that the "turning point" of his life came as a result of the Six-Day War, when he was thirteen. Israel's victory was "emotionally intoxicating" and triggered his lifelong obsession with Israeli security, and his fantasies of being part of it. He told fellow undergraduates at Stanford University that he had dual citizenship and was a colonel in the Israeli Army. Bragging and fanciful claims marked his years at Fletcher School of Law and Diplomacy at Tufts University in Boston, where he enrolled in 1977. He failed to earn his degree, and also failed in an attempt to join the CIA. In early 1981, Pollard sought a job as a defense analyst with the American Israel Public Affairs Committee (AIPAC), one of Washington's most effective lobbies. AIPAC officials found his bragging about access to top-secret information inappropriate and "weird"; one AIPAC official recalled that Pollard's story sounded "too incredible to be real. So we got rid of him." There was a feeling that Pollard was part of a "sting" operation attempting to set up AIPAC. He was clearly trouble.

Pollard also had been offering his services to Israel in 1980 and 1981, but no serious Israeli intelligence official would consider the recruitment of an openly pro-Israel American Jew who worked for the American intelligence community. There also was an unwritten law prohibiting the recruitment of any American Jew, pro-Israel or not. It was just too high-risk.

Pollard's repeated offers to spy for the State of Israel had unnerved the Israeli intelligence community. "He was turned back in 1980," a former Mossad operative said. "He's crazy; he's Jewish—'Don't take him.' It's like recruiting a Communist to spy [in the United States] for the KGB. He's automatically a suspect."

Rafi Eitan, the aggressive new director of LAKAM, decided to change the rules after the unproductive meetings with the President and his senior aides in Washington. He agreed with Sharon that the United States was holding back on intelligence that was essential to Israeli security—such as the KH-11 photography. "It was a basic suspicion," recalled one Israeli who had worked in Mossad with Eitan. "Whatever you get is not the real stuff—there is even stuff beyond."

Ari Ben-Menashe and his colleagues in the External Relations Department were also appalled when Eitan recruited Pollard in October 1981. Pollard was a member of a Navy team that visited Israel that fall to coordinate the exchange of intelligence with the Israeli Navy. Such visits were routine, and the Israelis had worked out a novel way of making their counterparts feel welcome: each American would be invited to an Israeli officer's home for dinner. "Guess who shows up at Pollard's dinner?" asked Ben-Menashe. "Rafi. He bagged him [Pollard] in one night. He didn't even pay him very well—just gives him this big story." Eitan needed Pollard, Ben-Menashe explained, "to access papers he already had knowledge of. He needed an analyst." His recruitment was viewed by military intelligence as "the worst fucking thing Rafi could have done."

By early 1982, Reuven "Rudi" Yerdor had been promoted to brigadier general and was in charge of Unit 8200, the Israeli communications intelligence service. Yerdor was a senior analyst who worked closely with his counterparts in the American National Security Agency, traveling to Washington every three months for liaison meetings. Yerdor's official title was deputy chief of staff for military intelligence in the Israeli Defense Force; his immediate superior was Major General Yehoshua Saguy, the head of Aman (military intelligence) and a deputy to Sharon who, like Sharon, was dismissed after the Sabra and Shatila massacre. Every senior officer understood that Saguy, as head of military intelligence, was directly responsible under military procedure for briefing the prime minister. But Saguy was known throughout the upper echelon of the Israeli military for his reluctance to challenge Sharon and his willingness to step aside and permit Sharon to be the main conduit for military intelligence to Begin and the Israeli cabinet.

Over the 1981–82 New Year's holiday, Yerdor was summoned by Saguy and given two packets of documents to evaluate: "Tell me what you think." The first set dealt with highly technical American intelligence describing a Soviet military system in the hands of the Arabs. The second documents, far less interesting to Yerdor, were copies of the daily and weekly summaries of worldwide NSA intercepts. "Rudi tells him the technical stuff is terrific," an Israeli official recalled, "but that 'we'll never get it in this form from the U.S.' As for the intercepts, 'These are less useful.'" Yerdor, as he later explained to a colleague, assumed that his government's intelligence services had recruited two people inside the United States—a step he found deplorable and shortsighted. Eventually, the material began flowing "in huge quantities," as Yerdor told his friend, and Yerdor "had to assign a special team to read and analyze it."

In February, Israel learned that the Soviets had decided to upgrade the Syrian air defense command and supply it with three battalions of SA-5s, their most advanced high-altitude antiaircraft missile. It was the first appearance in the Middle East of the system. The missiles remained under Soviet control, but they were assigned to protect Syria's short-range SS-21 missiles, which were capable of striking Israel. They also posed a threat to Israel's most advanced F-15 and F-16 fighter-bomber aircraft. It was an alarming escalation. An official request to the United States for intelligence on the capabilities of the SA-5 was made, but Yerdor was told, as he anticipated, that there was very little intelligence available on the system; it was too sensitive. "Two days later," an Israeli friend of Yerdor's said, "out of the blue sky, Rudi gets the full [U.S.] intelligence on the SA-5, which makes it clear that it is not as good as we feared." As for the source of the report, as Yerdor told his colleague, "this doesn't come" through normal channels.

In mid-May 1982, three weeks before the invasion of Lebanon, Yerdor's office was handed an astonishing assortment of invaluable American technical data about the air defense systems in Syria. It included materials that the U.S. intelligence community had never supplied to Israel: detailed information on side-looking radar, electronic maps, and precise frequency of operations for Syria's SA-6, SA-8, and advanced SA-3 surface-to-air missile systems. Yerdor again raised questions with General Saguy: "We don't get these materials and if we asked for it, we wouldn't get it." The Israeli Air Force, utilizing electronic countermeasures (ECM), would demolish the Syrian Air Force and destroy more than seventy Syrian missile launchers during the Lebanon war.

There was much more. "NSA intercepts begin arriving," one fully informed Israeli recalled. Rafi Eitan himself showed up at Yerdor's office and "throws him a daily intercept" dealing with the diplomatic activities of Sam Lewis. Yerdor told Eitan: "I wouldn't touch it with a ten-foot pole." Lewis, a career diplomat who would serve as ambassador until 1985, was widely known as a good friend of Israel but also was strongly opposed to Ariel Sharon and his policies.

Yerdor had little respect for Eitan, and worried about the long-range implications of Israeli intelligence activities in the United States, its best ally. He was convinced Eitan was driven by his personal ambition and his need to settle old scores with Yitzhak Hofi, the head of Mossad, and Avraham Shalom, Shin Beth's director.* He also was convinced, at least until the Pollard scandal became public, that Eitan had recruited two or more Americans; it wasn't clear how one person could have had as much access to such a variety of highly classified material as was flowing across his desk. Pollard, Yerdor learned later, had been cleared—despite his openly pro-Israel views—for access to the most sensitive intelligence in the U.S. government, and was using his office in Navy intelligence to place orders with abandon to classified archives throughout the Washington area.

Ben-Menashe, like Yerdor, remained convinced—even after Pollard's arrest and guilty plea—that Eitan had been working with more than one American. Under normal conditions, things were hectic in Ben-Menashe's Office of External Relations: Eitan's LAKAM operations in the United States produced a steady stream of routinely transferred scientific and technical documents—similar highly classified U.S. material had been arriving since the late 1950s, when the agency was set up. Now, illicitly obtained intelligence was flying so voluminously from LAKAM into Israeli intelligence that a special code name, JUMBO, was added to the security markings already on the documents. There were strict orders, Ben-Menashe recalled: "Anything marked JUMBO was not supposed to be discussed with your American counterparts."

---

* Hofi also was a critic of Ariel Sharon, and had been since they had served together as paratroopers in the Suez War. His dislike of Sharon manifested itself in unprecedented public criticism, reported in the Israeli press after the invasion of Lebanon, in which Hofi, former chief of staff Mordecai Gur, and two other retired army generals accused Sharon of insubordination and cowardice under fire on repeated occasions in the 1950s, including the Suez War.

After the Sabra and Shatila massacre, Sharon remained in Begin's cabinet, but as a minister without portfolio, and Moshe Arens, a former aeronautical engineer, was named defense minister. Israeli politics were in more disarray than usual over the next year; Menachem Begin's wife died in the spring, and a guilt-ridden Begin, who was in Washington at the time of her death, fell into a severe depression. He resigned as prime minister in September 1983 and was replaced by Yitzhak Shamir, a former senior Mossad operative and conservative member of the Likud coalition. Neither Labor nor Likud achieved a majority in the national elections in May 1984. A national unity coalition was negotiated over the next few months, with Shimon Peres and Shamir sharing power: Peres would serve as prime minister and Shamir as foreign minister until September 1986, when they would trade jobs. Yitzhak Rabin would serve as minister of defense throughout. Peres, Rabin, and Shamir became known as Israel's ruling troika.

Throughout the turmoil, Rafi Eitan stayed on the job—and so did Jonathan Pollard. A pattern for reporting was established: Pollard's intelligence would be summarized by Eitan and presented, without analysis or assessment, in a memorandum to the prime minister and minister of defense. By then, Pollard's material included essential KH-11 imagery as well as reporting and assessments from U.S. embassies and intelligence operatives inside Saudi Arabia, Jordan, and Egypt; such material is known in the diplomatic community as "third-party" information, and is never provided to outsiders. The top leadership, of course, knew what was going on. One former Israeli intelligence official recalled that Peres and Rabin, both very sophisticated in the handling of intelligence, were quick to ask, as the official put it, "Where are we getting this stuff?" They were told, the Israeli added, that Israeli intelligence " 'has a penetration into the U.S. intelligence community.' Both men let it go. No one said: 'Stop it here and now.' " Moshe Arens was viewed as far less sophisticated than Peres and Rabin about the nuances of intelligence. He did not raise any questions— "too dumb to ask," said the Israeli—but he was briefed on the American penetration by "intelligence guys who wanted to protect their ass."

After Pollard's arrest, the top leadership denied having any knowledge of his activities, and two internal commissions authorized by the cabinet and the Knesset that investigated the scandal also cleared the leadership of any direct knowledge. Pollard himself seemed to know better. In a pleading filed before he was given his life sentence in March 1987, he argued that his Israeli handlers told him that "Israel's dependence upon a 'special source' " had been mentioned at Israeli cabinet meetings. He also said that he was routinely provided with lists of intelligence items wanted; the lists were coordinated and "prioritized" by the heads of all the various military intelligence services. Much of the material he supplied, he stated, was satellite photographs and communication intercepts—material that any Israeli official would have to know "was not being transferred through official channels." Pollard's handlers in the United States, who included Aviem Sella by mid-1984, had even arranged for the Israeli government to provide, via its embassy in Washington, the most sophisticated photocopying machines for the reproduction of top-secret documents, including KH-11 satellite photographs. The photocopying machines arrived with special metal shielding to prevent the interception of electronic emanations.

Ari Ben-Menashe was aware of Rudi Yerdor's distress about the spying: "Yerdor was bitching about the fact that Eitan was compromising Israel's relations with the United States." Ben-Menashe understood much more: he had personal knowledge that Yitzhak Shamir, while serving as prime minister in 1983 and 1984, had authorized some of the Pollard material to be sanitized, retyped, and turned over to Soviet intelligence officials.

Ben-Menashe, an Iraqi Jew, had close ties to Shamir; in 1987, two years before his arrest in the United States and subsequent disaffection from Israel, he left the External Relations Department and went to work directly as an intelligence adviser for Shamir, then again serving as prime minister. In essence, he said, he conducted secret operations for Shamir. It was a step up. Ben-Menashe's ties to Shamir also were familial; his father served with Shamir in the fervently anti-British Stern Gang before the 1948 War of Independence.* Shamir, who viscerally disliked the United States, Ben-Menashe said, also "couldn't stand Begin and his moralistic approach to foreign relations. The first thing he [Shamir] decides"—upon becoming prime minister—"without any hesitation is to open the Soviet bloc to Israel." There was an immediate impact in the intelligence community, Ben-Menashe added: "A directive to the Mossad representative in Bucharest [Romania] to exchange information, to open things up. Nobody in the intelligence community would dare to do it without the approval of the prime minister."

The Soviets recognized the overture, Ben-Menashe said, and late in the year invited Israel to an intelligence conference in India to discuss the Pakistani nuclear weapons facility at Kahuta. In early 1984, while still acting prime minister, Shamir "authorized the exchange of intelligence with the Soviets on U.S. weapons systems. Suddenly," Ben-Menashe said, "we're exchanging information." Raw American intelligence was not handed over directly to the Soviets, but was reworked in an attempt to minimize the damage to American methods and agents. The exchange of intelligence paid an immediate dividend, beyond the easing of diplomatic tensions and the increased flow of Soviet immigrants to Israel, Ben-Menashe said. In late 1984 the Polish government permitted him, as a representative of the State of Israel, to travel to Warsaw and negotiate the sale of AK-47s and SA-7s, among other weapons, for shipment to Iran.

---

* Yair Stern considered the Jews' fight against the British to be more important than the world war against the Axis powers. The organization's leaders made a brief attempt in 1940 to broker an agreement with the Third Reich that would permit the illegal passage to Palestine of Jews from Germany and Europe to continue the fight against the British, whose war effort was supported by David Ben-Gurion and even the Irgun, a rival terrorist group that would be taken over by Menachem Begin in 1943. (Irgun's founder, David Raziel, in fact was serving as a high-ranking officer in British intelligence and wearing a British uniform when he was killed while on a mission in Iraq in 1941.) The Stern group, resisting pressure to fight with the Allies, sought direct negotiations at one point with Otto von Hentig, a representative of the German foreign ministry. Nothing came of it. In his memoirs, von Hentig wrote of meeting with a Jewish delegation (from Stern) that offered to cooperate with the Nazis and, in essence, go to war against their pro-Allied Zionist compatriots, if Hitler guaranteed the postwar independence of Jewish Palestine. Similar talks were held by Stern representatives with Benito Mussolini's Italy, calling on the Italians to provide transit camps and passage for Jewish refugees, as well as arms, in return for the Stern Gang's collaboration in expanding Italy's influence in the Middle East.

Ben-Menashe's account might seem almost too startling to be believed, had it not been subsequently amplified by a second Israeli, who cannot be named. The Israeli said that Pollard material was sanitized and dictated to a secretary before being turned over to the Soviets. Some material was directly provided to Yevgeni M. Primakov, the Soviet foreign ministry specialist on the Middle East who met publicly and privately with Shamir while he was prime minister. Shamir's turning to the Soviets was consistent with his personal and political beliefs, the Israeli said. While in Mossad in the 1950s and 1960s, Shamir was known for his efforts to improve relationships with his KGB counterparts. He left the intelligence service in the mid-1960s to join Begin's Herut Party and became speaker of the Knesset in 1977, when Begin became prime minister. He worked diligently to develop new ties with the Soviet Union, which he envisioned as a means of balancing, or offsetting, Israel's traditional reliance on the U.S. "Shamir has always been fascinated with authority and strong regimes," the Israeli said, "and very suspicious of democratic governments. He sees the U.S. as very soft, bourgeois, materialistic and effete."

For Shamir, the Israeli added, the relaying of the Pollard information to the Soviets was his way of demonstrating that Israel could be a much more dependable and important collaborator in the Middle East than the "fickle" Arabs: "What Arab could give you this?"

Shamir's unilateral decision to forward the material to the Soviets is now widely known in leading political circles in Israel, the Israeli source said. Rabin, who was close to the United States, went into a virtual "state of shock" upon being told, but kept his peace. Rabin and Peres, and their political advisers, understood that Shamir's action, if exposed, would mean the end of the increasingly shaky Likud coalition. They also realized, the Israeli source said, that the overall Israeli–United States relationship "would be at risk. So they kept quiet." Some officials of Mapam, the left-wing labor party with close ties to the Soviet bloc, also learned of Shamir's action and considered leaking that information to the press. The Mapam leaders "decided it was too explosive."

For his part, Shamir and his principals argued to their col-

leagues that his goal was to end the long-standing enmity between Israel and the Soviet Union and initiate some kind of
strategic cooperation. Shamir also claimed, the Israeli said, that
"he was not doing the United States such a disservice because
he's telling the Soviets that they cannot hide—the Americans
can see and hear everything."

One senior American intelligence official confirmed that there
have been distinct losses of human and technical intelligence
collection ability inside the Soviet Union that have been attributed, after extensive analysis, to Pollard. "The Israeli objective
[in the handling of Pollard] was to gather what they could and
let the Soviets know that they have a strategic capability—for
their survival and to get their people out [of the Soviet
Union]," one former CIA official said. "Where it hurts us is our
agents being rolled up and our ability to collect technical intelligence being shut down. When the Soviets found out what's
being passed"—in the documents supplied by Pollard to the
Israelis—"they shut down the source."

The Israeli officials most tarnished by the scandal were Rafi
Eitan and Aviem Sella, but Eitan did not suffer financially. He
was subsequently named to a high administrative position with
the Israel Chemicals Company, the largest state-owned enterprise in Israel. His surprising appointment was authorized by
none other than Ariel Sharon, who had been named minister of
trade and industry in 1984. As for Sella, he was promoted to
brigadier general after his return from the United States and
assigned as commander of Tel Nof, the site of Israel's nuclear-
ready air force squadron. After American protests, Sella instead was named head of the Israeli Defense Force staff college.
His prospects for further advancement in the air force were
bleak, and Sella retired.
    "They all decided Rafi would take the fall," one knowledge-
able American diplomat said, "and Sharon would take care of
him." The American, who conducted his own private inquiry
into the Pollard affair shortly after it became known, said that
the Israeli leadership agreed on a cover-up from the beginning,
despite the huge political differences between the parties.

"There is a national security doctrine in Israel that goes beyond everything—protect our government," he added. "If they had allowed it [the investigation] to go deeper than Rafi, it'd have blown up the [ruling] coalition. There was nothing to gain for Israel or the Labor Party by saying anything."

At one point, Rafi Eitan seemed to have second thoughts. He told an Israeli newspaper in early 1987, "All my actions, including the Pollard affair, were carried out with the knowledge of my superiors. I do not intend to be used as a sacrifice to cover up the knowledge and responsibility of others." (He changed his mind within a day, saying to an Israeli radio interviewer that all of the previously published statements attributed to him "were not made by me.")

The one aspect of the Pollard story that no one wanted revealed revolved around Aviem Sella. Sella was perhaps Israel's top air force expert in nuclear targeting and the delivery of nuclear weapons: it was his job to make sure that Israel's nuclear-armed F-16 aircraft could penetrate Soviet air defenses and reach their targets in the Soviet Union. Earlier in his career he had served as an F-4 pilot at Tel Nof, assigned to one of Israel's "black"—nuclear-capable—squadrons. Ariel Sharon's broadened view of Israeli national security and the Soviet threat had led to a dramatic upsurge in nuclear planning and nuclear targeting. The air force also was responsible for the advanced Jericho missile system, with its steadily increasing range. The new missile targets inside the Soviet Union required increased intelligence, and Sella's mission was to help Pollard gather the essential information and then evaluate it. Israel would need the most advanced American intelligence on weather patterns and communication protocols, as well as data on emergency and alert procedures. Any American knowledge of the electromagnetic fields that lie between Israel and its main targets in the Soviet Union also was essential to the targeting of the Jericho.

Sella's superb skill and knowledge of nuclear targeting blinded Eitan and the Israeli intelligence community to the fact that Sella was a pilot who knew nothing about running a covert operation. When Pollard did get into trouble in late 1985,

Sella had nothing to offer him—Sella's main concern was fleeing the United States as quickly as possible before he, too, was arrested and asked a lot of questions that neither he nor the Israeli government wanted asked.

Those Israelis who know of the Sella mission and the reasons behind it also believe that Jonathan Pollard had to understand what he was doing. "Pollard knew it," said one Sella friend. "Of course he knew it. We didn't need Pollard to bring us photographs of the PLO headquarters in Tunis." (The Israeli was referring to Pollard's claim that his intelligence had helped plan Israel's 1985 bombing of the PLO offices in Tunis.)

Pollard refused to cooperate with the U.S. Attorney's Office in Washington for six months before finally giving up Sella's name—and describing what he said was his involvement—as part of a plea bargain. It is not known whether the prosecutors in Washington realized at the time of the Pollard plea bargain that Sella's mission was linked to nuclear intelligence; nor is it even clear whether anyone in the U.S. government learned it later. Many of the government's submissions in the case, including an extensive presentation by Caspar Weinberger, were highly classified.

The government acknowledged that few involved in the case told the truth. It was that awkward situation that led them to insist that Sella be extradited to the United States. The Israeli government refused, and Sella was indicted in absentia in March 1987, in the U.S. District Court in Washington. In June 1990, Sella was declared a fugitive from justice.

Since his retirement, Sella has given friends and colleagues an account of his involvement that is more credible, but still far short of the whole story. While in Israel, he was recruited, he has said, for the job of trying to control Pollard, who was drowning the Israeli intelligence bureaucracy in documents. By 1984, when Sella was approached, he had almost completed his requirement for a Ph.D. in computer science at New York University; the obvious thought was that his technical training would be an asset in evaluating and perhaps winnowing down Pollard's materials. Sella knew, as he told colleagues, that Pollard had been recruited long before 1984—"the potato was in the oven," he said to one friend—but he was eager for the assignment: running a spy as important as Pollard would make his own climb to the top inevitable. Before taking the assignment, he checked with his superior, Major General Amos Lapidot, the air force chief of staff. Lapidot assured him, Sella has said, that Pollard was not a rogue—and clearance for his new assignment had been obtained from Yitzhak Rabin, the minister of defense. Once involved, Sella complained to a friend that Pollard "was running crazy." The spy, Sella said, "was giving him things he didn't want and didn't need."

Israel did make one direct attempt, nonetheless, to get the charges against the young colonel dismissed. In June 1986, shortly after Pollard gave up Sella's name, Israel hired Leonard Garment to represent the colonel. Garment, a former aide to Richard Nixon, was a prominent Washington attorney and private counsel to men such as former Attorney General Edwin Meese III. He also was a strong supporter of Israel, and under Nixon had occasionally become involved in high-level diplomacy.

In late June, Garment flew to Tel Aviv to interview Sella and speak with Israeli officials. His goal was to try to find some common ground between Washington and the government of Israel; to settle the matter before it led to even more damaging press. Sella's advisers in Israel included Chaim Joseph Zadok, a former minister of justice and elder statesman of the Labor Party, and government officials. They proposed that a factual proffer be offered the U.S. Justice Department, describing Sella's involvement—or lack of involvement. The document claimed that Sella had done nothing more than meet socially with Pollard. And Sella said that upon learning over dinner that Pollard was interested in forwarding documents to Israel, his only response was to suggest that "Pollard deal directly with the appropriate agency." The Israeli position, as outlined to Garment, was that the United States had no case against the colonel; there wasn't the slightest indication of spying on his part. Garment saw many state leaders while in Israel and even had dinner at the home of Shimon Peres. All assured him that they knew nothing of the Pollard matter.

After he had a long meeting with Sella and his brother in Tel Aviv, Garment began stalling for time; he refused to file the proffer, saying that it needed more work. Garment returned to Washington to try again to negotiate a diplomatic solution or find some way to come up with a document that could get his client off the hook without obstructing justice. After much communication back and forth, a six-man Israeli delegation arrived in Washington in August 1986 for a meeting with the Justice and State departments to resolve the issue. It was no ordinary group, but clear evidence that the necessity of protecting Sella reached to the top of the Israeli government. Its members were Chaim Zadok, the former justice minister; Meir Rosenne, a former Mossad official who was the Israeli ambassador to Washington; Rosenne's deputy, Elyakim Rubinstein, one of the brightest diplomats in Israel, who would become cabinet secretary; Ram Caspi, a prominent Labor Party lawyer and one of Shimon Peres's confidants; Avraham Shalom, the former head of Shin Beth (who had been forced to resign his post in late June because of cover-up charges in connection with the Shin Beth killing in 1984 of two Palestinian hijackers while in custody); and Hanan Bar-on, deputy director general of the Israeli foreign ministry. Caspi, Shalom, and Bar-on had been appointed by Peres immediately after Pollard's arrest to conduct an internal investigation. The three men reported within a week that Pollard was part of a rogue intelligence-gathering unit that operated without any government awareness.

Garment invited the six men to his home on the day before their meeting with Justice and State. They worked for hours on the proffer. Garment had drafted a memorandum on obstruction of justice under U.S. law in an attempt to persuade the Israelis to stop insisting that he file the proffer as initially written. The meeting went on past midnight, with Garment's wife, Suzanne, then a well-known Washington columnist for the *Wall Street Journal*, put in charge of typing drafts of the disputed proffer. At one point, according to a witness (not Garment), as Garment continued to demur, the inevitable question came: "What kind of a Jew are you?" Garment was incensed: "I'm an American citizen, too." What they wanted also made no sense in terms of protecting the client. Garment decided it

was time to let them know what he knew. He retrieved his
notes of the dinner conversation with Sella and read them to
the group. The Israelis listened quietly and then asked for a
few moments of privacy. When Garment returned, they demanded the Sella notes. "These are my notes," Garment told
them. They insisted. Garment held his ground. In that case,
they said, "you're discharged."

Garment lost his temper. He told the men that they would
never get the Sella notes and warned: "If any of you make a
move in my direction, I'll throw you in the pool." Everyone
settled down. It was later agreed that Garment would withdraw from the case, but do so quietly.

Garment's instinct for self-preservation—he was, after all, a
survivor of the Nixon White House—was at its most acute. He
did not know that Aviem Sella was a leading nuclear targeter,
he did not know that U.S. nuclear targeting secrets were involved in the Pollard affair, and he did not know that three of
the six men who negotiated with him over the Sella proffer had
been involved in an internal investigation and cover-up of the
Pollard scandal. What Garment did know, as he privately informed U.S. Attorney Joseph E. diGenova, who led the Pollard
prosecution, and Mark M. Richard, a deputy assistant attorney
general, was that he was leaving the case because he was not
sure whether his client was Aviem Sella or the Israeli government.

With his withdrawal, the Israeli government ended its attempt to protect Sella—in effect, ending Sella's career. Sella,
who retired from the air force in disillusionment and disappointment, remained in Israel, as of mid-1991 a fugitive from
American justice.

22

An Israeli Asset

By October 1986, Jonathan Pollard had yet to be sentenced and there were many in the U.S. intelligence community who were convinced that he had one and perhaps many more accomplices inside the government—men or women who were supplying Israel with the identification of highly classified documents that Pollard could then be assigned to retrieve. The hunt for "Mr. X," as the government called Pollard's alleged accomplice, had only begun.

Israel was in the news, and so was spying. The *Sunday Times* of London had every reason to anticipate that its October 5, 1986, revelation about Dimona, based on its interviews with Mordecai Vanunu, would be a sensation. It was the first inside account of the Israeli nuclear establishment, based on a publicly named source. It also was another story of betrayal involving Israel: Vanunu and Pollard were primarily driven not by financial gain (although both accepted money), but by the conviction that they were doing the right thing.

The intelligence communities of the world were riveted by the *Sunday Times* account. One key American nuclear intelligence official acknowledged that the Vanunu story and Pierre Pean's 1982 book on the early French involvement at Dimona "together presented the evidence that filled in all the question marks. What we and Z Division didn't know, they provided."

But the press paid little attention. The *Sunday Times*'s competitors on Fleet Street ignored the story, and so did much of the world's press. The *Washington Post* and the *New York Times* dismissed it in subsequent days with a few paragraphs buried inside their newspapers, and the major wire services treated it the same way.

Jerry Oplinger, the former White House aide, was appalled by the failure of the press to understand the importance of Vanunu. "I couldn't believe those guys. There was nothing [significant] in the *Times, Post,* and *Wall Street Journal,*" he said. "Everybody in the arms control business was amazed that there was nothing. To me and my close friends, it was really discouraging. Here is a fascinating and scary story, and even the press isn't interested."

Peter Hounam, the primary reporter and writer of the Vanunu story, knew it was the most important of his career. He expected anything, except apathy. There were not even any calls from the major newspapers in the United States. It might have been different, Hounam knew, if Mordecai Vanunu had been available in person. The *Sunday Times* had worked out a careful public relations campaign to help promote the story. There was to be a news conference on the day of publication (the newspaper would also announce that Vanunu had agreed to write a book and that syndication rights had been sold to *Stern,* the West German news magazine). But Vanunu had dropped out of sight the week before, and the *Sunday Times* was unable to produce him when he was most needed.

Vanunu, of course, had been duped by Israeli intelligence into leaving London on September 30 and lured to Rome, where he was abducted by the Mossad. His decision to walk away from the London newspaper world had followed publication of Vanunu's photograph in the *Sunday Mirror,* Britain's second-largest tabloid, and a hostile story the week before, on September 28. Israeli officials were quoted claiming that Vanunu had been fired from Dimona the year before "for attempting to copy documents." An Israeli press attaché added: "There is not, and there never has been, a scientist by this name working in nuclear research in Israel. I can confirm that a Mordecai Vanunu worked as a junior technician in the [Israeli] Atomic Energy Commission." The *Sunday Mirror* had attacked the credibility of Vanunu's photographs, quoting an unidentified nuclear weapons expert as saying that they could have been taken in an "egg factory." The *Mirror* also asked whether

Vanunu's account was "a hoax, or even something more sinister—a plot to discredit Israel."

The article had been given a lurid headline: "Strange Case of Israel and the Nuclear Conman." The alleged con man in the headline was not Vanunu, but Vanunu's agent, Oscar E. Guerrero, an opportunistic journalist from Colombia in South America who had befriended the hapless Vanunu in June, while he was still in exile in Australia. It was Guerrero who convinced Vanunu that his story and spectacular photographs were worth as much as $1 million. After failing to interest *Newsweek* magazine, Guerrero approached the London *Times* in late August, and within a few days, Peter Hounam was in Australia, interviewing Vanunu.

Guerrero, apparently fearful that he would be cut out of Vanunu's agreement with the *Sunday Times,* also approached the *Sunday Mirror*—known for its checkbook journalism—while Hounam and the *Sunday Times*'s "Insight Team" were preparing their story. It was that approach that put Ari Ben-Menashe and the Israeli intelligence community into the picture.

Hounam and the editors at the *Sunday Times* did not know that as they worked, Mordecai Vanunu had been compromised to the Israelis by a Fleet Street colleague named Nicholas Davies, the foreign editor of the *Daily Mirror*, sister newspaper of the *Sunday Mirror*. Davies's contact was Ari Ben-Menashe. He and Ben-Menashe had been partners in an international arms sales firm initially known as Ora Limited, which had operated out of Davies's London home since 1983. Ora Limited, set up with the approval of the Israeli government, according to Ben-Menashe, was designed to get arms flowing into Iran—one of many such undercover operations around the world. "Davies was my main backup on all the Iran arms sales," Ben-Menashe said.

Because of his ability to speak Farsi, Ben-Menashe had been assigned in November 1980 to a small working group inside the Israeli intelligence community that dealt with Iran, then an international outcast—like Israel—that needed arms for its war against Iraq. Ben-Menashe's assignment was to find ways of getting around the arms embargo. Front companies and credible people to run them were essential. "Nick had a friend in

the Mossad," Ben-Menashe recalled, and there was a casual
meeting in London. Davies accepted an invitation to visit
Israel; it was just a few more steps before he became an Israeli
asset. As a Catholic from northern England, Ben-Menashe said,
Davies was the perfect cutout, a well-dressed charmer with a
strong taste for the good life.

Ben-Menashe's files include hundreds of telexes and other
documents indicating that Ora Limited was actively involved
in arms trafficking with Iran at the highest levels. One 1987
cable, sent to Ayatollah Ali Akbar Hashemi Rafsanjani, provided terms for the sale to Iran of four thousand TOW missiles
at a cost of $13,800 each. The cable declared that a British citizen
named Nicholas Davies, as a representative of Ora Limited,
"will have the authority to sign contracts in Iran. . . ." Another series of documents revolved around the 1987 efforts of
Ora Limited to set up a communications company in Tucson,
Arizona, to be headed by Robert D. Watters, then a broadcast
engineer at the University of Arizona's television station. Watters, an expert on satellite voice communications, recalled
many meetings with Ben-Menashe in Tucson and many telephone conversations with Davies in London. "I thought Nick
was the money man," Watters said. "He was there representing
Ora."*

Davies, reached by telephone in London at a number listed
for Ora Limited, acknowledged that he knew Ben-Menashe but
denied any involvement in arms sales: "All I will say is just
keep investigating." Ben-Menashe, he added, was only a news
source: "He's got amazing information." At one time, he said,
he and Ben-Menashe had discussed collaborating on a book, but
the prospective publisher was not interested. Ben-Menashe was
now telling stories about him, Davies said, in revenge. "If any

---

* Watters wasn't surprised to learn that Davies was in the newspaper business: "He
called from what sounded like a very open room with lots of people talking and type-
writers going. I always wondered where he was." Before agreeing to set up the company on behalf of Ora Limited, Watters added, he sought to check out Ben-Menashe
and his London firm. Watters was also working under contract on a communications
project for the U. S. Border Control and, through a friend there, was put in touch with
officials of the U. S. Justice Department in Washington. "They said, 'Go ahead. Do
anything he wants. Just keep us informed,' " Watters said.

allegations are made in England," Davies warned, "I'll be seeing my solicitor."

But, in addition to the cable cited above, Ben-Menashe's allegations were explicitly confirmed by Janet Fielding, a London
actress who was the second wife of Nicholas Davies from 1982
to 1985. She said that she knew that Davies was selling arms in
partnership with Ben-Menashe at the same time he was serving
as foreign editor of the *Daily Mirror*. Eventually, she said in a
telephone interview, she became "appalled" by her then husband's activities. "Nick would try to tell me stuff [about the
arms sales] and I said I didn't want to know. I left him because
of it."

She had first known him as a journalist who had written
critically of the massacres at Sabra and Shatila during the 1982
Israeli invasion of Lebanon: "And then he gets involved with
Ari." She especially recalled, she said, serving Ben-Menashe
lunch at her home in late 1984: "I'd gone to the trouble of getting kosher salami and Ari didn't like it."

Asked whether she knew that Ben-Menashe was an Israeli
intelligence operative, Fielding responded, "It wasn't difficult
to put two and two together. Do you think I'm bloody stupid? I
shut my ears and walked"—out of the marriage.

Soon after Guerrero approached the *Sunday Mirror*, Ben-
Menashe said, Davies learned of it and immediately telephoned
him in Israel to tip him off: "The next I knew I was on the
night plane to London. Some shithead from Colombia was peddling the pictures in London. Nick arranged a meeting with
this 'hot' American journalist—me." At the meeting, Guerrero,
eager for another sale, displayed some of Vanunu's color photographs. Ben-Menashe's problem, he recalled, was that he simply had no idea what they showed or whether they were
significant. They would have to be seen, he knew, by experts in
Israel. "I told him I needed copies." Guerrero balked. "I said,
'You want some money? I have to know they're real.' I told him
Nick will vouch for me." Guerrero turned over copies of three
Vanunu photographs.

•   •   •

The fact of Vanunu's defection had been known for weeks by the top political leadership of Israel. There had been discussions, Ben-Menashe said, about what to do, with some officials urging Vanunu's assassination and the intelligence community recommending that he be ignored. It wasn't clear how much Vanunu knew or how much damage could be caused by a low-level Moroccan-born technician. It was Shimon Peres who ruled out assassination, Ben-Menashe said: "Peres said, 'Let's make him an example.'"

Vanunu's photographs, which had been shipped by Ben-Menashe directly to Israel—he was under strict orders to stay away from the Israeli embassy—created havoc. Ben-Menashe was told the next morning, "They're real." He was also told that Peres was personally handling the crisis. Ben-Menashe learned one of the reasons a few days later: there was fear that Vanunu knew that Israel had deployed nuclear land mines along the Golan Heights—and that he would talk about it. The land mines had been put in place in the early 1980s, when Vanunu was still working at Dimona.

That news propelled a major disinformation effort by Israel, Ben-Menashe said: "To stop every story. To put out the word that it's bullshit." Davies did his part at the *Sunday Mirror*, Ben-Menashe said, working directly with Robert Maxwell, publisher of the Mirror Group newspapers, the largest group of popular tabloids in Great Britain, which included the *Daily* and *Sunday Mirror*. Davies provided the framework for the September 28 Vanunu story, Ben-Menashe recalled, and then "it went to Maxwell. He was dealing directly with Maxwell." At one point, Ben-Menashe said, Davies set up a meeting for Ben-Menashe with Maxwell at his ninth-floor office. Maxwell made it clear at the brief session, Ben-Menashe recalled, that he understood what was to be done about the Vanunu story. "I know what has to happen," Maxwell told Ben-Menashe. "I have already spoken to your bosses."

Maxwell, Rupert Murdoch's fellow press baron and major competitor, was known for his closeness to Israel's top leadership. He subsequently became an owner of *Maariv*, the Israeli daily newspaper, and also briefly was owner of the Cytex Corporation, an Israeli-based supplier of high-tech printing equipment, whose senior executives included Yair Shamir, a former air force colonel and the son of Yitzhak Shamir.

The *Sunday Mirror* reporting and editing team that handled the Vanunu story had no contact with Nicholas Davies, whom they knew only as the foreign editor of the *Daily Mirror*. What the reporters did know, however, was that the story that appeared under their names had been dictated in tone and content by the newspaper's editor, Michael Malloy. There were heated debates with the *Mirror*'s reporting team, led by Tony Frost, insisting that the real story was not about Guerrero and his antics, as Malloy wanted to make it, but about the Vanunu photographs. Whatever Guerrero's problems, the Vanunu photographs could be real. If so, it was one hell of a story. The reporters recommended that the photographs be "splashed" across the front of the newspaper, with the accompanying story raising questions about their authenticity. But Malloy wanted none of Vanunu's photographs published and insisted on holding up Vanunu, and the *Sunday Times*, to ridicule.

The crunch came on the Thursday before publication, when Frost and a colleague named Mark Souster were ordered by Malloy to take the Vanunu photographs and data to the Israeli embassy. John C. Parker, then Malloy's senior deputy, understood that Maxwell himself had given the order. Parker and his colleagues were extremely concerned about what going to the embassy meant for Vanunu. It could lead to his arrest and even put his life in danger from assassination. "It's an editor's prerogative," Malloy told them, and the newspaper's staff did his bidding.

Frost knew that he and his colleagues had not participated in journalism's finest hour: "I was hoping one day that the full story would come out on this," he said.

Peter J. Miller, the *Sunday Mirror*'s senior news editor, who was fired by Maxwell in 1990 (Frost also was dismissed in the dispute), angrily complained that the newspaper's treatment of the Vanunu story had been turned around because of pressure from above. "The line we were instructed to take," Miller said, "cost the *Sunday Mirror* a world-beating exclusive."*

* Miller was fired in November 1990, after he was accused initially of neglect of duties and later with conspiring with another *Sunday Mirror* employee to sell a photo-

Parker, who left the *Mirror* in 1988 to publish *King of Fools*, a best-selling biography of the Duke of Windsor, also expressed bitterness over the handling of the Vanunu story. "The *Sunday Mirror* had the biggest story in the world at that time and it collapsed because of the line they took," he said. "It was a classic exercise by the Israelis in disinformation."

Malloy, who was forced out in 1988 as editor of the *Sunday Mirror*, acknowledged that he had discussed the handling of the Vanunu story with Maxwell, but said there was "nothing sinister or strange about Maxwell's involvement. I told Bob about it because of his involvement with Israel. He does have powerful friends there and close links." Told of the complaints by Parker, Miller, and Frost, Malloy said that he himself had misjudged the importance of the Vanunu photographs. "My news instincts were bad," Malloy, now a free-lance writer and novelist, explained. "It sounded to me like a setup." It was Maxwell, however, Malloy recalled, who ordered the staff to take the photographs to the Israeli embassy. "I think he [Maxwell] probably said, 'Oh, let the Israelis have a look at it,' and that's how it came about. It wasn't as if we were handing them to a foreign enemy."

Malloy also said he could not deny that he had invoked Maxwell's name in telling Miller, Parker, and Frost how to handle the story. Although he could not specifically recall doing so in the Vanunu case, Malloy said, "generally Maxwell was given a draft [of stories] in advance." Malloy also acknowledged that it was possible that Maxwell was not keeping him fully informed of his independent contacts, with the Israelis or others on the *Mirror* newspaper group, such as Nicholas Davies.* Maxwell

---

graph of Lady Diana, the Princess of Wales, dancing with John Travolta, the American actor, to rival publications after it had been printed in the *Mirror*. Miller, who was the publisher of a local London newspaper and magazine when interviewed, contested the firing before Britain's Industrial Tribunal, and in June 1991 won his case against Maxwell and the *Sunday Mirror*. The Tribunal, as of August 1991, was considering how much compensation to award Miller. Frost, now the deputy editor of the *Sunday Sun* in Newcastle, England, was also dismissed by Maxwell. He did not contest Maxwell's action against him.

  * Malloy said he knew nothing of Davies' ties to the Israelis but depicted him as serving as "sort of equerry for Maxwell. When Bob travels, he always has an entourage and Nick became part of that entourage." Davies, Malloy added, "always was a kind of entrepreneurial character—selling and importing on the side."

was in intelligence during the war," Malloy explained, "so he can be extremely disingenuous. So if he did know more than I knew, it's quite possible he wouldn't tell me."

Handling Robert Maxwell's *Sunday Mirror* was one thing, but the *Sunday Times* was still known to be at work on the Vanunu story—and the Israeli intelligence community had no clout at the top at the *Times*. "Those guys were not us," Ben-Menashe said. "They wanted the real story." The next step was to find Vanunu, still hiding out in London, and somehow manage to get him out of England. "We didn't know what hotel he was staying at," Ben-Menashe added. "We asked Nick to ask around and find out where the fuck he was. Nick did it, and we spotted him." Within days, the lonely Vanunu, who did not know about the land mines, Ben-Menashe said, was entrapped by the Mossad's Cindy Hanin Bentov and en route to Rome.

Ben-Menashe's involvement in the incident ended at that point, but he maintained his business ties with Davies until his arrest in New York in 1989. He initially sought to keep secret Davies's role in the ongoing arms sales, Ben-Menashe said, as any good intelligence operative would, but he decided to talk after Davies made no move to come to his defense. Davies, in fact, retained a New York attorney in a successful effort to resist being deposed by Ben-Menashe's attorneys in the case.

If he had chosen to do so, Ben-Menashe claimed, Davies could have proven to the American prosecutors that the sale of the C-130s to Iran had been sanctioned by the Israeli government.

Epilogue

For the men in the White House, the first day of President George Bush's Persian Gulf War couldn't have gone better. As America—and the world—watched on television, U.S. cruise missiles and Air Force and Navy planes struck their targets in downtown Baghdad and elsewhere in Iraq with precision. War seemed almost too easy. But the euphoria disappeared on the second day, as the Iraqi army carried out Saddam Hussein's pre-war pledge and fired eight Scud missiles at Israel from launchers that had supposedly been destroyed in the first hours of the war. Two Scuds landed in Tel Aviv and another near Haifa, and the world listened with dread to the initial, and erroneous, newscasts reporting that the Scud warheads contained nerve gas. Frightened Israelis, wearing gas masks, huddled in specially sealed above-ground rooms, waiting out the Iraqi bombardment; the streets below, as seen on television, were eerily quiet.

A senior American defense official rushed to Israel with a promise of future support, but it seemed inevitable that Israel would enter the Gulf War by sending its air force and its specially trained commando units into western Iraq, where the Scuds were located.

Adding to the tension was the fact that American intelligence had miscalculated in its predictions that Iraq had a limited number of Scud warheads and launchers—some estimates before the war put that number at fewer than 20. It had been thought that Iraq could launch its Scuds only from fixed launcher sites or from mobile launchers—no one had foreseen that Saddam Hussein's troops would convert a newly purchased fleet of flatbed trucks into makeshift launching pads.

General H. Norman Schwarzkopf, the American commander, eventually acknowledged that Iraq could have as many as fifteen battalions of launchers, each supplied with fifteen Scuds— a total of 225 missiles.

There was another element involved in those first hours, not known to the public but detected by an American satellite making its ninety-six-minute orbit around the earth. The satellite saw that Shamir had responded to the Scud barrage by ordering mobile missile launchers armed with nuclear weapons moved into the open and deployed facing Iraq, ready to launch on command. American intelligence picked up other signs indicating that Israel had gone on a full-scale nuclear alert that would remain in effect for weeks. No one in the Bush administration knew just what Israel would do if a Scud armed with nerve gas struck a crowded apartment building, killing thousands. All George Bush could offer Shamir, besides money and more batteries of Patriot missiles, was American assurance that the Iraqi Scud launcher sites would be made a priority target of the air war.

Such guarantees meant little; no Jews had been killed by poison gas since Treblinka and Auschwitz, and Israel, after all, had built its bomb so it would never have to depend on the goodwill of others when the lives of Jews were being threatened.

The escalation didn't happen, however; the conventionally armed Scud warheads caused—amazingly—minimal casualties, and military and financial commitments from the Bush administration rolled in. The government of Prime Minister Yitzhak Shamir received international plaudits for its restraint.

American officials were full of private assurances for months after the crisis that things had been under control; newsmen were told that Israel, recognizing the enormous consequence of a nuclear strike, would not have launched its missiles at Baghdad.

The fact is, of course, that no one in America—not even its President—could have dissuaded Shamir and his advisers from ordering any military actions they deemed essential to the protection of their nation. Such sovereignty isn't new or unusual. What is unusual is that one of America's most important allies

—a beleaguered ally surrounded by avowed enemies constantly threatening war—has secretly amassed a large nuclear arsenal while Washington looked the other way.

America's policy toward the Israeli arsenal, as we have seen in this book, was not just one of benign neglect: it was a conscious policy of ignoring reality.

By the mid-1980s, the technicians at Dimona had manufactured hundreds of low-yield neutron warheads capable of destroying large numbers of enemy troops with minimal property damage. The size and sophistication of Israel's arsenal allows men such as Ariel Sharon to dream of redrawing the map of the Middle East aided by the implicit threat of nuclear force. Israel also has been an exporter of nuclear technology and has collaborated on nuclear weapons research with other nations, including South Africa.

In September 1988, Israel launched its first satellite into orbit, bringing it a huge step closer to intercontinental missiles and a satellite intelligence capability—no more Jonathan Pollards would be needed to steal America's secrets. Scientists at Z Division concluded that the rocket booster that launched the Israeli satellite produced enough thrust to deliver a small nuclear warhead to a target more than six thousand miles away. Israeli physicists are still at the cutting edge in weapons technology and involved, as are their American and Soviet counterparts, in intensive research into nuclear bomb–pumped X-ray lasers, hydrodynamics, and radiation transport—the next generation of weaponry.

None of this has ever been discussed in the open in Israel, or in the Knesset. Meanwhile, Israeli field commanders have accepted nuclear artillery shells and land mines as battlefield necessities: another means to an end. The basic target of Israel's nuclear arsenal has been and will continue to be its Arab neighbors. Should war break out in the Middle East again and should the Syrians and the Egyptians break through again as they did in 1973, or should any Arab nation fire missiles again at Israel, as Iraq did, a nuclear escalation, once unthinkable except as a last resort, would now be a strong probability. Never again.

The Samson Option is no longer the only nuclear option available to Israel.

Acknowledgments

No author could have been blessed with a more intelligent, enthusiastic, or caring researcher, fact checker, editor, and colleague than Max Friedman of National Public Radio, an Oberlin College graduate who worked closely with me on this book for the past three years. He is a wonderful journalist.

Benjamin Frankel of Washington, a political scientist and an expert on national security, provided a seemingly unending tutelage on Israeli politics, history, and sociology.

Thomas W. Graham of the University of California at San Diego served as an in-house expert on the history of U.S. nonproliferation efforts, a subject few know better.

Thomas B. Cochran and Robert S. Norris graciously gave me a series of ad hoc, but expert, seminars on nuclear weapons and how they are made. Cochran is senior scientist and Norris is senior analyst with the Natural Resources Defense Council in Washington.

My longtime editor and friend Robert Loomis of Random House cared about this book and what it said, and how it said it. His help was essential. Esther Newberg, my agent, knew when to crack the whip and when to share a joke. It is a delight to be represented by someone of her integrity and intelligence. My thanks to Heather Shroder for her help in getting this book to foreign publishers.

Thanks, too, to Mrs. Miriam Borgenicht Klein for her help.

Notes

Few books have been written specifically on Israel's nuclear arsenal. The first and most politically insightful is *Israel and Nuclear Weapons*, by Fuad Jabber (published for the International Institute for Strategic Studies by Chatto & Windus, London, 1971). See also *Israel's Nuclear Arsenal*, by Peter Pry (Westview Press, Boulder, Colo., 1984); *Israeli Nuclear Deterrence*, by Shai Feldman (Columbia University Press, New York, 1982), and *Dimona: The Third Temple?* by Mark Gaffney (Amana Books, Brattleboro, Vt., 1989). The best reference work on the status of world proliferation is compiled and written by Leonard S. Spector, of the Carnegie Endowment in Washington, who publishes periodic updates. His most recent (with Jacqueline R. Smith) is *Nuclear Ambitions: The Spread of Nuclear Weapons, 1989–1990* (Westview Press, Boulder, Colo., 1990). And for the most recent Israeli view of the nuclear debate, see "Opaque Nuclear Proliferation," by Avner Cohen and Benjamin Frankel, *Journal of Strategic Studies*, Vol. 13, No. 3, September 1990, beginning at page 14.

1. A Secret Agreement

A full description of America's satellite capability and hardware, including an account of the KH-11, can be found in *American Espionage and the Soviet Target*, by Jeffrey Richelson (William Morrow, New York, 1987). The first journalistic report on the CIA's KK MOUNTAIN activities can be found in *Dangerous Liaison*, by Andrew and Leslie Cockburn (HarperCollins, New York, 1991); see Chapter 5, "Dirty Work on the Mountain." For an excellent discussion of President Jimmy Carter's troubles with the CIA's intelligence in Iran, see *All Fall Down*, by Gary Sick (Penguin Books, New York, 1985). There were many newspaper and magazine articles on the Geoffrey Prime spy scandal in Britain; see, for example, "The Treason of Geoffrey Prime," *Economist*, November 13, 1982, page 63. William Kampiles's travails similarly were fully reported. Richard Allen was first interviewed for this book on May 19, 1989, and many times thereafter. For a good account of the internal feuding in Israel over the bombing of the Iraqi reactor at Osirak, see *Israel's Secret Wars*, by Ian Black and Benny Morris (Grove Weidenfeld, New York, 1991), beginning at page 332. There have been many popular accounts of the raid itself; see, for example, *Two Minutes over Baghdad*, by Amos Perlmutter, Michael Handel, and Uri Bar-Joseph (Corgi Books, London, 1982). Also see *First Strike*, by Shlomo Nakdimon (Summit Books, New York, 1987, originally published by Yediot Ahronot/Eidanim, Tel Aviv, 1986). Menachem Begin's reaction to the raid can be found in the Israeli press for June 1982; see "Begin: Secret Atom

Bunker Also Was Destroyed in Raid," *Jerusalem Post*, June 12, 1981, page 1. The cited State Department study on Mozambique is entitled "Summary of Mozambican Refugee Accounts of Principally Conflict-Related Experience in Mozambique," submitted to the State Department in April 1988 by Robert Gersony, a consultant to the Bureau for Refugee Programs. William Bader was interviewed in Washington on June 3, 1991.

2. The Scientist

Not surprisingly, very little has been written about Ernst Bergmann. He is discussed in *Chaim Weizmann: A Biography by Several Hands*, in a chapter by R.H.S. Crossman, "The Prisoner of Rehovot," at page 333 (Atheneum, New York, 1963). See also *From These Men*, by Shimon Peres (Wyndham Books, New York, 1979), pages 185–201. An excellent magazine account of Bergmann's career was published in the weekly *Tel Aviv Magazine* of *Yediot Ahronot*, Israel's largest newspaper, in March 1991: "Who Forgot the Father of the Israeli Atom, and Why?" by Roni Hadar. The article, because of Israeli censorship, only hints at Bergmann's important role. The best biography (in English) of David Ben-Gurion is *Ben-Gurion*, by Michael Bar-Zohar (Adama Books, New York, 1977). Bar-Zohar is cited throughout the early portions of this book. The diaries of Moshe Sharett, *Personal Diary*, in Hebrew (Maariv, Tel Aviv, 1980) have been translated only in part. There are eight volumes in the original. Details of the early announcements of the Israeli Atomic Energy Commission can be found in Jabber and Pry. Bergmann's 1954 speech can be found in the *Daily Report* of the Foreign Broadcast Information Service for Tuesday, November 23, 1954, No. 227. Other details on Israel's early nuclear research program were provided by United Nations Ambassador Abba Eban in a speech on November 15, 1954; see page 335 et seq. of the official record for the General Assembly, Ninth Session. Ben-Gurion's remark about Israel being a "small spot" was cited in "The Hidden Debate," by Uri Bar-Joseph, *Journal of Strategic Studies*, June 1982, at page 212. Bar-Joseph's is one of many excellent scholarly articles on the Suez Crisis; see also "Israel's Relations with the Arabs," by Avi Shlaim, *Middle East Journal*, Spring 1983, beginning at page 180. Shlomo Aronson, an Israeli political scientist, has analyzed Israeli foreign policy in terms of its nuclear potential: see *Conflict and Bargaining in the Middle East* (Johns Hopkins University Press, Baltimore, 1978). The death of Aharon Katzir-Katchalsky was reported in the *Jerusalem Post*, June 1, 1972, "Leading Scientist Killed," page 3. Bergmann's quote about two atomic energies can be found in "Israelis Honor Atom Scientist," by James Feron, *New York Times*, May 14, 1966. Herman Mark was interviewed December 14, 1990, in Austin, Texas, and by telephone many times thereafter. Abe Feinberg was initially interviewed in New York on April 20, 1989, and many times in person and on the telephone thereafter. Bergmann's cited interview in 1969 was published in part in *A Tacit Alliance*, an excellent doctoral study of French-Israeli military ties by Sylvia K. Crosbie (Princeton University Press, Princeton, N.J., 1974). Bertrand Goldschmidt was interviewed in Paris on November 24, 1990. More details can be found in his memoir, *Atomic Rivals* (Rutgers University Press, New Brunswick, N.J., 1990), and his history of nuclear energy, *The Atomic Complex* (American Nuclear Society, La Grange Park, Ill., 1980).

3. The French Connection

The best account of France's role in the Israeli bomb is the cited *Les deux bombes*, by Pierre Pean (Fayard, Paris, 1982). The announcement of the Canadian-Indian reactor can be found in "Canada to Help Build Atom Research Reactor for India," by Grey Hamilton, *Toronto Globe and Mail*, April 30, 1956. Basic sources for the period leading up to the Suez war include the diaries of Ben-Gurion and Sharett, as well as *The Eisenhower Diaries*, Robert Ferrell, editor (W. W. Norton, New York, 1981), and de Gaulle's *Memoirs of Hope* (Simon & Schuster, New York, 1970). See also *Diary of the Sinai Campaign*, by Moshe Dayan (Weidenfeld & Nicholson, London, 1965), and *Suez*, by Hugh Thomas (Harper & Row, New York, 1966). The Bulganin threat during the Suez War can be found in contemporary newspaper accounts; especially see "Soviet Protests Canal Blockade," *New York Times*, November 5, 1956. The cited Peres biography is *Shimon Peres*, by Matti Golan (St. Martin's Press, New York, 1982). The French reactor at Marcoule is described in *Mechanical Engineering Magazine*, November 1959, at page 60 (no mention is made of its weapons capability, however). For the French view of the nuclear issue, see *The Balance of Terror*, by Pierre Gallois (Houghton Mifflin, Boston, 1961), page 137 et seq.

4. First Knowledge

The best account of the U-2 can be found in *Mayday*, by Michael R. Beschloss (Harper & Row, New York, 1986). Arthur Lundahl was interviewed in Bethesda, Maryland, on June 19, 1989, and many times by telephone afterward. Dino Brugioni was interviewed dozens of times by telephone at his home in Hartwood, Virginia, beginning on July 5, 1989. His account of the Auschwitz findings (cited in Chapter 7) can be found in "The Serendipity Effect of Aerial Reconnaissance," by Dino A. Brugioni, *Interdisciplinary Science Reviews*, Vol. 124, No. 1, 1989. America's difficulties in locating Soviet nuclear targets before the advent of the U-2 are described by David A. Rosenberg in "The Origins of Overkill: Nuclear Weapons and American Strategy, 1945–1960," *International Security*, Vol. 7, No. 3 (Spring 1983), pages 3–71. Andrew Goodpaster was interviewed by telephone in Washington on January 11, 1991.

5. Internal Wars

See Jabber for the generally held and mistaken view of the early resignations of the Israeli Atomic Energy Commission, as well as *Every Spy a Prince*, by Dan Raviv and Yossi Melman (Houghton Mifflin, Boston, 1990), page 69. Raviv and Melman, however, mention Binyamin Blumberg's important and early role in the Israeli bomb on the same page. Black and Morris also deal with Blumberg's little-known history. Ian Smart was interviewed in New York on July 23, 1989. He was then living in London. Thomas Graham was interviewed in Washington on May 15, 1989; his cited article is "The Economics of Producing Nuclear Weapons in Nth Countries," by Thomas W. Graham, in *Strategies for Managing Nuclear Proliferation*, edited by D. L. Brito, M. D. Intriligator, and A. E. Wick (Lexington Books, Lexington, Mass., 1983). Peres's boast about raising money can be found in the previously cited weekend magazine of *Yediot Ahronot*.

6. Going Public

John Finney was interviewed in Washington on April 18, 1989. The cited article was "U.S. Hears Israel Moves Toward A-Bomb Potential," *New York Times,* December 19, 1960, page 1. McCone's resignation and TV appearance were also on page 1 that day: "McCone to Resign as AEC Member." The cited Buchwald column (reprinted in part, with his permission) was published January 10, 1961, in the *New York Herald-Tribune,* "The Smashing Tailors of Beersheba." Walter Elder was interviewed in his suburban Virginia home on August 28, 1989, and many times by telephone thereafter. Armand Meyer was interviewed in Rosslyn, Virginia, on June 15, 1990. The cited Herter statement can be found in *The Alliance,* by Richard J. Barnet (Simon & Schuster, New York, 1983), page 179. Philip Farley was interviewed in Palo Alto, California, on October 30, 1989. Chapman Pincher was interviewed by telephone on March 28, 1991; the cited article is "Israel May Be Making an A-Bomb," London *Daily Express,* December 16, 1960, page 2. Myron Kratzer was interviewed in Washington in June 1989, and by telephone thereafter. The cited Freedom of Information documents are in the author's possession. Christian Herter's testimony to the Senate Foreign Relations Committee can be found in Vol. XIII, Part I, of the published Executive Sessions of the Senate Foreign Relations Committee (Historical Series), made public April 1984.

7. Dual Loyalty

The Strauss biography is *No Sacrifice Too Great,* by Richard Pfau (University Press of Virginia, Charlottesville, 1984.) There are many accounts of Oppenheimer's travails before the AEC; see *The Oppenheimer Hearing,* by John Major (Batsford, London, 1971). Strauss's test ban testimony was cited in *The Glory and the Dream,* by William Manchester (Little, Brown, Boston, 1973), page 985. Carl Kaysen was interviewed in Cambridge, Massachusetts, on November 11, 1989, and thereafter by telephone. William L. Strauss was interviewed by telephone on April 3, 1991; Alice Strauss was interviewed by telephone on May 6, 1991. Algie Wells was interviewed by telephone on March 29, 1991.

8. A Presidential Struggle

Abe Feinberg's role in presidential politics and fund-raising was initially reported in an unpublished dissertation, "Ethnic Linkage and Foreign Policy," by Etta Zablocki, Columbia University, 1983 (available through UMI dissertation information service, Ann Arbor, Mich.). Similar material was published in *The Lobby,* by Edward Tivnan (Simon & Schuster, New York, 1987), and *Truman and Israel,* by Michael J. Cohen (University of California Press, Berkeley, 1990). None of the accounts discusses Feinberg's relationship with the Israeli nuclear program. Clark Clifford was interviewed about Feinberg on April 8, 1991. Abraham Ribicoff was interviewed by telephone on November 5, 1990. Ben Bradlee and Arthur Schlesinger discussed President Kennedy on April 9, 1991. Kennedy's comments about campaign financing were made on October 4, 1961, according to Facts on File. A good account of Kennedy's efforts on campaign financing can be found in *Congressional Quarterly*'s "Congress and the Nation 1965–1968," Vol. II, "Political Finances," p. 444. Myer Feldman was interviewed in Washington on June 13, 1989, and many times thereafter. Jerome Weisner was interviewed by telephone on

June 27, 1991. Robert Komer was interviewed in Washington on April 3, 1989, and two times thereafter. William Crawford was interviewed in suburban Maryland on May 3, 1990. Israel's diversion of the Norwegian heavy water has been thoroughly researched and reported by Gary Milhollin, director of the Wisconsin Project on Nuclear Arms Control in Washington. Milhollin was the first to expose the issue, and has been more than generous in sharing his files and research. The explanation for the lack of a Shavit I can be found in "Publicity on Rocket Explained in Israel," *New York Times*, June 10, 1961. Paul Nitze was interviewed on October 9, 1990. Robert McNamara's cryptic conversation with the author took place on January 11, 1991. The more logical account of why the Israeli Atomic Energy Commission fell apart in the late 1950s was supplied by Yuval Neeman, minister of energy, in a conversation in Washington on April 15, 1991. Neeman would not discuss any current issues relating to Israel's nuclear capabilities. Floyd Culler was interviewed on November 30, 1989, in Palo Alto, California, and later by telephone. Phillips Talbot was interviewed briefly by telephone on April 8, 1991.

9. Years of Pressure

The declassified memorandum of the Kennedy talk with Golda Meir is available from the JFK Library in Boston and also can be found in *President Kennedy's Policy Toward the Arab States and Israel*, by Mordechai Gazit (Shiloah Center for Middle Eastern and African Studies, Tel Aviv University, 1983), page 108. The Gazit book provides invaluable background on Israeli policy in the Kennedy period. Much detail about Ben-Gurion's attitude and the history of that period, it should be noted again, comes from Michael Bar-Zohar's abridged biography. Daniel Ellsberg was interviewed in Washington on March 20, 1989. The most complete summary of Johnson's early ties to American Jews can be found in "Prologue," by Louis S. Gomolak, unpublished doctoral thesis (University of Texas, 1989), available through UMI dissertation information service.

10. The Samson Option

Excellent work on this period has been done by Shlomo Aronson, the Israeli political scientist and advocate of the deterrent value of Israel's nuclear arsenal. Moshe Dayan's *Maariv* article was summarized April 13, 1963, in the *New York Times*, "Israelis Warned on Arms Lag." Ben-Gurion's letter to the *Times* was published November 20, 1963. Theodore Taylor's paper was entitled "Can Nuclear Weapons Be Developed Without Full Testing?" It was a lecture given on December 11, 1988, at a workshop on Verification of Nuclear and Conventional Arms Reductions, Robin Brook Centre, St. Bartholomew's Medical College, London. The text of the lecture, with additional material, is reproduced in Theodore B. Taylor, "Nuclear Tests and Nuclear Weapons," in Benjamin Frankel, ed., *Opaque Nuclear Proliferation: Methodological and Policy Implications* (Frank Cass, London, 1991), pages 175–90. The cited White House papers are on file at the Lyndon B. Johnson Library in Austin. A number of books are useful on the background of international control of nuclear energy. See *The International Atomic Energy Agency and World Nuclear Order*, by Lawrence Scheinman (Resources for the Future, Washington, D.C., 1987) and *Nuclear Power Issues and Choices*, chaired by Spurgeon M. Keeny, Jr. (Ballinger Publishing Company, Cambridge, Mass., 1977). For a discussion of the Samson and Masada psychologies, see *A Psycho-History of Zionism*, by Jay Y. Gonen (Mason J. Charter, New York, 1975), Chapter 13. The cited Podhoretz article is entitled "The Abandonment of Israel" and appeared in the July 1976 issue of *Commentary*. The *New York Times* article on Bergmann appeared on June 14, 1966, and is cited above.

11. Playing the Game

The most comprehensive book on James Angleton is *Cold Warrior*, by Tom Mangold (Simon & Schuster, New York, 1991). Mangold shows that Angleton always had the support of Richard Helms in his paranoid treatment of defectors. Samuel Halpern was interviewed in his suburban Virginia home on April 29, 1991. The CIA's estimate on the "Consequences of Israeli Acquisition of Nuclear Capability" can be found in the Mordechai Gazit book cited above. For an excellent account of the making of the Chinese nuclear bomb, see *China Builds the Bomb*, by John Wilson Lewis and Xue Litai (Stanford University Press, Stanford, Calif., 1988). The material cited from Glenn Seaborg's *Stemming the Tide* (Lexington Books, Lexington, Mass., 1987) can be found in Chapter 13, "A Tale of Two Committees." The quote about India from McGeorge Bundy's *Danger and Survival* (Random House, New York, 1988) can be found on page 585. Seaborg describes the debate over the Gilpatric panel. Robert Kennedy's cited Senate speech was delivered on June 23, 1965; see the *Congressional Record* for that day at page 14566. The John Finney story was "Israel Permits U.S. to Inspect Atomic Reactor," *New York Times*, March 14, 1965, page 1.

12. The Ambassador

Walworth Barbour is rarely mentioned in any of the contemporary books about Israel or Middle East policies. One of the few to single out Barbour was Abba Eban, in his *Autobiography* (Random House, New York, 1977); Eban correctly described him as "corpulent, good-natured and brilliantly incisive," at page 297. Edward Dale was interviewed the first of many times at his home in Chapel Hill, North Carolina, on September 7, 1990. John Hadden was interviewed in Brunswick, Maine, on June 8, 1989, and many times thereafter by telephone. Peter Jessup was interviewed in Washington on March 20, 1989, and later by telephone. Carmelo Alba was interviewed in suburban Virginia on April 10, 1991. Herman Pollack was interviewed by telephone on May 21, 1991. Max Ben was initially interviewed by telephone from his home in St. Petersburg, Florida, on May 22, 1991, and thereafter. The late Robert Webber's widow, Clytie Webber, discussed her husband with the author on May 21, 1991. Eugene Braderman of Washington was interviewed twice by telephone about his 1960s visit to Israel, on October 1, 1990, and again the following April. The late Joseph Zurhellen was interviewed in New York on September 8, 1989. Arnold Kramish told of his meeting with Barbour in an interview on June 5, 1990. The cited Golda Meir comment about Barbour can be found in "Quiet Envoy to Israel," *New York Times*, April 3, 1971, one of the few times Barbour's name appeared in print while he was ambassador.

13. An Israeli Decision

Yigal Allon's boastful remarks made page 1 in the *New York Times* for December 11, 1967, "Allon Hints Israel Has Missiles." Moshe Dayan's Soviet

warning was published in *Frankfurter Allgemeine* on July 7, 1967. Walter Ros-
tow was interviewed at the LBJ Library in Austin, Texas, on October 14, 1990.
Kissinger's nuclear remarks can be found on page 397 (footnotes) in the Aron-
son book cited above. The cited *Time* magazine article is "How Israel Got the
Bomb," April 12, 1976. *The Plumbat Affair* was written by Elaine Davenport,
Paul Eddy, and Peter Gillman (J. B. Lippincott, Philadelphia, 1978).

14. A Presidential Gift

Dan Rather's question for the President came during a December 19, 1967,
news conference. The documents cited herein were released to the author
under the Freedom of Information Act; they are available from the LBJ Library. James Critchfield was interviewed April 13, 1989, and later by telephone. Harry McPherson was interviewed by telephone on May 8, 1991. Carl
Duckett was interviewed at his home in Hutchins, Virginia, on June 27, 1991.
There have been many published accounts of Richard Helms's aborted attempt to brief Johnson on the Israeli bomb; see "LBJ Was Told in '68 That
Israel Had Bomb," by John J. Fialka, *Washington Star*, March 1, 1978, page 1.
Paul Warnke was interviewed March 23, 1989, and later by telephone. Yitzhak
Rabin's account can be found at pages 141 and 142 of *The Rabin Memoirs* (Little,
Brown, Boston, 1979); Warnke somehow became Vornike in the Rabin book,
however. The late Harry Schwartz was interviewed July 14, 1989, at his home
near Easton, Maryland. The Rothschild pipeline deal was initially reported
July 18, 1959, in the *New York Times*, "Rothschild Investment Group To Operate Pipeline in Israel." Bill Moyers was interviewed by telephone on February 18, 1991.

15. The Tunnel

The best guide to the production of nuclear weapons is *U.S. Nuclear War-
head Production*, Vol. 2, by Thomas B. Cochran, William M. Arkin, Robert S.
Norris, and Milton M. Hoenig (Ballinger, Cambridge, Mass., 1987). The essen-
tial Vanunu story was "Revealed: The Secrets of Israel's Nuclear Arsenal,"
London *Sunday Times*, October 5, 1986. The story was written by the newspa-
per's "Insight" team, led by Peter Hounam. For an extensive analysis of
Vanunu, with additional information from his interviews with the *Sunday
Times*, see *The Invisible Bomb*, by Frank Barnaby (I. B. Tauris, London, 1989).
For details on Vanunu's life and his travails while being interviewed by the
Sunday Times in London, see *Triple Cross*, by Louis Toscano (Birch Lane Press,
New York, 1990). The use of robotics in the nuclear weapons production
process is briefly described in "Machining Hemispherical Shells," in the 1988
edition of *Research Highlights*, published by the Los Alamos National Labora-
tory. George Cowan was interviewed by telephone from New Mexico on
September 9, 1990; Hans Bethe was interviewed at his office at the California
Institute of Technology on January 21, 1991.

16. Prelude to War

Nixon's comments about the NPT were made September 8, 1968, in Pitts-
burg and September 11, 1968, in Charlotte, North Carolina. NSDM 6, apparently still classified, is in the author's possession. Morton Halperin was
interviewed in Washington on June 10, 1991. Charles Van Doren was interviewed in Washington on May 29, 1989. NSDM 32 also is in the author's

possession. Hedrick Smith's *New York Times* story was "U.S. Assumes the Israelis Have A-Bomb or Its Parts," July 19, 1970, page 1. Smith was interviewed about the story on May 9, 1991. Glenn Cella was interviewed March 31, 1989, and thereafter. David Long was interviewed by telephone on January 18, 1991; Curtis Jones was interviewed in Chapel Hill, North Carolina, on September 6, 1990. The Norris, Cochran, and Arkin essay is "History of the Nuclear Stockpile," *Bulletin of the Atomic Scientists,* August 1985. There have been many published accounts of Gerald Bull; a good one is "The Guns of Saddam," by William Scott Malone, David Halevy, and Sam Hemingway, *Washington Post,* Outlook Section, February 10, 1991. Israel's progress in laser-separated uranium was first reported by Robert Gillette in *Science Magazine,* March 22, 1974, "Uranium Enrichment: Rumors of Israeli Progress with Lasers." Nicholas Veliotes was first interviewed on June 20, 1989, in Washington. The Moshe Dayan quote about the end of the Third Temple can be found in the previously cited *Time* magazine article of April 12, 1976; it is also cited in Pry.

17. Nuclear Blackmail

There have been scores of analyses of the Yom Kippur War, besides the memoirs of the participants. For differing points of view, see "Kissinger and the Yom Kippur War," by Edward N. Luttwak and Walter Laqueur, *Commentary,* September 1974; "Arab-Israeli Conflict: Implications of Mass Destruction Weapons," by Avigdor Haselkorn, *Global Affairs,* Winter 1988; "The Relevance and Irrelevance of Nuclear Options in Conventional Wars: The 1973 October War," by Yair Evron, *Jerusalem Journal of International Relations,* Vol. 7, Nos. 1–2, 1984; and "The Soviet Nuclear Threat Toward the Close of the Yom Kippur War," by Yona Bandmann and Yishai Cordova, *Jerusalem Journal of International Relations,* Vol. 5, No. 1, 1980. Also see the works cited above by Shai Feldman and Shlomo Aronson. Mohammed Heikal was interviewed by telephone from his office in Cairo on July 3, 1991. Henry Kissinger describes his meeting with Ambassador Dinitz on page 493 in Chapter 11 of *Years of Upheaval* (Little, Brown, Boston, 1982). Despite many calls to his office and to his former colleagues in the U.S. government, Kissinger would not be interviewed about the 1973 war. Hermann Eilts was interviewed on July 10, 1991, by telephone from Boston. James Schlesinger was interviewed on April 25, 1989, in Washington; William Colby was interviewed on January 10, 1991, also in Washington. The Kalb brothers published the gist of their material on the 1973 war from *Kissinger* (Little, Brown, Boston, 1974) in the *New York Times Magazine,* June 23, 1974, "Twenty Days in October." Patrick Parker was interviewed in Washington in early December 1990. Orwin Talbott was interviewed by telephone from Annapolis, Maryland, his retirement home, on December 10, 1990, and again on June 20, 1991. Bruce Williams was interviewed in Washington on November 28, 1990. Kissinger's request for a CIA report on the Israeli nuclear arsenal was first reported by Benjamin Welles in the *Christian Science Monitor* for December 6, 1973, "Kissinger Orders CIA Study of Israel's A-weapons Capability." Duckett's problems with the 1974 estimate have been widely reported; see "How Israel Got the Bomb," by John Fialka, *Washington Monthly,* January 1979.

18. Injustice

John Fialka, then with the *Washington Star*, and David Burnham, then with the *New York Times*, have written extensively about the Zalman Shapiro case; see Burnham's "The Case of the Missing Uranium," *Atlantic*, April 1979. Both reporters, while raising repeated questions about Shapiro's actions, were careful to note that he had not been formally accused of any wrongdoing. For a different and more careless approach, see *The Unnatural Alliance*, by James Adams (Quartet Books, London, 1984), beginning at page 152 (Adams assumes that Shapiro was a Mossad asset). *Dangerous Liaison* doesn't do much better; see Chapter 4, "A Sword for Damocles." The documents and reports cited herein are available under the Freedom of Information Act; many thousands of them on NUMEC and its problems have been released. Zalman Shapiro was interviewed repeatedly by telephone from Pittsburgh, beginning on April 12, 1991. George Murphy was interviewed by telephone on May 30, 1989, and thereafter. James Lovett was interviewed on July 11, 1991. James Conran was interviewed on July 16, 1991. Victor Gilinsky was interviewed on June 12, 1989, in suburban Maryland, and thereafter by telephone. Cynthia Virostek was interviewed by telephone on July 17, 1991; she has assembled extensive files on NUMEC, and the author wishes to thank her for her generous help. Jody Powell's cited denial was published in the *New York Times* for October 26, 1977, "White House Discounts Allegations About Israeli Theft of Uranium," by Charles Mohr. Duckett's television appearance was on "Near Armageddon: The Spread of Nuclear Weapons in the Middle East," an ABC News Closeup, April 27, 1981. Henry Myers first discussed NUMEC and Shapiro with the author on November 17, 1980, and many times thereafter. Peter Stockton's first conversation with the author about Shapiro took place on January 26, 1988. Congressional funding for the cleanup of NUMEC was reported by United Press International, October 28, 1990, "Congress OKs Money for Cleanup of Nuclear Site." The estimate of more than one hundred kilograms of recovered uranium ("inventory gain") was provided by a senior technical official of the Nuclear Regulatory Commission who reviewed Babcock & Wilcox inventory reports to the NRC; such reports are available under the Freedom of Information Act.

19. The Carter Malaise

Ari Ben-Menashe initially contacted the author in August 1990 and was first interviewed in Cincinnati, Ohio, on April 11, 1991. He was subsequently interviewed in Washington and many more times by telephone. For a definitive account of the character of Menachem Begin, see *The Life and Times of Menachem Begin*, by Amos Perlmutter (Doubleday, Garden City, NY, 1987). Malcolm Toon was interviewed by telephone on May 20, 1991; his cable to Washington about the senatorial visit was made available under the Freedom of Information Act. The footnote about Vanunu and the senators' rebuff was reported in *Triple Cross*. George Rathjens was interviewed by telephone on March 25, 1989, and thereafter. Bergmann's speech in South Africa is cited in *The Unnatural Alliance*, among other places. Vorster's visit to Israel created a minor stir at the time: see "Vorster Visit to Israel Arouses Criticism," by Terence Smith, *New York Times*, April 18, 1976. The best account of the Carter administration's diplomacy on the 1977 Kalahari test was written by Murrey Marder and Don Oberdorfer of the *Washington Post;* see their story as syndicated in the *Philadelphia Inquirer* for September 4, 1977, "How the Powers Stopped a Test," page 1. The CIA's assessment of the attempted 1977 test was provided under the Freedom of Information Act to the Natural Resources Defense Council and made available to the press by the council on September 26, 1990. Harold Brown discussed the Israeli joint targeting request by telephone on April 26, 1991; he was previously interviewed in Washington on October 20, 1989.

20 An Israeli Test

There have been some excellent critiques of the White House's attempt, through the Ruina panel, to wish away the Israeli–South African test. See "The September 22, 1979, Mystery Flash: Did South Africa Detonate a Nuclear Bomb?" unpublished study by the Washington Office on Africa Educational Fund, May 21, 1985. The study was written by Ronald Walters of Howard University. See also an unpublished study by Gary Milhollin (available through the Wisconsin Project on Nuclear Arms Control): "The Vela Sighting in 1979." Stephen Green, in *Living by the Sword* (Amana Books, Brattleboro, Vt., 1988), dissects the Ruina report beginning at page 111. Gerald Oplinger was interviewed at his suburban Virginia home on January 9, 1991. Spurgeon Keeny was interviewed on March 24, 1989, in Washington and many times by telephone thereafter. Hodding Carter was interviewed by telephone on August 2, 1991. See Gary Sick (cited above) for details on the shah's visit to the United States. Jack Ruina was interviewed by telephone on August 2, 1991. John Scali was interviewed by telephone on August 6, 1991. Admiral Walters's bizarre explanation can be found in "Pretoria Suggests Cause of 'Explosion,' " by John F. Burns, *New York Times*, October 28, 1979. The cited P. W. Botha remark was on page 2 of the *Rand Daily Mail* for September 26, 1979: "SA Could Have Secret Weapon, Hints PW." The July 15, 1979, Ruina report was released by the Office of Science and Technology Policy in the White House and blandly entitled: "Ad Hoc Panel Report on the September 22 Event." Harold Agnew was interviewed by telephone on September 7, 1990. Louis Roddis was interviewed on May 7, 1991, and Donald Kerr was interviewed in Washington on February 13, 1991. Joseph Nye was briefly interviewed by telephone on January 2, 1991.

21. Israel's Nuclear Spy

The only book-length study of the Pollard affair is *Territory of Lies*, by Wolf Blitzer (Harper & Row, New York, 1989), which professionally summarizes all of the known and published information about the case. Blitzer, however, accepts far too much of Pollard's account at face value. Many of the essential details of Pollard's early life come from Blitzer and the press accounts at the time. Samuel Lewis was interviewed about the White House meeting on February 22, 1991. Sharon's strategic vision behind the Israeli invasion of Lebanon—and its folly—is most clearly spelled out in *Israel's Lebanon War*, by Ze'ev Schiff and Ehud Ya'ari (Simon & Schuster/Touchstone, New York, 1984). Sharon's December 15, 1981, speech is available in abridged form from the Israeli embassy in Washington; it initially was issued as an embassy press bulletin. For more on the Stern Gang, see *Wanted*, by Mordechai Schreiber (Shengold Publishers, New York, 1984), beginning at page 142.

22. An Israeli Asset

Peter Hounam was interviewed on July 30, 1991, by telephone from London, and thereafter. The cited *Sunday Mirror* article prominently featured a photograph of Vanunu next to an external photograph of the reactor at Dimona; the story itself, although vividly displayed, was buried deep inside the newspaper. Robert Watters was interviewed September 3, 1991, by telephone from Suva, Fiji, where he was on assignment as an electronics technician for the South Pacific Commission. Nicholas Davies (no relation to Nick Davies, a former reporter for the *Independent*) was interviewed by telephone from his home in London on July 26, 1991. Janet Fielding was interviewed by telephone from London on August 5, 1991. Peter Miller was interviewed by telephone from London on August 21 and 22, 1991. John Parker was interviewed in Washington on August 9, 1991. Tony Frost was interviewed by telephone from Newcastle, England, on August 6 and thereafter. The footnoted material about the Miller and Frost complaints against Maxwell came from the *U.K. Press Gazette* for April 29, 1991, "Sacked Mirror Man Finds Place in Sun," by Jean Morgan. Michael Malloy was interviewed by telephone on September 2, 1991, from the Passford House Hotel in Lymington, Hampshire, England, where he was on vacation.

Index

About the Author

SEYMOUR M. HERSH was born in Chicago in 1937 and graduated from the University of Chicago. He began his newspaper career as a police reporter for the City News Bureau in Chicago. After Army service, he was hired by United Press International in Pierre, South Dakota. In 1963 he joined the Associated Press in Chicago and in 1965 went to Washington for the AP to cover the Pentagon. He served as press secretary and speechwriter for Senator Eugene H. McCarthy in the famed "Children's Crusade"—the 1968 New Hampshire Democratic primary campaign against Lyndon Johnson. In 1969, as a free-lance journalist, Mr. Hersh wrote the first account of the My Lai massacre in South Vietnam, distributing five newspaper stories on the atrocity through Dispatch News Service. He was hired by the *New York Times* in 1972 and worked out of Washington and New York until his resignation in 1979 to write *The Price of Power*. In 1986, he rejoined the *Times*'s Washington bureau to write a series of critical articles about Panama's Manuel Noriega. He again joined the *Times* in Washington in September 1991, on a special assignment.

Mr. Hersh has won more than a dozen major journalism prizes. For his account of the My Lai massacre he earned the 1970 Pulitzer Prize for International Reporting, the George Polk Award, the Sigma Delta Chi Distinguished Service Award, and the Worth Bingham Prize. For his reporting on the secret B-52 bombing of Cambodia, he was accorded the Roy M. Howard Public Service Award and a second Polk Award in 1974. The next year he won the Drew Pearson Award, the John Peter Zenger Freedom of the Press Award, the Sidney Hillman Foundation Award, and a third Polk Award for his stories on the CIA and Chile and on CIA domestic spying. In 1981 he received a second Sigma Delta Chi Award and his fourth Polk Award for two articles in the *New York Times Magazine* on the involvement of former CIA agents in arms sales to Libya. He is also the recipient of the National Book Critics Circle Award and the *Los Angeles Times* Book Award for *The Price of Power: Kissinger in the Nixon White House.*

Mr. Hersh's previous books are *Chemical and Biological Warfare: America's Hidden Arsenal; My Lai 4: A Report on the Massacre and Its Aftermath; Cover-up: The Army's Secret Investigation of the Massacre of My Lai; The Price of Power: Kissinger in the Nixon White House;* and *"The Target Is Destroyed": What Really Happened to Flight 007 and What America Knew About It.* His articles have appeared in the *New Yorker,* the *New York Review of Books,* the *New York Times Magazine,* and the *New Republic.* He lives in Washington, D.C., with his wife and three children.